T0214508

Lecture Notes in Computer Science   11270

Commenced Publication in 1973
Founding and Former Series Editors:
Gerhard Goos, Juris Hartmanis, and Jan van Leeuwen

More information about this series at http://www.springer.com/series/7407

Carmen Graciani · Agustín Riscos-Núñez
Gheorghe Păun · Grzegorz Rozenberg
Arto Salomaa (Eds.)

Enjoying
Natural Computing

Essays Dedicated to Mario de Jesús Pérez-Jiménez
on the Occasion of His 70th Birthday

 Springer

Editors
Carmen Graciani
University of Seville
Sevilla
Spain

Agustín Riscos-Núñez
University of Seville
Sevilla
Spain

Gheorghe Păun
Romanian Academy
Bucharest
Romania

Grzegorz Rozenberg
Leiden University
Leiden
The Netherlands

Arto Salomaa
Turku Centre for Computer Science
Turku
Finland

ISSN 0302-9743   ISSN 1611-3349   (electronic)
Lecture Notes in Computer Science
ISBN 978-3-030-00264-0   ISBN 978-3-030-00265-7   (eBook)
https://doi.org/10.1007/978-3-030-00265-7

Library of Congress Control Number: 2018954069

LNCS Sublibrary: SL1 – Theoretical Computer Science and General Issues

Cover illustration: The drawing of the *Triana Bridge* on the front cover is the work of Augustín Riscos Núñez, Spain, based on a photograph by "Anual" (https://commons.wikimedia.org/wiki/User:Anual), with Creative Commons license "CC BY 3.0".

Photograph on p. V: The photograph of the honoree was taken by his daughter María Pérez-Barber, Spain. Used with permission.

This Springer imprint is published by the registered company Springer Nature Switzerland AG
The registered company address is: Gewerbestrasse 11, 6330 Cham, Switzerland

Mario de Jesús Pérez-Jiménez

Foreword

This festschrift is dedicated to Mario de Jesús Pérez-Jiménez on the occasion of his 70th birthday.

The title, *Enjoying Natural Computing*, reflects one of the guiding principles of Mario's functioning (in both his professional and his personal life): *once you choose to do something, enjoy doing it*. As a matter of fact, Mario is really successful in widely propagating this principle, e.g., it is very visible in the functioning of his Seville group. His contagious research enthusiasm, witnessed and enjoyed by his many scientific collaborators, must also be driven by this principle. A dominating feature of his character is his genuine altruism, a real devotion to the functioning of his friends and colleagues – this empathy for others is inexhaustible. His group tries to follow the "warning" which says: do not let Mario know that you need something, as then Mario is ready to drop everything and concentrate just on your problems.

His scientific credentials are impressive, as:

1. his research interests are wide, ranging from very theoretical problems from computational complexity theory to very applied problems and tasks, such as, the design of a programming language that facilitates in silico experiments in membrane computing,
2. he initiated a number of novel research directions as well as solving several very technically challenging problems.

In addition, Mario created "from scratch" an impressive research group in natural computing at the University of Seville. In fact, his group has become a sort of "pilgrimage venue" for researchers in membrane computing and other areas of natural computing. The "Brainstorming Week on Membrane Computing", organized annually by him since 2004, has become a famous meeting forum for researchers from all over the world. One can safely say that a big part of research problems (and their solutions) in the very active area of membrane computing originated during these meetings.

His achievements are well-recognized by the scientific community. A manifestation of this recognition was the overwhelming response to our invitations to contribute to this Festschrift. As a result, this volume contains contributions from researchers from 15 different countries. The contributions, which went through a thorough refereeing procedure, cover a wide spectrum of research areas, including membrane computing, spiking neural networks, phylogenetic networks, ant colonies optimization, workbench for biocomputing, reaction systems, entropy of computation, rewriting systems, and insertion-deletion systems. In this way, the volume reflects well the broad range of research interests of Mario.

Dear Mario:
Thank you for your collaboration and friendship.
We wish you continuous success and satisfaction in science in the years to come.

July 2018

Carmen Graciani
Gheorghe Păun
Agustín Riscos-Núñez
Grzegorz Rozenberg
Arto Salomaa

Contents

Chocolate P Automata

Artiom Alhazov[1], Rudolf Freund[2(✉)], Sergiu Ivanov[3], Marion Oswald[2],
and Sergey Verlan[4]

[1] Institute of Mathematics and Computer Science,
Academiei 5, 2028 Chişinău, Moldova
artiom@math.md

[2] Faculty of Informatics, TU Wien, Favoritenstraße 9–11, 1040 Vienna, Austria
{rudi,marion}@emcc.at

[3] IBISC, Université Évry, Université Paris-Saclay,
23 Boulevard de France, 91025 Évry, France
sergiu.ivanov@univ-evry.fr

[4] Laboratoire d'Algorithmique, Complexité et Logique, Université Paris Est Créteil,
61 Avenue du Général de Gaulle, 94010 Créteil, France
verlan@u-pec.fr

Abstract. We introduce several variants of input-driven tissue P
automata – we also will call them *chocolate automata* – where the rules
to be applied only depend on the input symbol. Both strings and multisets are considered as input objects; the strings are either read from
an input tape or defined by the sequence of symbols taken in, and the
multisets are given in an input cell at the beginning of a computation,
enclosed in a vesicle. Additional symbols generated during a computation are stored in this vesicle, too. An input is accepted when the vesicle
reaches a final cell and it is empty. The computational power of some
variants of input-driven tissue P automata (*chocolate automata*) is illustrated by examples and compared with the power of the input-driven
variants of other automata as register machines and counter automata.

1 Introduction

In the basic model of membrane systems as introduced at the end of the last
century by Gheorghe Păun, e.g., see [9,30], the membranes are organized in a
hierarchical membrane structure (i.e., the connection structure between the com-
partments/regions within the membranes being representable as a tree), and the
multisets of objects in the membrane regions evolve in a maximally parallel
way, with the resulting objects also being able to pass through the surrounding membrane to the parent membrane region or to enter an inner membrane.
Many variants of membrane systems, for obvious reasons mostly called *P systems*, have been investigated during nearly two decades, most of them being
computationally complete, i.e., being able to simulate the computations of register machines. If an arbitrary graph is used as the connection structure between
the cells/membranes, the systems are called *tissue P systems*, see [21].

© Springer Nature Switzerland AG 2018
C. Graciani et al. (Eds.): Pérez-Jiménez Festschrift, LNCS 11270, pp. 1–20, 2018.
https://doi.org/10.1007/978-3-030-00265-7_1

Instead of multisets of plain symbols coming from a finite alphabet, P systems quite often operate on more complex objects (e.g., strings, arrays), too. A comprehensive overview of different variants of (tissue) P systems and their expressive power is given in the handbook which appeared in 2010, see [32]. For a short view on the state of the art on the domain, we refer the reader to the P systems website [35] as well as to the Bulletin series of the International Membrane Computing Society [34].

The notion and concept of input-driven push-down automata goes back to the seminal paper [22] as well as the papers [6,10] improving the complexity measures shown in [22]. The main idea of input-driven push-down automata is that the input symbols uniquely determine whether the automaton pushes a symbol, pops a symbol, or leaves the pushdown unchanged. Input-driven push-down automata have been rediscovered at the beginning of this century under the name of visibly pushdown automata, see [3,4]. Since then, variants of input-driven push-down automata have gained growing interest, especially because closure properties and decidable questions of the language classes defined by these devices turn out to be similar to those of regular languages. Several new variants of input-driven automata have been developed, for example, using stacks or queues, see [5,19,20]. For complexity issues of input-driven push-down automata, the reader is referred to [24–27].

The so-called *point mutations*, i.e., *insertion*, *deletion*, and *substitution*, which mean inserting or deleting one symbol or replacing one symbol by another one in a string or multiset are very simple biologically motivated operations. For example, on strings graph-controlled insertion-deletion systems have been investigated in [13], and P systems using these operations at the left or right end of string objects were introduced in [16], where also a short history of using these point mutations in formal language theory can be found.

The operations of insertion and deletion in multisets show a close relation with the increment and decrement instructions in register machines. The power of changing states in connection with the increment and decrement instructions then can be mimicked by moving the whole multiset representing the configuration of a register machine from one cell to another one in the corresponding tissue system after the application of an insertion or deletion rule. Yet usually moving the whole multiset of objects in a cell to another one, besides maximal parallelism, requires *target agreement* between all applied rules, i.e., that all results are moved to the same target cell, e.g., see [15].

A different approach has been introduced in [2]: in order to guarantee that the whole multiset is moved even if only one point mutation is applied, the multiset is enclosed in a vesicle, and this vesicle is moved from one cell to another one as a whole, no matter if a rule has been applied or not. Requiring that one rule has to be applied in every derivation step, a characterization of the family of sets of (vectors of) natural numbers defined by partially blind register machines, which itself corresponds with the family of sets of (vectors of) natural numbers obtained as number (Parikh) sets of string languages generated by graph-controlled or matrix grammars without appearance checking, is obtained.

The idea of using vesicles of multisets has already been used in variants of P systems using the operations drip and mate, corresponding with the operations cut and paste well-known from the area of DNA computing, see [14]. Yet in that case, always two vesicles (one of them possibly an axiom available in an unbounded number) have to interact. In the model as introduced in [2] and also to be adapted in this paper, the rules are always applied to the same vesicle. The *point mutations*, i.e., *insertion, deletion*, and *substitution*, well-known from biology as operations on DNA, have also widely been used in the variants of *networks of evolutionary processors (NEPs)*, which consist of cells (processors) each of them allowing for specific operations on strings, and in each derivation step, after the application of a rule, allow the resulting string to be sent to another cell provided specific conditions (for example, random context output and input filters). A short overview on NEPs is given in [2], too.

In this paper, we now introduce input-driven tissue P automata – which we will also call *chocolate automata* – where the rules to be applied only depend on the input symbol. Taking strings as input objects, these are either read from an input tape or defined by the sequence of symbols taken in, and as a kind of additional storage we use a multiset of different symbols enclosed in a vesicle which moves from one cell of the tissue P system to another one depending on the input symbol; the input symbol at the same time also determines whether (one or more) symbols are added to the multiset in the vesicle or removed from there. The given input is accepted if the whole input has been read and the vesicle has reached a final cell and is empty at this moment. When using multisets as input objects, these are enclosed in the vesicle in the input cell at the beginning of a computation, which vesicle then will also carry the additional symbols. The given input multiset is accepted if no input symbols are present any more and the vesicle has reached a final cell and is empty at this moment.

As rules operating on the multiset enclosed in the vesicle when reading/consuming an input symbol we use insertion, deletion, and substitution of multisets, applied in the sequential derivation mode. As restricted variants, we consider systems without allowing substitution of multisets and systems only allowing symbols to be inserted or deleted (or substituted) as it is common when using point mutation rules.

Multiset automata have already been considered in [7], where models for finite automata, linear bounded automata, and Turing machines working on multisets are discussed. When dealing with multisets only, the tissue P automata considered in this paper can be seen as one of the variants of multiset pushdown automata as investigated in [18], where no checking for the emptiness of the multiset *memory* during the computation is possible. Various lemmas proved there then can immediately be adapted for our model. Moreover, also the input-driven variants can be defined in a similar manner, although input-driven multiset pushdown automata have not yet been considered in that paper.

We should also like to mention that the control given by the underlying communication structure of the tissue P system could also be interpreted as having a P system with only one membrane but using states instead. For a discussion on how to use and interpret features of (tissue) P systems as states we refer to [1], where also an example only using the point mutation rules insertion and deletion is given. Moreover, we will also consider another alternative model very common in the P systems area, i.e., P systems with antiport and symport rules, which were introduced in [29]; for overviews on P automata, we refer to [32], Chapter 5, [31], and [11]. One-membrane P systems using antiport rules in a sequential manner and with specific restrictions on the rules then are an adequate model for (input-driven) P automata, yet the restrictions are less visible than in the model of input-driven tissue P automata. On the other hand, when dealing with strings instead of multisets, the way how to read or define the input string in P systems with antiport rules has already been investigated thoroughly, e.g., see [8, 11, 28] for an overview.

The *sweet* title "chocolate automata"[1] is motivated by the following short story, fictive, but based on long-term experiences with the fruitful and inspiring meetings in Sevilla, known as the *Brainstorming Weeks on Membrane Computing*:

Preparing for the forthcoming week in Sevilla, expecting to meet many friends and colleagues as well as to have long nights of intensive discussions with his friends from Moldova, Artiom, Sergiu, and Sergey, Rudi thinks about how to fill his bag with a lot of chocolates. Moreover, a special birthday anniversary has to be celebrated, so some special chocolate cake is needed for this occasion. Starting to buy the cake, Rudi visits the famous Sacher in Vienna, and a big *Sacher Torte* as well as some other special Sacher sweets find their way into Rudi's *chocolate bag*.

A lot more sweets are expected to be needed, so Rudi at his home town Stockerau visits several stores to buy Austrian sweets like the famous *Mozart Kugeln*. With his *chocolate bag* well filled, Rudi now is ready and *happy* to start his journey from Vienna to Sevilla together with Marion. The friendly atmosphere established by Mario's Sevillan group immediately invites the teams from Austria – Rudi and Marion – and from Moldova – Artiom, Sergiu, and Sergey – to discuss new ideas on membrane computing. During the whole *Brainstorming Week*, a lot of chocolate is needed as brain fuel for the team members.

The famous churros are announced to be served in the middle of the week, during the morning coffee break; hence, to not interfere with this tradition, already on the second day the *Sacher Torte* is presented to Mario on the occasion of his special *birthday* anniversary, and he happily shares it with the participants of the meeting during the morning coffee break.

At the end of the *Brainstorming Week*, special *chocolate awards* are given to some participants: as usual, Artiom has had the most questions

---

[1] The idea of "chocolate automata" first came up in the relaxed atmosphere of the conference dinner at *AFL 2017*, the 15th International Conference on Automata and Formal Languages, taking place in Debrecen, Hungary, at the beginning of September, 2017; the ideas initiated there then were further developed during the *Brainstorming Week on Membrane Computing* at the beginning of February, 2018.

during all the talks, so he gets the *chocolate award* for the "most active participant in discussions". From all the young researchers present in Sevilla, Sergiu has contributed the most with new ideas especially on the last day, when results obtained during the current *Brainstorming Week* have been presented; therefore, he receives the *chocolate award* as the "most innovative young P scientist". During the closing ceremony, the members of the Sevillan group of *Mario* finally get a lot of chocolates as a special thank-you gift for their outstanding friendly organization.

After the *Brainstorming Week* Rudi returns home to Vienna together with Marion, with his *chocolate bag* being empty, but with his brain full of new "P ideas" obtained based on the discussions with the participants of the meeting, especially with his friends from Moldova.

Interpreting this story in an abstract way, the different chocolate sorts correspond to the different non-terminal symbols used as intermediate symbols during the computation. The events like going to a specific store as well as the coffee breaks and the award-giving events correspond with the terminal input symbols. There is no time condition on the sequence of these events except that chocolates have to be bought before they can be given away. This perfectly corresponds with the use of a mutiset bag (vesicle) as a storage, where the sequence does not matter as it is the case when dealing with strings stored in the stack of a pushdown automaton. Finally, the acceptance condition of empty vesicle at the end of the computation corresponds with having an empty *chocolate bag* at the end of the *Brainstorming Week*. Even several variants of the input-driven automata model can be derived from this *chocolate story*: for example, it is natural to buy several pieces in one store or to give away several chocolates at the same event, which nicely corresponds with putting more than one symbol into the vesicle or deleting more than one symbol from the vesicle at the same moment when reading/consuming an input symbol.

The rest of the paper now is structured as follows: In Sect. 2 we recall some well-known definitions from formal language theory. The main definitions for the model of (input-driven) tissue P automata as well as its variants to be considered in this paper are given in Sect. 3, and there we also present the definition of the alternative model of (input-driven) one-membrane P automata with (restricted) antiport rules; moreover we also give some first examples and results. Further illustrative examples and some more results, especially for input-driven tissue P automata are exhibited in Sect. 4. As upper bound for the family of sets of vectors of natural numbers accepted by input-driven tissue P automata we get the family of sets of vectors of natural numbers generated by partially blind register machines, and as upper bound for the family of sets of strings accepted by input-driven tissue P automata we get the family of sets of strings accepted by partially blind counter automata. A summary of the results obtained in this paper and an outlook to future research are presented in Sect. 5.

2 Prerequisites

We start by recalling some basic notions of formal language theory. An alphabet is a non-empty finite set of symbols. A finite sequence of symbols from an alphabet V is called a *string* over V. The set of all strings over V is denoted by V^*; the *empty string* is denoted by λ; moreover, we define $V^+ = V^* \setminus \{\lambda\}$. The *length* of a string x is denoted by $|x|$, and by $|x|_a$ we denote the number of occurrences of the symbol a in a string x.

A *multiset* M with underlying set A is a pair (A, f) where $f : A \to \mathbb{N}$ is a mapping, with $\mathbb{N}$ denoting the set of natural numbers (i.e., non-negative integers). If $M = (A, f)$ is a multiset then its *support* is defined as $supp(M) = \{x \in A \mid f(x) > 0\}$. A multiset is empty (respectively finite) if its support is the empty set (respectively a finite set). If $M = (A, f)$ is a finite multiset over A and $supp(M) = \{a_1, \ldots, a_k\}$, then it can also be represented by the string $a_1^{f(a_1)} \ldots a_k^{f(a_k)}$ over the alphabet $\{a_1, \ldots, a_k\}$ (the corresponding vector $(f(a_1), \ldots, f(a_k))$ of natural numbers is called Parikh vector of the string $a_1^{f(a_1)} \ldots a_k^{f(a_k)}$), and, moreover, all permutations of this string precisely identify the same multiset M (they have the same Parikh vector). The set of all multisets over the alphabet V is denoted by V°.

The family of all recursively enumerable sets of strings is denoted by RE, the corresponding family of recursively enumerable sets of Parikh vectors is denoted by $PsRE$. For more details of formal language theory the reader is referred to the monographs and handbooks in this area, such as [33].

2.1 Insertion, Deletion, and Substitution

For an alphabet V, let $a \to b$ be a rewriting rule with $a, b \in V \cup \{\lambda\}$, and $ab \neq \lambda$; we call such a rule a *substitution rule* if both a and b are different from λ and we also write $S(a, b)$; such a rule is called a *deletion rule* if $a \neq \lambda$ and $b = \lambda$, and it is also written as $D(a)$; $a \to b$ is called an *insertion rule* if $a = \lambda$ and $b \neq \lambda$, and we also write $I(b)$. The sets of all insertion rules, deletion rules, and substitution rules over an alphabet V are denoted by Ins_V, Del_V, and Sub_V, respectively. Whereas an insertion rule is always applicable, the applicability of a deletion and a substitution rule depends on the presence of the symbol a. We remark that insertion rules, deletion rules, and substitution rules can be applied to strings as well as to multisets. Whereas in the string case, the position of the inserted, deleted, and substituted symbol matters, in the case of a multiset this only means incrementing the number of symbols b, decrementing the number of symbols a, or decrementing the number of symbols a and at the same time incrementing the number of symbols b.

These types of rules and the corresponding notations can be extended by allowing more than one symbol on the left-hand and/or the right-hand side, i.e., $a, b \in V^*$, and $ab \neq \lambda$. The corresponding sets of all extended insertion rules, deletion rules, and substitution rules over an alphabet V are denoted by Ins_V^*, Del_V^*, and Sub_V^*, respectively.

2.2   Register Machines

Register machines are well-known universal devices for computing (generating or accepting) sets of vectors of natural numbers.

Definition 1. *A register machine is a construct* $M = (m, B, I, h, P)$ *where*

- *m is the number of registers,*
- *B is a set of labels bijectively labeling the instructions in the set P,*
- *I ⊆ B is the set of initial labels, and*
- *h ∈ B is the final label.*

  The labeled instructions of M in P can be of the following forms:

- $p : (ADD\,(r)\,, K)$, *with* $p \in B \setminus \{h\}$, $K \subseteq B$, $1 \le r \le m$.
  Increase the value of register r by one, and non-deterministically jump to one of the instructions in K.
- $p : (SUB\,(r)\,, K, F)$, *with* $p \in B \setminus \{h\}$, $K, F \subseteq B$, $1 \le r \le m$.
  If the value of register r is not zero then decrease the value of register r by one (decrement case) and jump to one of the instructions in K, otherwise jump to one of the instructions in F (zero-test case).
- $h : HALT$.
  Stop the execution of the register machine.

   A configuration *of a register machine is described by the contents of each register and by the value of the current label, which indicates the next instruction to be executed.*

In the accepting case, a computation starts with the input of a k-vector of natural numbers in its first k registers and by executing one of the initial instructions of P (labeled with $l \in I$); it terminates with reaching the *HALT*-instruction. Without loss of generality, we may assume all registers to be empty at the end of the computation.

By $\mathcal{L}(RM)$ we denote the family of sets of vectors of natural numbers accepted by register machines. It is well known (e.g., see [23]) that $PsRE = \mathcal{L}(RM)$.

Partially Blind Register Machines. In the case when a register machine cannot check whether a register is empty we say that it is partially blind: the registers are increased and decreased by one as usual, but if the machine tries to subtract from an empty register, then the computation aborts without producing any result (that is we may say that the subtract instructions are of the form $p : (SUB\,(r)\,, K, abort)$; instead, we simply will write $p : (SUB\,(r)\,, K)$.

Moreover, acceptance now by definition also requires all registers to be empty at the end of the computation, i.e., there is an implicit test for zero at the end of a (successful) computation, that is why we say that the device is partially blind. By $\mathcal{L}(PBRM)$ we denote the family of sets of vectors of natural numbers accepted by partially blind register machines. It is known (e.g., see [12]) that partially blind register machines are strictly less powerful than general register machines (hence, than Turing machines); moreover, $\mathcal{L}(PBRM)$ characterizes the Parikh sets of languages generated by graph-controlled or matrix grammars without appearance checking.

2.3 Counter Automata

Register machines can also be equipped with an input tape to be able to process strings, and the registers then are only used as auxiliary storage. We then call the registers *counters* and the automaton a *counter automaton* (we mention that in the literature slightly different definitions with respect to the instructions may be found). The additional instruction needed then is a *read instruction* reading one symbol from the input tape:

$$p : (read(a), K), \text{ with } p \in B \setminus \{h\}, K \subseteq B, \text{ and } a \in T.$$

T is the input alphabet, i.e., in sum we obtain a counter automaton as a construct

$$M = (m, B, I, h, P, T).$$

A counter automaton accepts an input $w \in T^*$ if and only if it starts in some initial state and with w on its input tape, and finally M reaches h having read the whole input string w. Without loss of generality, we again may assume all registers to be empty at the end of the computation.

It is well known (e.g., see [23]) that the family of string languages accepted by counter automata equals RE (in fact, only two counters are needed).

Partially Blind Counter Automata. As in the case of register machines, a counter automaton is called partially blind if it cannot check whether a register is empty, and acceptance by definition requires the whole input to be read and all counters to be empty at the end of the computation. For basic results on partially blind counter automata we refer to the seminal paper [17]. The family of string languages accepted by partially blind counter automata is denoted by $\mathcal{L}(PBCA)$.

2.4 Input-Driven Register Machines and Counter Automata

An input-driven register machine/counter automaton (an $IDRM^*$ and $IDCA^*$, respectively, for short) can be defined in the following way: any decrement of an input register r/any reading of a terminal symbol a is followed by *fixed* sequences of instructions on the working registers/counters only depending on the input register r/the terminal symbol a. If each such sequence is of length exactly one, then we speak of a real-time input-driven register machine/counter automaton (an $IDRM$ and $IDCA$, respectively, for short).

In the case of an $IDCA$, these sequences are of the form

$$p : (read(a), K) \to q : (\alpha(r), K_q),\ q \in K,$$

with $\alpha \in \{ADD, SUB\}$, $1 \le r \le m$, and they could be written as *one* extended instruction

$$p : (read(a), \alpha(r), \bigcup_{q \in K} K_q).$$

In a similar way, for an $IDCA^*$ we replace $\alpha(r)$ by the whole sequence of instructions following the reading of the input symbol a. A similar notation can be adapted for the case of a SUB-instruction on an input register instead of $read(a)$. Moreover, analogous definitions and notations hold for the partially blind variants of input-driven register machines/counter automata.

Remark 1. We emphasize that we have chosen a very restricted variant of what it means that the actions on the working registers only depend on the input symbol just read: no matter which label the read instruction $read(a)$ has, it must always be followed by the same sequence $\alpha(r)$; only the branching to labels from $\bigcup_{q \in K} K_q$ allows for taking different actions – in fact, read-instructions followed by the corresponding sequences of instructions – afterwards.   □

Remark 2. Allowing a set of initial labels as well as sets of labels in the ADD- and SUB-instructions may look quite unusual, but especially for the input-driven automata this feature turns out to be essential:

Assume we had allowed only one initial label i in any input-driven counter automaton. Now consider the finite multiset language $\{a, b\}$: assume there is an input-driven partially blind counter automaton accepting $\{a, b\}$. By definition, the instruction assigned to the initial label i must be a read instruction. With the initial label i, only *one* of the read instructions $read(a)$ or $read(b)$ can be assigned, hence, only a or only b can be accepted, a contradiction.

A similar argument holds for partially blind register machines taking the input set of two-dimensional vectors $\{(1, 0), (0, 1)\}$: the instruction assigned to i must be a SUB-instruction either on register 1 or on register 2, again leading to a contradiction.

On the other hand, with our more general definition, these sets are in $\mathcal{L}(IDCA^*)$ and $\mathcal{L}(IDRM^*)$, respectively. Still, in general we do not have closure under union, as the sequences of instructions after a read-instruction or a SUB-instruction in two different counter automata or register machines, respectively, need not be the same.   □

3   Tissue P Automata as Multiset Pushdown Automata

We now define a model of a tissue P automaton and its input-driven variants, first for the case of working with multisets as input objects:

Definition 2. *A* tissue P automaton *(a tPA* for short) is a tuple*

$$\Pi = (L, V, \Sigma, \Gamma, R, g, I, F)$$

where

- *L is a set of labels identifying in a one-to-one manner the $|L|$ cells of the tissue P system Π;*
- *V is the alphabet of the system;*
- *$\Sigma \subseteq V$ is the (non-empty) input alphabet of the system;*
- *$\Gamma \subseteq V$ is the (possibly empty) memory alphabet of the system, $\Gamma \cap \Sigma = \emptyset$;*
- *R is a set of rules of the form (i, p) where $i \in L$ and $p \in Ins_V^* \cup Del_V^* \cup Sub_V^*$, i.e., p is an extended insertion, deletion or substitution rule over the alphabet V; we may collect all rules from cell i in one set and then write $R_i = \{(i, p) \mid (i, p) \in R\}$, so that $R = \bigcup_{i \in L} R_i$; moreover, for the sake of conciseness, we may simply write $R_i = \{p \mid (i, p) \in R\}$, too;*
- *g is a directed graph describing the underlying communication structure of Π, $g = (N, E)$ with $N = L$ being the set of nodes of the graph g and the set of edges $E \subseteq L \times L$;*
- *$I \subseteq L$ is the set of labels of initial cells one of them containing the input multiset w at the beginning of a computation;*
- *$F \subseteq L$ is the set of labels of final cells.*

If in the definition above we take $p \in Ins_V \cup Del_V \cup Sub_V$ instead of $p \in Ins_V^* \cup Del_V^* \cup Sub_V^*$, then we speak of a *tPA* instead of a *tPA**.

A *tPA** Π now works as follows: The computation of Π starts with a vesicle containing the input multiset w in one of the initial cells $i \in I$, and the computation proceeds with derivation steps until a specific output condition is fulfilled.

In each derivation step, with the vesicle enclosing the multiset w being in cell k, one rule from R_k is applied to w and the resulting multiset in its vesicle is moved to a cell m such that $(k, m) \in E$.

As we are dealing with membrane systems, the classic output condition is to only consider halting computations; yet in case of automata, the standard acceptance condition is reaching a final state, which in our case means reaching a final cell h, and, moreover, the vesicle to be empty. We will combine these two conditions to define acceptance in this paper, as with the vesicle being empty no decrement rule can be applied any more and, moreover, it is guaranteed that we have "read the whole input". Only requiring the vesicle to be empty or else requiring to have reached a final cell with the vesicle containing no input symbol any more, are two other variants of acceptance.

The set of multisets accepted by Π is denoted by $Ps_{acc}(\Pi)$. The families of sets of vectors of natural numbers accepted by *tPA** and *tPA* with at most n cells are denoted by $\mathcal{L}_n(tPA^*)$ and $\mathcal{L}_n(tPA)$, respectively. If n is not bounded, we simply omit the subscript in these notations. In order to specify which rules are allowed in the *tPA** and *tPA*, we may explicitly specify I^*, D^*, S^* and I, D, S, respectively, to indicate the use of (extended) insertion, deletion, and substitution rules. For example, $\mathcal{L}(tPA, ID)$ then indicates that only insertion and deletion rules are used.

Remark 3. The model of a tPA^* comes very close to the model of a multiset pushdown automaton as introduced in [18]; in fact, the family of sets of vectors of natural numbers accepted by these multiset pushdown automata equals $\mathcal{L}(tPA^*)$. A formal proof would go far beyond the scope of this short paper, but the basic similarity of these two models becomes obvious when identifying the cells in the tPA^* with the states in the multiset pushdown automaton; moving the vesicle from one cell to another one corresponds to changing the states. As shown for the states of the multiset pushdown automata in [18], we could also restrict ourselves to only one initial as well as only one final cell in the general case, as this does not restrict the computational power of a tPA^*. On the other hand, for any of the following restricted variants this need not be true any more, especially for the input-driven variants defined later; in this context we also remind the arguments given in Remark 2.   □

The following result shows that having more than one rule in a cell is not necessary:

Lemma 1. *For any tPA^* Π there exists an equivalent tPA^* Π' such that every cell contains at most one rule.*

Proof (Sketch). Let $\Pi = (L, V, \Sigma, \Gamma, R, g, I, F)$ be a tPA^*. The equivalent tPA^* $\Pi' = (L', V, \Sigma, \Gamma, R', g', I', F')$ then is constructed as follows:

For every cell k with R_k containing n_k rules, instead of cell k we take n_k copies of that cell, cells $(k, 1), \ldots, (k, n_k)$, into Π', each of it containing one of the rules from R_k, say $p_{k,l}$, $1 \le l \le n_k$. The connection graph g then has to be enlarged to a graph g' containing all the edges

$$\{((k, l), (j, m)) \mid (k, j) \in g, 1 \le l \le n_k, 1 \le m \le n_j\}.$$

If cell k contains no rule, we rename it to cell $(k, 1)$, and no rule is contained in this cell, too.

The new sets of labels of initial and final cells are obtained by taking all copies of the original cell labels, i.e., we take

$$I' = \{(k, l) \mid (k \in I, 1 \le l \le n_k\},$$
$$F' = \{(k, l) \mid (k \in F, 1 \le l \le n_k\}.$$

We now immediately infer $Ps(\Pi) = Ps(\Pi')$.   □

Remark 4. Continuing the construction from Lemma 1, it is easy to show how to avoid having more than one final cell: we introduce a new final cell f', i.e., we take $F' = \{f'\}$, with this new cell not containing any rule; moreover, we add all edges

$$\{((k, l), f') \mid ((k, l), (j, m)) \in g', j \in F\}.$$

This new cell corresponds to the label of the final HALT instruction in a register machine or a counter automaton. As f' does not contain a rule, the computation will stop there in any case. $\square$

Remark 5. Having only one initial cell cannot be shown by only using a new structure: we may add two new cells i', i'' containing the rules $I(a)$ and $D(a)$, respectively, for some $a \in V$; the first one i' is used as the only new initial cell having one arc to the second one i'', i.e., (i', i''), from where to branch to the original initial cells as constructed in the proof of Lemma 1, i.e. we add all edges

$$\{(i'', (k, l)) \mid (k, l) \in I'\}.$$

Continuing the discussions from Remarks 2 and 3 we mention that this construction is not feasible for the input-driven variants to be defined in Subsect. 3.2. $\square$

The following result is based on the fact that the insertion, deletion, or substitution of a multiset over V can easily be simulated by a sequence of insertions and deletions:

Lemma 2. *For any tPA* Π there exists an equivalent tPA Π' even not using substitution rules.*

Now let $\mathcal{L}(mARB)$ denote the family of sets of multisets generated by arbitrary multiset grammars.

Corollary 1. $\mathcal{L}(tPA^*, IDS) = \mathcal{L}(tPA, ID) = \mathcal{L}(mARB) = \mathcal{L}(PBRM)$.

Proof (Sketch). The equality $\mathcal{L}(tPA^*, IDS) = \mathcal{L}(tPA, ID)$ follows from the definitions and Lemma 2.

The equality $\mathcal{L}(tPA^*, IDS) = \mathcal{L}(mARB)$ is a consequence of the observation discussed above in Remark 3 that $\mathcal{L}(tPA^*, IDS)$ corresponds to the family of sets of multisets accepted by multiset pushdwon automata as defined in [18]. In a similar way, interpreting the cells in a tissue P automaton as the states of a partially blind register machine and seeing the correspondence of the acceptance conditions, we also infer the equality $\mathcal{L}(tPA^*, IDS) = \mathcal{L}(PBRM)$. The details are left to the reader. $\square$

3.1   Accepting Strings

The tissue P automata defined above can also be used to accept sets of strings by assuming the input string to be given on a separate input tape, from where the symbols of the input string are read from left to right. As when going from register machines to counter automata, we use the additional instruction (*read instruction*) $read(a)$ with $a \in \Sigma$, Σ being the input alphabet. The corresponding automata then are defined as follows:

Definition 3. *A tissue P automaton for strings (a tPAL* for short) is a tuple*

$$\Pi = (L, V, \Sigma, \Gamma, R, g, I, F)$$

where L, V, Σ, Γ, R, g, I, F are defined as for a tPA^*, except that besides insertion, deletion, and substitution rules we also allow rules of the form $read(a)$ with $a \in \Sigma$, i.e., read instructions.

If we only take rules from $Ins_V \cup Del_V \cup Sub_V$ instead of $Ins_V^* \cup Del_V^* \cup Sub_V^*$, then we speak of a $tPAL$ instead of a $tPAL^*$.

A $tPAL^*$ Π works as follows: The computation of Π starts with the input string on the input tape as well as an empty vesicle in one of the initial cells $i \in I$, and the computation proceeds with derivation steps until the whole input string has been read and the vesicle has reached a final cell, again being empty at the end of the computation.

In each derivation step, with the vesicle enclosing the multiset w being in cell k, one rule from R_k is applied, either reading a symbol from the input tape or affecting w, and the resulting multiset in its vesicle then is moved to a cell m such that $(k, m) \in E$.

The set of strings accepted by Π is denoted by $L(\Pi)$. The families of sets of strings accepted by $tPAL^*$ and $tPAL$ with at most n cells are denoted by $\mathcal{L}_n(tPAL^*)$ and $\mathcal{L}_n(tPAL)$, respectively. If n is not bounded, we simply omit the subscript in these notations. In order to specify which rules are allowed in the $tPAL^*$ and $tPAL$, we again may explicitly specify I^*, D^*, S^* and I, D, S, respectively, to indicate the use of (extended) insertion, deletion, and substitution rules.

As for tissue P automata accepting multisets, also for the ones accepting strings we obtain some similar results as shown above:

Lemma 3. *For any $tPAL^*$ Π there exists an equivalent $tPAL^*$ Π' such that every cell contains at most one rule.*

Lemma 4. *For any $tPAL^*$ Π there exists an equivalent $tPAL$ Π' even not using substitution rules.*

Corollary 2. $\mathcal{L}(tPAL^*, IDS) = \mathcal{L}(tPAL, ID) = \mathcal{L}(PBCA)$.

3.2 Input-Driven Tissue P Automata

We now define the input-driven variants of tPA^* and tPA as well as $tPAL^*$ and $tPAL$:

Definition 4. *A tPA^* $\Pi = (L, V, \Sigma, \Gamma, R, g, I, F)$ is called* input-driven *(and called an IDtPA* for short) if the following conditions hold true:*

- *to each cell, (at most) one rule is assigned;*
- *any decrement of an input register r is followed by some fixed sequence of instructions on the working registers only depending on the input register r before a cell with the next decrement instruction on an input register is reached. Such a sequence of instructions may even be of length zero.*

If each such sequence is of length exactly one, then we speak of a real-time input-driven tPA^* (a rtIDtPA* for short).

Definition 5. *A tPAL* * $\Pi = (L, V, \Sigma, \Gamma, R, g, I, F)$ *is called* input-driven *(and called an* IDtPAL* *for short) if the following conditions hold true:*

- *to each cell, (at most) one rule is assigned;*
- *any reading of a terminal symbol a by a read instruction read(a) is followed by some fixed sequence of instructions on the working registers only depending on the terminal symbol a before a cell with the next read instruction is reached. Such a sequence of instructions may even be of length zero.*

If each such sequence is of length exactly one, then we speak of a real-time input-driven tPAL* (a rtIDtPAL* for short).

The corresponding families of sets of vectors of natural numbers and of sets of strings accepted by tissue P automata of type X with X being one of the types $IDtPA^*$, $IDtPA$, $rtIDtPA^*$, $rtIDtPA$ as well as $IDtPAL^*$, $IDtPAL$, $rtIDtPAL^*$, $rtIDtPAL$, are denoted by $\mathcal{L}(X)$.

Remark 6. As already discussed in Remark 1 for input-driven register machines and counter automata, we emphasize that we have chosen a very restricted variant of what it means that the actions on the multiset in the vesicle only depend on the input symbol just read: no matter in which cell we have the read instruction $read(a)$, it must always be followed by the same finite sequence of instructions not including read instructions. □

Remark 7. If we only have SUB-instructions on input registers/read instructions, i.e., if the $tPA^*/tPAL^*$ does not use the vesicle at all for storing any intermediate information of working registers, then such a $tPA^*/tPAL^*$ can be interpreted as a finite automaton accepting a regular multiset/string language. In this case, the condition of not having rules on the vesicle for symbols representing working registers, already subsumes the condition of the P automaton being input-driven. In fact, P systems of that kind exactly characterize the regular multiset/string languages. □

3.3   One-Membrane Antiport P Automata

The idea of using states instead of cells can also be "implemented" by using a well-investigated model of membrane systems using antiport rules:

Definition 6. *A one-membrane antiport P automaton (a 1APA* for short) is a tuple $\Pi = (V, \Sigma, \Gamma, Q, R, I, F)$ where*

- *V is the* alphabet *of the system;*
- *$\Sigma \subseteq V$ is the (non-empty)* input alphabet *of the system;*
- *$\Gamma \subseteq V$ is the (possibly empty)* memory alphabet *of the system, $\Gamma \cap \Sigma = \emptyset$;*
- *$Q \subseteq V$, $Q \cap (\Gamma \cup \Sigma) = \emptyset$, is the set of* states;
- *R is a set of rules of the form $pu \to qv$, $p, q \in Q$, $u \in (\Gamma \cup \Sigma)^*$, $v \in \Sigma^*$;*
- *$I \subseteq Q$ is the set of* initial *states;*
- *$F \subseteq Q$ is the set of* final *states.*

The $1APA^*$ can be seen as a membrane system consisting of only one membrane with the rules $pu \to qv$ interpreted as antiport rules $(pu, out; qv, in)$, i.e., the multiset pu leaves the membrane region and the multiset qv enters the membrane region.

Π starts with an input multiset w_0 together with one of the initial states p_0, i.e., with $w_0 p_0$ in its single membrane region, and then applies rules from R until a configuration with only $p_f \in F$ in the membrane region is reached, thus accepting the input multiset w_0.

For antiport P automata the acceptance of strings can be defined without needing an input tape as follows, e.g., see [28]: the rules in R now are of the form $pu \to qv$, $p, q \in Q$, $u \in \Gamma^*$ and $v \in (\Gamma \cup \Sigma)^*$, i.e., the input symbols are now taken from outside the membrane (from the environment); the sequence how the input symbols are taken in defines the input string (we may assume v to contain only one symbol from Σ; otherwise, if in one step several symbols are taken in, we have to take any permutation of these symbols, in which way several input strings are defined).

Using such rules and the interpretation of the input string as defined above, we obtain the model of a *one-membrane antiport P automaton for strings* (a $1APAL^*$ for short).

As in the preceding subsections we now can define specific variants of $1APA^*$ and $1APAL^*$, e.g., the corresponding input-driven automata. Yet as we have introduced these models especially to show the correspondence with an automaton model well-known in the area of P systems, we leave the technical details to the interested reader.

4   Examples and Results

The concepts of $IDtPA^*$ and $IDPBRM^*$ are closely related:

Theorem 1. $\mathcal{L}(IDtPA^*) \subseteq \mathcal{L}(PBRM^*)$ *and*
$$\mathcal{L}(IDtPA^*) = \mathcal{L}(IDtPA^*, ID) = \mathcal{L}(IDPBRM^*).$$

Proof (Sketch). The inclusion $\mathcal{L}(IDPBRM^*) \subseteq \mathcal{L}(PBRM^*)$ is obvious from the definitions.

The equality $\mathcal{L}(IDtPA^*, ID) = \mathcal{L}(IDPBRM^*)$ follows from the definitions of these types of input-driven automata: as already mentioned earlier, the cells in a tPA^* correspond to the states in a $PBRM$. The acceptance conditions – the vesicle being empty in a final cell in a tPA^* and all registers being empty in a $PBRM$ when reaching the final label – directly correspond to each other, too. Moreover, insertion and deletion rules directly correspond to ADD- and SUB-instructions. Finally, the conditions for the input-driven variants requiring the same actions for a consumed input symbol and the decrement of the corresponding register are equivalent, too.

The equality $\mathcal{L}(IDtPA^*) = \mathcal{L}(IDtPA^*, ID)$ follows from the possibility to simulate substitution rules by a sequence of insertion and deletion rules. This observation completes the proof.   □

Using similar arguments as in the preceding proof, now considering read instructions instead of decrements on input registers, we obtain the corresponding result for the string case:

Theorem 2. $\mathcal{L}(IDtPAL^*) \subseteq \mathcal{L}(PBCA^*)$ and
$$\mathcal{L}(IDtPAL^*) = \mathcal{L}(IDtPAL^*, ID) = \mathcal{L}(IDPBCA^*).$$

In the real-time variants, we cannot use substitution rules in the input-driven tissue P automata, as the simulation by deletion and insertion rules takes more than one step:

Theorem 3. $\mathcal{L}(rtIDtPA, ID) = \mathcal{L}(rtIDPBRM)$ and
$$\mathcal{L}(rtIDtPAL, ID) = \mathcal{L}(rtIDPBCA).$$

We now illustrate the computational power of input-driven tissue P automata accepting strings by showing how well-known string languages can be accepted. We remark that in all cases the automaton has only one initial label and one final label.

Example 1. The Dyck language L_D over the alphabet of brackets $\{[,]\}$ can easily be accepted by the $rtIDtPBCA$ M_D:

$$M_D = (1, B = \{1,2,3,4,5\}, l_0 = 1, l_h = 5, P, T = \{[,]\}),$$
$$P = \{1 : (read([), \{2\}), 2 : (ADD(1), \{1,3\}),$$
$$3 : (read(]), \{4\}), 4 : (SUB(1), \{1,3,5\}), 5 : HALT\}.$$

L_D can also be accepted by the corresponding $rtIDtPAL$ Π_D:

$$\Pi_D = (L = \{1,2,3,4,5\}, V, \Sigma, \Gamma, R, g = (L,E), I = \{1\}, F = \{5\}),$$
$$V = \{a_1, [,]\},$$
$$\Sigma = \{[,]\},$$
$$\Gamma = \{a_1\},$$
$$R = \{(1, read([)), (2, I(a_1)), (3, read(])), (4, D(a_1))\},$$
$$E = \{(1,2), (2,1), (2,3), (3,4), (4,1), (4,3), (4,5)\}.$$

The two constructions elaborated above implement the following definition of a well-formed bracket expression w over the alphabet of brackets $\{[,]\}$:

- for every prefix of w, the number of closing brackets] must not exceed the number of opening brackets [;
- the number of closing brackets] in w equals the number of opening brackets [.

Hence, during the whole computation, the (non-negative) difference between the number of opening and the number of closing brackets is stored as the number of symbols a_1; at the end, this number must be zero, which is guaranteed by the acceptance conditions.   □

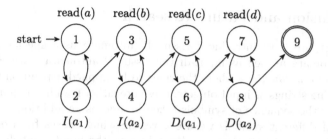

read(a)   read(b)   read(c)   read(d)

Fig. 1. Graphic representation of the $rtIDtPAL$ Π_{il}.

$\mathcal{L}(rtIDPBCA)$ even contains a non-context-free language:

Example 2. The language $L_{il} = \{a^n b^m c^n d^m \mid m, n \geq 1\}$ is not context-free, but accepted by the following $rtIDtPAL$ Π_{il}:

$$\Pi_{il} = (L = \{1, \ldots, 9\}, V, \Sigma, \Gamma, R, g = (L, E), I = \{1\}, F = \{9\}),$$
$$V = \{a_1, a_2, a, b, c, d\},$$
$$\Sigma = \{a, b, c, d\},$$
$$\Gamma = \{a_1, a_2\},$$
$$R = \{(1, read\,(a\,)), (2, I\,(a_1)), (3, read\,(b\,)), (4, I\,(a_2)),$$
$$(5, read\,(c\,)), (6, D\,(a_1)), (7, read\,(d\,)), (8, D\,(a_2))\},$$
$$E = \{(1, 2), (2, 1), (2, 3), (3, 4), (4, 3),$$
$$(4, 5), (5, 6), (6, 5), (6, 7), (7, 8), (8, 7), (8, 9)\}.$$

By this construction, we conclude $L_{il} \in \mathcal{L}(rtIDtPAL, ID)$. □

For the language considered in the next example we show that it is in $\mathcal{L}(rtIDtPAL^*)$, but we claim that it is not in $\mathcal{L}(rtIDtPAL)$:

Example 3. Let $k > 2$ and consider the string language $L_k = \{b_1^n \ldots b_k^n \mid n \geq 1\}$, which is not context-free, but accepted by the following $rtIDtPAL^*$ Π:

$$\Pi_k = (L = \{1, \ldots, 2k + 1\}, V, \Sigma, \Gamma, R, g = (L, E), I = \{1\}, F = \{2k + 1\}),$$
$$V = \{a_i, b_i \mid 1 \leq i \leq k\},$$
$$\Sigma = \{b_i \mid 1 \leq i \leq k\},$$
$$\Gamma = \{a_i \mid 1 \leq i \leq k\},$$
$$R = \{(1, read\,(b_1\,)), (2, I\,(a_2 \ldots a_k))\}$$
$$\cup \{(2j - 1, read\,(b_j\,)), (2j, D\,(a_j)) \mid 1 < j \leq k\},$$
$$E = \{(2j - 1, 2j), (2j, 2j - 1), (2j, 2j + 1) \mid 1 \leq j \leq k\}.$$

Without proof we claim that $L_k \notin \mathcal{L}(rtIDtPAL)$. □

5   Conclusion and Future Research

In this paper, we have introduced tissue P automata as a specific model of multiset automata as well as input-driven tissue P automata – which we also called *chocolate automata* – where the rules to be applied depend on the input symbol. Taking strings as input objects, these are either read from an input tape or defined by the sequence of symbols taken in, and as an additional storage of a multiset of different symbols we use a vesicle which moves from one cell of the tissue P system to another one depending on the input symbol; the input symbol at the same time determines whether (one or more) symbols are added to the multiset in the vesicle or removed from there and where the vesicle moves afterwards. The given input is accepted if it has been read completely and the vesicle has reached a final cell and/or is empty at this moment. When using multisets as input objects, these are enclosed in the vesicle in the input cell at the beginning of a computation, which vesicle then will also take the additional symbols. The given input multiset is accepted if no input symbols are present any more and the vesicle has reached a final cell and is empty at this moment.

As rules operating on the multiset enclosed in the vesicle when reading/consuming an input symbol we have used insertion, deletion, and substitution of multisets, working in the sequential derivation mode. As restricted variants, we have considered systems without allowing substitution of multisets and systems only allowing symbols to be inserted or deleted (or substituted).

We have shown how *chocolate automata* with multisets and strings can be characterized by input-driven register machines and input-driven counter automata, respectively. Moreover, we have exhibited some illustrative examples, for example, how the Dyck language or even some non-context-free languages can be accepted by simple variants of *chocolate automata*.

Several challenging topics remain for future research: for example, a characterization of the language classes accepted by several variants of tissue P automata accepting multisets or strings, especially for the input-driven variants (*chocolate automata*), introduced in this paper is still open.

As acceptance condition we have only considered reaching the final cell h with an empty vesicle. The other variants of acceptance, i.e., only requiring the vesicle to be empty or else requiring to have reached the final cell with the vesicle containing no input symbol any more, are to be investigated in the future in more detail.

Acknowledgements. The authors appreciate the helpful comments of the unknown referees.

References

1. Alhazov, A., Freund, R., Heikenwälder, H., Oswald, M., Rogozhin, Yu., Verlan, S.: Sequential P systems with regular control. In: Csuhaj-Varjú, E., Gheorghe, M., Rozenberg, G., Salomaa, A., Vaszil, Gy. (eds.) CMC 2012. LNCS, vol. 7762, pp. 112–127. Springer, Heidelberg (2013). https://doi.org/10.1007/978-3-642-36751-9_9

2. Alhazov, A., Freund, R., Ivanov, S., Verlan, S.: (Tissue) P systems with vesicles of multisets. In: Csuhaj-Varjú, E., Dömösi, P., Vaszil, Gy. (eds.) Proceedings 15th International Conference on Automata and Formal Languages. AFL 2017, 4–6 September 2017, Debrecen, Hungary, vol. 252, pp. 11–25. EPTCS (2017). https://doi.org/10.4204/EPTCS.252.6

3. Alur, R., Madhusudan, P.: Visibly pushdown languages. In: Babai, L. (ed.) Proceedings of the 36th Annual ACM Symposium on Theory of Computing, 13–16 June 2004, Chicago, IL, USA, pp. 202–211. ACM (2004). https://doi.org/10.1145/1007352.1007390

4. Alur, R., Madhusudan, P.: Adding nesting structure to words. J. ACM **56**(3), 16:1–16:43 (2009). https://doi.org/10.1145/1516512.1516518

5. Bensch, S., Holzer, M., Kutrib, M., Malcher, A.: Input-driven stack automata. In: Baeten, J.C.M., Ball, T., de Boer, F.S. (eds.) TCS 2012. LNCS, vol. 7604, pp. 28–42. Springer, Heidelberg (2012). https://doi.org/10.1007/978-3-642-33475-7_3

6. von Braunmühl, B., Verbeek, R.: Input-driven languages are recognized in log n space. In: Karpinski, M. (ed.) FCT 1983. LNCS, vol. 158, pp. 40–51. Springer, Heidelberg (1983). https://doi.org/10.1007/3-540-12689-9_92

7. Csuhaj-Varjú, E., Martín-Vide, C., Mitrana, V.: Multiset automata. In: Calude, C.S., Păun, Gh., Rozenberg, G., Salomaa, A. (eds.) WMC 2000. LNCS, vol. 2235, pp. 69–83. Springer, Heidelberg (2001). https://doi.org/10.1007/3-540-45523-X_4

8. Csuhaj-Varjú, E., Vaszil, Gy.: P automata or purely communicating accepting P systems. In: Păun, Gh., Rozenberg, G., Salomaa, A., Zandron, C. (eds.) WMC 2002. LNCS, vol. 2597, pp. 219–233. Springer, Heidelberg (2003). https://doi.org/10.1007/3-540-36490-0_14

9. Dassow, J., Păun, Gh.: On the power of membrane computing. J. UCS **5**(2), 33–49 (1999). https://doi.org/10.3217/jucs-005-02-0033

10. Dymond, P.W.: Input-driven languages are in log n depth. Inf. Process. Lett. **26**(5), 247–250 (1988). https://doi.org/10.1016/0020-0190(88)90148-2

11. Freund, R.: P automata: new ideas and results. In: Bordihn, H., Freund, R., Nagy, B., Vaszil, Gy. (eds.) Proceedings of Eighth Workshop on Non-Classical Models of Automata and Applications. NCMA 2016, 29–30 August 2016, Debrecen, Hungary, vol. 321, pp. 13–40. Österreichische Computer Gesellschaft (2016). https://shop.ocg.at/de/books.html

12. Freund, R., Ibarra, O., Păun, Gh., Yen, H.C.: Matrix languages, register machines, vector addition systems. In: Third Brainstorming Week on Membrane Computing, pp. 155–167 (2005). https://www.gcn.us.es/3BWMC/bravolpdf/bravol155.pdf

13. Freund, R., Kogler, M., Rogozhin, Yu., Verlan, S.: Graph-controlled insertion-deletion systems. In: Proceedings Twelfth Annual Workshop on Descriptional Complexity of Formal Systems. DCFS 2010, 8–10 August 2010, Saskatoon, Canada, pp. 88–98 (2010). https://doi.org/10.4204/EPTCS.31.11

14. Freund, R., Oswald, M.: Tissue P systems and (mem)brane systems with mate and drip operations working on strings. Electron. Notes Theor. Comput. Sci. **171**(2), 105–115 (2007). https://doi.org/10.1016/j.entcs.2007.05.011

15. Freund, R., Păun, Gh.: How to obtain computational completeness in P systems with one catalyst. In: Proceedings Machines, Computations and Universality 2013. MCU 2013, 9–11 September 2013, Zürich, Switzerland, pp. 47–61 (2013). https://doi.org/10.4204/EPTCS.128.13

16. Freund, R., Rogozhin, Yu., Verlan, S.: Generating and accepting P systems with minimal left and right insertion and deletion. Nat. Comput. **13**(2), 257–268 (2014). https://doi.org/10.1007/s11047-013-9396-3

17. Greibach, S.A.: Remarks on blind and partially blind one-way multicounter machines. Theor. Comput. Sci. **7**, 311–324 (1978). https://doi.org/10.1016/0304-3975(78)90020-8

18. Kudlek, M., Totzke, P., Zetzsche, G.: Multiset pushdown automata. Fundam. Inform. **93**(1–3), 221–233 (2009). https://doi.org/10.3233/FI-2009-0098

19. Kutrib, M., Malcher, A., Wendlandt, M.: Tinput-driven pushdown, counter, and stack automata. Fundam. Inform. **155**(1–2), 59–88 (2017). https://doi.org/10.3233/FI-2017-1576

20. Kutrib, M., Malcher, A., Wendlandt, M.: Queue automata: foundations and developments. In: Adamatzky, A. (ed.) Reversibility and Universality. ECC, vol. 30, pp. 385–431. Springer, Cham (2018). https://doi.org/10.1007/978-3-319-73216-9_19

21. Martín-Vide, C., Pazos, J., Păun, Gh., Rodríguez-Patón, A.: A new class of symbolic abstract neural nets: tissue P systems. In: Ibarra, O.H., Zhang, L. (eds.) COCOON 2002. LNCS, vol. 2387, pp. 290–299. Springer, Heidelberg (2002). https://doi.org/10.1007/3-540-45655-4_32

22. Mehlhorn, K.: Pebbling mountain ranges and its application to DCFL-recognition. In: de Bakker, J., van Leeuwen, J. (eds.) ICALP 1980. LNCS, vol. 85, pp. 422–435. Springer, Heidelberg (1980). https://doi.org/10.1007/3-540-10003-2_89

23. Minsky, M.L.: Computation: Finite and Infinite Machines. Prentice Hall, Englewood Cliffs (1967)

24. Okhotin, A., Salomaa, K.: Input-driven pushdown automata: nondeterminism and unambiguity. In: Bensch, S., Drewes, F., Freund, R., Otto, F. (eds.) Proceedings of Fifth Workshop on Non-Classical Models for Automata and Applications. NCMA 2013, 13–14 August 2013, Umeå, Sweden, vol. 294, pp. 31–33. Österreichische Computer Gesellschaft (2013). https://shop.ocg.at/de/books.html

25. Okhotin, A., Salomaa, K.: Input-driven pushdown automata with limited nondeterminism. In: Shur, A.M., Volkov, M.V. (eds.) DLT 2014. LNCS, vol. 8633, pp. 84–102. Springer, Cham (2014). https://doi.org/10.1007/978-3-319-09698-8_9

26. Okhotin, A., Salomaa, K.: Descriptional complexity of unambiguous input-driven pushdown automata. Theor. Comput. Sci. **566**, 1–11 (2015). https://doi.org/10.1016/j.tcs.2014.11.015

27. Okhotin, A., Salomaa, K.: State complexity of operations on input-driven pushdown automata. J. Comput. Syst. Sci. **86**, 207–228 (2017). https://doi.org/10.1016/j.jcss.2017.02.001

28. Oswald, M.: P automata. Ph.D. thesis, Faculty of Computer Science, TU Wien (2003)

29. Păun, A., Păun, Gh.: The power of communication: P systems with symport/antiport. New Gener. Comput. **20**(3), 295–306 (2002). https://doi.org/10.1007/BF03037362

30. Păun, Gh.: Computing with membranes. J. Comput. Syst. Sci. **61**(1), 108–143 (2000). https://doi.org/10.1006/jcss.1999.1693

31. Păun, Gh., Pérez-Jiménez, M.J.: P automata revisited. Theor. Comput. Sci. **454**, 222–230 (2012). https://doi.org/10.1016/j.tcs.2012.01.036

32. Păun, Gh., Rozenberg, G., Salomaa, A. (eds.): The Oxford Handbook of Membrane Computing. Oxford University Press, Oxford (2010)

33. Rozenberg, G., Salomaa, A. (eds.): Handbook of Formal Languages, vol. 1–3. Springer, Heidelberg (1997)

34. Bulletin of the International Membrane Computing Society (IMCS). http://membranecomputing.net/IMCSBulletin/index.php

35. The P Systems Website. http://ppage.psystems.eu/

Solving the N-Queens Puzzle
by Using Few Membranes

Bogdan Aman[1,2]($\boxtimes$) and Gabriel Ciobanu[1,2]

[1] Romanian Academy, Institute of Computer Science, Iaşi, Romania
bogdan.aman@iit.academiaromana-is.ro,gabriel@info.uaic.ro
[2] "A.I. Cuza" University of Iaşi, Iaşi, Romania

Abstract. The N-queens puzzle is a topic of several articles written by Mario Pérez-Jiménez and his collaborators. In this paper we present a family of polarizationless P systems with active membranes and 2-cooperation that provides all the possible solutions for this puzzle. The novelty consists in the method allowing a rather important reduction on the number of required membranes and computational steps for obtaining all the solutions of the N-queens problem.

1 Introduction

Membrane computing [15,17] is a well-known branch of natural computing aiming to abstract computing ideas and formal models from the structure and functioning of living cells, as well as from the organization of cells in tissues, organs or other higher order structures such as colonies of cells. The membrane systems (also known as P systems) are parallel and distributed computing models offering an approach to computation that is potentially superior to the one provided by conventional systems due to their inherent parallelism and nondeterminism. Computation is given by rewriting rules operating over multisets of objects (representing sets of objects with associated quantities) in cell-like compartmental architectures. Objects represent the formal counterpart of the molecular species (ions, proteins) floating inside cellular compartments, while the evolution rules represent the formal counterpart of the biochemical reactions.

Three main research directions are usually considered in membrane computing: modelling power [5,18], computational power in terms of the classical notion of Turing computability using a minimal quantity of ingredients [4], and efficiency in algorithmically solving (weak [2] or strong [3]) NP-complete problems in polynomial time (by using an exponential quantity of ingredients).

One such NP-complete problem is the N-queens problem, a generalization of the problem of putting eight non-attacking queens on a chessboard [7]. The fact that no queen threatens the other means that at most one of the N queens is placed on each row, column and diagonal. The N-queens problem was tackled by using P systems for the first time in [9] for the case $N = 4$, and a solution that included 65536 elementary membranes was proposed. By using depth-first search in membrane computing, the approach was improved in [10]. The speed of solving

© Springer Nature Switzerland AG 2018
C. Graciani et al. (Eds.): Pérez-Jiménez Festschrift, LNCS 11270, pp. 21–32, 2018.
https://doi.org/10.1007/978-3-030-00265-7_2

the N-queens problem by using membrane computing as a local search strategy was increased in [11]. A further increase in speed by reducing the number of communication rules was presented in [13]. These approaches involve representing the N-queens problem as a Boolean formula in conjunctive normal form, leading to a reduction to the satisfiability problem (shortly SAT). A different approach appeared in [8], where a construction of a dP system solving the N-queens problem is presented. The dP system uses the P system with active membranes as components, and the solution is mostly based on the one presented in [9].

In this paper, we propose a family of a variant of polarizationless P systems with active membranes [1] such that the N-th element of the family solves the N-queens puzzle. More precisely we use polarizationless P systems with active membranes and 2-cooperation (one membrane system for each value of N). In polarizationless P systems with active membranes [1], an object evolution rule is of form $[a \rightarrow v]_h$ such that a is a single object, not a multiset of objects; in this paper by 2-cooperation we understand that the object evolution rules are of form $[u \rightarrow v]_h$ such that u is a multiset of objects with at most two objects. A detailed overview summarizing the known results and variants for P systems with active membranes can be found in [16]. Our solution is such that the halting configuration encodes all the solutions of the puzzle. We use the massive parallelism to check the feasible solutions, and obtain the solution in a reduced number of steps by using a smaller number of membranes.

In order to find efficient solutions, the membrane systems are treated as deciding devices that respect the following conditions:

(1) all computations halt;
(2) two additional objects *yes* and *no* are used;
(3) exactly one of the objects *yes* (accepting computation) and *no* (rejecting computation) appears in the halting configuration; such an object should appear into a well recognizable output membrane which should be present in just one copy at the end of any computation.

Note that usually in membrane computing, the objects *yes* and *no* do not participate in the computation. However, since it does not affect the final configuration, this assumption is not imposed in this paper.

The paper is organized as follows: In Sect. 2 we define the polarizationless P systems with active membranes and 2-cooperation, and in Sect. 3 we present some complexity notions. Our family of P systems solving the N-queens problem is presented in Sect. 4. We exemplify how the approach works for an instance of the problem, namely for $N = 3$. Conclusion and references end the paper.

2 Membrane Systems

First of all, we present some terminology used in the sequel. A finite multiset over an alphabet O is a mapping $M : O \rightarrow \mathbb{N}$, where $\mathbb{N}$ is the set of nonnegative integers; $M(a)$ is said to be the multiplicity of $a \in O$ in M. We say that $M_1 \subseteq M_2$ if for all $a \in O$, $M_1(a) \leq M_2(a)$. The union or sum of two multisets over O is defined as $(M_1+M_2)(a) = M_1(a)+M_2(a)$, while the difference is defined for $M_2 \subseteq M_1$ as $(M_1 - M_2)(a) = M_1(a) - M_2(a)$ for all $a \in O$. The multiset M can also be represented by any permutation of a string $w = a_1^{M(a_1)} a_2^{M(a_2)} \ldots a_n^{M(a_n)} \in O^*$, where if $M(x) \neq 0$ then there exists j, $1 \leq j \leq n$, such that $x = a_j$. Given an alphabet O, we denote by O^* the sets of all finite strings of elements in O, including the empty string λ.

A membrane system is a structure of membranes arranged in either a cell-like tree [15], or a tissue-like graph [14], or a neural-like graph [12]. In this paper we use a tree structure given by polarizationless P systems with active membranes and 2-cooperation in which each membrane has a label, a unique *skin* membrane is the outermost part of the system, each region is delimited by a surrounding membrane and contains a multiset of objects and possibly some other membranes. We assume the membranes are labelled by natural numbers $\{1, \ldots, n\}$.

Definition 1. *A polarizationless P system with active membranes and 2-cooperation is a construct* $\Pi = (O, H, \mu, w_1, \ldots, w_n, R)$, *where*

1. $n \geq 1$ *is the initial degree of the system (i.e. number of membranes);*
2. O *is the alphabet of objects;*
3. H *is a finite set of labels for membranes;*
4. μ *is a membrane structure of n membrane bijectively labelled initially with elements of H;*
5. w_i *are strings over O describing the initial multisets of objects placed in the n regions of μ, for $1 \leq i \leq n$;*
6. R *is a finite set of evolution rules, where* $a, b, c \in O$, $u \in O^+$, $|u| \leq 2$, $v \in O^*$, $h \in H$, M_1, M_2 *denote (possibly empty) multisets of objects and membranes, while M_3 a (possibly empty) multiset of objects.*

   (a) $[u \rightarrow v]_h$ evolution(ev)

   The effect of applying this rule can be graphically represented as:

   $$M_1 \boxed{u\ M_2}_h \longrightarrow M_1 \boxed{v\ M_2}_h$$

   This is an evolution rule (associated with a membrane labelled with h) rewriting a non-empty multiset u into another, possible empty, multiset v.

   (b) $[a]_h \rightarrow b[\ ]_h$ communication (com)

   The effect of applying this rule can be graphically represented as:

   $$M_1 \boxed{a\ M_2}_h \longrightarrow M_1\, b \boxed{M_2}_h$$

   This communication rule (associated with a membrane labelled with h) sends an object a outside membrane h, and possibly rewriting it into an object b.

(c) $[a]_h \rightarrow [b]_h [c]_h$ division (div)

The effect of applying this rule can be graphically represented as:

$$M_1 \boxed{a\ M_3}_h \longrightarrow M_1 \boxed{b\ M_3}_h \boxed{c\ M_3}_h$$

A membrane labelled by h can be divided into two membranes having the same label h, possibly rewriting an object a into objects b and c, respectively.

These rules are applied according to the following principles:

- All the rules are applied in parallel and in a maximal manner. At one step, one object of a membrane can be used only by one rule (chosen in a nondeterministic way), and any object able to evolve by a rule (of any form) *should* evolve.
- All the objects and membranes not specified in a rule and which do not evolve remain unchanged (to the next step).
- At the same time, if a membrane labelled with h is divided and there are objects in this membrane which evolve by means of rules of type (a) or (b), then we suppose that evolution rules of type (a) and communication rules of type (b) are used first, and then the division is produced. This entire process takes only one step.
- The rules associated with a membranes labelled with h are used for all the copies of this membrane. At one step, a membrane labelled with h can be the subject of only one division rule.

The end of the computation is defined by the following halting condition: such a P system halts when no more rules can be applied in any of the regions.

3   The Efficiency of Membrane Systems

The membrane systems can be used as confluent deciding devices in which all the computations starting from the initial configuration evolve to the (same) answer/result. The solution designed in this paper will make sure that the computations are confluent. Note that we are not interested (only) in the existence of a solution for the N-queens puzzle, but finding (and storing) all the possible solutions (the queens arrangements) in an effective way. However, we treat the problem as a decision problem.

A family $\mathbf{\Pi}$, namely a collection of membrane systems $\mathbf{\Pi}(n)$, solves a decision problem if for each instance of size n of the problem there is a member of the family able to decide on the instance. In order to define the notion of uniformity, some notations are necessary:

- each instance of the decision problem is encoded as a string w over a suitable alphabet Σ;
- $\mathbf{\Pi}(n)$ is the membrane system of $\mathbf{\Pi}$ which solves the instances w of size n.

Other notions used here are defined as in [19].

Definition 2. *Let* $X = (I_X, \theta_X)$ *be a decision problem, and* $\mathbf{\Pi} = \{\mathbf{\Pi}(n) \mid w \in I_X, |w| = n, n \in \mathbb{N}\}$ *be a family of membrane systems.*

- $\mathbf{\Pi}$ *is said to be* polynomially uniform by Turing machines *if there exists a deterministic Turing machine working in polynomial time to construct the system* $\mathbf{\Pi}(n)$ *from the size* n *of an instance* $w \in I_X$.
- $\mathbf{\Pi}$ *is said to be* sound *with respect to* X *if the following holds: for each instance of the problem* $w \in I_X$, *if there exists an accepting computation of* $\mathbf{\Pi}(|w|)$, *then* $\theta_X(w) = 1$.
- $\mathbf{\Pi}$ *is said to be* complete *with respect to* X *if the following holds: for each instance of the problem* $w \in I_X$, *if* $\theta_X(w) = 1$, *then every computation of* $\mathbf{\Pi}(|w|)$ *is an accepting computation.*

Definition 3. *A decision problem* X *is solvable in* polynomial time *by a family of membrane systems* $\mathbf{\Pi} = \{\mathbf{\Pi}(n) \mid w \in I_X, |w| = n, n \in \mathbb{N}\}$ *if:*

- *The family* $\mathbf{\Pi}$ *is polynomially uniform by Turing machines.*
- *The family* $\mathbf{\Pi}$ *is polynomially bounded, namely there exists a natural number* $k \in \mathbb{N}$ *such that for each instance* $w \in I_X$, *every computation of* $\mathbf{\Pi}(|w|)$ *performs at most* $|w|^k$ *steps.*
- *The family* $\mathbf{\Pi}$ *is sound and complete with respect to* X.

Such a family $\mathbf{\Pi}$ *is said to provide a* uniform solution *to the problem* X.

4 A New Solution to N-Queens Problem

The solution presented in this paper consists of the following stages:

- *Generation stage*: using membrane division, all the possible arrangements of the queens on a chess board are generated;
- *Checking stage*: in each membrane, the system checks whether or not the queens are arranged in order to respect all the requirements;
- *Output stage*: the systems creates into an output membrane 0 the correct answer identified by an unique object *yes* or *no* in the halting configuration.

In order to reduce the computation overload, the generation and checking stages are performed in parallel (when this is possible) such that some solutions are immediately discarded without making any further computations over them. According to [20], for every decision problem we can associate a counting problem in a natural way by replacing the question "is there a solution?" with "how many solutions are there?". Even if the computation presented in this section is able to provide all the possible solutions, for the simplicity of the presentation we deal with the decision problems (and not with their corresponding counting problems).

Theorem 1. *The N-Queens problem can be solved by a uniform family of polarizationless P systems with active membranes and 2-cooperation in linear time.*

Proof. Let us consider a P system Π with active membranes having the initial configuration

$$[[l_{1,1}]_1]_0$$

and the alphabet

$$O = \{no, \overline{no}, \underline{no}, yes, \overline{yes}, \underline{yes}\} \cup \{q_{i,j}, \overline{q_{i,j}} \mid 1 \le i \le N,\ 1 \le j \le N\}$$
$$\cup \{l_{i,j}, l_{i,j}^a, l_{i,j}^b, l_{i,j}^c, l_{i,j}^d, \underline{l_{i,j}}, \overline{l_{i,j}} \mid 1 \le i \le N,\ 1 \le j \le N\}.$$

The P system Π with active membranes uses the set of rules R containing the following rules:

(i) $[l_{i,j} \rightarrow l_{i,j}^a l_{i,j}^b]_1$, for $1 \le i, j \le N$

These rules are used to start the checking phase for each location $l_{i,j}$ on the chess board, with $1 \le i \le N$ and $1 \le j \le N$. The checking phase tests if we can place or not a queen denoted by $q_{i,j}$ on a location $l_{i,j}$. This phase starts when an object $l_{i,j}$ is present inside a membrane labelled by 1. It is worth noting that the evolution starts with object $l_{i,j}$ in membrane 1, namely we start from the top left position of the board. The objects $l_{i,j}^a$ and $l_{i,j}^b$ are used in what follows to check if there exist a queen on the board attacking the current tested location $l_{i,j}$. Depending on the outcome of this test, we can decide to place a queen $q_{i,j}$ on location $l_{i,j}$.

(ii) $[q_{k,j} l_{i,j}^a \rightarrow q_{k,j} l_{i,j}^c]_1$, for $1 \le i, j \le N$ and $1 \le k < i$

Using these rules we check if for a location $l_{i,j}$ there is already placed a queen $q_{k,j}$ on the same column j. If this is the case, the queen $q_{k,j}$ remains on its position, while the object $l_{i,j}^a$ is rewritten to $l_{i,j}^c$. The presence of the object $l_{i,j}^c$ is used in what follows to signal that no queen can be placed on position $l_{i,j}$ because we would not obtain a valid solution. As the checking phase was started from the top left corner and will continue line by line in the next steps, there is no need to check if there is any queen on column j below line i, but just above line i. This is provided by using these rules only when $1 \le k < i$.

(iii) $[q_{k,t} l_{i,j}^a \rightarrow q_{k,t} l_{i,j}^c]_1$ if $|k - i| = |j - t|$, for $1 \le i, j \le N$, $1 \le k < i$ and $1 \le t \le N$

Using these rules we check if for a location $l_{i,j}$ there is already placed a queen $q_{k,t}$ on the same diagonal (left or right). If this is the case, the queen $q_{k,t}$ remains on its position, while the object $l_{i,j}^a$ is rewritten to $l_{i,j}^c$. As in the previous case, when checking the presence of a previous queen on the same column, the presence of the object $l_{i,j}^c$ is used to signal that no queen can be placed on position $l_{i,j}$ because we would not obtain a valid solution. There is no need to check if there is any queen on the same diagonal below line i, but just above line i. This is provided by using these rules only when $1 \le k < i$.

(iv) $[l_{i,j}^b \rightarrow l_{i,j}^d]_1$, for $1 \le i, j \le N$

While in the previous two steps we checked if there exist already any queen that attacks the current checked position l_{ij}, in parallel the object $l_{i,j}^b$ is changed to $l_{i,j}^d$ just to signal that the checking phase was performed. It should be noticed that if there is already a queen on the same column and another one on the same diagonal, only one of the two rules is chosen nondeterministically to change the object $l_{i,j}^a$ to $l_{i,j}^c$. This is due to the fact that the object $l_{i,j}^c$ only signals the presence of at least of a queen attacking the current position $l_{i,j}$, and we do not care how many queens attack the current position $l_{i,j}$.

(v) $[l_{i,j}^a l_{i,j}^d \to \overline{l_{i,j}}]_1$, for $1 \leq i,j \leq N$

The presence of both the objects $l_{i,j}^a$ and $l_{i,j}^d$ inside the same membrane labelled by 1 signals that in the previous checking phase no queen was found attacking the checked position $l_{i,j}$. This means that a new queen can be placed on the current position, fact that is provided by the creation of the object $\overline{l_{i,j}}$.

(vi) $[l_{i,j}^c l_{i,j}^d \to l_{i,j+1}]_1$, for $1 \leq i \leq N$ and $1 \leq j < N$

$[l_{i,N}^c l_{i,N}^d \to no]_1$, for $1 \leq i \leq N$

The presence of both the objects $l_{i,j}^c$ and $l_{i,j}^d$ inside the same membrane labelled by 1 signals that in the previous checking phase at least one queen was found attacking the checked position $l_{i,j}$. This means that a new queen cannot be placed on the current position. If we are not on the last column of the board, namely for $l_{i,j}$ it is the case that $1 \leq j < N$, then we move to the next location on the same line. This is denoted by the creation of the object $l_{i,j+1}$ that starts, in parallel with the current steps, a new checking phase to verify if another queen can be placed on position $l_{i,j+1}$. However, if we are on the last column of the board (namely $l_{i,N}$), then no queen can be placed on the current line and thus we stop the computation. This approach leads to a reduction on the number of performed steps and of the created resources during the computation.

(vii) $[\overline{l_{i,j}}]_1 \to [l_{i,j}]_1[l_{i,j+1}]_1$, for $1 \leq i \leq n$ and $1 \leq j < N$

$[\overline{l_{i,N}} \to l_{i,N}]_1$, for $1 \leq i \leq N$

The existence of an object $\overline{l_{i,j}}$ signals the fact that a new queen can be placed on the current position $l_{i,j}$. Before such a placement is done, we need to launch also a checking phase for the remaining squares of line i (to check if it can also be placed queens). If we are in the situation where $1 \leq j < N$ (namely we are not on the last position of a line), the object $\overline{l_{i,j}}$ is consumed and the current membrane is divided into two membranes. The first membrane contains the object $l_{i,j}$ that marks the fact that the queen is placed there, while in the new membrane a new object $l_{i,j+1}$ is added, marking that we check if on this position we can put a new queen. Notice that in this way, for each line, we check all the possible additions of new queens based on the queens added on the previous lines. If $j = N$, then we are on the last column of a line and no more checks need to be performed for the current line; so we simply rewrite $\overline{l_{i,j}}$ into $l_{i,j}$. This means that the checking phase is constructed in such a way that is no need to check if another queen is placed on the same line.

(viii) $[l_{i,j} \to q_{i,j}l_{i+1,1}]_1$, for $1 \leq i < N$ and $1 \leq j \leq N$

$[l_{N,j} \to q_{N,j}yes]_1$, for $1 \leq j \leq N$

The object $l_{i,j}$ can now be replaced by the object $q_{i,j}$ signalling that a new queen has been placed on the board. If $1 \leq i < N$ (namely we are not yet on the last line), once we placed the queen by creating the object $q_{i,j}$ we move to the first position of the next line to start a new checking phase. This move is performed by creating the object $l_{i+1,1}$ because it makes no sense to move on the other positions of the line $\overline{i}$ as we already placed a queen on this line. If $i = N$ (namely we are on the last line of the board), then beside the newly created object $q_{i,j}$ we also create an object yes that informs us that the current arrangement is a correct one.

(ix) $[no \rightarrow \overline{no}\ \underline{no}]_1$
$[\underline{no}]_1 \rightarrow [\ ]_1 no$
$[yes \rightarrow \overline{yes}\ \underline{yes}]_1$
$[\underline{yes}]_1 \rightarrow [\ ]_1 yes$
$[no\ no \rightarrow no]_0$
$[no\ yes \rightarrow yes]_0$
$[yes\ yes \rightarrow yes]_0$

As we treat this problem as a decision problem, these rules are needed to provide an unique answer in membrane 0 in the halting configuration. For this, only here, we need the communication rules to send the answer from each membrane 1 to the parent membrane 0. Once an object no is present inside a membrane, it is rewritten to the objects $\underline{no}$ and $\overline{no}$. The object $\underline{no}$ is used to communicate the answer no to the parent membrane 0, while the object $\overline{no}$ marks the end of the computation in membrane 1 and keeps track of the answer obtained. A similar approach is taken for each object yes inside a membrane 1. The last three rules are used to reduce the number of answers from membrane 0 to an unique answer in the halting configuration. Notice that these steps are applied in parallel with the other rules.

Analyzing the Computation. We describe how the polarizationless P systems with active membranes and 2-cooperation work in solving an instance of the N-Queens problem. The initial configuration is $[[l_{1,1}]_1]_0$.

The purpose of the evolution rules (i) is to initiate the checking phase for each one of the N^2 positions of the board, namely if a queen can be placed there or not depending on the existing queens already on the chess board. Since we start with the checking phase from the top-left corner, this means that there are no other queens placed on the board. This means that we can generate (by using the division rules of type (iv)) N membranes 1 such that each contains eventually a queen $q_{1,j}$ for $1 \leq j \leq N$. In order to generate a positive answer for placing a queen we need 5 steps; this means that the first N membranes are generated after at most $5 \cdot N$ steps.

Due to our rules, the checking stage is executed in parallel with the generation stage, and it takes at most $5 \cdot (N^2 - N)$ steps. This is since a positive answer needs 5 steps and, after checking first line of the board, only $N \cdot (N-1)$ positions are left as possible solutions for placing a queen. If all remaining evaluations would be negative, the minimum number of steps is given by $3 \cdot (N^2 - N)$ steps, due to the fact that a negative response is provided in 3 steps.

The output phase is also started in parallel with the checking stage. Once each object no or yes is created inside a membrane 1, then in at most 3 steps a copy of that object is communicated into membrane 0, while an object $\overline{no}$ or $\overline{yes}$ is kept in membrane 1. Considering the worst case scenario when 2^{N^2} membranes 1 are created, then in at most N^2 steps (by using the last three rules of type (ix)), a unique object yes or no remains inside membrane 0 as the final answer to the problem and the computation stops. However, due to the fact that the generation, checking and output phases are executed in parallel, the number of membranes and number of executed steps is much smaller.

Complexity. Let us analyze the necessary resources to construct $\Pi(w)$. The constructed system has:

- 2 membranes;
- 1 initial object;
- $9 \cdot N^2 + 6$ objects in the working alphabet;
- N^2 rules of type (i);
- $N^2 \cdot (N - 1)$ rules of type (ii);
- $N^3 \cdot (N - 1)$ rules of type (iii);
- N^2 rules of type (iv);
- N^2 rules of type (v);
- $N^2 + N$ rules of type (vi);
- $N^2 + N$ rules of type (vii);
- $N^2 + N$ rules of type $(viii)$;
- 7 rules of type (ix).

Therefore, the size of the constructed system of polarizationless P systems with active membranes and 2-cooperation is $\mathcal{O}(N^4)$.

It is easy to prove that the system $\Pi(w)$ constructed for an instance w always halts and creates in membrane 0 an object yes or no in the last step of the computation, object corresponding to the correct answer of the instance. The maximum number of steps for such a system is $6 \cdot N^2$, namely there exists a polynomial upper bound for the number of steps of the computation.

Sound and complete means that $\Pi(w)$ produces yes if and only if the given instance w has a solution. It can be easily noticed that, due to the way the system was designed (as detailed above) the computation of the system proceeds in such a way that the final answer is the same regardless of the maximal parallel and nondeterministic manner of applying the evolution rules. Therefore, the family Π solves the N-Queens problem in polynomial time according to Definition 3. $\square$

Example 1 (3 Queens Case). The evolution starts from the configuration $[[l_{1,1}]_1]_0$. It should be noticed that there is no need to check if there exist already queens in the system because we are at the beginning on the execution. However, in order to have a compact set of rules, we perform such a check.

$$[[l_{1,1}]_1]_0 \rightarrow [[l^a_{1,1} l^b_{1,1}]_1]_0$$
$$\rightarrow [[l^a_{1,1} l^d_{1,1}]_1]_0$$
$$\rightarrow [[\overline{l}_{1,1}]_1]_0$$
$$\rightarrow [[l_{1,1}]_1 [l_{1,2}]_1]_0$$

After performing the first check, it can be noticed that it is possible to place a queen on the board position $\{1,1\}$, this being provided by the created object $l_{1,1}$ on a fresh membrane 1.

$$\rightarrow [[q_{1,1}l_{2,1}]_1 \ [l_{1,2}^{a}l_{1,2}^{b}]_1]_0$$
$$\rightarrow [[q_{1,1}\overline{l_{2,1}^{a}}l_{2,1}^{b}]_1 \ [l_{1,2}^{a}l_{1,2}^{d}]_1]_0$$
$$\rightarrow [[q_{1,1}l_{2,1}^{c}l_{2,1}^{d}]_1 \ [\overline{l_{1,2}}]_1]_0$$
$$\rightarrow [[q_{1,1}l_{2,2}]_1 \ [l_{1,2}]_1 \ [\overline{l_{1,3}}]_1]_0$$

Since in the membrane containing the queen $q_{1,1}$ there is no way to place a queen $q_{2,1}$, we move to the position $l_{2,2}$ to check if this is appropriate for placing another queen.

$$\rightarrow [[q_{1,1}l_{2,2}^{a}l_{2,2}^{b}]_1 \ [q_{1,2}l_{2,1}]_1 \ [l_{1,3}^{a}l_{1,3}^{b}]_1]_0$$
$$\rightarrow [[q_{1,1}l_{2,2}^{c}l_{2,2}^{d}]_1 \ [q_{1,2}\overline{l_{2,1}^{a}}l_{2,1}^{b}]_1 \ [l_{1,3}^{a}l_{1,3}^{d}]_1]_0$$
$$\rightarrow [[q_{1,1}l_{2,3}]_1 \ [q_{1,2}l_{2,1}^{c}l_{2,1}^{d}]_1 \ [\overline{l_{1,3}}]_1]_0$$
$$\rightarrow [[q_{1,1}l_{2,3}^{a}l_{2,3}^{b}]_1 \ [q_{1,2}l_{2,2}]_1 \ [l_{1,3}]_1]_0$$
$$\rightarrow [[q_{1,1}l_{2,3}^{a}l_{2,3}^{d}]_1 \ [q_{1,2}l_{2,2}^{a}l_{2,2}^{b}]_1 \ [q_{1,3}l_{2,1}]_1]_0$$
$$\rightarrow [[q_{1,1}\overline{l_{2,3}}]_1 \ [q_{1,2}l_{2,2}^{c}l_{2,2}^{d}]_1 \ [q_{1,3}l_{2,1}^{a}l_{2,1}^{b}]_1]_0$$
$$\rightarrow [[q_{1,1}l_{2,3}]_1 \ [q_{1,2}l_{2,3}]_1 \ [q_{1,3}l_{2,1}^{a}l_{2,1}^{d}]_1]_0$$
$$\rightarrow [[q_{1,1}q_{2,3}l_{3,1}]_1 \ [q_{1,2}l_{2,3}^{a}l_{2,3}^{b}]_1 \ [q_{1,3}\overline{l_{2,1}}]_1]_0$$
$$\rightarrow [[q_{1,1}q_{2,3}l_{3,1}^{a}l_{3,1}^{b}]_1 \ [q_{1,2}l_{2,3}^{c}l_{2,3}^{d}]_1 \ [q_{1,3}l_{2,1}]_1 \ [q_{1,3}l_{2,2}]_1]_0$$
$$\rightarrow [[q_{1,1}q_{2,3}l_{3,1}^{c}l_{3,1}^{d}]_1 \ [q_{1,2}\,no]_1 \ [q_{1,3}q_{2,1}l_{3,1}]_1 \ [q_{1,3}l_{2,2}^{a}l_{2,2}^{b}]_1]_0$$

It should be noticed in the previous configuration that, by adding a queen $q_{1,2}$, there is no possibility to add another queen on row 2 of a board of size 3, and so the object no is created to stop the evolution of the membrane containing queen $q_{1,2}$.

$$\rightarrow [[q_{1,1}q_{2,3}\underline{l_{3,2}}]_1 \ [q_{1,2}\,\overline{no}\,\underline{no}]_1 \ [q_{1,3}q_{2,1}l_{3,1}^{a}l_{3,1}^{b}]_1 \ [q_{1,3}l_{2,2}^{c}l_{2,2}^{d}]_1]_0$$
$$\rightarrow [[q_{1,1}q_{2,3}l_{3,2}^{a}l_{3,2}^{b}]_1 \ [q_{1,2}\,\overline{no}]_1 \ [q_{1,3}q_{2,1}l_{3,1}^{c}l_{3,1}^{d}]_1 \ [q_{1,3}l_{2,3}]_1 \ no]_0$$
$$\rightarrow [[q_{1,1}q_{2,3}l_{3,2}^{c}l_{3,2}^{d}]_1 \ [q_{1,2}\,\overline{no}]_1 \ [q_{1,3}q_{2,1}\underline{l_{3,2}}]_1 \ [q_{1,3}l_{2,3}^{a}l_{2,3}^{b}]_1 \ no]_0$$
$$\rightarrow [[q_{1,1}q_{2,3}\underline{l_{3,3}}]_1 \ [q_{1,2}\,\overline{no}]_1 \ [q_{1,3}q_{2,1}l_{3,2}^{a}l_{3,2}^{b}]_1 \ [q_{1,3}l_{2,3}^{c}l_{2,3}^{d}]_1 \ no]_0$$
$$\rightarrow [[q_{1,1}q_{2,3}l_{3,3}^{a}l_{3,3}^{b}]_1 \ [q_{1,2}\,\overline{no}]_1 \ [q_{1,3}q_{2,1}l_{3,2}^{c}l_{3,2}^{d}]_1 \ [q_{1,3}\,no]_1 \ no]_0$$
$$\rightarrow [[q_{1,1}q_{2,3}l_{3,3}^{c}l_{3,3}^{d}]_1 \ [q_{1,2}\,\overline{no}]_1 \ [q_{1,3}q_{2,1}l_{3,3}]_1 \ [q_{1,3}\,\overline{no}\,\underline{no}]_1 \ no]_0$$
$$\rightarrow [[q_{1,1}q_{2,3}\,no]_1 \ [q_{1,2}\,\overline{no}]_1 \ [q_{1,3}q_{2,1}l_{3,3}^{a}l_{3,3}^{b}]_1 \ [q_{1,3}\,\overline{no}]_1 \ no\,no]_0$$
$$\rightarrow [[q_{1,1}q_{2,3}\,\overline{no}\,\underline{no}]_1 \ [q_{1,2}\,\overline{no}]_1 \ [q_{1,3}q_{2,1}l_{3,3}^{c}l_{3,3}^{d}]_1 \ [q_{1,3}\,\overline{no}]_1 \ no]_0$$
$$\rightarrow [[q_{1,1}q_{2,3}\,\overline{no}]_1 \ [q_{1,2}\,\overline{no}]_1 \ [q_{1,3}q_{2,1}\,\overline{no}\,\underline{no}]_1 \ [q_{1,3}\,\overline{no}]_1 \ no\,no]_0$$
$$\rightarrow [[q_{1,1}q_{2,3}\,\overline{no}]_1 \ [q_{1,2}\,\overline{no}]_1 \ [q_{1,3}q_{2,1}\,\overline{no}]_1 \ [q_{1,3}\,\overline{no}]_1 \ no\,no]_0$$
$$\rightarrow [[q_{1,1}q_{2,3}\,\overline{no}]_1 \ [q_{1,2}\,\overline{no}]_1 \ [q_{1,3}q_{2,1}\,\overline{no}]_1 \ [q_{1,3}\,\overline{no}]_1 \ no]_0$$

As expected, there is no possible way to arrange three queens on a board of size three, and the unique answer provided inside membrane 0 is given by the object no. Notice also that in the final configuration, all the membranes labelled by 1 contain the object $\overline{no}$, marking the fact that none of those arrangements are valid. Thus, only 5 membranes and 29 steps are needed to provide the answer for a chess board of dimension 3. This is an improvement with respect to the solution provided by other approaches; for instance, in [9] are necessary 512 membranes and 117 steps.

5 Conclusion

In this paper we defined polarizationless P systems with active membranes and 2-cooperation to solve the N-queens problem. Our solution is such that the halting configuration encodes all the solutions of the puzzle. According to [21], the membrane division cannot be avoided; the only possibility is to use elementary division (as done in this paper) such that each correct arrangement of the queens is kept in a separate membrane.

We use the massive parallelism specific to membrane computing to check the feasible solutions, and obtain the solution in a reduced number of steps by using a small number of membranes. The necessary resources and the number of computational steps for obtaining all the solutions of the puzzle are polynomial in N. We exemplified our approach for the case $N = 3$, and show that only 5 membranes and 29 steps are needed to provide a correct answer. This results represents an improvement with respect to other existing solutions.

References

1. Alhazov, A., Pan, L.: Polarizationless P systems with active membranes. Grammars **7**, 141–159 (2004)
2. Aman, B., Ciobanu, G.: Solving a weak NP-complete problem in polynomial time by using mutual mobile membrane systems. Acta Inform. **48**(7–8), 409–415 (2011)
3. Aman, B., Ciobanu, G.: Efficiently solving the bin packing problem through bio-inspired mobility. Acta Inform. **54**(4), 435–445 (2017)
4. Aman, B., Ciobanu, G.: Turing completeness using three mobile membranes. In: Calude, C.S., Costa, J.F., Dershowitz, N., Freire, E., Rozenberg, G. (eds.) UC 2009. LNCS, vol. 5715, pp. 42–55. Springer, Heidelberg (2009). https://doi.org/10.1007/978-3-642-03745-0_12
5. Aman, B., Ciobanu, G.: Describing the immune system using enhanced mobile membranes. Electron. Notes Theor. Comput. Sci. **194**(3), 5–18 (2008)
6. Bell, J., Stevens, B.: A survey of known results and research areas for N-queens. Discrete Math. **309**(1), 1–31 (2009)
7. Bezzel, M.: Proposal of 8-queens problem. Berl. Schachzeitung **3**, 363 (1848). Submitted under the author name "Schachfreund"
8. Buño, K.C., Cabarle, F.G.C., Calabia, M.D., Adorna, H.N.: Solving the N-queens problem using dP systems with active membranes. Theor. Comput. Sci. **736**, 1–14 (2018)
9. Gutiérrez-Naranjo, M.A., Martínez-del Amor, M.A., Pérez-Hurtado, I., Pérez-Jiménez, M.J.: Solving the N-queens puzzle with P systems. In: Gutiérrez-Escudero, R., Gutiérrez-Naranjo, M.A., Păun, G., Pérez-Hurtado, I., Riscos-Núñez, A. (eds.) 7th Brainstorming Week on Membrane Computing, pp. 199–210. Fénix Editora, São Paulo (2009)

10. Gutiérrez-Naranjo, M.A., Pérez-Jiménez, M.J.: Depth-first search with P systems. In: Gheorghe, M., Hinze, T., Păun, G., Rozenberg, G., Salomaa, A. (eds.) CMC 2010. LNCS, vol. 6501, pp. 257–264. Springer, Heidelberg (2010). https://doi.org/10.1007/978-3-642-18123-8_20

11. Gutiérrez-Naranjo, M.A., Pérez-Jiménez, M.J.: Local search with P systems - a case study. Int. J. Nat. Comput. Res. **2**, 47–55 (2011)

12. Ionescu, M., Păun, Gh., Yokomori, T.: Spiking neural P systems. Fundam. Inform. **71**, 279–308 (2006)

13. Maroosi, A., Muniyandi, R.C.: Accelerated execution of P systems with active membranes to solve the N-queens problem. Theor. Comput. Sci. **551**, 39–54 (2014)

14. Martín-Vide, C., Păun, Gh., Pazos, J., Rodríguez-Patón, A.: Tissue P systems. Theor. Comput. Sci. **296**, 295–326 (2003)

15. Păun, Gh.: Computing with membranes. J. Comput. Syst. Sci. **61**, 108–143 (2000)

16. Păun, Gh.: Active membranes. In: [17], pp. 282–301

17. Păun, Gh., Rozenberg, G., Salomaa, A. (eds.): The Oxford Handbook of Membrane Computing. Oxford University Press, Oxford (2010)

18. Peng, H., Wang, J., Shi, P., Pérez-Jiménez, M.J., Riscos-Núñez, A.: Fault diagnosis of power systems using fuzzy tissue-like P systems. Integr. Comput.-Aided Eng. **24**(4), 401–411 (2017)

19. Pérez-Jiménez, M.J., Riscos-Núñez, A., Romero-Jiménez, A., Woods, D.: Complexity-membrane division, membrane creation. In: [17], pp. 302–336 (2010)

20. Valencia-Cabrera, L., Orellana-Martín, D., Riscos-Núñez, A., Pérez-Jiménez, M.J.: Counting membrane systems. In: Gheorghe, M., Rozenberg, G., Salomaa, A., Zandron, C. (eds.) CMC 2017. LNCS, vol. 10725, pp. 74–87. Springer, Cham (2018). https://doi.org/10.1007/978-3-319-73359-3_5

21. Zandron, C., Ferretti, C., Mauri, G.: Solving NP-complete problems using P systems with active membranes. In: Antoniou, I., Calude, C.S., Dinneen, M.J. (eds.) Unconventional Models of Computation, pp. 289–301. Springer, Heidelberg (2001). https://doi.org/10.1007/978-1-4471-0313-4_21

A Model of Antibiotic Resistance Evolution Dynamics Through P Systems with Active Membranes and Communication Rules

Fernando Baquero[1], Marcelino Campos[1,2], Carlos Llorens[3], and José M. Sempere[2(✉)]

[1] Department of Microbiology, IRYCIS, Ramon y Cajal University Hospital, Madrid, Spain
baquero@bitmailer.net
[2] Department of Information Systems and Computation, Universitat Politècnica de València, Valencia, Spain
{mcampos,jsempere}@dsic.upv.es
[3] Biotechvana, Valencia, Spain
carlos.llorens@biotechvana.com

Abstract. In this work we describe a model of antibiotic resistance evolution dynamics based on a membrane computing approach. The model was implemented in a simulator tool first proposed in [3], with a naive set of rules and characteristics. In this paper, we describe the improvements over the first version of the model, we introduce new P system rules to manage all the elements of the system, and we explain a scenario in order to illustrate the experiments that can be carried out in the proposed framework.

1   Introduction

P systems were proposed by Păun in 1998 [7] and gave birth to the membrane computing research area [9]. Basically, P systems are computational models inspired by eukaryotic cells and the exchange of biomolecules and information that is carried out through the physical membranes that structure the organelles of the cell. The computational ingredients of P systems are: (1) the arrangement of different regions organized in a tree-like structure, (2) a set of rules that guide the operation of the model during any computation, and (3) a set of objects that evolve and move throughout the structure of the system. The model can be defined non-deterministic and working in a maximally parallel manner. Hence, the interest in using it for the resolution of highly complex problems and with a stochastic component. In fact, membrane computing has proven to be a useful and versatile tool in systems biology, giving rise to different models in different areas such as ecology [5], bioprocesses [2] or the mechanisms for genetic regulation [1], to name a few areas of interest. A compendium of some works on systems biology addressed by membrane computing is [8], while other bio-applications of

C. Graciani et al. (Eds.): Pérez-Jiménez Festschrift, LNCS 11270, pp. 33–44, 2018.
https://doi.org/10.1007/978-3-030-00265-7_3

membrane computing have been shown in [4]. In this work, we propose a modeling of the population dynamics of bacteria referred to the evolution of antibiotic resistance. Antibiotic resistance is a priority problem in Public Health. As it has been described in [12]: *"Antimicrobial resistance (AMR) with a wide range of infectious agents is a growing public health threat of broad concern to countries and multiple sectors. Increasingly, governments around the world are beginning to pay attention to a problem so serious that it threatens the achievements of modern medicine. A post-antibiotic era, in which common infections and minor injuries can kill, far from being an apocalyptic fantasy, is instead a very real possibility for the 21st century."* That is why the study of possible scenarios where resistance to antibiotics behaves epidemically is of great interest. Our work is oriented to the efficient design of a computational simulator of such scenarios as it has already been tested in [3].

The structure of this work is as follows: In Sect. 2, we formally define P systems with active membranes and we explain its semantics. We define a cell-like P system with active membranes and communication rules to model the population dynamics related to the antibiotic resistance evolution in bacteria. In Sect. 3, we describe a scenario to test the proposed model, and in Sect. 4 we report some experimental results from the described model. Finally, we state some conclusions about this work.

2 Basic Concepts

In this section we introduce basic concepts about P systems. We assume that the reader is familiar with the basic concepts of membrane computing. If this is not the case, we recommend the reading of [10,11]. In this work we use cell-like P systems with active membranes and without polarization that are defined as follows.

Definition 1. *A P system with active membranes of degree $m \geq 1$ is defined by the tuple $\Pi = (V, H, \mu, w_1, w_2, \cdots, w_m, R, i_0)$ where*

1. *V is the alphabet of objects*
2. *H is the alphabet of labels for membranes*
3. *μ is the initial membrane structure, of degree m, with all membranes labeled with elements of H and no polarizations. A membrane with label h is represented as $[\ ]_h$*
4. *$w_1, w_2, \cdots, w_m$ are strings over V specifying the multiset of objects present in the compartment of μ*
5. *R is a finite set of rules of the following types*
   (a) $[v \rightarrow w]_h$ with $v, w \in V^*$ (evolution rules)
   (b) $v[\ ]_h \rightarrow [w]_h$ with $v, w \in V^*$ ('in' communication rules)
   (c) $[v]_h \rightarrow w[\ ]_h$ with $v, w \in V^*$ ('out' communication rules)
   (d) $[v]_h \rightarrow [\ [w]_j]_h$ with $v, w \in V^*$ (membrane creation with object evolution)
6. *$i_0 \in \{0, \cdots, m\}$ indicates the region where the result of a computation is obtained (0 represents the environment).*

The rules of the P system are applied in a non-deterministic maximally parallel manner. The computation of the system finishes whenever no rule can be applied. A configuration of the system at time t during a computation is defined by the membrane structure μ_t and the multisets of objects at every region in μ_t.

2.1 Modifications of the System Used in the Model Definition

We are going to specify some of the components of the P system that have been previously defined, since to perform the simulation of the model we have introduced some modifications on the rules and the way in which the system works, that is, how the rules are applied in each step of computing. Fundamentally, we will specify the rules, the object alphabets and the working manner of the system.

Alphabets and Membranes

In each region of the system there are two parameters that can regulate the application of the rules within the region: the *capacity* and the *occupation*. We consider that the alphabet V is partitioned into two alphabets V_c and V_{nc} so that $V = V_c \cup V_{nc}$, with $V_c \cap V_{nc} = \emptyset$. V_c denotes the set of objects that consume capacity of the membrane when they enter into the region delimited by it, while V_{nc} is the rest of objects. Each object from V_c consumes one unit of the capacity of the membrane. In addition, we will consider that the internal membranes of a region also consume only one unit, independently of its internal structure and the objects it may contain. In this way, if in the region delimited by the membrane h with a capacity γ there is a occupation index of δ objects and membranes then we will denote it as $[\ ]_h^{\gamma - \delta}$. We will call *effective capacity* the difference between capacity and occupation. Observe that the effective capacity of a membrane is always greater than or equal to zero, and we will not allow negative values. This concept is dynamic since the occupation of a membrane can vary depending on the communication rules that are executed during the computation.

Another aspect in which we will make distinction is with respect to the objects that can be duplicated in the membrane duplication rules that we will explain later. Again, we will define a partition of the alphabet V into two sets V_d and V_{nd} so that $V = V_d \cup V_{nd}$, with $V_d \cap V_{nd} = \emptyset$. Here, V_d denotes the set of objects that are duplicated in a membrane duplication, while objects from V_{nd} are not replicated.

Rules

The rules at every region are ordered by priorities in the usual manner. In addition, we can associate to each rule a numerical parameter that identifies its suitability in terms of its possible application or not in a computation step. Therefore, we can define the *suitability* function: $\mathcal{P} : R \to [0, 1]$ that approximates our model to a probabilistic/stochastic model in a way similar to PDP systems [6], although in our case we only use a cell-like P system instead of a multienvironment P system with active membranes. This function allows the application of the rules to only a subset of the objects. For example, if a rule

$a \rightarrow b$ has a suitability index of 0.5 and there are two objects a in the region, then only one object a will be transformed into b according to the rule application (always taking this fact on average over the number of times we apply that rule in that configuration).

Next we will describe the semantics of the rules that we have defined in our model. Some of them differ slightly from the semantics that have been habitually assigned to them, while others are new rules that adapt to the needs of the reality that is intended to model:

1. evolution rules: $[u_i]_j^\alpha \rightarrow [u_i']_j^{\alpha'}$
   In the membrane j the multiset u_i is substituted by the multiset u_i'. The effective capacity of the membrane is adjusted according to the multisets u_i and u_i', and the elements from V_c and V_{nc}.

2. 'in' object communication rules: $[u_i[\ ]_j^\alpha]_k^\beta \rightarrow [[u_i']_j^{\alpha'}]_k^{\beta'}$
   The effective capacity of the membrane j may be decreased and the effective capacity of membrane k may be increased according to the multisets u_i and u_i', and the elements from V_c and V_{nc}.

3. 'out' object communication rules: $[[u_i]_j^\alpha]_k^\beta \rightarrow [u_i'[\ ]_j^{\alpha'}]_k^{\beta'}$
   The effective capacity of the membrane j may be increased and the effective capacity of membrane k may be decreased according to the multisets u_i and u_i', and the elements from V_c and V_{nc}.

4. 'between' object communication rules: $[[u_i]_j^\alpha[\ ]_k^\beta]_p^\omega \rightarrow [[\ ]_j^{\alpha'}[u_i']_k^{\beta'}]_p^\omega$
   The effective capacity of the membrane j may be increased and the effective capacity of membrane k may be decreased according to the multisets u_i and u_i', and the elements from V_c and V_{nc}. Observe that, at the membrane p, the effective capacity ω does not change since the membranes j and k remain inside the membrane p.

5. membrane dissolution rules (removing content): $[[u_i]_k^\alpha]_p^\beta \rightarrow [\ ]_p^{\beta'}$
   If the membrane k has all the objects of the multiset u_i, it is dissolved and the objects and membranes contained inside disappear. The effective capacity of p is increased due to the dissolution of k.

6. membrane dissolution rules (leaving the content): $[[u_i]_k^\alpha]_p^\beta \rightarrow [w]_p^{\beta'}$
   If the membrane k contains the objects denoted by u_i, it is dissolved and all the objects inside (denoted by w) remain in the membrane p. The effective capacity of the membrane p changes according to the multiset w, and the elements from V_c and V_{nc}, and the disappearance of the membrane k.

7. 'in' membrane communication rules: $[[\ ]_i^\alpha[\ ]_j^\beta]_k^\omega \rightarrow [[[\ ]_i^\alpha]_j^{\beta'}]_k^{\omega'}$
   If the membranes i and j are in the region k, the membrane i is introduced into the membrane j. The effective capacities of membranes j and k are changed according to the new membrane structure.

8. 'out' membrane communication rules: $[[[\ ]_i^\alpha]_j^\beta]_k^\omega \rightarrow [[\ ]_i^\alpha[\ ]_j^{\beta'}]_k^{\omega'}$
   If the membrane j contains the membrane i, the membrane i is pushed out of the membrane j. The effective capacities of membranes j and k are changed according to the new membrane structure.

9. 'between' membrane communication rules: $[[[\ ]_i^\alpha]_j^\beta[\ ]_k^\omega]_l^\gamma \rightarrow [[\ ]_j^{\beta'}[[\ ]_i^\alpha]_k^{\omega'}]_l^\gamma$
   If the membrane j and k are in the same region and the membrane j contains

the membrane i, the membrane i is moved from the membrane j to the membrane k. The effective capacities of membranes j and k are changed according to the new membrane structure. Observe that the capacity of membrane l does not change.

10. membrane duplication rules: $[[\ ]_i^\alpha]_j^\beta \rightarrow [[\ ]_i^{\alpha'}[\ ]_i^{\alpha''}]_j^{\beta'}$

The membrane i duplicates itself. The effective capacity of membrane j is changed according to the new membrane structure. For the membrane i the process is the following: We start with one membrane i and we finish with two membranes i. All the membranes and the objects inside i belonging to V_d, are duplicated while the objects belonging to V_{nd} are distributed non-deterministically between the two copies of i.

Computation Mode

We define a parameter ψ that denotes the computation mode of the system. We consider three different computation modes that are regulated according to the effective capacity of every membrane. Observe that the effective capacity allows the population regulation of the simulated system. In other works such as [5] the population regulation is carried out by the objects defined in the alphabets of the P system.

We have considered three different computation modes that we describe as follows:

- $\psi = 1$

All the rules are executed according to the priorities and the function $\mathcal{P}$ provided that they can be executed and the effective capacity of the membranes are not exceeded.

- $\psi = 2$

All the rules are executed according to the priorities and the function $\mathcal{P}$. When a rule is applied if a membrane exceeds its effective capacity receiving objects or membranes, some elements generated by the rules are nondeterministically removed to preserve the membrane effective capacity to zero.

- $\psi = 3$

All the rules are executed according to the priorities and the function $\mathcal{P}$. At the end of a calculation step, the membranes with their exceeded effective capacity eliminate the objects and the membranes proportionally to their quantity until the effective capacity is set to zero.

3   Description of a Scenario

With the objective of testing the proposed system, we are going to model a scenario where the rules, objects and structures are adapted to those described in the previous section. We model two populations: a hospital and a community. Each population contains hosts and each host contains bacteria. Guests can move from one population to another and bacteria can spread from one host to another. Different types of antibiotics are administered to the guests that can kill the bacteria. Bacteria can have some resistance genes that allow them to survive an antibiotic. An antibiotic removes some intestinal bacteria and other bacteria can occupy this place while the intestinal bacteria are recovering.

Before beginning to define the scenario more formally, we must take into account some details. First, the capacity of the membranes, especially in the hosts, is essential for the dynamics of the simulation; a host has a finite capacity to contain bacteria. On the other hand, bacteria have a very high level of growth but bacteria can not replicate if there is no space. Then, when we apply antibiotic to a host and eliminate bacteria, a new space appears and can be affected by other bacteria. And second, to make a meaningful simulation, we need many membranes: in a hospital there are many patients, in a community many people, and a host can have three billion bacteria. For a simulation, these numbers are intractable. To solve this problem we made two decisions: for the number of hosts the important is the proportion of people between the hospital and the community. We can take a single sample but we must maintain the proportion of a host in the hospital for one hundred people in the community. Another decision we have made is that we consider only one small sample of bacteria instead of the 3 billion that a host can have. The main reason for this decision is that each bacterium is represented by a membrane in the P system and the practical computability of the simulation could be compromised if all the bacteria are encoded. Taking a representative sample of the elements of the scenario seems an appropriate approach to obtain significant results.

We will detail the scenario taking into account the following aspects:

1. One step of computation is equivalent to one hour in the real time. One step simulates one hour because *E. coli* usually takes about an hour to divide into optimal conditions, being one of the fastest bacteria to do so. Therefore, one hour is a significant unit of time to work.
2. There are two populations, one hospital with one hundred hosts and one community with ten thousand hosts.
3. Every four steps (four hours) the hospital and the community exchange one host.
4. We work with the bacteria of the intestine. The five types of bacteria studied are EC (*Escherichia coli*), EF1 and EF2 (*Enteroccocus faecium*), KP (*Klebsiella pneumoniae*) and PA (*Pseudomonas aeruginosa*). These bacteria represent the 1% of all the bacteria in the intestine.
5. In this scenario there are three types of antibiotics: A1 (*aminopenicillins*), A2 (*cefotaxime*) and A3 (*fluoroquinolones*).
6. An antibiotic treatment consists in one dose every 6 hours for a seven days. Each dose tries to kill the 30% of the bacteria in the first hour and a 15% in the second hour.
7. The 20% of the hosts in the hospital are under treatment, as well as the 1.3% in the community.
8. At the hospital, the 30% of the treatments are for antibiotic A1, 40% for antibiotic A2, and 30% for the A3 antibiotic. In the community, the 75% of the treatments are antibiotic A1, 5% of antibiotic A2 and 20% of antibiotic A3.

9. When a host is treated with antibiotic A1, the 25% of the bacteria in the intestine dies, with the antibiotic A2 dies 20% and for the antibiotic A3 the 10%. These bacteria take two months to recover their normal number. Meanwhile, this space can be occupied by EC, EF1, EF2, KP and PA.
10. A bacterium can have two different types of resistance, a static resistance (resistances in the genome) or a mobile resistance (resistances in plasmids or transposons).
11. A bacterium can only contain two mobile resistances.
12. The static resistance AR1 resists the antibiotic A1, AR2 resists the antibiotic A2 and AR3 resists the antibiotic A3.
13. The mobile resistance PAR1 resists A1 and the resistance PAR2 resists A1 only at the 10% if the resistance is in EC, KP, or PA and A2 if the resistance is in EC, KP or PA. The resistance PAR2 resists only A2 if it is in EF1 or EF2.
14. Each host starts with the bacteria configuration shown in Table 1:

Table 1. Table of bacteria configuration

Bacteria	Number	Static resistance	Mobile resistance
EC	5000	No resistance	No resistance
EC	2500	No resistance	PAR1
EC	1000	AR3	No resistance
EC	100	AR3	PAR1
EF1	995	AR2	No resistance
EF2	200	AR2 and AR3	PAR1
KP	200	AR1 and AR3	PAR2
PA	5	AR1	PAR2

15. A mobile resistance can move between EC and KP with a rate of 0.0001, between EF1 and EF2 with a rate of 0.0001, from PA to EC or KP at a rate of 0.000000001 and from EC or KP to PA at a rate of 0.000000001. Mobile resistance movements between bacteria of the same type can also be considered. For example, the movement rate from PA to PA is 0.0001.
16. There is a possibility by mutation that a bacterium without AR3 genetic resistance takes this resistance at a rate of 0.00000001.
17. When one host propagates to another, it passes the 0.1% of EC, EF1, EF2, KP, and PA. In one hour, the 5% of the hospital hosts extended other hosts and the 1% in the community.
18. The growth of each bacterium is different. Growth 1 represents that in one hour, if there is space, the bacteria double their number. EC has growth 1, EF1 and EF2 have 0.85, KP has 0.9 and PA has 0.15. A resistance in a bacterium means an additional cost for growth because every element must be replicated in mitosis. In this scenario we put a penalty of 0.03 (subtracted from the growth rate) for each AR3, PAR1 and PAR2.

4   Experiments and Results

For experimentation, we write the scenario described above in a XML language created expressly for the simulator of this calculation model. We perform 50,000 steps because for the study of resistances in bacteria this number of steps is needed to show significant results. The simulator uses the computation mode $\psi = 3$ of the model. The initial membrane structure for the simulation is showed in the Fig. 1.

The proposed P system described in Sect. 2 was created to simulate scenarios with bacteria. This means that in a computation there is a large number of membranes, and to be able to execute a simulation we need to work with membranes with multiplicity. When we use membranes with multiplicity and rules with suitability, the power of the multiplicity is lost because we separate the membranes to apply the rules. For example, if we have a membrane with multiplicity two and we apply a rule with 0.5 of suitability, the rule is only executed in one of the two membranes and the result produces two different membranes with multiplicity one. After some calculation steps, some membranes appear that represent exactly the same bacteria but are not represented with only one membrane with multiplicity. To solve this problem, at the end of each step, we check all the membranes that do not have inside other membranes (in this case the bacteria), and we fuse the equivalent membranes in only one membrane with multiplicity that is equal to the sum of the fused membranes.

From the simulation, we obtain two types of results: the first is the counting of each object and membrane in the hospital and the community (the elements in the contained membranes are also counted), and the second is the test, a test

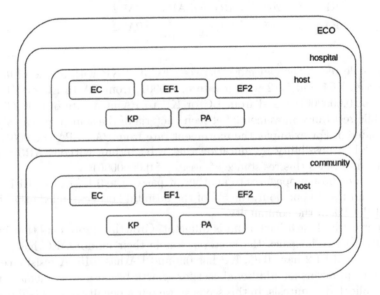

Fig. 1. Initial membrane structure for the described scenario.

is defined by two sets of elements: what is *necessary* and what is *forbidden*. A membrane passes the test if it contains all the necessary elements and none of the elements is forbidden. So, we can count the number of membranes that pass the test (for example, how many EC bacteria have a resistance but do not have another). In this scenario, we focused the study on two points: the evolution of the bacteria in the hospital and the evolution of the resistance of the EC in the hospital.

In the Fig. 2, we can see the evolution of the bacteria in the hospital. The x axis in the graph represents the calculation steps (one step simulates one hour), and the y axis represents the number of elements that we analyze. The bacteria in smaller number are PA, these bacteria have resistance to A1 and A2, but they have a very low fitness in front of the fitness of the other bacteria. The PA bacteria are outside the graph due to its low number with respect to the other bacteria. The next two bacteria are EF1 and EF2. Although EF1 and EF2 have the same physical state, EF2 appear in greater numbers because, at the beginning, EF2 bacteria have resistance to all antibiotics and EF1 only to A2. The KP bacteria have resistance to all antibiotics but they appear in more quantity than EF1 because their fitness is a little higher than EF2. Finally, the EC have the highest growth among all the bacteria under study. It is because they have the best physical form and, at the beginning, some EC have resistance to A3 and A1.

We must say that some resistances are transferred throughout the experiment. The most important are EF1 that take the resistance PAR1 from EF2. In addition, EF1 still do not have resistance to A3 (they can take this resistance by mutation, but with very little probability). The other important resistance acquisition is the resistance of EC to A2. EC can take this resistance from KP

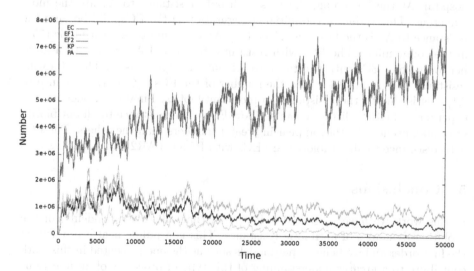

Fig. 2. Evolution of the bacteria in the hospital along about 70 month.

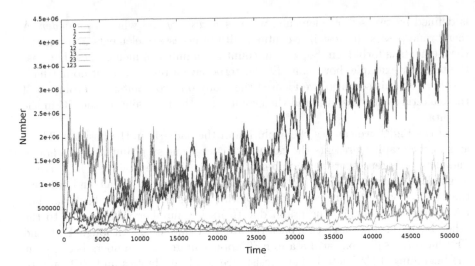

Fig. 3. Evolution of the EC bacteria depending of their resistances in the hospital along about 70 month. For this study we take into account the static resistance AR3 and the mobile resistances PAR1 and PAR2. 0 shows EC without AR3, PAR1 and PAR2, 1 shows EC with PAR1, 2 shows EC with PAR2, 3 shows EC with AR3, 12 shows EC with PAR1 and PAR2, 13 shows EC with PAR1 and AR3, 23 shows EC with PAR2 and AR3 and 123 shows EC with PAR1, PAR2 and AR3.

and, with less probability, from PA. When the EC take resistance to A2 they take resistance to all the antibiotics.

The Fig. 3 shows the evolution of the resistance of the EC bacteria in the hospital. At the beginning, the ECs with only resistance to A1 are the more numerous. This is due to the initial configuration of the ECs, and because the resistance to A1 is the best one, given that A1 is the most used antibiotic (75% in the community). The ECs with resistance to A1 and A3 start with a number lower than ECs with resistance to A1 but they grow faster. The ECs with resistance to A1 and A3 exceed the number of the ECs with only resistance to A1, this is due to the resistance to more antibiotics. Finally, throughout the experiment, little by little we can see how ECs with resistance to all antibiotics grow and, eventually, they appear in greater numbers than the others. The ECs with resistance to all antibiotics are ECs with PAR1, PAR2 and AR3.

5   Conclusions

In this work we have presented a P system that allows the modeling of the evolution dynamics of antibiotic resistance. This is a public health problem of the first order and we believe that models such as the one presented in this work contribute to a greater understanding of this type of processes of an infectious nature. The first approach we made with this type of systems was published in [3]. However, subsequent refinements of the model and its adjustments led us to a substantial modification of the model with the aim of giving it a greater capacity to represent the real problem as well as greater computational benefits. The main modifications that we have been incorporating since our initial proposal has been exposed in this work.

The first conclusion we can reach is that P systems are a useful tool when dealing with some problems of Systems Biology, such as the one we have discussed in this paper. In addition, the formalization of the P systems allows a fairly intuitive understanding of what happens in the system, even for those scientists and professionals who do not have a great knowledge about computer models. In our case, the explanation of the gene transfer could be done in a very graphic way, assimilating some regions of the system to the carriers of the resistance and the populations in interaction as regions at the same level.

This work allows us to continue advancing towards more complex simulators that allow a greater understanding of reality.

Acknowledgements. Our work would not have been possible without the previous contributions of the community in P systems that allowed us to formulate this model as a valid tool and, in some cases, the best tool for modeling biological processes. In particular, all the works on ecological systems of the Natural Computing Group of the University of Seville, led by Prof. Mario de Jesús Pérez-Jiménez, have been our source of inspiration to address the design of our model.

José M. Sempere is indebted to Mario for his generosity and sincere friendship during all these years. This anniversary is a good opportunity to convey to Mario my gratitude for his human qualities, scientific rigor and ethical standards that I have been fortunate to witness and share. My sincere congratulations and best wishes for all that we still have left to share.

References

1. Barbacari, N., Profir, A., Zelinschi, C.: Gene regulatory network modeling by means of membrane computing. In: Proceedings of the 7th International Workshop on Membrane Computing WMC 2006. LNCS, vol. 4361, pp. 162–178 (2006)
2. Besozzi, D., Cazzaniga, P., Cocolo, S., Mauri, G., Pescini, D.: Modeling diffusion in a signal transduction pathway: the use of virtual volumes in P systems. Int. J. Found. Comput. Sci. **22**(1), 89–96 (2011)
3. Campos, M.: A membrane computing simulator of trans-hierarchical antibiotic resistance evolution dynamics in nested ecological compartments (ARES). Biol. Direct **10**(1), 41 (2015)
4. Ciobanu, G., Păun, Gh., Pérez-Jiménez, M.J.: Applications of Membrane Computing. Springer, Heidelberg (2006). https://doi.org/10.1007/3-540-29937-8
5. Colomer, M.A., Margalida, A., Sanuy, D., Pérez-Jiménez, M.J.: A bio-inspired model as a new tool for modeling ecosystems: the avian scavengeras a case study. Ecol. Model. **222**(1), 33–47 (2011)
6. Colomer, M.A., Martínez-del-Amor, M.A., Pérez-Hurtado, I., Pérez-Jiménez, M.J., Riscos-Núñez, A.: A uniform framework for modeling based on P systems. In: Li, K., Nagar, A.K., Thamburaj, R. (eds.) IEEE Fifth International Conference on Bio-Inspired Computing: Theories and Applications (BIC-TA 2010), vol. 1, pp. 616–621 (2010)

7. Dassow, J., Păun, Gh.: On the power of membrane computing. TUCS Technical Report No. 217 (1998)
8. Frisco, P., Gheorghe, M., Pérez-Jiménez, M.J. (eds.): Applications of Membrane Computing in Systems and Synthetic Biology. ECC, vol. 7. Springer, Cham (2014). https://doi.org/10.1007/978-3-319-03191-0
9. Păun, Gh.: Computing with membranes. J. Comput. Syst. Sci. **61**(1), 108–143 (2000)
10. Păun, Gh.: Membrane Computing: An Introduction. Springer, Heidelberg (2002). https://doi.org/10.1007/978-3-642-56196-2
11. Păun, Gh., Rozenberg, G., Salomaa, A. (eds.): The Oxford Handbook of Membrane Computing. Oxford University Press, Oxford (2010)
12. World Health Organization: Antimicrobial Resistance: Global Report on Surveillance (2014)

Small Spiking Neural P Systems
with Structural Plasticity

Francis George C. Cabarle[1,2], Ren Tristan A. de la Cruz[1], Henry N. Adorna[1],
Ma. Daiela Dimaano[1], Faith Therese Peña[1], and Xiangxiang Zeng[2,3(✉)]

[1] Department of Computer Science, University of the Philippines Diliman,
Diliman, 1101 Quezon City, Philippines
{fccabarle,radelacruz,hnadorna,mndimaano,ffpena}@up.edu.ph
[2] School of Information Science and Technology, Xiamen University,
Xiamen 361005, Fujian, China
xzeng@xmu.edu.cn
[3] Departamento de Inteligencia Artificial, Universidad Politécnica de Madrid (UPM),
Boadilla del Monte, 28660 Madrid, Spain

Abstract. Spiking neural P systems or SN P systems are computing models inspired by spiking neurons. The SN P systems variant we focus on are SN P systems with structural plasticity or SNPSP systems. Unlike SN P systems, SNPSP systems have a dynamic topology for creating or removing synapses among neurons. In this work we construct small universal SNPSP systems: 62 and 61 neurons for computing functions and generating numbers, respectively. We then provide some new directions, e.g. parameters to consider, in the search for such small systems.

1 Introduction

In this work we continue the search for small universal systems concerning variants of spiking neural P systems (in short, SN P systems) as in [5,10,13,17] to name a few. Investigations on the power, efficiency, and applications of SN P systems and variants is a very active area, with a recent survey in [12]. The specific class of SN P systems we focus here are spiking neural P systems with structural plasticity (or SNPSP systems) from [3] with further works in [1,2,14] to name a few. SNPSP systems are inspired by the ability of neurons to add or delete synapses (the edges) among neurons (the nodes in the graph). Computations in SNPSP systems proceed with a dynamic topology in contrast with SN P systems and their many variants with static topologies. This way, even with simplified types of rules, SNPSP systems can be "useful" by controlling the *flow* of information (in the form of spikes) in the system by using rules to create or remove synapses. This work is structured as follows: Sect. 2 provides preliminaries for our results; Sects. 3 and 4 provide our results with SNPSP systems having 62 and 61 neurons for computing functions and generating numbers, respectively. In Sect. 5 we discuss why such numbers of neurons are "small enough" and provide ideas, e.g. parameters, for future research on small universal systems.

© Springer Nature Switzerland AG 2018
C. Graciani et al. (Eds.): Pérez-Jiménez Festschrift, LNCS 11270, pp. 45–56, 2018.
https://doi.org/10.1007/978-3-030-00265-7_4

2 Preliminaries

We assume that the reader has basic knowledge in formal language and automata theory, and membrane computing. We only briefly mention notations and definitions relevant to what follows. More information can be found in various monographs, e.g. [11].

A register machine is a construct of the form $M = (m, H, l_0, l_f, I)$ where m is the number of registers, H is a finite set of instruction labels, l_0 and l_f are the start and final (or halt) labels, respectively, and I is a finite set of instructions bijectively labelled by H. Instructions have the following forms:

- $l_i : (ADD(r), l_j, l_k)$, add 1 to register r, then nondeterministically apply either instruction labelled by l_j or by l_k,
- $l_i : (SUB(r), l_j, l_k)$, if register r is nonempty then subtract 1 from r and apply l_j, otherwise apply l_k,
- $l_f : FIN$, halts the computation of M.

A register machine is deterministic if all ADD instructions are of the form $l_i : (ADD(r), l_j)$. To generate numbers, M starts with all registers empty, i.e. storing the number zero. The computation of M starts by applying l_0 and proceeds to apply instructions as indicated by the labels. If l_f is applied, the number n stored in a specified register is said to be computed by M. If computation does not halt, no number is generated. It is known that register machines are computationally universal, i.e. able to generate all sets of numbers that are Turing computable. To compute Turing computable functions, introduce arguments $n_1, n_2, \ldots, n_k$ in specified registers $r_1, r_2, \ldots, r_k$, respectively. The computation of M starts by applying l_0. If l_f is applied, the value of the function is placed in a specified register r_t, with all registers different from r_t being empty. In this way, the partial function computed is denoted by $M(n_1, n_2, \ldots, n_k)$.

The universality of register machines that compute functions is define as follows [10,15]: Let $\varphi_0, \varphi_1, \ldots$ be a fixed and admissible enumeration of all unary partial recursive functions. A register machine M_u is (strongly) universal if there is a recursive function g such that for all natural numbers x, y we have $\varphi_x(y) = M_u(g(x), y)$. The numbers $g(x)$ and y are introduced in registers 1 and 2 as inputs, respectively, with the result obtained in a specified output register.

As in [10], we use the universal register machine $M_u = (8, H, l_0, l_f, I)$ from [6] with the 23 instructions in I and respective labels in H given in Fig. 1. The machine from [6] which contains a separate instruction that checks for zero in register 6 is replaced in [10] with $l_8 : (SUB(6), l_9, l_0)$, $l_9 : (ADD(6), l_{10})$. It is important to note that as in [10], and without loss of generality, a modification is made in M_u because SUB instructions on the output register 0 are not allowed in the construction from [4]. A new register 8 is added and we obtain register machine M'_u by replacing l_f of M_u with the following instructions: $l_f : (SUB(0), l_{22}, l'_f)$, $l_{22} : (ADD(8), l_f)$, $l'_f : FIN$.

A spiking neural P system with structural plasticity or SNPSP system Π of degree $m \geq 1$ is a construct $\Pi = (O, \sigma_1, \ldots, \sigma_m, syn, in, out)$, where $O = \{a\}$ is

$l_0 : (SUB(1), l_1, l_2),$ $l_1 : (ADD(7), l_0),$ $l_2 : (ADD(6), l_3),$

$l_3 : (SUB(5), l_2, l_4),$ $l_4 : (SUB(6), l_5, l_3),$ $l_5 : (ADD(5), l_6),$

$l_6 : (SUB(7), l_7, l_8),$ $l_7 : (ADD(1), l_4),$ $l_8 : (SUB(6), l_9, l_0),$

$l_9 : (ADD(6), l_{10}),$ $l_{10} : (SUB(4), l_0, l_{11}),$ $l_{11} : (SUB(5), l_{12}, l_{13}),$

$l_{12} : (SUB(5), l_{14}, l_{15}),$ $l_{13} : (SUB(2), l_{18}, l_{19}),$ $l_{14} : (SUB(5), l_{16}, l_{17}),$

$l_{15} : (SUB(3), l_{18}, l_{20}),$ $l_{16} : (ADD(4), l_{11}),$ $l_{17} : (ADD(2), l_{21}),$

$l_{18} : (SUB(4), l_0, l_f),$ $l_{19} : (SUB(0), l_0, l_{18}),$ $l_{20} : (ADD(0), l_0),$

$l_{21} : (ADD(3), l_{18}),$ $l_f : FIN.$

Fig. 1. The universal register machine from [6]

the alphabet containing the *spike symbol* a, and $\sigma_1, \ldots, \sigma_m$ are *neurons* of Π. A neuron $\sigma_i = (n_i, R_i)$, $1 \leq i \leq m$, where $n_i \in \mathbb{N}$ indicates the initial number of spikes in σ_i written as string a^{n_i} over O; R_i is a finite set of rules with the following forms:

1. **Spiking Rule:** $E/a^c \rightarrow a$ where E is a regular expression over O and $c \geq 1$.
2. **Plasticity Rule:** $E/a^c \rightarrow \alpha k(i, N)$ where $c \geq 1$, $\alpha \in \{+, -, \pm, \mp\}$, $N \subset \{1, \ldots, m\}$, and $k \geq 1$.

The set of *initial synapses* between neurons is $syn \subset \{1, \ldots, m\} \times \{1, \ldots, m\}$, with $(i, i) \notin syn$, and in, out are neuron labels that indicate the input and output neurons, respectively. When $L(E) = \{a^c\}$, rules can be written with only a^c on their left-hand sides. The semantics of SNPSP systems are as follows. For every time step, each neuron of Π checks if any of their rules can be applied. Activation requirements of a rule are specified as E/a^c at the left-hand side of every rule. A rule $r \in R_i$ of σ_i is applied if the following conditions are met: the a^n spikes in σ_i is described by E of r, i.e. $a^n \in L(E)$, and $n \geq c$. When r is applied, $n - c$ spikes remain in σ_i. If σ_i can apply more than one rule at a given time, exactly one rule is nondeterministically chosen to be applied. When a spiking rule is applied in neuron σ_i at time t, all neurons σ_j such that $(i, j) \in syn$ receive a spike from σ_i at the same step t.

When a plasticity rule $E/a^c \rightarrow \alpha k(i, N)$ is applied in σ_i, the neuron performs one of the following actions depending on α and k: For $\alpha = +$, add at most k synapses from σ_i to k neurons whose labels are specified in N. For $\alpha = -$, delete at most k synapses that connect σ_i to neurons whose labels are specified in N. For $\alpha = \pm$ (resp., $\alpha = \mp$), at time step t perform the actions for $\alpha = +$ (resp., $\alpha = -$), then in step $t + 1$ perform the actions for $\alpha = -$ (resp., $\alpha = +$).

Let $P(i) = \{j \mid (i, j) \in syn\}$, be the set of neuron labels such that $(i, j) \in syn$. If a plasticity rule is applied and is specified to add k synapses, there are cases when σ_i can only add less than k synapses: when most of the neurons in N already have synapses from σ_i, i.e. $|N - P(i)| < k$. A synapse is added from σ_i to each of the remaining neurons specified in N that are not in $P(i)$. If $|N - P(i)| = 0$

then there are no more synapses to add. If $|N - P(i)| = k$ then there are exactly k synapses to add. When $|N - P(i)| > k$ then nondeterministically select k neurons from $N - P(i)$ and add a synapse from σ_i to the selected neurons.

We note the following important semantic of plasticity rules: when synapse (i, j) is added at step t then σ_j receives one spike from σ_i also at step t.

Similar cases can occur when deleting synapses. If $|P(i)| < k$, then only less than k synapses are deleted from σ_i to neurons specified in N that are also in $P(i)$. If $|P(i)| = 0$, then there are no synapses to delete. If $|P(i) \cap N| = k$ then exactly k synapses are deleted from σ_i to neurons specified in N. When $|P(i) \cap N| > k$, nondeterministically select k synapses from σ_i to neurons in N and delete the selected synapses. A plasticity rule with $\alpha \in \{\pm, \mp\}$ activated at step t is applied until step $t + 1$: during these steps, no other rules can be applied but the neuron can still receive spikes.

Π is synchronous, i.e. at each step if a neuron can apply a rule then it must do so. Neurons are locally sequential, i.e. they apply at most one rule each step, but Π is globally parallel, i.e. all neurons can apply rules at each step. A *configuration* of Π indicates the distribution of spikes among the neurons, as well as the synapse dictionary *syn*. The initial configuration is described by $n_1, n_2, \ldots, n_m$ for each of the m neurons, and the initial *syn*. A *transition* is a change from one configuration to another following the semantics of rule application. A sequence of transitions from the initial configuration to a halting configuration, i.e. where no more rules can be applied, is referred to as a *computation*.

At each computation, if σ_{out} fires at steps t_1 and t_2 for the first and second time, respectively, then a number $n = t_2 - t_1$ is said to be computed by the system. When the system receives or sends a spike to the environment, denote with "1" or "0" each step when the system sends or does not send (resp., receives or does not receive) a spike, respectively. This way, the spike train $10^{n-1}1$ denotes the system receiving or sending 2 spikes with interval n between the spikes.

3   A Small SNPSP System for Computing Functions

In this section we provide a small and universal SNPSP system that can compute functions. The system will follow the same design as in [10] for simulating M'_u: the system takes in the input spike train $10^{g(x)-1}10^{y-1}1$, where the numbers $g(x)$ and y are the inputs of M'_u. After taking in the input spike train, simulation of M'_u begins by simulating instruction l_0 until instruction l_f is encountered which ends the computation of M'_u. Finally, the system output is a spike train $10^{\varphi_x(y)-1}1$ corresponding to the output of $\varphi_x(y)$ of M'_u. Each neuron is associated with either a register or a label of an instruction of M'_u. If register r contains number n, the corresponding σ_r has $2n$ spikes. Simulation of M'_u starts when two spikes are introduced to σ_{l_0}, after σ_1 and σ_2 are loaded with $2g(x)$ and $2y$ spikes, respectively. If M'_u halts with r_8 containing $\varphi_x(y)$ then σ_8 has $2\varphi_x(y)$ spikes. Figures 2 and 3 are the modules associated with the ADD and SUB instructions, respectively. These modules have $\sigma_{l'_i}$ and $\sigma_{l''_i}$ referred to as *auxiliary neurons*, and such neurons do not correspond to registers or instructions. Instead of using rules of the form $a^s \to \lambda$, i.e. forgetting rules of standard SN P systems in [4], our systems only use plasticity rules of the form $a \to -1(l_i, \emptyset)$. In this way, deleting a non-existing synapse simply consumes spikes and nothing else, hence simulating a forgetting rule.

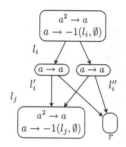

Fig. 2. ADD module

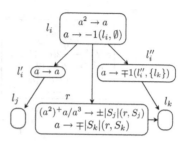

Fig. 3. SUB module

Module ADD in Fig. 2 simulates the instruction $l_i : (ADD(r), l_j)$. The first instruction of M is an ADD instruction and is labeled l_0. Let us assume that the simulation of the module starts at time t. Initially, l_i contains 2 spikes and all other neurons are empty. At time t, neuron l_i uses the rule $a^2 \to a$ to send one spike each to l_i' and l_i''. At time $t+1$, neurons l_i' and l_i'' each fire a spike, and both r and l_j each receive 2 spikes. At the next step, neuron l_j activates in order to simulate the next instruction.

Module SUB in Fig. 3 simulates the instruction $l_i : (SUB(r), l_j, l_k)$. Initially, l_i contains 2 spikes and all other neurons are empty. When the simulation starts at time t, neuron l_i uses the rule $a^2 \to a$ to send one spike each to l_i', l_i'', and r. At time $t+1$, neuron l_i' fires a spike to l_j. At the same time, neuron l_i'' deletes its synapse to l_k and waits until time $t+2$ to add the same synapse, thus sending one spike to l_k.

In the case σ_r was not empty before it received a spike from l_i, neuron r now contains at least three spikes which corresponds to register σ_r containing the value of at least 1. Neuron r in this case uses the rule $(a^2)^+ a/a^3 \to \pm|S_j|(r, S_j)$, where $S_j = \{j \mid j$ is the second element of the triple in a SUB instruction on register $r\}$. If this rule was used, neuron l_j receives a total of 2 spikes at time $t+1$. At $t+2$, neuron l_j is activated and continues the simulation of the next instruction. At the same time, neuron l_i'' sends a spike to σ_{l_k} which σ_{l_k} removes at $t+3$ using its rule $a \to -1(l_k, \emptyset)$.

In the case where σ_r was empty before receiving a spike from σ_{l_i}, this corresponds to register r containing the value 0. Neuron r uses the rule $a \to \mp|S_k|(r, S_k)$, where $S_k = \{k \mid k$ is the third element of the triple in a SUB instruction on register $r\}$. At $t+1$, neuron r deletes its synapse to σ_{l_k}. At $t+2$, neuron l_k receives 2 spikes in total – one from σ_r and from $\sigma_{l_i''}$ – and is activated in the next step in order to simulate the next instruction. Also at $t + 2$, neuron l_j removes the spike it received from $\sigma_{l'_i}$ using its rule $a \to -1(l_j, \emptyset)$.

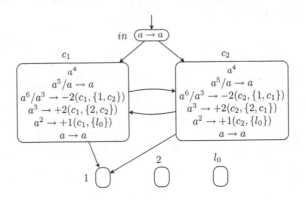

Fig. 4. *INPUT* module

Module *INPUT* as seen in Fig. 4 loads $2g(x)$ and $2y$ spikes to σ_1 and σ_2, respectively. The module begins its computation after σ_{in} receives the first spike from the input spike train $10^{g(x)-1}10^{y-1}1$. We assume that the simulation of the INPUT module starts at time t when σ_{in} sends spikes to σ_{c_1} and σ_{c_2}. At this point, both σ_{c_1} and σ_{c_2} have 5 spikes and each use the rule $a^5/a \to a$. At $t + 1$, σ_1 receives 2 spikes, so σ_{c_1} and σ_{c_2} receive a spike from each other. Since σ_{c_1} and σ_{c_2} each have 5 spikes again, they use the same rules again. Neurons c_1 and c_2 continue to send spikes to σ_1 and to each other in a loop. This loop continues until both neurons receive a spike again from σ_{in}, at this point they have 6 spikes each. Note that this spike from σ_{in} is from the second spike in the input spike train.

In the next step, σ_{c_1} and σ_{c_2} use rules $a^6/a^3 \to -2(c_1, \{1, c_2\})$ and $a^6/a^3 \to -2(c_2, \{1, c_1\})$, respectively, to delete their synapses to each other and to σ_1. Neurons c_1 and c_2 each have 3 spikes now, so they create synapses and send one spike to each other and σ_2. Both neurons have one spike each so they use rule $a \to a$ to send a spike to σ_2 and each other in a loop similar to the previous one. Once both neurons receive a spike from σ_{in} for the third and last time, the loop is broken. Neurons c_1 and c_2 each have 2 spikes now so they use rules $a^2 \to +1(c_1, \{l_0\})$ and $a^2 \to +1(c_2, \{l_0\})$ to create a synapse and send a spike to σ_{l_0}. At the next step, σ_{l_0} activates and the simulation of M'_u begins.

Module *OUTPUT* in Fig. 5 is activated when instruction l_f is executed by M'_u. Recall that M'_u stores its result in output register 8. We assume that at some time t, instruction l_f is executed so M'_u halts. Also at t, and for simplicity, σ_8 contains $2n$ spikes corresponding to the value n stored in register 8 of M'_u. Actually, and as mentioned at the beginning of this section, register 8 stores the number $\varphi_x(y)$ and hence σ_8 stores $2\varphi_x(y)$ spikes.

Neuron l_f sends a spike to σ_8 and σ_{out}. At $t + 1$, neuron *out* applies rule $a \to a$ and sends the first of two spikes to the environment. Neuron 8 now

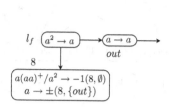

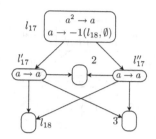

Fig. 5. $OUTPUT$ module.

Fig. 6. $ADD\text{-}ADD$ module to simulate l_{17} : $(ADD(2), l_{21})$ and l_{21} : $(ADD(3), l_{18})$.

with $2n + 1$ spikes applies rule $a(aa)^+/a^2 \rightarrow -1(8, \emptyset)$ to consume 2 spikes. Neuron 8 continues to use this rule until only 1 spike remains, then uses the rule $a \rightarrow \pm 1(8, out)$ to send a spike to σ_{out}. At the next step, σ_8 deletes its synapse to σ_{out}, while σ_{out} sends a spike to the environment for the second and last time. In this way, the system produces an output spike train of the form $10^{2n-1}1$ corresponding to the output of M_u'. The breakdown of the 86 neurons in the system are as follows:

- 9 neurons for registers 0 to 8,
- 25 neurons for 25 instruction labels l_0 to l_{22} with l_f and l_f',
- 48 neurons for 24 ADD and SUB instructions,
- 3 neurons in the $INPUT$ module, 1 neuron in the $OUTPUT$ module.

This number can be reduced by some "code optimizations", exploiting some particularities of M_u' similar to what was done in [10]. We observe the case of two consecutive ADD instructions. In M_u', there is one pair of consecutive ADD instructions, i.e. l_{17} : $(ADD(2), l_{21})$ and l_{21} : $(ADD(3), l_{18})$. By using the module in Fig. 6 to simulate the sequence of two consecutive ADD instructions, we save the neuron associated with l_{21} and 2 auxiliary neurons.

A module for the sequence of $ADD\text{-}SUB$ instructions is in Fig. 7. We save the neurons associated with l_6, l_{10}, and one auxiliary neuron for each pair. There are two sequences of $ADD\text{-}SUB$ instructions, i.e. l_5 : $(ADD(5), l_6)$, l_6 : $(SUB(7), l_7, l_8)$, l_9 : $(ADD(6), l_{10})$ and l_{10} : $(SUB(4), l_0, l_{11})$.

To further reduce the number of neurons, we use similar techniques as in [17] to decrease neurons by sharing one or two auxiliary neurons among modules. Consider the case of two ADD modules: As shown in Proposition 3.1 in [17], l_2 : $(ADD(6), l_3)$ and l_9 : $(ADD(6), l_{10})$ can share one auxiliary neuron without producing "wrong" simulations. Now consider the case of two SUB instructions: We follow the same grouping using Proposition 3.2 in [17] to make sure that two SUB modules follow only the "correct" simulations of M_u'. All modules associated with the instructions in each of the following groups can share 2 auxiliary neurons:

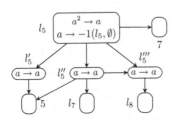

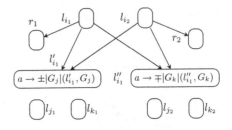

Fig. 7. *ADD-SUB* module to simulate l_5 : $(ADD(5), l_6)$ and l_6 : $(SUB(7), l_7, l_8)$.

Fig. 8. *SUB-SUB* module

1. l_0 : $(SUB(1), l_1, l_2)$, l_4 : $(SUB(6), l_5, l_3)$, l_6 : $(SUB(7), l_7, l_8)$, l_{10} : $(SUB(4), l_0, l_{11})$, l_{11} : $(SUB(5), l_{12}, l_{13})$, l_{13} : $(SUB(2), l_{18}, l_{19})$, l_{15} : $(SUB(3), l_{18}, l_{20})$.
2. l_3 : $(SUB(5), l_2, l_4)$, l_8 : $(SUB(6), l_9, l_0)$, l_f : $(SUB(0), l_{22}, l'_f)$.
3. l_{14} : $(SUB(5), l_{16}, l_{17})$, l_{18} : $(SUB(4), l_0, l_{22})$, l_{19} : $(SUB(0), l_0, l_{18})$.
4. l_{12} : $(SUB(5), l_{14}, l_{15})$.

In order to allow the sharing of auxiliary neurons between SUB modules in the system, the rules of auxiliary neurons must be changed as shown in Fig. 8. The rule in l'_i auxiliary neurons is changed to $a \to \pm|G_j|(r, G_j)$, where $G_j = \{j \mid j$ is the second element of the triple in a SUB instruction within the same group$\}$. Similarly, the rule in l''_i auxiliary neurons is changed to $a \to \mp|G_k|(r, G_k)$, where $G_k = \{k \mid k$ is the third element of the triple in a SUB instruction within the same group$\}$. As such, in the first group we have G_j as $\{l_0, l_1, l_5, l_7, l_{12}, l_{18}\}$ and G_k as $\{l_2, l_3, l_8, l_{11}, l_{13}, l_{19}, l_{20}\}$.

These groupings allow the saving of 20 neurons, however only 16 neurons are saved since l_6 : $(SUB(7), l_7, l_8)$ and l_{10} : $(SUB(4), l_0, l_{11})$ are already used in the *ADD-SUB* module in Fig. 7. This gives a total decrease of 17 neurons. Together with the 3 neurons saved by the module in Fig. 6, as well as the 4 neurons saved by the module in Fig. 7, an improvement is achieved from 86 to 62 neurons which we summarize as follows.

Theorem 1. *There is a universal SNPSP system for computing functions having 62 neurons.*

4   A Small SNPSP System for Generating Numbers

In this section, an SNPSP system Π is said to be universal as a generator of a set of numbers as in [10], according to the following framework: Let $\varphi_0, \varphi_1, \ldots$ be a fixed and admissible enumeration of partial recursive functions in unary. Encode the xth partial recursive function φ_x as a number given by $g(x)$ for some recursive function g. We then introduce from the environment the sequence $10^{g(x)-1}1$ into Π. The set of numbers generated by Π is $\{m \in \mathbb{N} \mid \varphi_x(m)$ is defined$\}$.

We consider the same strategy from [10]. First, from the environment we introduce the spike train $10^{g(x)-1}1$ and load $2g(x)$ spikes in σ_1. Second, non-deterministically load a natural number m into σ_2 by introducing $2m$ spikes in σ_2, and send the spike train $10^{m-1}1$ out to the environment to generate the number m. Third and lastly, to verify if φ_x is defined for m we start the register machine M_u in Fig. 1 with the values $g(x)$ and m in registers 1 and 2, respectively. If M_u halts then so does Π, thus $\varphi_x(m)$ is defined. Note the main difference between generating numbers and computing functions: we do not require a separate $OUTPUT$ module but we need to nondeterministically generate the number m. Since no $OUTPUT$ module is needed we can omit register 8, and computation simply halts after $l_{18} : (SUB(4), l_0, l_f)$. The combined $INPUT\text{-}OUTPUT$ module is given in Fig. 9.

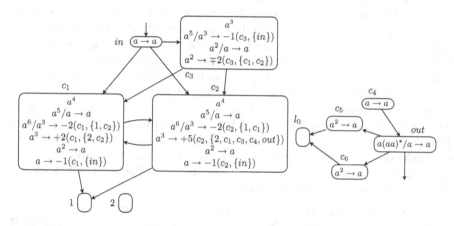

Fig. 9. $INPUT\text{-}OUTPUT$ module

Module $INPUT\text{-}OUTPUT$ loads $2g(x)$ and $2m$ spikes to σ_1 and σ_2, respectively. The module is activated when σ_{in} receives a spike from the environment. Neurons c_1, c_2, and c_3 initially contain 4, 4, and 3 spikes respectively. Assume the module is activated at t and σ_{in} sends one spike each to σ_{c_1}, σ_{c_2}, and σ_{c_3}. At this point, both c_1 and c_2 have 5 spikes and they use the rule $a^5/a \to a$. At $t+1$, neuron 1 receives 2 spikes, and c_1 and c_2 will receive a spike from each other. Neurons c_1 and c_2 continue to spike at σ_1 and to each other in a loop until they receive a spike again from in. When σ_{in} fires a spike for the second and last time at some $t+x$, neurons c_1, c_2, and c_3 now have 6, 6, and 5 spikes, respectively. At $t+x+1$, neurons c_1 and c_2 use rules $a^6/a^3 \to -2(c_1, \{1, c_2\})$ and $a^6/a^3 \to -2(c_2, \{1, c_1\})$, respectively. They each delete their synapses to σ_1 and consume 3 spikes so 3 spikes remain. At the same time σ_{c_3} uses the rule $a^5/a^3 \to -1(c_3, \{in\})$ and consumes 3 spikes. Now σ_{c_3} has 2 spikes and nondeterministically chooses between two rules.

If σ_{c_3} applies $a^2/a \to a$ at $t+x+2$, it sends one spike each to σ_{c_1} and σ_{c_2}. At the same time, σ_{c_1} applies $a^3 \to +2(c_1, \{2, c_2\})$ to create synapses and send spikes to σ_2 and σ_{c_2}. Neuron c_2 applies $a^3 \rightarrow +5(c_2, \{2, c_1, c_3, c_4, out\})$ to create synapses and send spikes to $\sigma_2, \sigma_{c_1}, \sigma_{c_3}, \sigma_{c_4}$, and σ_{out}. Since σ_{c_1} and σ_{c_2} received one spike from each other and one spike from σ_{c_3}, they both apply $a^2 \rightarrow a$ at $t + x + 3$. If σ_{c_3} continues to apply $a^2/a \rightarrow a$, neurons c_1 and c_2 continue to send one spike to each other, σ_{c_4}, and σ_{out}, as well as load σ_2 with 2 spikes. If σ_{c_3} applies $a^2 \rightarrow \mp 2(c_3, \{c_1, c_2\})$ instead then it ends the loop between σ_{c_1} and σ_{c_2}. Neurons c_1 and c_2 receive a spike from each other but do not receive a spike from σ_{c_3}. At the next step both neurons do not fire a spike and instead apply $a \rightarrow -1(c_1, \{in\})$ to simply consume their spikes.

Now we verify the operation of the remainder of the module. When σ_{c_2} applies $a^3 \rightarrow +5(c_2, \{2, c_1, c_3, c_4, out\})$ at $t + x + 2$, it sends a spike each to σ_{c_4} and σ_{out} for the first time. At $t + x + 3$, neuron c_4 sends a spike to σ_{out}, followed by the sending of a spike of σ_{out} to the environment for the first time. Note that σ_{c_4} and σ_{out} also receive one spike each from σ_{c_2} at $t + x + 3$ due to $a^2 \rightarrow a$. At the next step, σ_{c_4} and σ_{out} have 1 and 2 spikes, respectively. If σ_{c_3} continues to apply $a^2/a \rightarrow a$ then σ_{c_2} continues to fire spikes to σ_{c_4} and σ_{out}. Neuron out does not fire since it accumulates an even number of spikes from σ_{c_2} and σ_{c_4}.

Once σ_{c_3} applies $a^2 \rightarrow \mp 2(c_3, \{c_1, c_2\})$ to end the loop between σ_{c_1} and σ_{c_2}, neurons c_4 and out do not receive a spike from σ_{c_2}. Neuron c_4 fires a spike to σ_{out} so now σ_{out} has an odd number of spikes. At the next step, σ_{out} fires a spike to the environment for the second and last time. Neuron out also sends a total of two spikes each to σ_{c_5} and σ_{c_6}. Once σ_{c_5} and σ_{c_6} collect two spikes each they fire a spike to σ_{l_0} to start the simulation of M_u. The modified module for halting and simulating l_{18}, since register 8 is not required, is in Fig. 10. The following is the breakdown of the 81 neurons in the system:

- 8 neurons for 8 registers (the additional register 8 is omitted),
- 22 neurons for 22 labels (l_f is omitted), 42 neurons for 21 ADD and SUB instructions, 1 neuron for the special SUB instruction (Fig. 10),
- 8 neurons in the $INPUT\text{-}OUTPUT$ module.

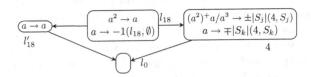

Fig. 10. Module for simulating $l_{18} : (SUB(4), l_0, l_f)$ without l_f.

As in Sect. 3, we can decrease by 7 the number of neurons by using the optimizations in Figs. 6 and 7. We can also use the method in [17] and the module shown in Fig. 8 to share auxiliary neurons. A neuron is saved in two ADD modules, and we follow a similar grouping for the 12 SUB instructions where we save 12 neurons. A total of 20 neurons are saved. Using the results above, an improvement is made from 81 to 61 neurons. The breakdown is as follows, and the result summarized afterwards.

- 8 neurons for 8 registers, 19 neurons for 19 labels (l_6, l_{10}, and l_{21} are saved),
- 25 neurons for *ADD* and *SUB* instructions, 1 neuron for the special *SUB* instruction, and 8 neurons in the *INPUT-OUTPUT* module.

Theorem 2. *There is a universal number generating SNPSP system having 61 neurons.*

5 Discussions and Final Remarks

We report our preliminary work on small universal SNPSP systems with 62 and 61 neurons for computing functions and generating numbers, respectively. Of course these numbers can still be reduced but here we note some observations on results for small SN P systems and their variants. While the numbers obtained in this work are still "large", we argue that the technique used in this work and as in [10,17] and more recently in [5,13], which here we denote as the *Korec simulation* technique, seems closer to biological reality: each neuron is associated either with an instruction or a register only. In this technique, neurons also have "fewer" rules making them more similar to the systems in [16] as compared to smaller systems in [7–9] with "super neurons", i.e. neurons having a fixed but "large" number of rules. The Korec simulation can also bee seen as a normal form, i.e. observing a simplifying set of restrictions. While it is interesting to pursue the search for systems with the smallest number of neurons, we think it is also interesting to search for systems with a small number of neurons and rules in the neurons. Korec simulation can also be extended to other register machines given in [6].

The smallest systems due to Korec simulation must have $m + n$ neurons as mentioned in [8]. In this work as in others using Korec simulation, simulating M_u or M_u' means having 34 and 30 neurons, respectively. Hence, results in this work and in [5,10,13,17] are approximately double these numbers but it is still open how to further reduce them without violating the Korec simulation. Perhaps including a parameter k where each neuron has no more than k rules could be considered in future works. In our results, all neurons in our modules have $k = 2$ except for the c_i neurons in the *INPUT* module. Such neurons can be replaced with neurons having at most 2 rules, but it remains open how to do this in our systems and in others without increasing the number of neurons "significantly".

Lastly, this work is only concerned with SNPSP systems having neurons that produce at most one spike each step. It remains to be seen how small the system can become if neurons produce more than one spike each step, e.g. using synapse weights as in [1] and extended spiking rules as in [7,8,13].

Acknowledgements. The first three authors are grateful for the ERDT project (DOST-SEI), Project 171722 PhDIA and Semirara Mining Corp. Professorial Chair (UP Diliman OVCRD). X. Zeng is supported by Juan de la Cierva position (code: IJCI-2015-26991) and the National Natural Science Foundation of China (Grant Nos. 61472333, 61772441, 61472335). The authors are grateful for useful comments from two anonymous referees.

References

1. Cabarle, F.G.C., Adorna, H.N., Pérez-Jiménez, M.J.: Asynchronous spiking neural P systems with structural plasticity. In: Calude, C.S., Dinneen, M.J. (eds.) UCNC 2015. LNCS, vol. 9252, pp. 132–143. Springer, Cham (2015). https://doi.org/10.1007/978-3-319-21819-9_9
2. Cabarle, F.G.C., Adorna, H.N., Pérez-Jiménez, M.J.: Sequential spiking neural P systems with structural plasticity based on max/min spike number. Neural Comput. Appl. 27(5), 1337–1347 (2016)
3. Cabarle, F.G.C., Adorna, H.N., Pérez-Jiménez, M.J., Song, T.: Spiking neural p systems with structural plasticity. Neural Comput. Appl. 26(8), 1905–1917 (2015)
4. Ionescu, M., Păun, Gh., Yokomori, T.: Spiking neural P systems. Fundam. Inform. 71(2, 3), 279–308 (2006)
5. Kong, Y., Jiang, K., Chen, Z., Xu, J.: Small universal spiking neural P systems with astrocytes. ROMJIST 17(1), 19–32 (2014)
6. Korec, I.: Small universal register machines. Theor. Comput. Sci. 168(2), 267–301 (1996)
7. Neary, T.: Three small universal spiking neural P systems. Theor. Comput. Sci. 567(C), 2–20 (2015)
8. Pan, L., Zeng, X.: A note on small universal spiking neural P systems. In: Păun, G., Pérez-Jiménez, M.J., Riscos-Núñez, A., Rozenberg, G., Salomaa, A. (eds.) WMC 2009. LNCS, vol. 5957, pp. 436–447. Springer, Heidelberg (2010). https://doi.org/10.1007/978-3-642-11467-0_29
9. Pan, T., Shi, X., Zhang, Z., Xu, F.: A small universal spiking neural P system with communication on request. Neurocomputing 275, 1622–1628 (2018)
10. Păun, A., Păun, G.: Small universal spiking neural P systems. BioSystems 90(1), 48–60 (2007)
11. Păun, G.: Membrane Computing: An Introduction. Springer, Heidelberg (2002). https://doi.org/10.1007/978-3-642-56196-2
12. Rong, H., Wu, T., Pan, L., Zhang, G.: Spiking neural P systems: theoretical results and applications. In: Graciani, C. et al. (eds.) Pérez-Jiménez Festschrift. LNCS, vol. 11270, pp. 256–268. Springer, Heidelberg (2018)
13. Song, T., Pan, L., Păun, G.: Spiking neural P systems with rules on synapses. Theor. Comput. Sci. 529, 82–95 (2014)
14. Song, T., Pan, L.: A normal form of spiking neural P systems with structural plasticity. Int. J. Swarm Intell. 1(4), 344–357 (2015)
15. Zeng, X., Lu, C., Pan, L.: A weakly universal spiking neural P system. In: Proceedings of the Bio-Inspired Computing Theories and Applications (BICTA), pp. 1–7. IEEE (2009)
16. Zeng, X., Pan, L., Pérez-Jiménez, M.: Small universal simple spiking neural P systems with weights. Sci. China Inf. Sci. 57(9), 1–11 (2014)
17. Zhang, X., Zeng, X., Pan, L.: Smaller universal spiking neural P systems. Fundam. Inform. 87(1), 117–136 (2008)

Approximating Polygons for Space-Filling Curves Generated with P Systems

Rodica Ceterchi[1]([✉]), Atulya K. Nagar[2], and K. G. Subramanian[2]

[1] Faculty of Mathematics and Computer Science, University of Bucharest,
14 Academiei St., 010014 Bucharest, Romania
rceterchi@gmail.com
[2] Faculty of Science, Liverpool Hope University, Hope Park, Liverpool L16 9JD, UK

Abstract. In the novel area of membrane computing, the bio-inspired computing models with the generic name of P systems have turned out to be a convenient framework for handling different kinds of problems and for developing suitable solutions. One such problem area is generation of geometric patterns of approximations of space-filling curves encoded as words over appropriate chain code symbols. Parallel chain code P systems with rewriting in parallel of words in the regions using context-free rules have been shown to generate the languages of chain code words representing the finite approximation patterns of the well-known space-filling Peano and Hilbert curves. Here we consider the approximating polygons that converge to the space-filling curves of Hilbert and construct a parallel chain code P system generating these approximating polygons. We also construct a parallel chain code P system for generating the approximating polygons corresponding to another space-filling curve, known as Lebesgue's curve, which is almost everywhere differentiable unlike any other space-filling curve.

1 Introduction

The field of membrane computing has had a rapid growth, both in terms of theoretical results and application areas, with numerous lines of study [7,16,23,25] being proposed and successfully carried out. These studies reveal the flexibility and richness of the new computing models in this field with the generic name of P systems, originally formulated by Păun [15] in his seminal work inspired by the membrane structure and functioning of the living cells. P systems based on rewriting, again initially considered by Păun [14], with objects being strings over a given alphabet and evolution rules being string transformation rules such as those of a Chomsky grammar [17,18] have also been extensively investigated including several variants [6] being introduced, with different types of objects and rewriting rules. Extending the rewriting P systems to two-dimensions, array objects and array-rewriting rules are considered in the P systems introduced in

---

K. G. Subramanian—Honorary Visiting Professor.

© Springer Nature Switzerland AG 2018
C. Graciani et al. (Eds.): Pérez-Jiménez Festschrift, LNCS 11270, pp. 57–65, 2018.
https://doi.org/10.1007/978-3-030-00265-7_5

[2] and as an application, the problem of generation of floor-design patterns is dealt with in [8].

On the other hand, chain code pictures in the two-dimensional plane, in their basic version, are described by words over the symbols l, r, u, d, with the symbols respectively depicting the movement along a unit line from a point q in the chain code picture with integer coordinates to the left, right, up and down neighbours of q. In other words, the symbols l, r, u, d are interpreted as instructions for drawing a unit line respectively to the left, right, up or down direction from the current position in the chain code picture. In [13], a chain code picture generating grammar model was introduced and subsequently has been investigated by many researchers. Linking chain code picture grammars and P systems, specifically string-rewriting ones called rewriting chain code P systems, were proposed in [24] with context-free grammar type rules in the regions and the terminal alphabet $\{l, r, u, d\}$ with the interpretation mentioned earlier. In [4], rewriting in parallel mode was employed and parallel chain code P systems were proposed.

Space-filling curves constitute a fascinating area of mathematics with intense research activity relating to these curves having taken place in the past [9, 19–21] and continuing to take place even in the present day, both in theory and applications [10–12, 22]. Peano's and Hilbert's curves are two well-known and well-investigated space-filling curves. Chain code P systems are constructed in [24], with a sequential mode of rewriting, to generate the patterns of approximations of the Peano space-filling curve, encoding the patterns over $\{l, r, u, d\}$. Parallel chain code P systems are considered in [4] involving a parallel mode of rewriting, again generating chain code words over $\{l, r, u, d\}$ representing approximations of the Peano and the Hilbert space-filling curves. Those P systems have an advantage of a reduction in the number of membranes in comparison with the chain code P systems described in [24].

We consider here the sequence of approximating polygons of the Hilbert curve (see, for example, [19], p. 22) and construct a parallel chain code P system for generating the set of these approximating polygons. Among other space-filling curves considered in the literature, Lebesgue's space-filling curve is an interesting curve ([19], p. 69: Chap. 5). We also construct a parallel chain code P system for generating the set of approximating polygons of Lebesgue's curve.

2   Basic Definitions and Results

For basic notions recalled here and also for unexplained notions we refer to [4, 5, 13, 14, 17, 18, 23].

A chain code picture is basically composed of horizontal and vertical unit lines in the plane, joining points in the plane with integer coordinates. On tracing all the unit lines of a chain code picture starting from a point which is an end of a unit line and ending also at a similar point in the picture, we can associate a word over the symbols $\{l, r, u, d\}$, called the chain code word, with the symbols being interpreted as standing for moves from a point in the picture along a horizontal or vertical unit line and reaching the left, right, up or down neighbour of the point. A chain code picture language is a set of chain code words, with each word corresponding to a chain code picture. For formal definitions relating to chain code pictures we refer to [5,13].

We now recall the parallel chain code P system and for more formal details we refer to [4].

An alphabet V is a finite set of symbols and a string (also known as a word) w over V is a finite sequence of symbols from V. The set of all words over V, including the empty word λ is denoted by V^*. A context-free parallel chain code P system of degree $n, n \geq 1$, consists of a membrane structure μ with each membrane labelled in a one-to-one way with $1, 2, \ldots, n$. Initially, each membrane or region has a finite set possibly empty $L_i, 1 \leq i \leq n$, of strings over a set N of nonterminals and the set Σ of chain-code symbols l, r, u, d. Each region has a finite set (which can also be empty) $R_i, 1 \leq i \leq n$, of context-free rules of the form $A \to \alpha(tar)$, where $A \in N$, $\alpha \in (N \cup \Sigma)^*$. Each rule has an attached target $tar \in \{here, out, in\}$ (in general, $here$ is omitted) specifying the region where the result of the rewriting should be placed in the next step: $here$ means that the result remains in the same region where the rule was applied, out means that the string has to be sent to the region immediately surrounding the region where it has been produced, and in means that the string should go to one of the directly inner membranes, if any exists. We write a parallel chain code P system as $\Pi = (N, \Sigma, \mu, L_1, \cdots, L_n, R_1, \cdots, R_n, i_0)$ where i_0 is the output membrane. In a computation of Π, each string in every region is rewritten by all possible rules at a time; if no rule can rewrite a string, then it remains unchanged. When a computation halts, no rules can be applied in the regions, it is a *successful* computation and the strings generated over the terminal alphabet Σ collected in the output membrane constitute the chain code picture language generated by the P system Π. The set of all chain code picture languages generated by context-free parallel chain code P systems with n membranes is denoted by $PCCP_n(CF)$.

3   Generation of Hilbert Words

While Peano discovered the first space-filling curve, Hilbert was the first to give a geometrical generating procedure. Representing the geometric patterns as strings of symbols, the problem of generation of these strings by L systems is considered in [21]. We recall in this section the P system with parallel rewriting [4], which generates the Hilbert words which correspond to the chain code pictures (Fig. 1) defining the Hilbert space-filling curve in the limit. The Hilbert curve patterns can be represented by picture description words over the alphabet $\Sigma = \{l, r, u, d\}$ as follows: The first approximation is given by $H_1 = urd$ and for $n > 1$, the subsequent approximations are given by
$H_n = g_1(H_{n-1})uH_{n-1}rH_{n-1}dg_2(H_{n-1})$ where g_1 and g_2 are homomorphisms on $\Sigma = \{l, r, u, d\}$ given by $g_1(u) = r, g_1(d) = l, g_1(l) = d, g_1(r) = u, g_2(u) = l, g_2(d) = r, g_2(l) = u, g_2(r) = d$. The finite approximations of the Hilbert curve, $H_n, n \geq 1$, are called *Hilbert words*.

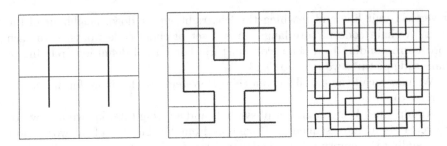

Fig. 1. The first three patterns of the sequence defining the Hilbert curve

We consider the context-free parallel chain code P system Π_H given by

$$\Pi_H = (\{A, B, C, D\}, \{l, r, u, d\}, [_1[_2]_2]_1, \{A\}, \emptyset, \emptyset, R_1, \emptyset, 2)$$

where R_1 is the union of the sets of rules:
$\{A \to BuArAdC, B \to ArBuBlD, C \to DlCdCrA, D \to CdDlDuB\}$, with target indication *here*, and $\{A \to \lambda, B \to \lambda, C \to \lambda, D \to \lambda\}$, with target indication *in*.

We have proven in [4] the following theorem.

Theorem 1. *The P system Π_H produces in membrane 2 the Hilbert words.*

4   Approximating Polygons for the Hilbert Curve

We first informally state the notion of the approximating polygons of the Hilbert curve, following [1]. The "final" Hilbert curve starts in the lower left corner of the unit square, passes through every point of the unit square and terminates in the lower right corner. As for the subsquares, the Hilbert curve has a similar property, namely, entering each subsquare in one particular corner, and exiting the subsquare in one of the corners that shares a common edge with the entry corner. Connecting the entry and exit corners with a polygon, we obtain an approximating polygon of the Hilbert curve. Different approximating polygons are obtained depending on the refinement level of the subsquares. The approximating polygons of the Hilbert curve ([19], p. 22: Fig. 2.6.1) converge uniformly to the Hilbert curve and can be expressed in terms of the chain code symbols l, r, u, d. The words corresponding to the first three approximating polygons of the Hilbert curve are

$$H_1 = urrd.$$

$$H_2 = ruulurrdurrdlddr,$$

$$H_3 = urrdruulruuldlluruulurrdurrdlddr$$

$$ruulurrdurrdlddrdlluldddrlddrurrd$$

The first two members of these approximating polygons are given in Fig. 2. For $n \geq 1$, we have the recurrence relation

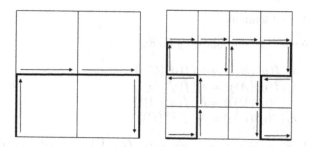

Fig. 2. The first two approximating polygon patterns of the sequence defining the Hilbert curve

$$H_{n+1} = \delta_1(H_n)H_nH_n\delta_2(H_n)$$

where

$$\delta_1(u) = r, \delta_1(r) = u, \delta_1(d) = l, \delta_1(l) = d,$$

$$\delta_2(u) = l, \delta_2(l) = u, \delta_2(d) = r, \delta_2(r) = d.$$

The context-free parallel chain code P system Π_{APH} generating the words $H_n, n \geq 1$ corresponding to the approximating polygons of the Hilbert curve is given by

$$\Pi_{APH} = (\{A, B, C, D\}, \{l, r, u, d\}, [_1[_2]_2]_1, \{A\}, \emptyset, R_1, \emptyset, 2)$$

where R_1 contains the following four rules with target indication *here*:

$$A \rightarrow BuArrAdC, \quad B \rightarrow ArBuuBlD,$$

$$C \rightarrow DlCddCrA, \quad D \rightarrow CdDllDuB,$$

and the following four rules with target indication *in*:

$$A \rightarrow \lambda, B \rightarrow \lambda, C \rightarrow \lambda, D \rightarrow \lambda.$$

Theorem 2. *The P system Π_{APH} given above produces in membrane 2 the words H_n, where H_n is the $n-$th approximating polygon of the Hilbert Curve.*

Let us denote by η the morphism given by the four rewriting rules with target *here*, and by f the morphism given by the four rewriting rules with target *in*. We will prove by induction that $f(\eta^n(A))) = H_n$.

Proof. Consider the alphabet $\Theta = \{A, B, C, D\} \cup \Sigma$ where $\Sigma = \{l, r, u, d\}$ and the morphisms $\eta : \Theta^* \rightarrow \Theta^*$ given by $A \rightarrow BuArrAdC, B \rightarrow ArBuuBlD, C \rightarrow DlCddCrA, D \rightarrow CdDllDuB, u \rightarrow u, d \rightarrow d, r \rightarrow r, l \rightarrow l$ and $f : \Theta^* \rightarrow \Sigma^*$ given by $A \rightarrow \lambda, B \rightarrow \lambda, C \rightarrow \lambda, D \rightarrow \lambda, u \rightarrow u, d \rightarrow d, r \rightarrow r, l \rightarrow l$. We have to prove that $f(\eta^n(A)) = H_n, n \geq 1$.

First a technical lemma:

Lemma 1. *For $n \geq 1$, the following hold:*

$$f(\eta^n(A)) = \delta_1(f(\eta^n(B))) = \delta_2(f(\eta^n(C)))$$
$$f(\eta^n(B)) = \delta_1(f(\eta^n(A))) = \delta_2(f(\eta^n(D)))$$
$$f(\eta^n(C)) = \delta_1(f(\eta^n(D))) = \delta_2(f(\eta^n(A)))$$
$$f(\eta^n(D)) = \delta_1(f(\eta^n(C))) = \delta_2(f(\eta^n(B)))$$

Proof. By induction. For $n = 1$, we have $f(\eta(A)) = urrd$, $f(\eta(B)) = ruul$, $f(\eta(C)) = lddr$, $f(\eta(D)) = dllu$, and the rest is straightforward computation. We suppose the equalities hold for n. To prove the first equality:

$$f(\eta^{n+1}(A)) = f(\eta^n(BuArrAdC))$$
$$= f(\eta^n(B))uf(\eta^n(A))rrf(\eta^n(A))df(\eta^n(C))$$
$$= \delta_1(f(\eta^n(A)))u\delta_1(f(\eta^n(B)))rr\delta_1(f(\eta^n(B)))d\delta_1(f(\eta^n(D)))$$
$$= \delta_1(f(\eta^n(A)))\delta_1(r)\delta_1(f(\eta^n(B)))\delta_1(u)\delta_1(u)\delta_1(f(\eta^n(B)))\delta_1(l)\delta_1(f(\eta^n(D)))$$
$$= \delta_1(f(\eta^n(ArBuuBlD))) = \delta_1(f(\eta^{n+1}(B))).$$

The other equalities follow by similar computations, and $\delta_1^2 = \delta_2^2 = 1_\Sigma$.   □

Back to the Proof of Theorem. For $n = 1$ we have $f(\eta(A)) = urrd = H_1$. We suppose that $f(\eta^n(A)) = H_n$, and we compute for $n + 1$:

$$f(\eta^{n+1}(A)) = f(\eta^n(BuArrAdC))$$
$$= f(\eta^n(B))uf(\eta^n(A))rrf(\eta^n(A))df(\eta^n(C))$$
$$= \delta_1(f(\eta^n(A)))uf(\eta^n(A))rrf(\eta^n(A))d\delta_2(f(\eta^n(A)))$$
$$= \delta_1(H_n)uH_nrrH_nd\delta_2(H_n) = H_{n+1},$$

where we have used the lemma and the induction hypothesis.   □

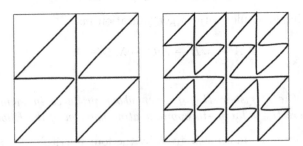

Fig. 3. The first two approximating polygon patterns of the sequence defining the Lebesgue curve

5   Lebesgue's Space-Filling Curve and Approximating Polygons

Another interesting space-filling curve is the Lebesgue's space-filling curve which is differentiable almost everywhere ([19], p. 78: Theorem 5.4.2) unlike the space-filling curves of Peano and Hilbert which are nowhere differentiable. In [19], a sequence of approximating polygons ([19], p. 81: Fig. 5.5.3) is constructed with the sequence of these continuous curves converging to Lebesgue's space-filling curve. In addition to the chain code symbols, we consider an additional symbol f_{ne} corresponding to a move along the diagonal of a unit square from the lower left corner to the opposite corner. Thus for a unit square $ABCD$ in the plane with the corners A, B, C, D having integer coordinates $(i, j), (i+1, j), (i+1, j+1), (i, j+1)$ respectively, we denote by the symbols f_{ne}, l, d moves along the diagonal from A to C, along the side from B to A (or C to D) and along the side D to A (or C to B)respectively. In terms of these symbols, we can represent by words, the approximating polygons of the Lebesgue's curve [19]. The first two members of these approximating polygons are given in Fig. 3. The corresponding words are

$$L_1 = f_{ne}lf_{ne}ddf_{ne}lf_{ne}$$

$$L_2 = f_{ne}lf_{ne}ddf_{ne}lf_{ne}llf_{ne}lf_{ne}ddf_{ne}lf_{ne}$$

$$ddddf_{ne}lf_{ne}ddf_{ne}lf_{ne}llf_{ne}lf_{ne}ddf_{ne}lf_{ne}$$

For $n \geq 1$,

$$L_{n+1} = L_n l^{2^n} L_n d^{2^{n+1}} L_n l^{2^n} L_n.$$

We consider the context-free parallel chain code P systems with a small modification and call them context-free parallel chain code like P systems. The modification is that we include the symbol f_{ne} in the set of terminal symbols. In fact we need here only the symbols l, d along with f_{ne}. The context-free parallel chain code like P system Π_{APL} generating the words L_n, $n \geq 1$ corresponding to the approximating polygons of the Lebesgue's curve is given by

$$\Pi_{APL} = (\{A, B, D\}, \{f_{ne}, l, d\}, [_1[_2]_2]_1, \{A\}, \emptyset, R_1, \emptyset, 2)$$

where R_1 contains the following three rules with target indication *here*:

$$A \rightarrow ABADDABA, \quad B \rightarrow BB, \quad D \rightarrow DD,$$

and the following three rules with target indication *in*:

$$A \rightarrow f_{ne}, B \rightarrow l, D \rightarrow d.$$

Theorem 3. *The P system Π_{APL} defined above produces in membrane 2 the words L_n corresponding to the approximating polygons of the Lebesgue curve.*

Proof. We denote by η the morphism given by the rules with target indication *here*, and by f the morphism given by the rules with target indication *in*. We have to show that for any $n \geq 1$, $f(\eta^n(A)) = L_n$, the n-th approximating polygon of the Lebesgue curve. We will do this by induction.

For $n = 1$, we have $f(\eta(A)) = L_1$ by straightforward computations.

Suppose now the relation is true for n, and we compute for $n + 1$:

$$f(\eta^{n+1}(A)) = f(\eta^n(ABADDABA))$$
$$= f(\eta^n(A))f(\eta^n(B))f(\eta^n(A))f(\eta^n(D))f(\eta^n(D))f(\eta^n(A))f(\eta^n(B))f(\eta^n(A))$$
$$= f(\eta^n(A))l^{2^n}f(\eta^n(A))d^{2^{n+1}}f(\eta^n(A))l^{2^n}f(\eta^n(A))$$
$$= L_n l^{2^n} L_n d^{2^{n+1}} L_n l^{2^n} L_n = L_{n+1}.$$

$\square$

6   Conclusions

P systems involving rewriting in parallel are constructed for generation of the chain code words over the basic chain code symbols and/or an additional symbol corresponding to approximate polygons of Hilbert's and Lebesgue's curves. Also in [3], we have considered the problem of generation with parallel chain code P systems of the approximation patterns of a variant of Peano's curve due to Wunderlich [19]. It will be of interest to construct P systems of a similar kind to generate the sequence of geometric approximation patterns that define Lebesgue's curve. The first two members of this sequence are given in [19] in Fig. 5.5.1 (p. 79) and Fig. 5.5.2 (p. 80). We leave this problem open. Also, another interesting problem for future study as pointed out by one of the reviewers is to model in terms of P systems, a practical application of Hilbert or Lebesgue curve.

Acknowledgements. We thank the anonymous referees for their valuable suggestions and comments which greatly helped to improve the paper.

The first author wishes to thank Mario for a long lasting friendship and a fruitful working relationship.

All the authors join in saying: Happy Birthday, Mario!

References

1. Bader, M., Schraufstetter, S., Vigh, C.A., Behrens, J.: Memory efficient adaptive mesh generation and implementation of multigrid algorithms using Sierpiński curves. Int. J. Comput. Sci. Eng. **4**(1), 12–21 (2008)
2. Ceterchi, R., Mutyam, M., Păun, G., Subramanian, K.G.: Array-rewriting P systems. Natural Comput. **2**, 229–249 (2003)
3. Ceterchi, R., Nagar, A.K., Subramanian, K.G.: Chain code P system generating a variant of the Peano space-filling curve (2018, submitted)
4. Ceterchi, R., Subramanian, K.G., Venkat, I.: P systems with parallel rewriting for chain code picture languages. In: Beckmann, A., Mitrana, V., Soskova, M. (eds.) CiE 2015. LNCS, vol. 9136, pp. 145–155. Springer, Cham (2015). https://doi.org/10.1007/978-3-319-20028-6_15

5. Drewes, F.: Some Remarks on the generative power of collage grammars and chain-code grammars. In: Ehrig, H., Engels, G., Kreowski, H.-J., Rozenberg, G. (eds.) TAGT 1998. LNCS, vol. 1764, pp. 1–14. Springer, Heidelberg (2000). https://doi.org/10.1007/978-3-540-46464-8_1
6. Ferretti, C., Mauri, G., Păun, G., Zandron, C.: On three variants of rewriting P systems. Theor. Comput. Sci. **301**, 201–215 (2003)
7. Gheorghe, M., Păun, G., Pérez Jiménez, M.J., Rozenberg, G.: Research frontiers of membrane computing: open problems and research topics. Int. J. Found. Comput. Sci. **24**(5), 547–624 (2013)
8. Isawasan, P., Venkat, I., Muniyandi, R.C., Subramanian, K.G.: A membrane computing model for generation of picture arrays. In: Badioze Zaman, H. (ed.) IVIC 2015. LNCS, vol. 9429, pp. 155–165. Springer, Cham (2015). https://doi.org/10.1007/978-3-319-25939-0_14
9. Kitaev, S., Mansour, T., Seebold, P.: The Peano curve and counting occurrences of some patterns. J. Autom. Lang. Combin. **9**(4), 439–455 (2004)
10. Lawder, J.K., King, P.J.H.: Using space-filling curves for multi-dimensional indexing. In: Lings, B., Jeffery, K. (eds.) BNCOD 2000. LNCS, vol. 1832, pp. 20–35. Springer, Heidelberg (2000). https://doi.org/10.1007/3-540-45033-5_3
11. Lebesgue, H.: Leçons sur l'Intégration et la recherche des fonctions primitives. Bull. Am. Math. Soc. **36**, 463–468 (1930)
12. Mokbel, M.F., Aref, W.G.: Space-filling curves. In: Shekhar, S., Xiong, H. (eds.) Encyclopedia of GIS. Springer, Boston (2008)
13. Maurer, H.A., Rozenberg, G., Welzl, E.: Using string languages to describe picture languages. Inf. Control **54**, 155–185 (1982)
14. Păun, G.: Computing with membranes. J. Comput. Syst. Sci. **61**, 108–143 (2000)
15. Păun, G.: Membrane Computing: An Introduction. Springer, Heidelbrg (2000)
16. Păun, G., Rozenberg, G., Salomaa, A.: The Oxford Handbook of Membrane Computing. Oxford University Press Inc., New York (2010)
17. Rozenberg, G., Salomaa, A. (eds.): Handbook of Formal Languages (3 Volumes). Springer, Berlin (1997). https://doi.org/10.1007/978-3-642-59126-6
18. Salomaa, A.: Formal Languages. Academic Press, London (1973)
19. Sagan, H.: Space-Filling Curves. Springer, New York (1994). https://doi.org/10.1007/978-1-4612-0871-6
20. Seebold, P.: Tag system for the Hilbert curve. Discret. Math. Theor. Comput. Sci. **9**, 213–226 (2007)
21. Siromoney, R., Subramanian, K.G.: Space-filling curves and infinite graphs. In: Ehrig, H., Nagl, M., Rozenberg, G. (eds.) Graph Grammars 1982. LNCS, vol. 153, pp. 380–391. Springer, Heidelberg (1983). https://doi.org/10.1007/BFb0000120
22. Skubalska-Rafajowicz, E.: Applications of the space - filling curves with data driven measure - preserving property. Nonlinear Anal.: Theory, Methods Appl. **30**(3), 1305–1310 (1997)
23. Subramanian, K.G.: P systems and picture languages. In: Durand-Lose, J., Margenstern, M. (eds.) MCU 2007. LNCS, vol. 4664, pp. 99–109. Springer, Heidelberg (2007). https://doi.org/10.1007/978-3-540-74593-8_9
24. Subramanian, K.G., Venkat, I., Pan, L.: P systems generating chain code picture languages In: Proceedings of Asian Conference on Membrane Computing, pp. 115–123 (2012)
25. Zhang, G., Pan, L.: A survey of membrane computing as a new branch of natural computing. Chin. J. Comput. **33**(2), 208–214 (2010)

A Logical Representation of P Colonies: An Introduction

Luděk Cienciala[1], Lucie Ciencialová[1], Erzsébet Csuhaj-Varjú[2(✉)], and Petr Sosík[1]

[1] Institute of Computer Science and Research Institute of the IT4Innovations Centre of Excellence, Silesian University in Opava, Opava, Czech Republic
{ludek.cienciala,lucie.ciencialova,petr.sosik}@fpf.slu.cz

[2] Faculty of Informatics, ELTE Eötvös Loránd University, Budapest, Hungary
csuhaj@inf.elte.hu

Abstract. We introduce a new way of representation of computation in P colonies. It is based on logical values, propositional logic and rule-based systems. A configuration of a P colony is transformed into a data structure based on a system of stacks. We present a conversion of conditions of applicability of rules, programs, multisets of programs and complete computational steps as propositional formulas in the disjunctive normal form. This representation allows, among others, to derive new results concerning the complexity of execution of computational steps of a P colony.

1 Introduction

P colonies, introduced in [5], are variants of very simple tissue-like P systems, where the cells (agents) have only one region and they interact with their joint shared environment by using programs, i.e., by finite collections of rules of special forms. The extraordinary simplicity of these constructs is demonstrated by some of their important characteristics.

At any step of their functioning, both the agents and the environment are represented by a finite number of objects, elements of an object-alphabet. (We note that the environment has an infinite number of occurrences of a special symbol, called the environmental symbol as well.) The agents in the P colony have constant capacity and each agent has the same capacity, i.e., at any computational step every agent is represented by a constant number of objects and this number is the same for any agent. Furthermore, the agents can change their contents (the objects at their disposal) and the objects in the environment by using very simple rules, namely, evolution rules (an object inside the agent is changed for some other object) or communication rules (an object inside the agent is exchanged with object located in the environment). There exists one other type of rules as well, the so-called checking rule. A checking rule consists of either two evolution rules or of two communication rules, written as r_1/r_2. Rule r_1 has higher priority than r_2, i.e., if r_1 is applicable, then it has to be

C. Graciani et al. (Eds.): Pérez-Jiménez Festschrift, LNCS 11270, pp. 66–76, 2018.
https://doi.org/10.1007/978-3-030-00265-7_6

used, otherwise r_2 has to be applied. The change of the contents of the agents and the change of the current environment is performed by programs. Every agent has a finite set of programs, and each program consists of as many rules as the capacity of the agent. When a program is applied, all of its rules should be used in parallel. At every step, as many agents perform a program in parallel as possible. These synchronized actions of the agents correspond to a configuration change of the P colony. A finite sequence of configuration changes following each other and starting from the so-called initial configuration is a computation. The result of the computation is the number of copies of a distinguished object, called the final object, occurring in the environment in a final configuration of the P colony, which is usually a halting configuration.

During the years, P colonies have been studied in detail; for summaries consult [1,4]. These investigations mainly focused on studying P colonies as computing devices; a large number of results prove that even though P colonies are very simple computing devices they are computationally complete even with restricted size parameters.

In this paper we study P colonies from other aspect, namely, we provide a representation of P colonies in terms of logical values, propositional logic and rule-based systems. The startpoint of our approach is that the applicability conditions of rules, programs, multisets of programs can be given as propositional formulas in disjunctive normal form and the computational step is obtained by using a rule-based system.

Obviously, if an evolution rule of the form $a \rightarrow b$ is to be applied by an agent, then object a should be present inside the agent. Analogously, if a communication rule $c \leftrightarrow d$ is to be applied by an agent, then object c should be present inside the agent and object d should appear in the environment. To perform rules and programs, the configuration of the P colony has to satisfy such conditions.

To continue the concept of logical representation of P colonies, a configuration of a P colony is transformed into a system of stacks with logical values. Elements of these stacks are then used as variables in the propositional formulas and thus a configuration defines an interpretation of the formulas. The computational step corresponds to a transition of a rule-based production system. Using this approach, we may solve several problems concerning P colonies. In this paper, we proved that the decision problem whether a configuration C is a halting configuration of a P colony Π without checking rules is in **P**, and if Π is with checking rules then it is in **NP**.

The logical representation of P colonies we provide and the approach we propose allow to apply many results known in propositional logic to resolve open problems in P colony theory. We close the paper with two open problems and a short discussion of the possible applications of this new approach.

2   Preliminaries and Basic Notions

Throughout the paper we assume the reader to be familiar with the basics of formal language theory and membrane computing, more information can be found in [6,7].

For an alphabet Σ, the set of all words over Σ (including the empty word, ε), is denoted by Σ^*. The length of a word $w \in \Sigma^*$ is denoted by $|w|$ and $|w|_a$ denotes the number of occurrences of the symbol $a \in \Sigma$ in w.

A multiset of objects M is a pair $M = (O, f)$, where O is an arbitrary (not necessarily finite) set of objects and f is a mapping $f : O \to \mathbb{N}$; f assigns to each object in O its multiplicity in M. Any multiset of objects M with the set of objects $O = \{x_1, \ldots x_n\}$ can be represented as a string w over alphabet O with $|w|_{x_i} = f(x_i)$; $1 \le i \le n$. Obviously, all words obtained from w by permuting the letters can also represent the same multiset M, and ε represents the empty multiset.

2.1 P Colonies

The original concept of a P colony was introduced in [5] and presented in a developed form in [2,3].

Definition 1. *A P colony of capacity k, $k \ge 1$, is a construct $\Pi = (O, e, f, V_E, A_1, \ldots, A_n)$, where*

- *O is an alphabet, its elements are called objects;*
- *$e \in O$ is the basic (or environmental) object of the P colony;*
- *$f \in O$ is the final object of the P colony;*
- *V_E is a finite multiset over $O - \{e\}$, called the initial state (or the initial content) of the environment;*
- *A_i, $1 \le i \le n$, are agents, where each agent $A_i = (O_i, P_i)$ is defined as follows:*
  - *O_i is a multiset consisting of k objects over O, the initial state (or initial content) of the agent;*
  - *$P_i = \{p_{i,1}, \ldots, p_{i,k_i}\}$ is a finite set of programs, where each program consists of k rules. Each rule is in one of the following forms:*
    - *$a \to b$, called an evolution rule;*
    - *$c \leftrightarrow d$, called a communication rule;*
    - *r_1/r_2, called a checking rule; r_1, r_2 are evolution rules or communication rules.*

We add some brief explanations to the components of the P colony. We first note that throughout the paper, we use term "object a is inside agent A" and term "$a \in w$, where w is the state of agent A" as equivalent.

The first type of rules associated to the programs of the agents, the *evolution rules*, are of the form $a \to b$. This means that object a inside the agent is rewritten to (evolved to be) object b. The second type of rules, the *communication rules*, are of the form $c \leftrightarrow d$. If such a communication rule is performed, then object c inside the agent and object d in the environment swap their location, i.e., after executing the rule, object d appears inside the agent and object c is located in the environment.

The third type of rules are the checking rules. A checking rule is formed from two rules of one of the two previous types. If a checking rule r_1/r_2 is performed, then the rule r_1 has higher priority to be executed over the rule r_2. This means that the agent checks whether or not rule r_1 is applicable. If the rule can be executed, then the agent must use this rule. If rule r_1 cannot be applied, then the agent uses rule r_2.

The program determines the activity of the agent: the agent can change its state and/or the state of the environment.

The environment is represented by a finite number (zero included) of copies of non-environmental objects and a countably infinite copies of the environmental object e.

In every step, if a program is applied, then each object inside the agent is affected by its execution. Depending on the rules in the program, the program execution may affect the environment as well. *This interaction between the agents and the environment is the key factor of the functioning of the P colony.*

The functioning of the P colony starts from its initial configuration (initial state). The *initial configuration* of a P colony is an $(n + 1)$-tuple of multisets of objects present in the P colony at the beginning of the computation. It is given by the multisets O_i for $1 \leq i \leq n$ and by multiset V_E. Formally, the *configuration* of the P colony Π is given by $(w_1, \ldots, w_n, w_E)$, where $|w_i| = k$, $1 \leq i \leq n$, w_i represents all the objects present inside the i-th agent, and $w_E \in (O - \{e\})^*$ represents all the objects in the environment different from object e. A configuration $(w_1, \ldots, w_n, w_E)$ *contains* a configuration $(w'_1, \ldots, w'_n, w'_E)$ *iff* $w'_E \subseteq w_E$ and $w'_i \subseteq w_i$, $1 \leq i \leq n$.

At each *step of the computation* (at each transition), the state of the environment and that of the agents change in the following manner:

In the *maximally parallel* derivation mode a maximal number of agents performs one of its applicable (non-deterministically chosen) programs simultaneously. This means that applicable programs are added to the multiset of applied programs, one program per agent, in an arbitrary order, until no more programs can be added due to the trade-offs between them. Then the multiset of programs is applied.

The other derivation mode is the *sequential* derivation mode. In this case one agent uses one of its programs at a time. If more than one agent is able to apply at least of its programs, then the acting agent is non-deterministically chosen. If the number of applicable programs for the agent is higher than one, then the agent non-deterministically chooses one of these programs.

A transition between configurations C_1 and C_2 is denoted by $C_1 \Rightarrow C_2$. A configuration C is called *alive* if there is another configuration $C' \neq C$ such that $C \Rightarrow C'$. Otherwise, the configuration is called *dead*. Note that a dead configuration is either halting (the P colony cannot apply any rule), or else each valid multiset of applicable rules (subject to the derivation mode) leads the P colony to the same configuration.

A sequence of transitions starting in the initial configuration is called a *computation*. A computation is said to be *halting* if a configuration is reached where no program can be applied. With a halting computation, we associate a *result* which is given as the number of copies of the objects f present in the environment in the halting configuration.

Because of the non-determinism in choosing the programs, starting from the initial configuration we obtain several computations, hence, with a P colony we can associate a set of numbers, denoted by $N(\Pi)$, computed by all possible halting computations of the given P colony.

In the original model (see [5]) the number of objects inside each agent is set to two. Therefore, the programs were formed from only two rules. Moreover, the initial configuration was defined as $(n+1)$-tuple $(ee, \ldots, ee, \varepsilon)$ so the environment of the P colony is "empty", i.e., without an input information at the beginning of the computation.

The number of agents in a given P colony is called the degree of Π; the maximal number of programs of an agent of Π is called the height of Π.

3   Logical Representation of P Colonies

In this section we introduce a new way of representation of the concept of a P colony. First, we briefly explain the idea. To represent existence (or non-existence) of objects in the P colony, we use value 1 (or 0). Let a be an object in the P colony ($a \in O$) and suppose that there are three copies of such object placed in the environment. We construct a stack called "a" and put value 0 into the bottom of stack. For every copy of object a in the environment, we push one copy of 1 to the stack. The presence of object a can be expressed as literal a interpreted as TRUE, otherwise it is FALSE.

a	1	1	1	0

An agent of capacity k is represented by an array of $|O|$ stacks. The sum of 1s in all stacks is k. For example, agent A_1 with capacity 3 working with alphabet $O = \{e, a, b, c,\}$ and with objects aae inside the agent has following representation:

$A_1 : a$	1	1	0
b	0
c	0
e	1	0

The presence of object a inside the agent A_i can be expressed as literal $A_i[a]$. or more precisely, as an interpretation of this literal.

In these terms we describe how one step of the computation in the whole system is done: We divide the process into two phases – in the first phase a multiset of programs is chosen randomly from the set of all multisets containing one applicable program per each agent which can apply at least one program. In the second phase we check the actual applicability of each program in the selected multiset in relation to the number of objects needed for the execution of the programs. Now we describe the process in detail.

A rewriting rule $a \rightarrow b$ of agent A_i is applicable if there is an object a inside the agent A_i. It means that the rule is applicable if literal $A_i[a]$ is true. The communication rule $a \leftrightarrow b$ is applicable if there is an object a inside the agent and object b in the environment. In terms of logic we can write the condition as $A_1[a] \wedge b$. If $b = e$ we may omit b in the condition (there is always some copy of e in the environment). A condition of applicability of a rewriting or a communication rule will be called *elementary condition of applicability*.

We can express the condition of applicability for checking rule r_1/r_2 as $c_1 \vee c_2$ where r_1, r_2 are rewriting or communication rules with conditions of applicability c_1, c_2. Notice that we speak of applicability, and not the way of application: r_1/r_2 is applicable if at least one of r_1 and r_2 is applicable, that is, if $c_1 \vee c_2$ is TRUE. If r_1 is applicable, then r_1/r_2 can be applied. If r_2 is applicable but r_1 is not applicable, then checking rule r_1/r_2 can be applied as well. If both r_1 and r_2 are applicable, then r_1/r_2 is also applicable, in this case we apply r_1.

Lemma 1. *Given a program $p_{i,l}$, the condition of its applicability $c_{i,l}$ can be expressed in a disjunctive normal form with 2^d conjunctions, where d is the number of checking rules in the program.*

Proof. The condition of applicability of the programs is $c_{i,l} : c_1 \wedge c_2 \wedge \cdots \wedge c_k$, where c_x is the condition of applicability of the x-th rule in the program. A condition is in the form:

$A_i[a]$ (rewriting rule),

$A_i[a] \wedge b$ (communication rule),

$c_{x_1} \vee c_{x_2}$ (checking rule).

If the program contains a checking rule, then we can write the condition $c_{i,l}$ in the disjunctive normal form (DNF) $c_{i,l} : (c_1 \wedge c_2 \wedge \cdots \wedge c_{j_1} \wedge c_{j+1} \wedge \cdots \wedge c_k) \vee (c_1 \wedge c_2 \wedge \cdots \wedge c_{j_2} \wedge c_{j+1} \wedge \cdots \wedge c_k)$. (Notice that c_{j_1} and c_{j_2} are the conditions for applicability of the two subrules of the checking rule.)

If there are d checking rules in the program, then the formula contains a conjunction of d disjunctions and $k - d$ elementary conditions (i.e., literals or conjunction of literals). Its conversion to DNF results in a disjunction of 2^d conjunctions of k-tuples of elementary conditions of applicability.

Furthermore, consider a k-tuple of elementary rules corresponding to a conjunction. Generally, j rules ($1 \leq j \leq k$) may depend on the presence of the same object a inside the agent, hence the program is applicable only if the agent contains at least j objects a. To indicate that some objects should be present in several copies, we introduce a literal $A_i[a][j]$, $1 \leq j \leq k$, which is TRUE when the j-th position in the stack "a" of agent A_i exists and contains 1. Similarly, $b[j]$ is the literal which is TRUE when the j-th position in stack "b" is 1, i.e., when the environment contains at least j objects b.

Therefore, in each conjunction in the final DNF of the condition $c_{i,l}$, literals $A_i[a]$ must be substituted/indexed for $A_i[a][j]$, where j is the order of occurrence of $A_i[a]$ in the conjunction. Similarly, each literal b is substituted for $b[j]$. $\square$

Given a DNF representing the applicability of a program $p_{i,l}$ with d checking rules, without any change in its satisfiability, we can re-order the conjunctions in DNF due to decreasing priority among rules as follows:

0. Conjunctions with elementary conditions for the first rule in all d checking rules.
1. Conjunctions with elementary condition for the second rule in one checking rule, and for the first rule in the remaining checking rules.
2. Conjunctions with elementary conditions for the second rule in two checking rules, and for the first rule in the remaining checking rules.

   $\vdots$

d. Conjunctions with elementary conditions for the second rule in all d checking rules.

This reordering induced by checking rules is crucial for the process of correct execution of one computational step of the P colony, as it is described after Lemma 2. In this process, conjunctions in DNF are evaluated in the left-to-right order, which ensures that the first elementary rule in checking rules has always priority over the second elementary rule.

Clearly, the logical condition whether an agent A_i can be active (i.e., is able to apply some of its programs) can be expressed as a disjunction of conditions for all programs of that agent: $c_i = c_{i,1} \lor c_{i,2} \lor \cdots \lor c_{i,k_i}$, where k_i is the number of programs of the agent A_i.

Lemma 2. *Given a P colony Π as in Definition 1, the condition whether Π can perform a computational step can be expressed in a DNF with $\sum_{i=1}^{n} \sum_{j=1}^{k_i} 2^{d_{i,j}}$ conjunctions, where $d_{i,j}$ is the number of checking rules in the program $p_{i,j}$.*

Proof. A P colony can perform a computational step (regardless of the sequential or parallel mode) if at least one of its agents can apply some program. Hence, the condition of applicability of a computational step of the colony Π is the disjunction of conditions $c_{i,l}$ for all programs of all agents of Π. By Lemma 1, these conditions are already in the DNF, so their disjunction leads to a greater DNF. The total number of conjunctions in the resulting DNF is just the sum of individual DNF's, and the statement follows again by Lemma 1.   □

The process of execution of one computational step of the P colony in logical representation under maximally parallel mode can be now completed as follows.

1st phase:

(a) For each program $p_{i,j}$ in the colony construct the formula $c_{i,j}$ of its applicability as described in Lemma 1.
(b) For each agent A_i choose one the formulas $c_{i,j}$, $1 \le j \le k_i$, which is TRUE in the actual configuration (the configuration interprets all literals). If an agent has no such formula, then it cannot apply any program.

(c) In each chosen $c_{i,j}$ in the DNF (ordered by their priorities induced by checking rules) find the first conjunction which is TRUE and add it to a resulting multiset M of formulas (corresponding to the multiset of applicable programs).

(d) If the multiset M is empty, then the configuration is halting. Otherwise, construct a disjunction c_M of all conjunctions in M (the order of conjunctions is random).

2nd phase:

(a) Re-index literals a for all $a \in O$ (corresponding to objects in the environment) to $a[j]$ using the total order of occurrence of a in the whole formula c_M. This is necessary as the limited amount of environmental objects may cause trade-offs among chosen programs.

(b) Re-interpret all conjunctions in the formula c_M. Some of them may be now FALSE, while the whole formula remains TRUE.

(c) Apply (in parallel) all sequences of elementary rules corresponding to those conjunctions which are still TRUE.

The execution of a multiset of rules can be understood as an action of a rule-based production system: as sensory precondition we use condition of applicability and an action can be constructed from functions push and pop as it is usual for stacks. Function $\text{push}(x)$ means put 1 to the top of stack x. Function $\text{pop}(x)$ means remove 1 from the top of stack x.

Let us show one step of computation for simple P colony $\Pi = (O, e, f, V_E, A_1)$ with capacity two and one agent and with $O = \{a, b, c, d, e, f\}$, $w_E = \varepsilon$, $A_1 = (ee, \{\langle a \leftrightarrow c/c \leftrightarrow d; \ c \leftrightarrow f/a \leftrightarrow e \rangle; \ \langle a \to b; \ e \leftrightarrow b \rangle\})$.

Let us construct a condition of applicability of the program $\langle a \to b; \ e \leftrightarrow b \rangle$: It is formed from one rewriting and one communication rule.

rule	elementary condition of applicability
$a \to b$	$A_1[a]$
$e \leftrightarrow b$	$A_1[e] \wedge b$

The condition of applicability of the program after the substitution (indexing) of literals is $A_1[a][1] \wedge A_1[e][1] \wedge b[1]$.

The condition of applicability of the program $\langle a \leftrightarrow c/c \leftrightarrow d; \ c \leftrightarrow f/a \leftrightarrow e \rangle$ is formed from two checking rules, each formed from two communication rules.

rule	elementary condition of applicability
$a \leftrightarrow c$	$c_{11} : A_1[a] \wedge c$
$c \leftrightarrow d$	$c_{12} : A_1[c] \wedge d$
$c \leftrightarrow f$	$c_{21} : A_1[c] \wedge f$
$a \leftrightarrow e$	$c_{22} : A_1[a]$
$a \leftrightarrow c/c \leftrightarrow d$	$(A_1[a] \wedge c) \vee (A_1[c] \wedge d)$
$c \leftrightarrow f/a \leftrightarrow e$	$(A_1[c] \wedge f) \vee A_1[a]$

The condition of applicability of the program is formed from four conjunctions: $c_{11} \wedge c_{21}$ with highest priority, $c_{12} \wedge c_{21}$ and $c_{11} \wedge c_{22}$, and $c_{12} \wedge c_{22}$ with lowest priority. After indexing of literals we obtain

$$(A_1[a][1] \wedge c[1] \wedge A_1[c][1] \wedge f[1]) \vee$$
$$\vee (A_1[c][1] \wedge d[1] \wedge A_1[c][2] \wedge f[1]) \vee$$
$$\vee (A_1[a][1] \wedge c[1] \wedge A_1[a][2]) \vee$$
$$\vee (A_1[c][1] \wedge d[1] \wedge A_1[a][1])$$

Rules for execution of programs are:

- if $A_1[a][1] \wedge c[1] \wedge A_1[c][1] \wedge f[1]$ then $(\text{pop}(A_1[a]) \wedge \text{push}(A_1[c]) \wedge \text{pop}(c) \wedge$ $\text{push}(a) \wedge \text{pop}(A_1[c]) \wedge \text{push}(A_1[f]) \wedge \text{pop}(f) \wedge \text{push}(c))$
- if $A_1[c][1] \wedge d[1] \wedge A_1[c][2] \wedge f[1]$ then $(\text{pop}(A_1[c]) \wedge \text{push}(A_1[d]) \wedge \text{pop}(d) \wedge$ $\text{push}(c) \wedge \text{pop}(A_1[c]) \wedge \text{push}(A_1[f]) \wedge \text{pop}(f) \wedge \text{push}(c))$
- if $A_1[a][1] \wedge c[1] \wedge A_1[a][2]$ then $(\text{pop}(A_1[a]) \wedge \text{push}(A_1[c]) \wedge \text{pop}(c) \wedge \text{push}(a) \wedge$ $\text{pop}(A_1[a]) \wedge \text{push}(A_1[e]) \wedge \text{push}(a))$
- if $A_1[c][1] \wedge d[1] \wedge A_1[a][1]$ then $(\text{pop}(A_1[c]) \wedge \text{push}(A_1[d]) \wedge \text{pop}(d) \wedge \text{push}(c) \wedge$ $\text{pop}(A_1[a]) \wedge \text{push}(A_1[e]) \wedge \text{push}(a))$

The logical representation of P colonies, particularly the conditions of applicability of (multisets of) rules allows for a clearer view of complexity of the process of execution of a P colony. Here we focus on the problem whether a given configuration is halting. This problems amounts to checking whether there exists an applicable multiset of programs.

Theorem 1. *Consider a P colony Π without checking rules, and a configuration C of Π. The problem whether C is a halting configuration is in* **P**.

Proof. If no checking rules are present then, by Lemma 1, each condition $c_{i,l}$ corresponding to an applicability of a program $p_{i,l}$, $1 \leq i \leq n$, $1 \leq l \leq k_i$, consists of a single conjunction. By Lemma 2, the formula – condition of applicability of a computational step of Π is a DNF consisting of $\sum_{i=1}^{n} k_i$ conjunctions, each containing at most $2k$ literals. Therefore, the size of the formula is polynomial in the size of description of the P colony Π, and so is the algorithm for its construction and interpretation. $\square$

Theorem 2. *Consider a P colony Π with checking rules, and a configuration C of Π. The problem whether C is a halting configuration is in* **NP**.

Proof. In presence of checking rules, each condition $c_{i,l}$ corresponding to an applicability of a program $p_{i,l}$, $1 \leq i \leq n$, $1 \leq l \leq k_i$, is expressed in DNF consisting of up to 2^k conjunctions (Lemma 1). One could argue that the size of the formula is smaller before its conversion to the DNF. However, the conversion seems necessary since all literals in the formula must be indexed (see the proof of Lemma 1) to interpret the formula correctly, and this is done only after the conversion to the DNF.

By Lemma 2, the formula – condition of applicability of a computational step of Π is a DNF consisting of $\sum_{i=1}^{n} \sum_{j=1}^{k_i} 2^{d_{i,j}} = \mathcal{O}(n2^k)$ conjunctions, each conjunction containing at most $2k$ literals, where $1 \leq d_{i,j} \leq k$ is the number of checking rules in the program $p_{i,j}$. Therefore, the size of the formula (in number of literals) is $\mathcal{O}(nk2^k)$. $\square$

Open Problem 1. Consider the problem "is a given configuration of a P colony with checking rules halting?" Is the problem NP-complete? We conjecture yes but no proof is known yet.

Open Problem 2. How complex is the problem to decide whether a given configuration of a P colony is dead or alive? (Consult Sect. 2.1 for the definition of a dead configuration.)

4 Conclusions

In this paper we introduced a concept of logical representation of P colonies, particularly the transformation of applicability of its rules and computational steps into propositional formulas. A configuration of a P colony is transformed into a system of stacks with logical values. Elements of these stacks are then used as variables in the mentioned propositional formulas and thus a configuration defines an interpretation of the formulas. The application of a computational step then can be viewed as a transition of a rule-based production system.

The logical representation of P colonies allows to apply many results known in propositional logic to resolve open problems concerning P colonies. Particularly, it allows to convert the conditions of applicability of programs and multisets of programs into the form of logical formulas in DNF. This transformation, in turn, results in a straightforward characterization of computational complexity of execution of computational steps of a P colony. Some of them may characterize the borderline between P and NP, although the proof is not known yet. Many related problems remain open, two of which are mentioned in the previous section.

Acknowledgments. This work was supported by The Ministry of Education, Youth and Sports from the National Programme of Sustainability (NPU II) project IT4Innovations excellence in science - LQ1602, by SGS/13/2016 and by Grant No. 120558 of the National Research, Development, and Innovation Office - NKFIH, Hungary.

References

1. Ciencialová, L., Csuhaj-Varjú, E., Cienciala, L., Sosík, P.: P colonies. Bull. Int. Membr. Comput. Soc. **1**(2), 119–156 (2016)
2. Csuhaj-Varjú, E., Kelemen, J., Kelemenová, A., Păun, Gh., Vaszil, Gy.: Computing with cells in environment: P colonies. J. Mult.-Valued Log. Soft Comput. **12**(3–4 Spec. Iss.), 201–215 (2006)
3. Kelemen, J., Kelemenová, A.: On P colonies, a biochemically inspired model of computation. In: Proceedings of the 6th International Symposium of Hungarian Researchers on Computational Intelligence, Budapest TECH, Hungary, pp. 40–56 (2005)
4. Kelemenová, A.: P colonies. In: Păun, Gh., Rozenberg, G., Salomaa, A. (eds.) The Oxford Handbook of Membrane Computing, Chap. 23.1, pp. 584–593. Oxford University Press, Oxford (2010)

5. Kelemen, J., Kelemenová, A., Păun, Gh.: Preview of P colonies: a biochemically inspired computing model. In: Workshop and Tutorial Proceedings, Ninth International Conference on the Simulation and Synthesis of Living Systems (Alife IX), Mass, Boston, pp. 82–86 (2004)
6. Păun, Gh., Rozenberg, G., Salomaa, A. (eds.): The Oxford Handbook of Membrane Computing. Oxford University Press Inc., New York (2010)
7. Rozenberg, G., Salomaa, A. (eds.): Handbook of Formal Languages I-III. Springer, Heidelberg (1997). https://doi.org/10.1007/978-3-642-59126-6

The Fair Proportion Is a Shapley Value on Phylogenetic Networks Too

Tomás M. Coronado[1,2], Gabriel Riera[1,2], and Francesc Rosselló[1,2(✉)]

[1] Department of Mathematics and Computer Science,
University of the Balearic Islands, 07122 Palma, Spain
{t.martinez,gabriel.riera,cesc.rossello}@uib.edu
[2] Balearic Islands Health Research Institute (IdISBa), 07010 Palma, Spain

Abstract. The Fair Proportion of a species in a phylogenetic tree is a very simple measure that has been used to assess its genetic value relative to the overall phylogenetic diversity represented by the tree. It has recently been proved by Fuchs and Jin to be equal to the Shapley Value of the coalitional game that sends each subset of species to its rooted Phylogenetic Diversity in the tree. We prove in this paper that this result extends to the natural translations of the Fair Proportion and the rooted Phylogenetic Diversity to rooted phylogenetic networks. We also generalize to rooted phylogenetic networks the expression for the Shapley Value of the unrooted Phylogenetic Diversity game on a phylogenetic tree established by Haake, Kashiwada and Su.

1 Introduction

The assessment of the genetic value of individual species, with the purpose of ranking them in order to increase the efficiency of the allocation of conservation actions, is an important problem in conservation biology [3]. The Fair Proportion of a species in a rooted phylogenetic tree, introduced by Redding and Mooers in [14], is one of the simplest measures proposed in this connection. Recall that, in a phylogenetic tree, the length of an arc quantifies the evolutionary distance between the species represented by the nodes at its ends, and the sum of all these lengths is a measure of the global phylogenetic diversity of the set of species at the leaves of the tree [5]. Then, the Fair Proportion apportions this global diversity among these leaves by equally dividing the length of each arc among its descendant leaves. However, although this index is very easy to define, it is not immediately obvious that it ranks species in a sound and meaningful way.

The Shapley Value of a species in a phylogenetic tree, introduced by Haake, Kashiwada and Su in [9], is another such individual phylogenetic diversity measure. It is based on a well-known and well-understood solution from cooperative game theory to the problem of apportioning the global value of a game among its players. In this way, it provides a meaningful distribution of the global diversity of a phylogenetic tree among its leaves, at the cost of being defined through

© Springer Nature Switzerland AG 2018
C. Graciani et al. (Eds.): Pérez-Jiménez Festschrift, LNCS 11270, pp. 77–87, 2018.
https://doi.org/10.1007/978-3-030-00265-7_7

quite a complex formula that involves a sum of an exponential number of terms. Nevertheless, in what Steel called an "interesting and not immediately obvious" result [17, p. 141], Fuchs and Jin proved in [6] that Fair Proportions and Shapley Values are exactly the same on rooted phylogenetic trees, thus providing an individual phylogenetic diversity index which is easy to define and compute and which ranks species in a meaningful way.

In this note we extend Fuchs and Jin's result to rooted phylogenetic networks, graphical models of evolutionary histories that allow the inclusion of reticulate processes like hybridizations, recombinations or lateral gene transfers [10]. More specifically, we show that if we define the Fair Proportion of a leaf in a rooted phylogenetic network exactly as if we were in a phylogenetic tree—by splitting up the length of each arc equally among all its descendant leaves and then adding up the leaf's share of the lengths of all its ancestor arcs—then it turns out to be equal to the subnet Shapley Value of the leaf in the network as defined by Wicke and Fischer in [18]. We also extend to rooted phylogenetic networks the simple expression for the unrooted phylogenetic Shapley Value established by Haake, Kashiwada and Su in [9], thus showing in particular that it can be computed efficiently also on rooted phylogenetic networks.

2   Preliminaries

Let Σ be a finite set of labels. A Σ-$rDAG$ is a rooted directed acyclic graph with its *leaves* (its nodes of out-degree 0) bijectively labeled in Σ. We shall denote the sets of nodes and arcs of a Σ-rDAG N by $V(N)$ and $E(N)$, respectively, and we shall always identify its leaves with their corresponding labels. A Σ-rDAG is *arc-weighted*, or simply *weighted*, when it is endowed with a mapping $\omega : E(N) \to \mathbb{R}_{\geqslant 0}$ that assigns a weight, or *length*, $\omega(e) \geqslant 0$ to every arc e.

Given two nodes u, v in a Σ-rDAG N, we say that u is a *parent* of v when $(u, v) \in E(N)$, and that u is an *ancestor* of v, or that v is a *descendant* of u, when there exists a directed path from u to v in N. The *cluster* $C(e)$ of $e \in E(N)$ is the set of descendant leaves of its end node and we shall denote by $\kappa(e)$ the number of elements of $C(e)$. If $a \in C(e)$, we shall also say that e is an *ancestor arc* of a.

A *phylogenetic network* on Σ is a Σ-rDAG without *elementary* nodes (that is, without nodes of in-degree $\leqslant 1$ and out-degree 1). A node in a phylogenetic network is of *tree type* when its in-degree is 0 (the *root*) or 1, and a *reticulation* when its in-degree is at least 2. A *phylogenetic tree* is a phylogenetic network without reticulations. Let us emphasize, thus, that all our phylogenetic trees are rooted, unless otherwise explicitly stated. Given a phylogenetic network N on Σ and a subset $X \subseteq \Sigma$, we shall denote by $N(X)$ the subgraph of N induced by the set of all the ancestors of the leaves in X; it is an X-rDAG, with the same root as N.

Let T be a weighted phylogenetic tree on Σ. The *Fair Proportion* of $a \in \Sigma$ in T [14] is

$$FP_T(a) = \sum_{e:\, a \in C(e)} \frac{\omega(e)}{\kappa(e)}.$$

For every $X \subseteq \Sigma$, the *rooted Phylogenetic Diversity* $rPD_T(X)$ of X in T [5] is the *total weight* of $T(X)$, that is, the sum of the lengths of its arcs:

$$rPD_T(X) = \sum_{e:\, X \cap C(e) \neq \emptyset} \omega(e),$$

and the *unrooted Phylogenetic Diversity* $uPD_T(X)$ of X in T [5] is the total weight of the smallest unrooted subtree of T containing the leaves in X, or, equivalently, the total weight of the subtree of $T(X)$ rooted at the lowest common ancestor $LCA_T(X)$ of X.

A *coalitional game* on a set Σ is simply a set function $W : \mathcal{P}(\Sigma) \to \mathbb{R}$ that assigns a value to each "coalition" $X \subseteq \Sigma$. For every $a \in \Sigma$, the *Shapley Value* $SV_a(W)$ on a of a coalitional game W on Σ [15] is a weighted average of the marginal contribution of a to the value, under W, of each coalition $X \subseteq \Sigma$ containing it:

$$SV_a(W) = \sum_{a \in X \subseteq \Sigma} \frac{(|X| - 1)!(|\Sigma| - |X|)!}{|\Sigma|!} (W(X) - W(X \setminus \{a\})).$$

The *Shapley value* of the game W is then the vector $(SV_a(W))_{a \in \Sigma}$.

The use of coalitional games to study phylogenetic diversity was initiated by Nehring and Puppe in [12]. For the specific applications and interpretation of the Shapley Value in phylogenetics, see [9] and [13, Sect. 9.2].

3   The Fair Proportion Is a Shapley Value

Let N be a weighted phylogenetic network on Σ. We define the *Fair Proportion* of $a \in \Sigma$ in N, $FP_N(a)$, exactly as if N were a phylogenetic tree: we split the length of each arc equally among all its descendant leaves, and then we add up a's share of the lengths of all its ancestor arcs:

$$FP_N(a) = \sum_{e:\, a \in C(e)} \frac{\omega(e)}{\kappa(e)}.$$

In particular, if N is a phylogenetic tree, this Fair Proportion corresponds to the one recalled in the previous section. Our goal in this section is to show that, as it already happens on phylogenetic trees [6], this Fair Proportion is the Shapley Value of a certain "phylogenetic diversity" coalitional game: namely, of $rPSD_N : \mathcal{P}(\Sigma) \to \mathbb{R}$ on Σ, where, for every $X \subseteq \Sigma$, $rPSD_N(X)$ is the *rooted*

Phylogenetic Subnet Diversity of X in N in the sense of [18, Definition 6], which is defined as the total weight of $N(X)$:

$$rPSD_N(X) = \sum_{e:\, X \cap C(e) \neq \emptyset} \omega(e);$$

in particular, $rPSD_N(\emptyset) = 0$. Notice that if T is a phylogenetic tree, then $rPSD_T$ corresponds to Faith's rooted Phylogenetic Diversity rPD_T.

For every $a \in \Sigma$, let its *rooted subnet Shapley Value* in N be the Shapley Value of $rPSD_N$ on a:

$$SV_N(a) = \sum_{a \in X \subseteq \Sigma} \frac{(|X| - 1)!(|\Sigma| - |X|)!}{|\Sigma|!} \left(rPSD_N(X) - rPSD_N(X \setminus \{a\}) \right).$$

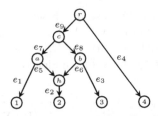

Fig. 1. The phylogenetic network used in Example 1.

Example 1. Consider the phylogenetic network N depicted in Fig. 1 and let the lengths of its arcs be $w_i = \omega(e_i)$, for every $i = 1, \ldots, 9$. The reticulation in it would represent that species "2" is the product of some interchange of genetic material between ancestor species a and b. Then:

$$\kappa(e_1) = \kappa(e_2) = \kappa(e_3) = \kappa(e_4) = \kappa(e_5) = \kappa(e_6) = 1$$
$$\kappa(e_7) = \kappa(e_8) = 2, \ \kappa(e_9) = 3$$

$$rPSD_N(1) = w_1 + w_7 + w_9$$
$$rPSD_N(2) = w_2 + w_5 + w_6 + w_7 + w_8 + w_9$$
$$rPSD_N(3) = w_3 + w_8 + w_9; \quad rPSD_N(4) = w_4$$
$$rPSD_N(1,4) = w_1 + w_4 + w_7 + w_9$$
$$rPSD_N(2,3) = w_2 + w_3 + w_5 + w_6 + w_7 + w_8 + w_9$$
$$rPSD_N(2,4) = w_2 + w_4 + w_5 + w_6 + w_7 + w_8 + w_9$$
$$rPSD_N(3,4) = w_3 + w_4 + w_8 + w_9$$
$$rPSD_N(1,2,3) = w_1 + w_2 + w_3 + w_5 + w_6 + w_7 + w_8 + w_9$$
$$rPSD_N(1,2,4) = w_1 + w_2 + w_4 + w_5 + w_6 + w_7 + w_8 + w_9$$
$$rPSD_N(1,3,4) = w_1 + w_3 + w_4 + w_7 + w_8 + w_9$$
$$rPSD_N(2,3,4) = w_2 + w_3 + w_4 + w_5 + w_6 + w_7 + w_8 + w_9$$

So, the Shapley Values of the leaves of N are:

$$SV_N(1) = \frac{1}{4}\big(rPSD_N(1) - rPSD_N(\emptyset)\big)$$

$$+\frac{1}{12}\big(rPSD_N(1,2) - rPSD_N(2) + rPSD_N(1,3) - rPSD_N(3)$$

$$+rPSD_N(1,4) - rPSD_N(4)\big)$$

$$+\frac{1}{12}\big(rPSD_N(1,2,3) - rPSD_N(2,3) + rPSD_N(1,2,4)$$

$$-rPSD_N(2,4) + rPSD_N(1,3,4) - rPSD_N(3,4)\big)$$

$$+\frac{1}{4}\big(rPSD_N(1,2,3,4) - rPSD_N(1,2,3)\big)$$

$$= \frac{1}{4}(w_1 + w_7 + w_9) + \frac{1}{12}(3w_1 + 2w_7 + w_9) + \frac{1}{12}(3w_1 + w_7) + \frac{1}{4}w_1$$

$$= w_1 + \frac{1}{2}w_7 + \frac{1}{3}w_9 = \frac{\omega(e_1)}{\kappa(e_1)} + \frac{\omega(e_7)}{\kappa(e_7)} + \frac{\omega(e_9)}{\kappa(e_9)} = FP_N(1)$$

$$SV_N(3) = w_3 + \frac{1}{2}w_8 + \frac{1}{3}w_9 = \frac{\omega(e_3)}{\kappa(e_3)} + \frac{\omega(e_8)}{\kappa(e_8)} + \frac{\omega(e_9)}{\kappa(e_9)} = FP_N(3)$$

(by symmetry)

$$SV_N(2) = \frac{1}{4}\big(rPSD_N(2) - rPSD_N(\emptyset)\big)$$

$$+\frac{1}{12}\big(rPSD_N(1,2) - rPSD_N(1) + rPSD_N(2,3)$$

$$-rPSD_N(3) + rPSD_N(2,4) - rPSD_N(4)\big)$$

$$+\frac{1}{12}\big(rPSD_N(1,2,3) - rPSD_N(1,3) + rPSD_N(1,2,4)$$

$$-rPSD_N(1,4) + rPSD_N(2,3,4) - rPSD_N(3,4)\big)$$

$$+\frac{1}{4}\big(rPSD_N(1,2,3,4) - rPSD_N(1,3,4)\big)$$

$$= \frac{1}{4}(w_2 + w_5 + w_6 + w_7 + w_8 + w_9)$$

$$+\frac{1}{12}(3w_2 + 3w_5 + 3w_6 + 2w_7 + 2w_8 + w_9)$$

$$+\frac{1}{12}(3w_2 + 3w_5 + 3w_6 + w_7 + w_8) + \frac{1}{4}(w_2 + w_5 + w_6)$$

$$= w_2 + w_5 + w_6 + \frac{1}{2}w_7 + \frac{1}{2}w_8 + \frac{1}{3}w_9$$

$$= \frac{\omega(e_2)}{\kappa(e_2)} + \frac{\omega(e_5)}{\kappa(e_5)} + \frac{\omega(e_6)}{\kappa(e_6)} + \frac{\omega(e_7)}{\kappa(e_7)} + \frac{\omega(e_8)}{\kappa(e_8)} + \frac{\omega(e_9)}{\kappa(e_9)} = FP_N(2)$$

$$SV_N(4) = \frac{1}{4}\big(rPSD_N(4) - rPSD_N(\emptyset)\big)$$

$$+\frac{1}{12}\big(rPSD_N(1,4) - rPSD_N(1) + rPSD_N(2,4)$$

$$-rPSD_N(2) + rPSD_N(3,4) - rPSD_N(3)\big)$$

$$+\frac{1}{12}\big(rPSD_N(1,2,4) - rPSD_N(1,2) + rPSD_N(1,3,4)$$

$$-rPSD_N(1,3) + rPSD_N(2,3,4) - rPSD_N(2,3)\big)$$

$$+\frac{1}{4}\big(rPSD_N(1,2,3,4) - rPSD_N(1,2,3)\big)$$

$$= \frac{1}{4}w_4 + \frac{3}{12}w_4 + \frac{3}{12}w_4 + \frac{1}{4}w_4 = w_4 = \frac{\omega(e_4)}{\kappa(e_4)} = FP_N(4)$$

So, if N is *ultrametric* (all paths from the root to leaves have the same length) and *time-consistent* (any reticulation and its parents are at the same distance from the root), then $w_7 = w_8$, $w_1 = w_2 = w_3$, $w_5 = w_6 = 0$, $w_7 = w_8$, and $w_4 = w_9 + w_7 + w_1$ and it is straightforward to check that the leaf with the largest SV is 4.

In the simple phylogenetic network considered in the previous example, the rooted subnet Shapley Value of each leaf was equal to its Fair Proportion. Next theorem establishes that it is always the case.

Theorem 1. *For every weighted phylogenetic network N on Σ and for every $a \in \Sigma$, $FP_N(a) = SV_N(a)$.*

Proof. Let $|\Sigma| = n$. For every $X \subseteq \Sigma$ containing a,

$$rPSD_N(X) - rPSD_N(X \setminus \{a\}) = \sum_{e:\, X \cap C(e) \neq \emptyset} \omega(e) - \sum_{\substack{e:\, (X \setminus \{a\}) \cap C(e) \\ \neq \emptyset}} \omega(e) = \sum_{e:\, X \cap C(e) = \{a\}} \omega(e).$$

Then,

$$SV_N(a) = \sum_{k=1}^{n} \frac{(k-1)!(n-k)!}{n!} \sum_{|X|=k, a \in X} \left(rPSD_N(X) - rPSD_N(X \setminus \{a\})\right)$$

where

$$\sum_{|X|=k, a \in X} \left(rPSD_N(X) - rPSD_N(X \setminus \{a\})\right) = \sum_{|X|=k, a \in X} \sum_{e:\, X \cap C(e) = \{a\}} \omega(e)$$

$$= \sum_{e:\, a \in C(e)} |\{Y \subseteq \Sigma \setminus C(e) \mid |Y| = k-1\}| \cdot \omega(e) = \sum_{e:\, a \in C(e)} \binom{n - \kappa(e)}{k-1} \omega(e).$$

Therefore,

$$SV_N(a) = \sum_{k=1}^{n} \left(\frac{(k-1)!(n-k)!}{n!} \sum_{e:\, a \in C(e)} \binom{n - \kappa(e)}{k-1} \omega(e) \right)$$

$$= \sum_{e:\, a \in C(e)} \left(\omega(e) \sum_{k=1}^{n} \frac{(k-1)!(n-k)!}{n!} \binom{n - \kappa(e)}{k-1} \right)$$

$$= \sum_{e:\, a \in C(e)} \left(\omega(e) \sum_{j=0}^{n-1} \frac{j!(n-j-1)!}{n!} \binom{n - \kappa(e)}{j} \right) = \sum_{e:\, a \in C(e)} \frac{\omega(e)}{\kappa(e)}$$

where the last equality is a consequence of Lemma 6.15 in [17], which establishes that, for every $1 \leqslant m \leqslant n$,

$$\sum_{j=0}^{n-1} \frac{j!(n-j-1)!}{n!} \binom{n-m}{j} = \frac{1}{m}.$$

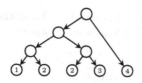

Fig. 2. A multilabeled tree.

Remark 1. A *multilabeled tree* (a *MUL-tree*, for short) on Σ is a rooted tree with its leaves labeled in Σ. The difference with usual phylogenetic trees is that the leaf labeling in a MUL-tree need not be bijective and, thus, more than one leaf may be assigned the same label. MUL-trees include *area cladograms* [7] and *gene trees* [8] as special instances. Given a MUL-tree T, if, for every label $a \in \Sigma$ assigned to more than one leaf, we remove all leaves labeled with a together with the arcs ending in them and we add a new reticulation h_a, a new leaf labeled with a, new arcs from the parents of the former leaves labeled with a to h_a, and a new arc (h_a, a), we obtain a phylogenetic network uniquely determined by T, which we call *associated* to T. For instance, the phylogenetic network in Fig. 1 is associated to the MUL-tree depicted in Fig. 2.

This representation of MUL-trees as phylogenetic networks allows the translation to the MUL-trees setting of the concepts developed so far. So, let T be a weighted MUL-tree. For every arc e in it, let $C(e)$ be the set of labels of its descendant leaves and $\kappa(e) = |C(e)|$ the number of different labels assigned to descendant leaves of e. For every label $a \in \Sigma$, let its *Fair Proportion* in T be

$$FP_T(a) = \sum_{e:a \in C(e)} \frac{\omega(e)}{\kappa(e)}.$$

Notice that now we split each $\omega(e)$ equally among the different labels of e's descendant leaves, without taking into account their multiplicities, that is, disregarding how many leaves are assigned to each given label. Then, if, for every $X \subseteq \Sigma$, we define its *MUL-Phylogenetic Diversity* in T as

$$mPD_T(X) = \sum_{e:\, X \cap C(e) \neq \emptyset} \omega(e),$$

Theorem 1 applied to the phylogenetic network associated to T implies that FP_T is the Shapley Value of mPD_T.

4   The Unrooted Subnet Shapley Value on a Rooted Phylogenetic Network

Consider the following two further set functions on Σ associated to a phylogenetic network N on Σ: for every $X \subseteq \Sigma$,

- The *Cophenetic Value* $\Phi_N(X)$ is 0 if $X = \emptyset$ and the sum of the lengths of the arcs that are ancestors of all leaves in X otherwise:

$$\Phi_N(X) = \sum_{e:\, X \subseteq C(e)} \omega(e) \qquad \text{if } X \neq \emptyset.$$

- The *unrooted Phylogenetic Subnet Diversity* $uPSD_N(X)$ is the difference

$$uPSD_N(X) = rPSD_N(X) - \Phi_N(X) = \sum_{\substack{e:\, X \cap C(e) \neq \emptyset \\ X \not\subseteq C(e)}} \omega(e).$$

So, if T is a phylogenetic tree, Φ_T is equal to the usual cophenetic value of a set of leaves X [1,16], that is, the total weight of the path going from the root of T to the lowest common ancestor of X, and $uPSD_T$ is equal to Faith's unrooted Phylogenetic Diversity uPD_T recalled in Sect. 2.

For every $a \in \Sigma$, let its *unrooted subnet Shapley Value* in N be the Shapley Value of $uPSD_N$ on a,

$$uSV_N(a) = \sum_{a \in X \subseteq \Sigma} \frac{(|X| - 1)!(|\Sigma| - |X|)!}{|\Sigma|!} \big(uPSD_N(X) - uPSD_N(X \setminus \{a\})\big),$$

and let its *cophenetic Shapley Value* in N be the Shapley Value of Φ_N on a,

$$cSV_N(a) = \sum_{a \in X \subseteq \Sigma} \frac{(|X| - 1)!(|\Sigma| - |X|)!}{|\Sigma|!} \big(\Phi_N(X) - \Phi_N(X \setminus \{a\})\big).$$

By the additivity of Shapley Values (cf. Axiom 3 in [15] or (4) in [9, Sect. 2.4]), the equality $rPSD_N = uPSD_N + \Phi_N$ implies that

$$SV_N = uSV_N + cSV_N.$$

Our goal is to obtain an expression for uSV_N that generalizes to rooted phylogenetic networks the expression for uPD_T on phylogenetic trees T established in [9]. We do it by using Theorem 1 and the following expression for cSV_N.

Lemma 1. *For every weighted phylogenetic network N on Σ and for every $a \in \Sigma$,*

$$cSV_N(a) = \frac{1}{n} rPSD_N(\Sigma) - \sum_{e:\, a \notin C(e)} \frac{\omega(e)}{n - \kappa(e)}.$$

Proof. Let $|\Sigma| = n$. To simplify the notations, we shall omit the subscripts N in Φ_N and cSV_N. For every $\{a\} \subsetneq X \subseteq \Sigma$

$$\Phi(X) - \Phi(X \setminus \{a\}) = \sum_{e:\, X \subseteq C(e)} \omega(e) - \sum_{e:\, (X \setminus \{a\}) \subseteq C(e)} \omega(e) = -\sum_{\substack{e:\, a \notin C(e) \\ (X \setminus \{a\}) \subseteq C(e)}} \omega(e)$$

while

$$\Phi(\{a\}) - \Phi(\emptyset) = \sum_{e:\, a \in C(e)} \omega(e) = rPSD_N(\Sigma) - \sum_{e:\, a \notin C(e)} \omega(e).$$

Then,

$$
cSV(a) = \sum_{k=1}^{n} \frac{(k-1)!(n-k)!}{n!} \sum_{|X|=k, a \in X} (\Phi(X) - \Phi(X \setminus \{a\}))
$$
$$
= \frac{1}{n} (\Phi(\{a\}) - \Phi(\emptyset)) + \sum_{k=2}^{n} \frac{(k-1)!(n-k)!}{n!} \sum_{|X|=k, a \in X} (\Phi(X) - \Phi(X \setminus \{a\}))
$$

and, for every $k \geqslant 2$,

$$
\sum_{|X|=k, a \in X} (\Phi(X) - \Phi(X \setminus \{a\})) = - \sum_{|X|=k, a \in X} \sum_{\substack{e: a \notin C(e) \\ (X \setminus \{a\}) \subseteq C(e)}} \omega(e)
$$
$$
= - \sum_{e: a \notin C(e)} |\{Y \subseteq C(e) \mid |Y| = k-1\}| \cdot \omega(e) = - \sum_{e: a \notin C(e)} \binom{\kappa(e)}{k-1} \omega(e).
$$

Therefore,

$$
cSV(a) = \frac{1}{n} \left(rPSD_N(\Sigma) - \sum_{e: a \notin C(e)} \omega(e) \right)
$$
$$
- \sum_{k=2}^{n} \left(\frac{(k-1)!(n-k)!}{n!} \sum_{e: a \notin C(e)} \binom{\kappa(e)}{k-1} \omega(e) \right)
$$
$$
= \frac{1}{n} rPSD_N(\Sigma) - \sum_{k=1}^{n} \left(\frac{(k-1)!(n-k)!}{n!} \sum_{e: a \notin C(e)} \binom{\kappa(e)}{k-1} \omega(e) \right)
$$
$$
= \frac{1}{n} rPSD_N(\Sigma) - \sum_{e: a \notin C(e)} \left(\omega(e) \sum_{k=1}^{n} \frac{(k-1)!(n-k)!}{n!} \binom{\kappa(e)}{k-1} \right)
$$
$$
= \frac{1}{n} rPSD_N(\Sigma) - \sum_{e: a \notin C(e)} \frac{\omega(e)}{n - \kappa(e)}
$$

using again Lemma 6.15 in [17], which finishes the proof.

Replacing the expressions for cSV_N and $rCSV_N$ given in Theorem 1 and the last lemma, respectively, in $uCSV_N = rCSV_N - cSV_N$, we obtain the following result:

Theorem 2. *For every weighted phylogenetic network N on Σ and for every $a \in \Sigma$,*

$$
uSV_N(a) = \frac{1}{n} \sum_{e: a \in C(e)} \frac{n - \kappa(e)}{\kappa(e)} \cdot \omega(e) + \frac{1}{n} \sum_{e: a \notin C(e)} \frac{\kappa(e)}{n - \kappa(e)} \cdot \omega(e).
$$

It is not difficult to check that this expression corresponds to the one given in [9, Theorem 4] when N is a rooted phylogenetic tree.

5   Conclusions

In this note we have generalized to rooted phylogenetic networks two results on Shapley Values for phylogenetic trees: the equality of the rooted phylogenetic Shapley Value with the Fair Proportion, and the simple expression of the unrooted phylogenetic Shapley Value in terms of the lengths and the cardinalities of arcs' clusters. This note is accompanied by the GitHub page https://github.com/biocom-uib/Shapley-networks that contains several Python scripts to compute the indices considered here on phylogenetic networks represented in extended Newick format [2].

We would like to call the reader's attention on the fact that Theorem 1 is easily generalized to coalitional games $W : \mathcal{P}(\Sigma) \rightarrow \mathbb{R}$ for which there exist a set E and two mappings $C : E \rightarrow \mathcal{P}(\Sigma)$ and $\omega : E \rightarrow \mathbb{R}$ such that

$$W(X) = \sum_{e:\, X \cap C(e) \neq \emptyset} \omega(e).$$

For such a game W, the proof of Theorem 1 *mutatis mutandis* shows that its Shapley value on $a \in \Sigma$ is simply

$$SV_a(W) = \sum_{e:\, a \in C(e)} \frac{\omega(e)}{|C(e)|}.$$

For instance, a Shapley Value of this type can be used to assess the importance of a question in an exam, one of the main goals of Item Response Theory [4], as follows. Let Σ be the set of questions in an exam and let E be the set of students taking this exam. Assume that all questions in the exam are worth the same score. For every student e, let $C(e)$ be the set of questions correctly answered in her exam and set $\omega(e) = 1/|E|$. For every set of questions X, let $W(X) = \sum_{e:\, X \cap C(e) \neq \emptyset} \omega(e)$, which is equal to the fraction of students that answered correctly at least one question in X. Then, as we have just seen, the Shapley Value of this game on a given question a is

$$SV_a(W) = \frac{1}{|E|} \sum_{e:\, a \in C(e)} \frac{1}{|C(e)|}.$$

This Shapley Value measures the contribution of question a to the global success in the exam, increasing with the number of students who answered the question correctly but decreasing with the grades they obtained.

If different questions may have different scores, then it would be sensible to take as $\omega(e)$ the total score of the exam divided by $|E|$, in which case $W(X)$, for a set of questions X, would be the sum of grades of the students who answered correctly some question in X, averaged by the global number of students. For another, recent use of the Shapley Value in the classification of items in an exam, see [11].

Acknowledgements. This research was partially supported by the Spanish Ministry of Economy and Competitiveness and the ERDF through project DPI2015-67082-P (MINECO/FEDER). We thank I. García and the reviewers for their helpful suggestions on several aspects of this paper.

References

1. Cardona, G., Mir, A., Rotger, L., Rosselló, F., Sánchez, D.: Cophenetic metrics for phylogenetic trees, after Sokal and Rohlf. BMC Bioinf. **14**, 3 (2013)
2. Cardona, G., Rosselló, F., Valiente, G.: Extended Newick: it is time for a standard representation of phylogenetic networks. BMC Bioinf. **9**, 532 (2008)
3. Diniz, J.: Phylogenetic diversity and conservation priorities under distinct models of phenotypic evolution. Conserv. Biol. **18**, 698–704 (2004)
4. Embretson, S., Reise, S.: Item Response Theory. Psychology Press, London (2013)
5. Faith, D.: Conservation evaluation and phylogenetic diversity. Biol. Conserv. **61**, 1–10 (1992)
6. Fuchs, M., Jin, E.Y.: Equality of Shapley value and fair proportion index in phylogenetic trees. J. Math. Biol. **71**, 1133–1147 (2015)
7. Ganapathy, G., Goodson, B., Jansen, R., Le, H., Ramachandran, V., Warnow, T.: Pattern identification in biogeography. IEEE/ACM Trans. Comput. Biol. Bioinf. **3**, 334–346 (2006)
8. Gregg, W., Ather, S., Hahn, M.: Gene-tree reconciliation with MUL-trees to resolve polyploidy events. Syst. Biol. **66**, 1007–1018 (2017)
9. Haake, C.-J., Kashiwada, A., Su, F.E.: The Shapley value of phylogenetic trees. J. Math. Biol. **56**, 479–497 (2008)
10. Huson, D., Rupp, R., Scornavacca, C.: Phylogenetic Networks: Concepts, Algorithms and Applications. Cambridge University Press, Cambridge (2010)
11. Lutsenko, M., Shadrinceva, N.: Shapley weights of test items. Vestnik Sankt-Petersburgskovo Universiteta, Seriya 10, 13, pp. 300–312 (2017, in Russian)
12. Nehring, K., Puppe, C.: A theory of diversity. Econometrica **70**, 1155–1198 (2002)
13. Moretti, S., Patrone, F.: Transversality of the Shapley value. Top **16**, 1–41 (2008)
14. Redding, D., Mooers, A.: Incorporating evolutionary measures into conservation prioritization. Conserv. Biol. **20**, 1670–1678 (2006)
15. Shapley, L.: A value for n-person games. In: Kuhn, H., Tucker, A. (eds.) Contributions to the Theory of Games, Vol. II, Annals of Mathematical Studies, vol. 28, pp. 307–317. Princeton University Press (1953)
16. Sokal, R., Rohlf, F.: The comparison of dendrograms by objective methods. Taxon **11**, 33–40 (1962)
17. Steel, M.: Phylogeny: Discrete and Random Processes in Evolution. SIAM, Philadelphia (2016)
18. Wicke, K., Fischer, M.: Phylogenetic diversity and biodiversity indices on phylogenetic networks. Math. Biosci. **298**, 80–90 (2018)

Deterministic Parsing with P Colony Automata

Erzsébet Csuhaj-Varjú[1], Kristóf Kántor[2], and György Vaszil[2(⊠)]

[1] Department of Algorithms and Their Applications, Faculty of Informatics,
ELTE Eötvös Loránd University, Pázmány Péter sétány 1/c,
Budapest 1117, Hungary
csuhaj@inf.elte.hu
[2] Department of Computer Science, Faculty of Informatics,
University of Debrecen, Kassai út 26, Debrecen 4028, Hungary
{kantor.kristof,vaszil.gyorgy}@inf.unideb.hu

Abstract. We investigate the possibility of the deterministic parsing (that is, parsing without backtracking) of languages described by (generalized) P colony automata. We define a subclass of these computing devices satisfying a property which resembles the LL(k) property of context-free grammars, and study the possibility of parsing the characterized languages using a k symbol lookahead, as in the LL(k) parsing method for context-free languages.

1 Introduction

The computational model called P colony is similar to tissue-like membrane systems. In P colonies, multisets of objects are used to describe the contents of cells and the environment, and these multisets are processed by the cells in the corresponding colony using rules which enable the evolution of the objects present in the cells or the exchange of objects between the environment and the cells. These computing agents have a very confined functionality: they can store a restricted amount of objects at a given time (this is called the capacity of the cell; every cell has the same capacity) and they can process a restricted amount of information. The way of information processing is very simple: The rules are either of the form $a \to b$ (for changing an object a into an object b inside the cell), or $a \leftrightarrow b$ (for exchanging an object a inside a cell with an object b in the environment). A program is a rule set with exactly the same number of rules as the capacity of the cell. When a program is executed, the k rules (the capacity of the cell) that it contains are applied to the k objects simultaneously. A configuration of a P colony with n cells is a an n-tuple of multisets of objects, those which are present inside the cells. During a computational step, a maximal number of cells of the P colony execute one of their programs in parallel. A computation ends when the P colony reaches one of its final configurations (usually given as the set of halting configurations, that is, when no program can be applied by any of the cells).

C. Graciani et al. (Eds.): Pérez-Jiménez Festschrift, LNCS 11270, pp. 88–98, 2018.
https://doi.org/10.1007/978-3-030-00265-7_8

There are many theoretical results concerning P colonies. Despite the fact that they are extremely simple computing systems, they are computationally complete, even with very restricted size parameters and other syntactic or functioning restrictions. For these, and more topics, results, see [4,5,7–10,12,13,17,18] and for summaries consult [6,22].

P colony automata were introduced in [3]. They are called automata, because they accept string languages by assuming an initial input tape with an input string in the environment. The available types of rules are extended by so-called tape rules. These types of rules in addition to manipulating the objects as their non-tape counterparts, also read the processed objects from the input tape.

To overcome the difficulty that different tape rules can read different symbols in the same computational step, generalized P colony automata were introduced in [19] and studied further in [20,21]. The main idea of this computational model was to get the process of input reading closer to other kinds of membrane systems, especially to antiport P systems and P automata. The latter, introduced in [14] (see also [11]) are P systems using symport and antiport rules (see [23]), characterizing string languages.

This generality is used in the generalized P colony automata theory, that is, the idea of characterizing strings through the sequences of multisets processed during computations. A computation in this model defines accepted multiset sequences, which are transformed into accepted symbol sequences/strings. In this model there is no input string, but there are tape rules and non-tape rules equally for evolution and communication rules. In a single computational step, this system is able to read more than one symbol, thus reading a multiset. This way generalized P colony automata are able to avoid the conflicts present in P colony automata, where simultaneous usage of tape rules in a single computational step can arise problems. After getting the result of a computation, that is, the accepted sequence of multisets, it is possible to map them to strings in a similar way as shown in P automata.

In [19], some basic variants of the model were introduced and studied from the point of view of their computational power. In [20,21] we continued the investigations structuring our results around the capacity of the systems, and different types of restrictions imposed on the use of tape rules in the programs.

The concept of a P colony automata has been developed into another direction as well, namely, those variants have been introduced and studied where the environment consists of a string and the communication rules of the cells are for substituting (replacing a symbol with another symbol), inserting, or erasing symbols of the current environmental string [2]. These constructs are called APCol systems (Automaton-like P colonies). Notice that this model essentially differs from the generalized P colony automaton since the whole environment is given in advance and in the form of a string. APCol systems are also able to obtain the full computational power, i.e., they are computationally complete [4,5].

Since P colony automata variants accept languages, different types of characterizations of their language classes are of interest. One possible research direction could be investigating their parsing properties in terms of programs and rules of the (generalized) P colony automata. In this paper we study the possibility of deterministically parsing the languages characterized by these devices. We define the so-called LL(k) condition for these types of automata, which enables deterministic parsing with a k symbol lookahead, as in the case of context-free LL(k) languages, and present an initial result showing that using generalized P colony automata we can deterministically parse context-free languages that are not LL(k) in the "original" sense.

2 Preliminaries and Definitions

Let V be a finite alphabet, let the set of all words over V be denoted by V^*, and let ε be the empty word. The number of occurrences of a symbol a in w where $a \in V$ is denoted by $|w|_a$.

A multiset over a set V is a mapping $M : V \to \mathbb{N}$ where $\mathbb{N}$ denotes the set of non-negative integers. This mapping assigns to each object $a \in V$ its multiplicity $M(a)$ in M. The set $supp(M) = \{a \mid M(a) \geq 1\}$ is the support of M. If V is a finite set, then M is called a finite multiset. A multiset M is empty if its support is empty, $supp(M) = \emptyset$. The set of finite multisets over the alphabet V is denoted by $\mathcal{M}(V)$. A finite multiset M over V will also be represented by a string w over the alphabet V with $|w|_a = M(a)$, $a \in V$, the empty multiset will be denoted by $\emptyset$.

We say that $a \in M$ if $M(a) \geq 1$, and the cardinality of M, $card(M)$ is defined as $card(M) = \Sigma_{a \in M} M(a)$. For two multisets $M_1, M_2 \in \mathcal{M}(V)$, $M_1 \subseteq M_2$ holds, if for all $a \in V$, $M_1(a) \leq M_2(a)$. The union of M_1 and M_2 is defined as $(M_1 \cup M_2) : V \to \mathbb{N}$ with $(M_1 \cup M_2)(a) = M_1(a) + M_2(a)$ for all $a \in V$, the difference is defined for $M_2 \subseteq M_1$ as $(M_1 - M_2) : V \to \mathbb{N}$ with $(M_1 - M_2)(a) = M_1(a) - M_2(a)$ for all $a \in V$.

A *genPCol automaton* of capacity k and with n cells, $k, n \geq 1$, is a construct

$$\Pi = (V, e, w_E, (w_1, P_1), \ldots, (w_n, P_n), F)$$

where

- V is an *alphabet*, the alphabet of the automaton, its elements are called *objects*;
- $e \in V$ is the *environmental object* of the automaton, the only object which is assumed to be available in an arbitrary, unbounded number of copies in the environment;
- $w_E \in (V - \{e\})^*$ is a string representing a multiset from $\mathcal{M}(V - \{e\})$, the multiset of objects different from e which is found in the environment initially;
- $(w_i, P_i), 1 \leq i \leq n$, specifies the i-th *cell* where w_i is (the representation of) a multiset over V, it determines the initial contents of the cell, and its cardinality $|w_i| = k$ is called the *capacity* of the system. P_i is a set of *programs*, each program is formed from k rules of the following types (where $a, b \in V$):
    - *tape rules* of the form $a \xrightarrow{T} b$, or $a \xleftrightarrow{T} b$, called rewriting tape rules and communication tape rules, respectively; or

- *nontape rules* of the form $a \rightarrow b$, or $a \leftrightarrow b$, called rewriting (nontape) rules and communication (nontape) rules, respectively.

A program is called a *tape program* if it contains at least one tape rule.

- F is a set of *accepting configurations* of the automaton which we will specify in more detail below.

A genPCol automaton reads an input word during a computation. A part of the input (possibly consisting of more than one symbol) is read during each configuration change: the processed part of the input corresponds to the multiset of symbols introduced by the tape rules of the system.

A *configuration* of a genPCol automaton is an $(n+1)$-tuple $(u_E, u_1, \ldots, u_n)$, where $u_E \in \mathcal{M}(V - \{e\})$ is the multiset of objects different from e in the environment, and $u_i \in \mathcal{M}(V)$, $1 \leq i \leq n$, are the contents of the i-th cell. The *initial configuration* is given by $(w_E, w_1, \ldots, w_n)$, the initial contents of the environment and the cells. The elements of the set F of *accepting configurations* are given as configurations of the form $(v_E, v_1, \ldots, v_n)$, where

- $v_E \in \mathcal{M}(V - \{e\})$ denotes a multiset of objects different from e being in the environment, and
- $v_i \in \mathcal{M}(V)$, $1 \leq i \leq n$, is the contents of the i-th cell.

In order to describe the functioning of genPCol automata, let us define the following multisets. Let r be a rewriting or a communication rule (tape or nontape), and let us denote by $left(r)$ and $right(r)$ the objects on the left and on the right side of r, respectively. Let also, for $\alpha \in \{left, right\}$ and for any program p, $\alpha(p) = \bigcup_{r \in p} \alpha(r)$ where the union denotes multiset union (as defined above), and for a rule r and a program $p = \langle r_1, \ldots, r_k \rangle$, the notation $r \in p$ denotes the fact that $r = r_j$ for some j, $1 \leq j \leq k$.

Moreover, for any tape program p we also define the multiset of symbols $read(p) = \bigcup_{r \in p, r = a \xrightarrow{T} b, b \neq e} right(r) \cup \bigcup_{r \in p, r = a \xleftrightarrow{T} b, a \neq e} left(r)$, the multiset of symbols (different from e) on the right side of rewriting tape rules and on the left side of communication tape rules. If p is not a tape program, that is, p contains no tape rules, then $read(p) = \emptyset$.

For all communication rules r of the program p, let $export(p) = \bigcup_{r \in p} left(r)$ and $import(p) = \bigcup_{r \in p} right(r)$, the multiset of objects that are sent out to the environment and brought inside the cell when applying the program p, respectively.

Moreover, $create(p) = \bigcup_{r \in p} right(p)$ for the rewriting rules r of p, that is, $create(p)$ is the multiset of symbols produced by the rewriting rules of program p.

Let $c = (u_E, u_1, \ldots, u_n)$ be a configuration of a genPCol automaton Π, and let $U_E = u_E \cup \{e, e, \ldots\}$, thus, the multiset of objects found in the environment (together with the infinite number of copies of e, denoted as $\{e, e, \ldots\}$, which are always present). The *sequence of programs*

$$(p_1, \ldots, p_n) \in (P_1 \cup \{\#\}) \times \ldots \times (P_n \cup \{\#\})$$

is *applicable in configuration c*, if the following conditions hold.

- The selected programs are applicable in the cells (the left sides of the rules contain the same symbols that are present in the cell), that is, for each $1 \leq i \leq n$, if $p_i \in P_i$ then $left(p_i) = u_i$;
- the symbols to be brought inside the cells by the programs are present in the environment, that is, $\bigcup_{p_i \neq \#, 1 \leq i \leq n} import(p_i) \subseteq U_E$;
- the set of selected programs is maximal, that is, if any $p_i = \#$ is replaced by some $p_i' \in P_i$, $1 \leq i \leq n$, then the above conditions are not satisfied any more.

The set of all applicable sequences of programs in the configuration $c = (u_E, u_1, \ldots, u_n)$ is denoted by App_c, that is,

$$App_c = \{P_c = (p_1, \ldots, p_n) \in (P_1 \cup \{\#\}) \times \ldots \times (P_n \cup \{\#\}) \mid \text{ where } P_c$$
$$\text{is a sequence of applicable programs in the configuration } c\}.$$

A configuration c is called *a halting configuration* if the set of applicable sequences of programs is the singleton set $App_c = \{(p_1, \ldots, p_n) \mid p_i = \# \text{ for all } 1 \leq i \leq n\}$.

Let $c = (u_E, u_1, \ldots, u_n)$ be a configuration of the genPCol automaton. By applying a sequence of applicable programs $P_c \in App_c$, the configuration c is *changed* to a configuration $c' = (u_E', u_1', \ldots, u_n')$, denoted by $c \overset{P_c}{\Longrightarrow} c'$, if the following properties hold:

- If $(p_1, \ldots, p_n) = P_c \in App_c$ and $p_i \in P_i$, then $u_i' = create(p_i) \cup import(p_i)$, otherwise, if $p_i = \#$, then $u_i' = u_i$, $1 \leq i \leq n$. Moreover,
- $U_E' = U_E - \bigcup_{p_i \neq \#, 1 \leq i \leq n} import(p_i) \cup \bigcup_{p_i \neq \#, 1 \leq i \leq n} export(p_i)$ (where U_E' again denotes $u_E' \cup \{e, e, \ldots\}$ with an infinite number of copies of e).

Thus, in genPCol automata, we apply the programs in the maximally parallel way, that is, in each computational step, every component cell nondeterministically applies one of its applicable programs. Then we collect all the symbols that the tape rules "read" (these multisets are denoted by $read(p)$ for a program p above): this is the multiset read by the system in the given computational step.

For any P_c sequence of applicable programs in a configuration c, $read(P_c)$ denotes the multiset of objects read by the tape rules of the programs of P_c, that is,

$$read(P_c) = \bigcup_{p_i \neq \#, \ (p_1, \ldots, p_n) = P_c} read(p_i).$$

Then we can also define the set of multisets which can be read in any configuration of the genPCol automaton Π as

$$in(\Pi) = \{read(P_c) \mid P_c \in App_c\}.$$

Remark 1. Although the set of configurations of a genPCol automaton Π can be infinite (because the multiset corresponding to the contents of the environment is not necessarily finite), the set $in(\Pi)$ is always finite. To see this, note that the applicability of a program by a component cell also depends on the contents of the particular component. Since at most one program can be applied in a component in one computational step, and the number of programs associated to each component is finite, the number of different sequences of applicable programs in any configuration, that is, the cardinality of the set App_c is finite.

A successful computation defines this way an accepted sequence of multisets: $u_1u_2\ldots u_s$, $u_i \in in(\Pi)$, for $1 \le i \le s$, that is, the sequence of multisets entering the system during the steps of the computation.

Let $\Pi = (V, e, w_E, (w_1, P_1), \ldots, (w_n, P_n), F)$ be a genPCol automaton. The *set of input sequences accepted by* Π is defined as

$$A(\Pi) = \{u_1u_2\ldots u_s \mid u_i \in in(\Pi),\ 1 \le i \le s,\ \text{and there is a configuration}$$
$$\text{sequence } c_0, \ldots, c_s,\ \text{with } c_0 = (w_E, w_1, \ldots, w_n),\ c_s \in F,\ c_s \text{ halting,}$$
$$\text{and}\quad c_i \overset{P_{c_i}}{\Longrightarrow} c_{i+1}\ \text{with } u_{i+1} = read(P_{c_i})\ \text{for all } 0 \le i \le s-1\}.$$

Let Π be a genPCol automaton, and let $f : in(\Pi) \to 2^{\Sigma^*}$ be a mapping, such that $f(u) = \{\varepsilon\}$ if and only if u is the empty multiset.

The *language accepted by* Π with respect to f is defined as

$$L(\Pi, f) = \{f(u_1)f(u_2)\ldots f(u_s) \in \Sigma^* \mid u_1u_2\ldots u_s \in A(\Pi)\}.$$

The class of languages accepted by generalized PCol automata with capacity k and with mappings from the class $\mathcal{F}$ is denoted

- by $\mathcal{L}(\text{genPCol}, \mathcal{F}, \text{com-tape}(k))$ when all the communication rules are tape rules,
- by $\mathcal{L}(\text{genPCol}, \mathcal{F}, \text{all-tape}(k))$ when all the programs must have at least one tape rule, and
- by $\mathcal{L}(\text{genPCol}, \mathcal{F}, *(k))$ when programs with any kinds of rules are allowed.

Let V and Σ be two alphabets, and let $\mathcal{M}_{FIN}(V) \subseteq \mathcal{M}(V)$ denote the set of finite subsets of the set of finite multisets over an alphabet V. Consider a mapping $f : D \to 2^{\Sigma^*}$ for some $D \in \mathcal{M}_{FIN}(V)$. We say that $f \in \mathcal{F}_{TRANS}$, if for any $v \in D$, we have $|f(v)| = 1$, and we can obtain $f(v) = \{w\}$, $w \in \Sigma^*$ by applying a deterministic finite transducer to any string representation of the multiset v, (as w is unique, the transducer must be constructed in such a way that all string representations of the multiset v as input result in the same $w \in \Sigma^*$ as output, and moreover, as f should be nonerasing, the transducer produces a result with $w \ne \varepsilon$ for any nonempty input).

Besides the above defined class of mappings, we also use the so called permutation mapping. Let $f_{perm} : \mathcal{M}(V) \to 2^{\Sigma^*}$ where $V = \Sigma$ be defined as follows. For all $v \in \mathcal{M}(V)$, we have

$$f_{perm}(v) = \{a_{\sigma(1)}a_{\sigma(2)}\ldots a_{\sigma(s)} \mid v = a_1a_2\ldots a_s \text{ for some permutation}$$
$$\sigma \text{ of } \{1, \ldots, s\}\ \}.$$

We denote the language classes that can be characterized with these types of input mappings as $\mathcal{L}_X(\text{genPCol}, Y(k))$, where $X \in \{perm, \text{TRANS}\}$, $Y \in \{\text{com-tape, all-tape}, *\}$.

Now we recall an example from [20] to demonstrate the above defined notions.

Example 1. Let $\Pi = (\{a, b, c\}, e, \emptyset, (ea, P), F)$ be a genPCol automaton where

$$P = \{p_1 : \langle e \to a, a \overset{T}{\leftrightarrow} e \rangle, \ p_2 : \langle e \to b, a \overset{T}{\leftrightarrow} e \rangle, \ p_3 : \langle e \to b, b \overset{T}{\leftrightarrow} a \rangle,$$

$$p_4 : \langle e \to c, b \overset{T}{\leftrightarrow} a \rangle, \ p_5 : \langle a \to b, b \overset{T}{\leftrightarrow} a \rangle, \ p_6 : \langle a \to c, b \overset{T}{\leftrightarrow} a \rangle\}$$

with all the communication rules being tape rules. Let $F = \{(v, ca) \mid a \notin v\}$ be the set of final configurations.

The initial configuration of this systems is $c_0 = (\emptyset, ea)$. Since the number of components is just one, the sequences of applicable programs are one element "sequences". The set of sequences of programs applicable in the initial configuration contains two elements, $App_{c_0} = \{(p_1), (p_2)\}$.

A possible computation of this system is the following:

$$(\emptyset, ea) \Rightarrow (a, ea) \Rightarrow (aa, ea) \Rightarrow (aaa, eb) \Rightarrow (aab, ba) \Rightarrow (bba, ba) \Rightarrow (bbb, ac)$$

where the first three computational steps read the multiset containing an a, the last three steps read a multiset containing a b, thus the accepted multiset sequence of this computation is $(a)(a)(a)(b)(b)(b)$.

It is not difficult to see that similarly to the one above, the computations which end in a final configuration (a configuration which does not contain the object a in the environment) accept the set of multiset sequences

$$A(\Pi) = \{(a)^n (b)^n \mid n \geq 1\}.$$

The set of multisets which can be read by Π is $in(\Pi) = \{a, b\}$ (where a and b denote the multisets containing one copy of the object a and b, respectively).

If we consider f_{perm} as the input mapping, we have

$$L(\Pi, f_{perm}) = \{a^n b^n \mid n \geq 1\}.$$

On the other hand, if we consider the mapping $f_1 \in \mathcal{F}_{\text{TRANS}}$ where $f_1 : in(\Pi) \to 2^{\Sigma^*}$ with $\Sigma = \{c, d, e, f\}$ and $f_1(a) = \{cd\}$, $f_1(b) = \{ef\}$, we get the language

$$L(\Pi, f_1) = \{(cd)^n (ef)^n \mid n \geq 1\}.$$

The computational capacity of genPCol automata was investigated in [19–21]. It was shown that with unrestricted programs systems of capacity *one* generate any recursively enumerable language, that is,

$$\mathcal{L}_X(\text{genPCol}, *(k)) = \mathcal{L}(\text{RE}), \ k \geq 1, \ X \in \{perm, TRANS\}.$$

A similar result holds for all-tape systems with capacity at least two.

$$\mathcal{L}_X(\text{genPCol}, \text{all-tape}(k)) = \mathcal{L}(\text{RE}) \text{ for } k \geq 2, \ X \in \{perm, TRANS\}.$$

3   P Colony Automata and the LL(k) Condition

Let $U \subset \Sigma^*$ be a finite set of strings over some alphabet Σ. Let $\mathrm{FIRST}_k(U)$ denote the set of length k prefixes of the elements of U for some $k \geq 1$, that is, let

$$\mathrm{FIRST}_k(U) = \{pref_k(u) \in \Sigma^* \mid u \in U\}$$

where $pref_k(u)$ denotes the string of the first k symbols of u if $|u| \geq k$, or $pref_k(u) = u$ otherwise.

Definition 1. Let $\Pi = (V, e, w_E, (w_1, P_1), \ldots, (w_n, P_n), F)$ be a genPCol automaton, let $f : in(\Pi) \to 2^{\Sigma^*}$ be a mapping as above, and let $c_0, c_1, \ldots, c_s$ be a sequence of configurations with $c_i \implies c_{i+1}$ for all $0 \leq i \leq s - 1$.

We say that the P colony Π is LL(k) for some $k \geq 1$ with respect to the mapping f, if for any two distinct sets of programs applicable in configuration c_s, $P_{c_s}, P'_{c_s} \in App_{c_s}$ with $P_{c_s} \neq P'_{c_s}$, the next k symbols of the input string that is being read determines which of the two sequences are to be applied in the next computational step, that is, the following holds.

Consider two computations

$$c_s \xrightarrow{P_{c_s}} c_{s+1} \xrightarrow{P_{c_{s+1}}} \ldots \xrightarrow{P_{c_{s+m}}} c_{s+m+1}, \text{ and } c_s \xrightarrow{P'_{c_s}} c'_{s+1} \xrightarrow{P'_{c_{s+1}}} \ldots \xrightarrow{P'_{c_{s+m'}}} c'_{s+m'+1}$$

where $u_{c_s} = read(P_{c_s})$ and $u_{c_{s+i}} = read(P_{c_{s+i}})$ for $1 \leq i \leq m$, and similarly $u'_{c_s} = read(P'_{c_s})$ and $u'_{c_{s+i}} = read(P'_{c_{s+i}})$ for $1 \leq i \leq m'$, thus, the two sequences of input multisets are

$$u_{c_s} u_{c_{s+1}} \ldots u_{c_{s+m}} \text{ and } u'_{c_s} u'_{c_{s+1}} \ldots u'_{c_{s+m'}}.$$

Assume that these sequences are long enough to "consume" the next k symbols of the input string, that is, for w and w' with

$$w \in f(u_{c_s})f(u_{c_{s+1}}) \ldots f(u_{c_{s+m}}) \text{ and } w' \in f(u'_{c_s})f(u'_{c_{s+1}}) \ldots f(u'_{c_{s+m'}}),$$

either $|w| \geq k$ and $|w'| \geq k$, or if $|w| < k$ (or $|w'| < k$), then c_{s+m+1} (or $c_{s+m'+1}$) is a halting configuration.

Now, the P colony Π is LL(k), if for any two computations as above,

$$\mathrm{FIRST}_k(w) \cap \mathrm{FIRST}_k(w') = \emptyset.$$

The class of context-free LL(k) languages will be denoted by $\mathcal{L}(\mathrm{CF,LL}(k))$ (see for example the monograph [1] for more details), while the languages characterized by genPCol automata satisfying the above defined condition, with input mapping of type f_{perm} or $f \in TRANS$, will be denoted by $\mathcal{L}_X(\mathrm{genPCol,LL}(k))$, $X \in \{perm, TRANS\}$.

Let us illustrate the above definition with an example.

Example 2. Let $\Pi = (\{a,b,c,d,f,g,e\}, e, \emptyset, (ea, P_1), F)$ where

$$P_1 = \{\langle e \to b, a \overset{T}{\leftrightarrow} e \rangle, \langle e \to e, b \overset{T}{\leftrightarrow} a \rangle, \langle e \to c, a \overset{T}{\leftrightarrow} e \rangle, \langle e \to f, a \overset{T}{\leftrightarrow} e \rangle,$$

$$\langle e \to d, c \overset{T}{\leftrightarrow} b \rangle, \langle b \to c, d \overset{T}{\leftrightarrow} e \rangle, \langle e \to g, f \overset{T}{\leftrightarrow} b \rangle, \langle b \to f, g \overset{T}{\leftrightarrow} e \rangle\} \text{ and}$$

$$F = \{(v, ce), (v, fe) \mid v \in V^*, b \notin v\}.$$

The language characterized by Π is

$$L(\Pi, f_{perm}) = \{a\} \cup \{(ab)^n a(cd)^n \mid n \geq 1\} \cup \{(ab)^n a(fg)^n \mid n \geq 1\}.$$

To see this, consider the possible computations of Π. The initial configuration is $(\emptyset, ea)$ and there are three possible configurations that can be reached, namely (we denote by $\Rightarrow_u$ a configuration change during which the multiset of symbols u was read by the automaton)

1. $(\emptyset, ea) \Rightarrow_a (a, ce)$,
2. $(\emptyset, ea) \Rightarrow_a (a, fe)$,
3. $(\emptyset, ea) \Rightarrow_a (a, be)$.

The first two cases are non-accepting states, but the derivations cannot be continued, so let us consider the third one.

$$(a, be) \Rightarrow_b (b, ea) \Rightarrow_a (ba, be) \Rightarrow_b (bb, ea) \Rightarrow_a \ldots \Rightarrow_b (b^i, ea).$$

At this point, the computation can follow two different paths again, either

$$(b^i, ae) \Rightarrow_a (b^i a, ec) \Rightarrow_c (b^{i-1} ac, db) \Rightarrow_d (b^{i-1} acd, ce) \Rightarrow_c \ldots \Rightarrow_d (ac^i d^i, ce),$$

or

$$(b^i, ae) \Rightarrow_a (b^i a, ef) \Rightarrow_f (b^{i-1} af, gb) \Rightarrow_g (b^{i-1} afg, fe) \Rightarrow_f \ldots \Rightarrow_g (af^i g^i, fe).$$

In the first phase of the computation, the system produces copies of b and sends them to the environment, then in the second phase these copies of b are exchanged to copies of cd or copies of fg. The system can reach an accepting state when all the copies of b are used, that is, when an equal number of copies of ab and either of cd or of fg were produced.

Note that the system satisfies the LL(1) property, the symbol that has to be read, in order to accept a desired input word, determines the set of programs that has to be used in the next computational step.

As a consequence of the above example, we can state the following.

Theorem 1. *There are context-free languages in $\mathcal{L}_X(genPCol,LL(1))$, $X \in \{perm, TRANS\}$, which are not in $\mathcal{L}(CF,LL(k))$ for any $k \geq 1$.*

Proof. The language $L(\Pi, f_{perm}) \in \mathcal{L}_{perm}(genPCol,LL(1))$ from Example 2 is not in $\mathcal{L}(CF,LL(k))$ for any $k \geq 1$. If we consider the mapping $f_1 \in TRANS$, $f_1 : \{a,b,c,d,f,g\} \to \{a,b,c,d,f,g\}$ with $f_1(x) = x$ for all $x \in \{a,b,c,d,f,g\}$, then $L(\Pi, f_1) = L(\Pi, f_{perm})$, thus, $\mathcal{L}_{TRANS}(genPCol,LL(1))$ also contains the non-LL(k) context-free language.

4   Conclusions

P systems and their variants are able to describe powerful language classes, thus their applicability in the theory of parsing or analyzing syntactic structures are of particular interest, see, for example [15,16]. For example, in [15], so-called active P automata (P automata with dynamically changing membrane structure) were used for parsing, utilizing the dynamically changing membrane structure of the P automaton for analyzing the string. In addition to studying the suitability of P system variants for parsing different types of languages, developing well-known notions like LL(k) property for these models are of interest as well, since the results demonstrate the boundaries of the original concepts. In this paper we have started investigations in this direction, namely we studied the possibility of deterministically parsing languages characterized by P colony automata. We provided the definition of an LL(k)-like property for (generalized) P colony automata, and showed that languages which are not LL(k) in the "original" context-free sense for any $k \geq 1$ can be characterized by LL(1) P colony automata with different types of input mappings. The properties of these language classes for different values of k and different types of input mappings are open to further investigations. Our investigations confirmed that concepts, questions related to parsing are of interest in P systems theory.

Acknowledgments. The work of E. Csuhaj-Varjú was supported in part by the National Research, Development and Innovation Office of Hungary, NKFIH, grant no. K 120558. The work of K. Kántor and Gy. Vaszil was supported in part by the National Research, Development and Innovation Office of Hungary, NKFIH, grant no. K 120558 and also by the construction EFOP-3.6.3-VEKOP-16-2017-00002, a project financed by the European Union, co-financed by the European Social Fund.

References

1. Aho, A.V., Ulmann, J.D.: The Theory of Parsing, Translation, and Compiling, vol. 1. Prentice-Hall, Englewood Cliffs (1973)
2. Cienciala, L., Ciencialová, L., Csuhaj-Varjú, E.: Towards P colonies processing strings. In: Macías Ramos, L.F., Martínez Del Amor, M.A., Păun, G., Pérez Hurtado, I., Riscos Nuñez, A., Valencia Cabrera, L. (eds.) Twelfth Brainstorming Week on Membrane Computing, pp. 103–118. Fénix Editora (2014)
3. Cienciala, L., Ciencialová, L., Csuhaj-Varjú, E., Vaszil, G.: PCol automata: recognizing strings with P colonies. In: Martínez Del Amor, M.A., Păun, G., Pérez Hurtado, I., Riscos Nuñez, A. (eds.) Eighth Brainstorming Week on Membrane Computing, Sevilla, 1–5 February 2010, pp. 65–76. Fénix Editora (2010)
4. Cienciala, L., Ciencialová, L., Csuhaj-Varjú, E.: P colonies processing strings. Fundam. Inform. **134**(1–2), 51–65 (2014)
5. Cienciala, L., Ciencialová, L., Csuhaj-Varjú, E.: A class of restricted P colonies with string environment. Nat. Comput. **15**(4), 541–549 (2016)
6. Cienciala, L., Ciencialová, L., Csuhaj-Varjú, E., Sosík, P.: P colonies. Bull. Int. Membr. Comput. Soc. **1**(2), 119–156 (2016)

7. Cienciala, L., Ciencialová, L., Kelemenová, A.: On the number of agents in P colonies. In: Eleftherakis, G., Kefalas, P., Păun, G., Rozenberg, G., Salomaa, A. (eds.) WMC 2007. LNCS, vol. 4860, pp. 193–208. Springer, Heidelberg (2007). https://doi.org/10.1007/978-3-540-77312-2_12

8. Cienciala, L., Ciencialová, L., Kelemenová, A.: Homogeneous P colonies. Comput. Inform. **27**(3), 481–496 (2008)

9. Ciencialová, L., Cienciala, L.: Variation on the theme: P colonies. In: Kolăr, D., Meduna, A. (eds.) Proceedings of the 1st International Workshop on Formal Models, Ostrava, pp. 27–34 (2006)

10. Ciencialová, L., Csuhaj-Varjú, E., Kelemenová, A., Vaszil, G.: Variants of P colonies with very simple cell structure. Int. J. Comput., Commun. Control. **4**(3), 224–233 (2009)

11. Csuhaj-Varjú, E., Oswald, M., Vaszil, G.: P automata. In: Păun, G., Rozenberg, G., Salomaa, A. (eds.) The Oxford Handbook of Membrane Computing. Oxford University Press, Inc., Oxford (2010)

12. Csuhaj-Varjú, E., Kelemen, J., Kelemenová, A.: Computing with cells in environment: P colonies. Mult.-Valued Log. Soft Comput. **12**(3–4), 201–215 (2006)

13. Csuhaj-Varjú, E., Margenstern, M., Vaszil, G.: P colonies with a bounded number of cells and programs. In: Hoogeboom, H.J., Păun, G., Rozenberg, G., Salomaa, A. (eds.) WMC 2006. LNCS, vol. 4361, pp. 352–366. Springer, Heidelberg (2006). https://doi.org/10.1007/11963516_22

14. Csuhaj-Varjú, E., Vaszil, G.: P automata or purely communicating accepting P systems. In: Păun, G., Rozenberg, G., Salomaa, A., Zandron, C. (eds.) WMC 2002. LNCS, vol. 2597, pp. 219–233. Springer, Heidelberg (2003). https://doi.org/10.1007/3-540-36490-0_14

15. Bel-Enguix, G., Gramatovici, R.: Parsing with active P automata. In: Martín-Vide, C., Mauri, G., Păun, G., Rozenberg, G., Salomaa, A. (eds.) WMC 2003. LNCS, vol. 2933, pp. 31–42. Springer, Heidelberg (2004). https://doi.org/10.1007/978-3-540-24619-0_3

16. Bel Enguix, G., Nagy, B.: Modeling syntactic complexity with P systems: a preview. In: Ibarra, O.H., Kari, L., Kopecki, S. (eds.) UCNC 2014. LNCS, vol. 8553, pp. 54–66. Springer, Cham (2014). https://doi.org/10.1007/978-3-319-08123-6_5

17. Freund, R., Oswald, M.: P colonies working in the maximally parallel and in the sequential mode. In: Zaharie, D., et al. (eds.) Seventh International Symposium on Symbolic and Numeric Algorithms for Scientific Computing (SYNASC 2005), 25–29 September 2005, Timisoara, Romania, pp. 419–426. IEEE Computer Society (2005)

18. Freund, R., Oswald, M.: P colonies and prescribed teams. Int. J. Comput. Math. **83**(7), 569–592 (2006)

19. Kántor, K., Vaszil, G.: Generalized P colony automata. J. Autom., Lang. Comb. **19**(1–4), 145–156 (2014)

20. Kántor, K., Vaszil, G.: Generalized P colony automata and their relation to P automata. In: Gheorghe, M., Rozenberg, G., Salomaa, A., Zandron, C. (eds.) CMC 2017. LNCS, vol. 10725, pp. 167–182. Springer, Cham (2018). https://doi.org/10.1007/978-3-319-73359-3_11

21. Kántor, K., Vaszil, G.: On the classes of languages characterized by generalized P colony automata. Theor. Comput. Sci. **724**, 35–44 (2018)

22. Kelemenová, A.: P colonies. In: Păun, G., Rozenberg, G., Salomaa, A. (eds.) The Oxford Handbook of Membrane Computing, pp. 584–593. Oxford University Press, Inc., Oxford (2010)

23. Păun, A., Păun, G.: The power of communication: P systems with symport/antiport. New Gener. Comput. **20**(3), 295–306 (2002)

ACORD: Ant Colony Optimization and BNF Grammar Rule Derivation

Luis Fernando de Mingo López[1]([⊠]), Nuria Gómez Blas[1],
Juan Castellanos Peñuela[2], and Alberto Arteta Albert[3]

[1] Departamento de Sistemas Informáticos,
Escuela Técnica Superior de Ingeniería de Sistemas Informáticos,
Universidad Politécnica de Madrid, Alan Turing sn, 28031 Madrid, Spain
{fernando.demingo,nuria.gomez.blas}@upm.es
[2] Departamento de Inteligencia Artificial, Universidad Politécnica de Madrid,
Campus de Montegancedo, 28660 Boadilla del Monte, Madrid, Spain
juan.castellanos@upm.es
[3] Department of Computer Science, Troy University,
University Avenue, Troy, AL 36081, USA
aarteta@troy.edu

Abstract. Ant Colony Systems have been widely employed in optimization issues primarily focused on path finding optimization, such as Travelling Salesman Problem. The first algorithm was aiming to search for an optimal path in a graph, based on the behavior of ants seeking a path between their colony and a source of food. Besides, ant colony optimization algorithms have been applied to many combinatorial optimization problems, ranging from quadratic assignment to protein folding or routing vehicles and a lot of derived methods have been adapted to dynamic problems in real variables, stochastic problems, multi-targets and parallel implementations. The main advantage lies in the choice of the edge to be explored, defined using the idea of pheromone. This article proposes the use of Ant Colony Systems to explore a Backus-Naur form grammar whose elements are solutions to a given problem. Similar studies, without using Ant Colonies, have been used to solve optimization problems, such as Grammatical Swarm (based on Particle Swarm Optimization) and Grammatical Evolution (based on Genetic Algorithms). Proposed algorithm opens the way to a new branch of research in Swarm Intelligence, which until now has been almost non-existent, using ant colony algorithms to solve problems described by a grammar. (All source code in R is available at https://github.com/fernando-demingo/ACORD-Algorithm).

This research has been partially supported by European project *Regulation Study in the Adoption of the autonomous driving in the European Urban Nodes* (AUTOC-ITS): INEA/CEF/TRAN/M2015/1143746. Action No: 2015-EU-TM-0243-S and by Spanish project *Integración de Sistemas Cooperativos para Vehículos Autómos en Tráfico Compartido* (CAV): TRA2016-78886-C3-3-R.

C. Graciani et al. (Eds.): Pérez-Jiménez Festschrift, LNCS 11270, pp. 99–113, 2018.
https://doi.org/10.1007/978-3-030-00265-7_9

1   Introduction

A large number of different algorithms have been developed to find suboptimal solutions for the traveling salesman problem (TSP) in polynomial time. Examples are nearest neighbor, greedy, insertion heuristics, christofides, 2-opt and 3-opt. The non-deterministic metaheuristics like simulated annealing (SA) [1,2], tabu search [3], genetic algorithms (GA) [4] and particle swarm optimization (PSO) [5] have also been used, giving better results than previously mentioned deterministic algorithms. There are efficient algorithms for the TSP but the research continues on different metaheuristic algorithms [6].

Ant colony optimization (ACO) is another metaheuristic that was successfully used for the TSP [7]. The effectiveness of the ACO has been improved by use of different types of hybridization, like addition of local searchers or combining ACO with GA [8,9], differential evolution (DE) [10] or kangaroo algorithm [11]. These types of hybridization methods usually have a drawback of complexity of implementation and computation time penalty. It has also been shown that, although adding a local searcher is a good approach in the majority of cases, it may prevent ACO from finding the optimal solution [12]. A very interesting hybridization of ACO is given by [13] were scout ants, which search the solution space in a more systematic way, are added to the algorithm. Multi-colony systems [14] have been developed, as well as variations of the basic ACO like elitist ant colony, rank based ant colony system and min-max ant system (MMAS) to improve the performance on the TSP [15] in a more natural way, with different pheromone strategies. All these variations have the problem of becoming trapped in local optima due to the fact that they increase the efficiency by making their search more greedy by intensifying the search near the best found solution. Min-max ant system (MMAS) [16] tries to solve this problem by bounding the pheromone values and resetting the pheromone trail if better solutions have not been found in a large number of iterations. Minimum pheromone threshold strategy (MPTS) is another approach to avoid early stagnation applied to the quadratic assignment problems [17]. MPTS adds an additional minimum threshold value and if a pheromone value falls below, it is set to the maximal allowed value of the pheromone trail. Thus the MPTS avoids reinitialization of the pheromone trail like in the MMAS and explores the solution search space more systematically. Another interesting approach is in introducing variable pheromone sensitivity within population of ants [18].

Grammatical Evolution [19,20] is an evolutionary algorithm approach to automatic program generation, which evolves strings of binary values, and uses a grammar in BNF (Backus-Naur Form) notation to map those strings into programs, which can then be evaluated. The modular design behind GE means that any search algorithm can be used to evolve a population of binary strings, and after mapping each individual onto a program using GE, any program/algorithm can be used to evaluate those individuals.

The life-cycle of a Grammatical Evolution [21] run is as follows: a chosen Search Engine (typically a variable-length genetic algorithm) creates a population of individuals. Each of these strings represents a potential solution for the problem to be solved, and therefore needs to be evaluated so that a fitness score can be attributed to each (that is, how well does the program that each string represents fairs on the current problem). To that end, these strings will be mapped onto programs by GE, through the use of a Language Specification (typically a BNF grammar). The resulting programs can then be evaluated through a Problem Specification (for example, an interpreter), which will attribute each program a fitness score. These scores can then be sent back to the search engine, which will use then to evolve a new population of individuals, which will also need to be evaluated.

This cycle goes on until a predefined stop condition is met (usually if a solution is found, or if a maximum number of evaluations has been reached). This process is based on the idea of a Genotype to Phenotype mapping: an individual comprised of binary values (genotype) is evolved, and, before being evaluated, is subjected to a mapping process to create a program (phenotype), which is then evaluated by a fitness function. This creates two distinct spaces, a search space and a solution space.

Typically, the language specification is done through a BNF context-free grammar. A BNF grammar is represented by a tuple (N, T, P, S), where T is a set of Terminal symbols, i.e., items that can appear in legal sentences of the grammar, and N is a set of Non-Terminal symbols, which are temporary items used in the generation of terminals. P is a set of Productions that map the non-terminal symbols to a sequence of terminal (or non-terminal) symbols, and S is a Start Symbol, from which all legal sentences must be generated.

O'Neill et al. [22,23] have successfully applied GE to predicting corporate bankruptcy, forecasting stock indices, bond credit ratings, and other financial applications. GE has also been used with a classic predator-prey model [24] to explore the impact of parameters such as predator efficiency, niche number, and random mutations on ecological stability [25]. It is possible to structure a GE grammar that for a given function/terminal set is equivalent to genetic programming.

Grammatical Swarm is based on a particle swarm learning algorithm coupled to a grammatical evolution genotype/phenotype mapping [22] to generate programs in a language [26]. The update equations for the swarm algorithm are those from Particle Swarm Optimization, with additional constraints placed on the velocity and particle location dimension values, such that maximum velocities v_{max} are bound to $[-255, 255]$, and each dimension is bound to the range $[0, 255]$. Note that this is a continuous swarm algorithm with real-valued particle vectors. The standard grammatical evolution mapping function is adopted, with the real-values in the particle vectors being rounded up or down to the nearest integer value for the mapping process.

Grammatical Swarm results demonstrate that it is possible to successfully generate programs using the Grammatical Swarm technique. [23] presented an analysis of the Grammatical Swarm approach on the dynamics of the search. It is found that restricting the search to the generation of complete programs, or with the use of a ratchet constraint forcing individuals to move only if a fitness improvement has been found, can have detrimental consequences for the swarms performance and dynamics.

O'Neill et al. [22] examine the application of grammatical swarm to classification problems, and illustrates the particle swarm algorithms' ability to specify the construction of programs. Each individual particle represents choices of program construction rules, where these rules are specified using a Backus Naur Form grammar. The results demonstrate that it is possible to generate programs using the grammatical swarm technique with a performance similar to the grammatical evolution evolutionary automatic programming approach.

2   Ant Colony Optimization Overview

The ACO algorithm is based on mimicking the behavior of ants colony while gathering food. Each ant starts from the nest and walks towards food until it reaches an intersection, where it has to decide which path to select. In the beginning this choice is random, but after some time the majority of ants will be moving along the optimal path. This happens because of the colony's collective intelligence. Each ant, as he moves, deposits chemical called pheromone thus marking the route taken. Pheromone trail evaporates as time passes. Accordingly, a shorter path will have more pheromone because it will have less time to evaporate before it is deposited again. Each ant chooses paths that have more pheromone so shorter routes will be selected with higher and higher probabilities until practically all ants go along shortest path. But, it case of dynamic change, some new obstacle or new passage, ants will quickly adopt to new situation.

Ant colony algorithms are an iterative, probabilistic metaheuristic for finding solutions to combinatorial optimization problems [27]. They are based on the foraging mechanism employed by real ants attempting to find a short path from their nest to a food source. While foraging, the ants communicate indirectly via pheromone, which they use to mark their respective paths and which attracts other ants. In the ant algorithm, artificial ants use virtual pheromone to update their path through the decision graph. Ants of the later iterations use the pheromone marks of previous good ants as a means of orientation when constructing their own solutions, which ultimately result in focusing the ants on promising parts of the search space.

Ant algorithms were first proposed by Dorigo and colleagues [27–29] as a multi-agent approach to difficult combinatorial optimization problems such as the traveling salesman problem, the quadratic assignment problem, routing in communications networks, graph coloring and so on. Ant algorithms were inspired by the observation of real ant colonies. Ants are social insects, that is, insects that live in colonies and whose behavior is directed more to the survival of the colony as a whole than to that of a single individual component of the colony. Social insects have captured the attention of many scientists because of the high structuration level their colonies can achieve, especially when compared to the relative simplicity of the colony's individuals. An important and interesting behavior of ant colonies is their foraging behavior, and, in particular, how ants can find the shortest paths between food sources and their nest.

While walking from food sources to the nest and vice versa, ants deposit on the ground a substance called pheromone, forming in this way a pheromone trail. Ants can smell pheromone, and when choosing their way, they tend to choose, in probability, paths marked by strong pheromone concentrations. The pheromone trail allows the ants to find their way back to the food source (or to the nest). Also, it can be used by other ants to find the location of the food sources found by their nest-mates. This form of indirect communication mediated by pheromone laying is known as stigmergy [30]. As defined by [30] in his work on Bellicositermes Natalensis and Cubitermes, stigmergy is the stimulation of the workers by the very performances they have achieved.

In the double bridge experiment described by [31] (see Fig. 1), the bridge's branches have different length. The first ants to arrive at the food source are those that took the two shortest branches, so that, when these ants start their return trip, more pheromone is present on the short branch than on the long branch, stimulating successive ants to choose the short branch. In this case, the importance of initial random fluctuations is much reduced, and the stochastic pheromone trail following behavior of the ants coupled to differential branch length is the main mechanism at work.

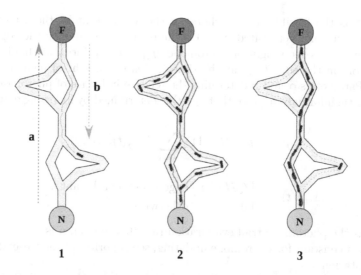

Fig. 1. Ant colony double bridge experiment. The first ants to arrive at the food source are those that took the two shortest branches, so that, when these ants start their return trip, more pheromone is present on the short branch than on the long branch, stimulating successive ants to choose the short branch.

Ant Colony Optimization is implemented as a team of intelligent agents which simulate the ants behavior, walking around the graph representing the problem to solve using mechanisms of cooperation and adaptation. Ant Colony algorithm requires to define the following:

- The problem needs to be represented appropriately, which would allow the ants to incrementally update the solutions through the use of a probabilistic transition rules, based on the amount of pheromone in the trail and other problem specific knowledge. It is also important to enforce a strategy to construct only valid solutions corresponding to the problem definition.
- A problem-dependent heuristic function η that measures the quality of components that can be added to the current partial solution.
- A rule set for pheromone updating, which specifies how to modify the pheromone value τ.
- A probabilistic transition rule based on the value of the heuristic function η and the pheromone value τ that is used to iteratively construct a solution.

ACO was first introduced using the Travellng Salesman Problem (TSP). Starting from its start node, an ant iteratively moves from one node to another. When being at a node, an ant chooses to go to a unvisited node at time t with a probability given by:

$$p_{i,j}^k(t) = \frac{[\tau_{i,j}(t)]^\alpha [\eta_{i,j}(t)]^\beta}{\sum_{l \in N_i^k} [\tau_{i,l}(t)]^\alpha [\eta_{i,l}(t)]^\beta}, \ j \in N_i^k \tag{1}$$

where N_i^k is the feasible neighborhood of the ant k, that is, the set of cities which ant k has not yet visited; $\tau_{i,j}(t)$ is the pheromone value on the edge (i,j) at the time t, α is the weight of pheromone; $\eta_{i,j}(t)$ is a priori available heuristic information on the edge (i,j) at the time t, β is the weight of heuristic information. Parameters α and β determine the relative influence of pheromone trail and heuristic information. Note that $\tau_{i,j}(t)$ is determined by following equations:

$$\tau_{i,j}(t) = \rho \tau_{i,j}(t-1) + \sum_{k=1}^{n} \Delta \tau_{i,j}^k(t), \ \forall (i,j) \tag{2}$$

$$\Delta \tau_{i,j}(t)^k = \begin{cases} Q/L_k(t) & \text{edge } i,j \text{ chosen by ant } k \\ 0 & \text{otherwise} \end{cases} \tag{3}$$

where ρ is the pheromone trail evaporation rate $(0 < \rho < 1)$, n is the number of ants, Q is a constant for pheromone updating, see Algorithm 1 for a pseudo-code implementation.

Figure 2 shows some chosen random iteration for a given a TSP problem in France. The more red in edges the more pheromone concentration. Iteration 4 shows obtained solution. The moving of ants provides the parallel and independent search of the route with the help of dynamical change of pheromone trail. The ant represents an elementary unit with the ability to learn, and due to collective-cooperative work with other members of population, it is able to find acceptable solution to the given problem. The lower number of ants allows the individual to change the path much faster. The higher number of ants in population causes the higher accumulation of pheromone on edges, and thus an individual keeps the path with higher concentration of pheromone with a high probability. The great advantage over the use of exact methods is that ACO algorithm provides relatively good results by a comparatively low number of iterations, and is therefore able to find an acceptable solution in a comparatively short time, so it is useable for solving problems occurring in practical applications.

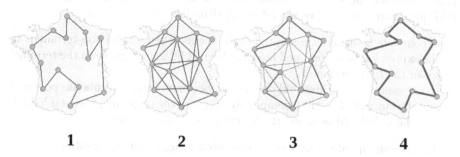

1   **2**   **3**   **4**

Fig. 2. Ant colony optimization for TSP. The artificial ants have memory; they can remember the cities they have visited and therefore they would not select those cities again. The artificial ants are not completely blind; they know the distances between two cities and prefer to choose the nearby cities from their positions.

Algorithm 1. Pseudo-code for the Ant Colony System algorithm.

1: Initialize
2: **while** stopping criterion not satisfied **do**
3:     Position each ant in a starting node
4:     **repeat**
5:         **for** Each ant **do**
6:             Choose next node by applying the state transition rule
7:             Apply step by step pheromone update
8:         **end for**
9:     **until** every ant has built a solution
10:     update best solution
11:     Apply offline pheromone update
12: **end while**

---

3   ACORD Algorithm

Ant colony algorithms have proven to be a useful alternative for solving routing problems. Proposed algorithm takes advantage of this feature to find the solution to an optimization problem, defined by a fitness function, in which individuals belong to the language generated by a BNF grammar. The algorithm makes use of:

(a) a BNF grammar that represents possible solutions to the problem,

(b) of a fitness function to evaluate such elements and

(c) its structure is based on the classical algorithm of ant colonies.

The grammar is used in a developmental process to construct a solution by applying production rules, beginning from the start symbol of the grammar. Beginning from the left hand side of the genome, ants are used to select appropriate rules for the left most non-terminal in the developing solution from the BNF grammar, until one of the following situations arise:

- A complete solution is generated. This occurs when all the non-terminals in the expression being mapped are transformed into elements from the terminal set of the BNF grammar.
- In the event that a threshold on the number of wrapping events has occurred and the individual is still incompletely mapped, the mapping process is halted, and the individual assigned the lowest possible fitness value.

Pheromone update stage can be evaluated using following equation:

$$\Delta\tau_{xy}^k = \begin{cases} QL_k & \text{if ant } k \text{ uses edge } xy \text{ in its tour} \\ 0 & \text{otherwise} \end{cases} \tag{4}$$

where L_k is the fitness of the solution generated by ant (or a 0 value is individual is incompletely mapped) and Q is a constant.

The Santa Fe Ant model problem has been extensively used to investigate, test and evaluate evolutionary computing systems and methods over the past two decades. There is however no literature on its program structures that are systematically used for fitness improvement, the geometries of those structures and their dynamics during optimization. The trail is embedded in a toroidally connected grid of 32×32 cells. The food trail of 144 cells (89 containing food and 55 being gaps in the trail with no food). There are 10 left and 11 right turns of the trail. The objective of the Santa Fe ant problem is to evolve a program that can navigate this trail, finding all the food using a specified amount of energy.

The Santa Fe ant problem is sometimes used as a representative problem, usually among a suite of other problems. Common cases for this use are as a performance benchmark and to show the viability of metaheuristics or new methods. The problem has similarly been used to show the viability of Analytic Programming [32], Cartesian Genetic Programming, Grammatical Evolution and Constituent Grammatical Evolution [33]. The problem has been used to study generalization ability [34] and negative slope coefficient [35].

The BNF for the Santa Fe Ant Trail is as follows:

```
N = {<code>, <line>, <if-statement>, <op>,
     <expr>}
T = {left(), right(), move(), food_ahead(),
     else, if, {, }, (, ), ;}
S = <code> | <expr>
```

Table 1. BNF grammars used to solve the Santa Fe Trail problem.

BNF-O'Neill grammar definition

```
<code> :: = <line> |<code><line>
<line> :: = <if-statement> | <op>
<if-statement> :: = if (food_ahead()) {
                        <line>
                    } else {
                        <line>
                    }
<op> :: =    left(); | right(); | move();
```

BNF-Koza grammar definition

```
<expr> :: = <line> | <expr><line>
<line> :: = <if-statement> | <op>
<if-statement> :: = if(food_ahead()) {
                        <expr>
                    } else {
                        <expr>
                    }
<op> :: =    left(); | right(); | move();
```

Note that starting symbol could be `<code>` (O'Neil grammar definition) or `<expr>` (Koza grammar definition). And P can be represented as shown in Table 1.

The performance of the proposed algorithm has been benchmarked against the Grammatical Evolution algorithm using the Santa Fe Trail problem. Two distinct benchmarks have been performed for the following situation when GE uses the standard BNF grammar definition mentioned in the Grammatical Evo-

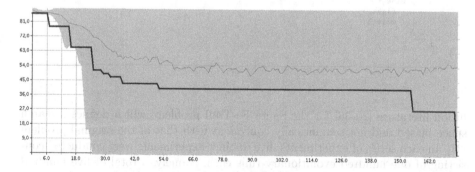

Fig. 3. Fitness (vertical) vs # iteration (horizontal) in Sata Fe Trail problem solved using ACORD algorithm, according to grammar in Table 1 (BNF-O'Neill). Final results in Table 2. (Figure Legend: dark blue - best fitness, royal blue – average fitness, powder blue – variance fitness). (Color figure online)

Table 2. Best solution using ACORD algorithm with grammar in Table 1 (BNF-O'Neill).

```
if(food_ahead()) {
    move();
} else {
    right();
    if(food_ahead()) {
        move();
    } else {
        if(food_ahead()) {
            if(food_ahead()) {
                move();
            } else {
                move();
                if(food_ahead()) {
                    right();
                } else {
                    move();
                }
            }
        } else {
            if(food_ahead()) {
                if(food_ahead()) {
                    move();
                } else {
                    move();
                    right();
                }
            } else {
                if(food_ahead()) {
                    move();
                } else {
                    left();
                }
                left();
            }
        }
        if(food_ahead()) {
            if(food_ahead()) {
                left();
            } else {
                right();
            }
        } else {
            right();
            move();
        }
    }
}
```

lution literature [20, 36] for the Santa Fe Trail problem, which defines a search space biased and not semantically equivalent with that of the original problem [37]. In each series of experiments, five distinct experiments were conducted consisting of one hundred evolutionary runs each. Namely, a total of five hundred evolutionary runs were performed for each algorithm (Fig. 3).

Proposed ant colony algorithm was successful at finding a solution in the Santa Fe Trail problem with very high success rates, ranging from 85% to 94%

with an average success rate of 90%. The code for the best solution is shown in listing 2.

Table 3 shows the detailed results of the experiments. The column Best shows the best value of all five experiments. Runs is the number of evolutionary runs performed in the experiment, Steps, the required steps of the best solution found in the particular experiment, Success, how many evolutionary runs (percentage) found a solution, and Average Success, the average success rate of all five experiments.

Table 3. Grammatical results in Santa Fe Trail.

	Exp1	Exp2	Exp3	Exp4	Exp5	**Best**
GE with BNF-Koza						
Runs	100	100	100	100	100	100
Steps	393	375	393	377	337	337
Success	85%	93%	89%	94%	87%	94%
Average	**90%**					
GE with BNF-O'Neill						
Runs	100	100	100	100	100	100
Steps	419	507	415	541	479	415
Success	8%	11%	10%	6%	13%	13%
Average	**10%**					
ACORD Algorithn						
Runs	100	100	100	100	100	100
Steps	609	609	607	609	607	607
Success	80%	76%	75%	81%	74%	81%
Average	**78%**					

The experimental results show that proposed algorithm obtains good results compared to Grammatical Evolution in terms of success rate whether the later uses a BNF grammar definition (BNF-Koza) which defines a search space semantically equivalent with that used in the original problem [37], or whether it uses a BNF grammar definition (BNF-O'Neill) which defines a biased search space. In contrast, proposed algorithm is able to find much better solutions in terms of the required steps.

The poor performance of GE using BNF-Koza can be explained if we take into account that this grammar definition defines a search space semantically equivalent with that of the original problem, which is very large, making it difficult for GE to find a solution. Instead, BNF-O'Neill defines a smaller search space and biases the search to areas where a solution can be found more easily (with higher success rate) but with the cost of excluding other areas where more efficient programs could be found (using less steps). This is the reason why GE using BNF-O'Neill didn't find solutions with less than 607 steps. In order to support the last argument, a series of five new experiments of one hundred evolutionary runs each was conducted, setting the steps limit to 606. In these experiments the success rate of GE was 0%, providing further experimental evidence that GE using BNF-O'Neill cannot find solutions with less than 607 steps.

Furthermore, Georgiou and Teahan [38] tried to solve the Santa Fe Trail problem using random search as the search mechanism of Grammatical Evolution instead of the standard steady-state genetic algorithm. Their results show that using the search space defined by the BNF-O'Neill grammar definition, GE with random search has a success rate of 50% in finding a solution. Instead, the success rate of GE with random search using the search space defined by the BNF-Koza grammar definition is just 1.4%. These results further support the claim that the BNF-O'Neill grammar definition defines a different search space than the BNF-Koza grammar definition, where solutions can be found more easily.

The promising results of proposed algorithm benchmarking on the Santa Fe Trail problem raises the question whether it can improve GE in other problems as well.

4   Conclusion

Ant colony algorithms have proven to be a useful alternative for solving routing problems. Proposed algorithm takes advantage of this feature to find the solution to an optimization problem in which candidates belong to the language generated by a BNF grammar. Virtual ants walk through the derivation rules as if it were a graph. This idea is inspired by the works of Grammatical Evolution and Grammatical Swarm, based on the desire to separate genotype from phenotype. Therefore, the search space can be restricted, and knowledge of the domain of the problem can be incorporated. It is also possible to test convergence in some versions of the ant colony algorithm (i.e. it is able to find the overall optimal in finite time). The first evidence of an ant colony convergence algorithm was made in [39], the graph-based ant system algorithm, and then algorithms for Ant Colony Systems. Like most metaheuristics, it is very difficult to estimate the theoretical speed of convergence.

This new algorithm opens the way to a new branch of research in Swarm Intelligence, which until now has been almost non-existent, using ant colony algorithms to solve problems described by a grammar. Proposed algorithm is able through its conditional behaviour-switching feature to focus the search in more useful areas by decreasing the actual search space without using domain knowledge of the problem in question and without changing semantically the original search space.

Acknowledgments. History of all great works is to witness that no great work was ever done without either the active or passive support a person's surrounding and one's close quarters. We are highly thankful to our learned faculty, and friend, **Mr. Mario Pérez Jiménez** for his active guidance throughout these years.

References

1. Wang, Z., Geng, X., Shao, Z.: An effective simulated annealing algorithm for solving the traveling salesman problem. J. Comput. Theor. Nanosci. **6**(7), 1680–1686 (2009)
2. Meer, K.: Simulated annealing versus metropolis for a TSP instance. Inf. Process. Lett. **104**(6), 216–219 (2007)
3. Gendreau, M., Laporte, G., Semet, F.: A tabu search heuristic for the undirected selective travelling salesman problem. Eur. J. Oper. Res. **106**(2–3), 539–545 (1998)
4. Liu, F., Zeng, G.: Study of genetic algorithm with reinforcement learning to solve the TSP. Expert. Syst. Appl. **36**(3), 6995–7001 (2009)
5. Shi, X.H., Liang, Y.C., Lee, H.P., Lu, C., Wang, Q.X.: Particle swarm optimization-based algorithms for TSP and generalized TSP. Inf. Process. Lett. **103**(5), 169–176 (2007)
6. Rego, C., Gamboa, D., Glover, F., Osterman, C.: Traveling salesman problem heuristics: leading methods, implementations and latest advances. Eur. J. Oper. Res. **211**(3), 427–441 (2011)
7. Kollin, F., Bavey, A.: Ant colony optimization Algorithms: pheromone techniques for TSP. Technical report, KTH, School of Computer Science and Communication (CSC) (2017)
8. Lee, Z.J., Su, S.F., Chuang, C.C., Liu, K.H.: Genetic algorithm with ant colony optimization (GA-ACO) for multiple sequence alignment. Appl. Soft Comput. **8**(1), 55–78 (2008)
9. Moslehi, G., Khorasanian, D.: A hybrid variable neighborhood search algorithm for solving the limited-buffer permutation flow shop scheduling problem with the makespan criterion. Comput. Oper. Res. **52**(PB), 260–268 (2014)
10. Xiao, J., Li, L.: A hybrid ant colony optimization for continuous domains. Expert Syst. Appl. **38**(9), 11072–11077 (2011)
11. Xiang, W., Yin, J., Lim, G.: An ant colony optimization approach for solving an operating room surgery scheduling problem. Comput. Ind. Eng. **85**(C), 335–345 (2015)
12. Neumann, F., Sudholt, D., Witt, C.: Rigorous analyses for the combination of ant colony optimization and local search. In: Dorigo, M., Birattari, M., Blum, C., Clerc, M., Stützle, T., Winfield, A.F.T. (eds.) ANTS 2008. LNCS, vol. 5217, pp. 132–143. Springer, Heidelberg (2008). https://doi.org/10.1007/978-3-540-87527-7_12
13. Gan, R., Guo, Q., Chang, H., Yi, Y.: Improved ant colony optimization algorithm for the traveling salesman problems. J. Syst. Eng. Electron. **21**(2), 329–333 (2010)
14. Jovanovic, R., Tuba, M., Simian, D.: Comparison of different topologies for island-based multi-colony ant algorithms for the minimum weight vertex cover problem. WSEAS Trans. Comput. **9**(1), 83–92 (2010)
15. Stutzle, T., Dorigo, M.: ACO algorithms for the traveling salesman problem. In: Evolutionary Algorithms in Engineering and Computer Science: Recent Advances in Genetic Algorithms, Evolution Strategies, Evolutionary Programming, Genetic Programming and Industrial Applications. Wiley, Hoboken (1999)
16. Stützle, T., Hoos, H.H.: MAX-MIN ant system. Futur. Gener. Comput. Syst. **16**(9), 889–914 (2000)
17. Wong, K.Y., See, P.C.: A new minimum pheromone threshold strategy (MPTS) for max-min ant system. Appl. Soft Comput. **9**(3), 882–888 (2009)

18. Pintea, C.M., Chira, C., Dumitrescu, D., Pop, P.C.: Sensitive ants in solving the generalized vehicle routing problem. J. Comput., Commun. Control. **6**(4), 228–231 (2012)
19. Ryan, C., Collins, J.J., Neill, M.O.: Grammatical evolution: evolving programs for an arbitrary language. In: Banzhaf, W., Poli, R., Schoenauer, M., Fogarty, T.C. (eds.) EuroGP 1998. LNCS, vol. 1391, pp. 83–96. Springer, Heidelberg (1998). https://doi.org/10.1007/BFb0055930
20. O'Neill, M., Ryan, C.: Grammatical Evolution: Evolutionary Automatic Programming in an Arbitrary Language. Kluwer Academic Publishers, Norwell (2003)
21. Nicolau, M.: Understanding grammatical evolution: initialisation. Genet. Program. Evolvable Mach. **18**(4), 467–507 (2017)
22. O'Neill, M., Brabazon, A.: Grammatical swarm. In: Deb, K. (ed.) GECCO 2004. LNCS, vol. 3102, pp. 163–174. Springer, Heidelberg (2004). https://doi.org/10.1007/978-3-540-24854-5_15
23. O'Neill, M., Brabazon, A.: Grammatical swarm: the generation of programs by social programming. Nat. Comput. **5**(4), 443–462 (2006)
24. Grimme, C., Schmitt, K.: Inside a predator-prey model for multi-objective optimization: a second study. In: Proceedings of the 8th Annual Conference on Genetic and Evolutionary Computation. GECCO 2006, pp. 707–714. ACM, New York (2006)
25. Alfonseca, M., Soler Gil, F.J.: Evolving a predator-prey ecosystem of mathematical expressions with grammatical evolution. Complexity **20**(3), 66–83 (2015)
26. Dempsey, I., O'Neill, M., Brabazon, A.: Foundations in Grammatical Evolution for Dynamic Environments, 1st edn. Springer Publishing Company, Incorporated, Heidelberg (2009). https://doi.org/10.1007/978-3-642-00314-1
27. Bonabeau, E., Dorigo, M., Theraulaz, G.: Swarm Intelligence: From Natural to Artificial Systems. Oxford University Press, Oxford (1999)
28. Dorigo, M., Maniezzo, V., Colorni, A.: The ant system: optimization by a colony of cooperating agents. IEEE Trans. Syst. Man Cybern. Part B **26**(1), 29–41 (1996)
29. Dorigo, M., Stützle, T.: Ant Colony Optimization. Bradford Company, Scituate (2004)
30. Grassé, P.P.: La reconstruction du nid et les coordinations interindividuelles chez Bellicositermes natalensis et Cubitermes sp. La théorie de la stigmergie: essai d'interprétation du comportement des termites constructeurs. Insectes Sociaux **6**, 41–83 (1959)
31. Goss, S., Aron, S., Deneubourg, J., Pasteels, J.: Self-organized shortcuts in the Argentine ant. Naturwissenschaften **76**(12), 579–581 (1989)
32. Oplatková, Z., Zelinka, I.: Investigation on artificial ant using analytic programming. In: Proceedings of the 8th Annual Conference on Genetic and Evolutionary Computation. GECCO 2006, pp. 949–950. ACM, New York (2006)
33. Georgiou, L., Teahan, W.J.: Constituent grammatical evolution. In: Proceedings of the Twenty-Second International Joint Conference on Artificial Intelligence - Volume. IJCAI 2011, vol. 2, pp. 1261–1268. AAAI Press (2011)
34. Kushchu, I.: Genetic programming and evolutionary generalization. Trans. Evol. Comput. **6**(5), 431–442 (2002)
35. Poli, R., Vanneschi, L.: Fitness-proportional negative slope coefficient as a hardness measure for genetic algorithms. In: Proceedings of the 9th Annual Conference on Genetic and Evolutionary Computation. GECCO 2007, pp. 1335–1342. ACM, New York (2007)
36. O'Neill, M., Ryan, C.: Grammatical evolution. IEEE Trans. Evol. Comput. **5**(4), 349–358 (2001)

37. Koza, J.R.: Genetic programming as a means for programming computers by natural selection. Stat. Comput. **4**(2), 87–112 (1994)
38. Georgiou, L., Teahan, W.J.: Grammatical evolution and the santa fe trail problem. In: Filipe, J., Kacprzyk, J. (eds.) ICEC 2010 - Proceedings of the International Conference on Evolutionary Computation, (part of the International Joint Conference on Computational Intelligence IJCCI 2010), Valencia, Spain, 24–26 October 2010, pp. 10–19. SciTePress (2010)
39. Gutjahr, W.J.: A graph-based ant system and its convergence. Futur. Gener. Comput. Syst. **16**(8), 873–888 (2000)

Membrane Computing as a Modelling Tool: Looking Back and Forward from Sevilla

Manuel García-Quismondo, Carmen Graciani$^{(\boxtimes)}$, and Agustín Riscos-Núñez

Research Group on Natural Computing,
Department of Computer Science and Artificial Intelligence,
Universidad de Sevilla, Avda. Reina Mercedes s/n, 41012 Sevilla, Spain
{mgarciaquismondo,cgdiaz,ariscosn}@us.es

Abstract. This paper is a tribute to Prof. Mario de Jesús Pérez-Jiménez. An overview of modelling applications in membrane computing has been compiled, trying to narrate it from a historical perspective and including numerous bibliographical references. Since being exhaustive was obviously out of scope, this quick tour on almost two decades of applications is biased, paying special attention to the contributions in which Prof. Pérez-Jiménez and members of his research group were involved.

1 Introduction

Membrane computing (MC) is a computational discipline that takes inspiration from molecular and cellular biology. Therefore, it seems natural to consider membrane computing as a valuable modelling framework for biological processes. In this sense, several authors considered the possibility to "return some meaningful information to Biology" (see Chap. 1 in [36]) from the very initial stages of this discipline. The majority of the initial research lines in membrane computing were devoted to theoretical results investigating the computational power of different classes of P systems: either proving their Turing completeness or exploring their equivalence with elements of classical formal language hierarchies. However, from the onset the curiosity to work towards applications has been also present. The first book fully devoted to applications in membrane computing appeared in 2006 [19], although applications were carried out since 2000, as we will mention later. For a more up-to-date overview of applications of membrane computing, please visit the *P systems web page* [3] and the *Bulletin of the International Membrane Computing Society* [1]. Interested readers are also advised to refer to two of the most recent volumes: *Applications of Membrane Computing in Systems and Synthetic Biology* [26] and *Real-life Applications with Membrane Computing* [50]. There are also several other overviews of modelling applications, e.g. [30,37,38].

© Springer Nature Switzerland AG 2018
C. Graciani et al. (Eds.): Pérez-Jiménez Festschrift, LNCS 11270, pp. 114–129, 2018.
https://doi.org/10.1007/978-3-030-00265-7_10

This paper presents a historical (and obviously non-exhaustive) overview of computational modelling approaches within membrane computing, with a special focus on the contributions in which RGNC[1] members were involved.

1.1 Computational Modelling

Computational modelling and simulation are nowadays a cornerstone of the scientific method. Everything starts in Nature, when we identify some physical or biological phenomenon that attracts our interest for some reason. Usually, such intriguing phenomena can be seen as *complex systems*, in the sense that we can describe them as a collection of elements (let us call them "players") that interact following relatively simple rules, exhibiting a complex behaviour of the system as a whole. This behaviour is commonly referred to as emergent, and means that the evolution of the system displays some special properties that are not trivially deduced from the local dynamics of its components.

The first subjective decision to take when designing a model is to determine which are the *relevant* ingredients (players, features, variables) that will compose this model. Judging which ingredients are significant enough to be included is a decision linked to the reason why the phenomenon is of interest. More precisely, Regev and Shapiro explain in [43] that a *good* model should combine the following key desirable properties: relevant, readable, extensible and computationally tractable. Thus, we have to find the balance between two conflicting goals. On the one hand, we should capture as many ingredients as possible to yield a relevant and realistic model. On the other hand, we should try to keep the model as simple as possible, so that it is easy to interpret and work with.

A fundamental stage in the design of a model is validation. To this aim, we need software simulation tools that allow us to run virtual experiments, in order to carry out a reliable analysis of its dynamics under various initial conditions. This is where the concept of practical feasibility comes into play.

2 Historical Overview of Modelling Works in MC

We would like to initiate the narrative of the time line on a very significant event: the Workshop on Multiset Processing that was held in Curtea de Argeş in 2000. This is commonly accepted as the origin of the series of workshops on membrane computing (which later on evolved and gave rise in 2010 to the International Conference on Membrane Computing).

At that time, the limits of the field of membrane computing were still undefined, and the attendants to the meeting came from a variety of backgrounds.

---

[1] RGNC stands for *Research Group on Natural Computing* from Universidad de Sevilla, also known in the MC community as "Sevilla team".

2.1 In the Beginning, There Was ...

During the above-mentioned workshop, what could be considered as the precursors of future works in the field of modelling in membrane computing were presented.

Banâtre et al. presented a contribution entitled *Gamma and the Chemical Reaction Model: Fifteen Years After* [7]. Gamma was originally proposed in 1986 as a formalism for the definition of concurrent programs. The basic idea underlying the formalism is to describe computation as a form of chemical reaction on a collection of elementary pieces of data. Indeed, the chemical abstract machine paradigm (*CHAM – CHemical Abstract Machine –*, introduced by Berry and Boudol in early 1990s) already includes the notion of "membrane" as a container of elements that react among them.

Nishida presented a contribution entitled *Multiset and K-Subset Transforming Systems* [31], where he provided an example illustrating how to model a chaotic discrete dynamical system by means of a *K*-subset transforming system. He also provided theoretical results proving the expressive power of this kind of systems. Moreover, one year later, he participated again in the Workshop on Membrane Computing, presenting another application case study: a model for the light reactions of the photosynthesis [32]. There are a couple of observations on this paper: on the one hand, he mentioned a computer simulator as a natural addition to the theoretical model. On the other hand, he suggested the idea to go beyond standard multisets, using multiplicities on any semiring K.

Last, but not least, Suzuki et al. presented a contribution entitled *Artificial Life Applications of a Class of P Systems: Abstract Rewriting Systems on Multisets* [45]. We will refer to this, together with some related works, in the next section.

2.2 The Dawn of Brainstorming Era

The second significant event that we would like to highlight is the Brainstorming Week on Membrane Computing (BWMC). Its first edition was held in Tarragona (Spain) in February 2003.

The Brainstorming Week is a meeting where participants can freely exchange ideas and open problems. It is much more dynamic than a standard workshop or conference, in the sense that the program is proactively set during the gathering and is made up of provocative talks about works in progress that will later on become papers, after fruitful discussions and joint work sessions in a friendly atmosphere. Except for this first edition, the BWMC has been held annually since 2004 in Sevilla (Spain), organised by the RGNC.

In the proceedings volume that was produced after the first meeting, we can find several applications in the form of computational models.

Suzuki and Tanaka revisit in [47] their proposal to use *Abstract rewriting systems on multisets* as a versatile modelling framework able to capture not only dynamics of chemical reactions (e.g. Brusselator model) and population dynamics in a tri-trophic ecological system (both of them already hinted in [45]), but also other applications in medicine such as inflammatory response.

In particular, Suzuki and his collaborators have presented during the Fourth Workshop on Membrane Computing, held later the same year, a model of the p53[2] signalling network [46].

The authors presented a very simple model using a few multiset rewriting rules, allowing symbols to move along two regions: nucleus and cytoplasm. The goal of the paper is to show that the use of P systems as an alternative to traditional rate equation models is useful and practically feasible. The proceedings are available for download via [3], however interested readers may also refer to the chapter "Modeling p53 Signaling Pathways by Using Multiset Processing", in [19].

One can also find in the Brainstorming proceedings an interesting joint work by Ardelean and Besozzi [4], where the authors propose to pay attention to mechano-sensitive channels from a membrane computing perspective.

The idea is further developed in [11,12], where one can find several considerations about the ingredients or features that should be integrated in a P system variant to be considered as a competitive modelling framework. They already mention the idea of adding *variable parameters* associated with a membrane (in their case related to membrane tension), whose changes are determined by environmental conditions. They point out that this concept is similar to the role of electrical charges in P systems with active membranes [34]. They also acknowledge the advantage of considering rules able to interact with objects at both sides of the membrane, similar to the approach in [9,10]. In particular, for mechano-sensitive channels it is straightforward that the concentration of reactants should be taken into account in the rules, and the authors cite how Suzuki and Tanaka defined their rules as pairs of the type [*condition, action*].

Another aspect that should be taken into account in order to capture the dynamics of biological processes is the replacement of maximal parallelism by some alternative semantics that express a probabilistic behaviour, and consequently the dependence on software tools to run multiple simulations [5,6,13].

2.3   Reaching Maturity

In 2003, the Institute for Scientific Information (ISI) listed the seminal paper of membrane computing [35] as *fast breaking paper*. In addition, membrane computing was selected as a *fast emerging area* in computer science. Let us try to keep track of the lines of work related to the modelling of phenomena in membrane computing, which were gradually gaining strength in those first years. Indeed, we can notice an important milestone in 2005, when the collective volume [19] was elaborated. There were several teams working on different approaches, but sharing similar interests.

---

[2] The p53 protein is closely related to the control of the *apoptosis* process (also known as "programmed cell death"), and therefore is quite relevant in cancer research.

For example, the teams from Universities of Verona and Milano-Bicocca, leaded by Prof. Vincenzo Manca and Prof. Giancarlo Mauri, respectively, have a long tradition in this direction, both in DNA and membrane computing. Their work has produced not only a large number of publications, but also the development of the corresponding software tools and environments for modelling, as well as many PhD Theses: G. Franco *Biomolecular Computing Combinatorial Algorithms and Laboratory Experiments* (2006), L. Bianco *Membrane Models of Biological Systems* (2007), and A. Castellini *Algorithms and Software for Biological MP Modeling by Statistical and Optimization Techniques* (2010).

In 2005, Mario laid the foundation stone of the Sevilla team modelling contributions. More precisely, he designed in collaboration with Romero-Campero (who was at that time one of his PhD students) a model of the Epidermal growth factor receptor (EGFR) signalling network, using *Continuous P systems* [40]. In this framework, objects multiplicity is represented by positive real numbers, and at each instant rules are considered to be applied a positive real number of times. The concept of *computation step* is formally replaced by an *evolution function* working over matrices of real numbers, although in the software simulator it is obviously necessary to work with an approximation. The robustness of this model was studied in [41].

Continuous P Systems

In [40] a continuous variant of P systems was introduced to model the epidermal growth factor receptor (EGFR) signalling cascade. In contrast to the models developed so far, these systems could evolve in every instant by applying a maximal set of rules a positive real number of times each. Another significant difference was that they worked with *continuous multisets*, a mapping from an alphabet Σ to $\mathbb{R}^+$, the set of non-negative real numbers. The rules that are used are of the form

$$\mathcal{R}_l = \{r : u \, [\, v \,]_l \xrightarrow{\mathcal{K}_r} u' \, [\, v' \,]_l\}$$

where u, v, u', v' are standard multisets (i.e. with natural multiplicities) and $\mathcal{K}_r$ is the function that determines the number of times that the rule will be applied, depending on the multiplicities of objects in the current configuration. This variant was inspired by the fact that in vivo chemical reactions evolve in a continuous way following a rate that depends on the concentration of the reactants (mass action law).

The rules, used to model protein-protein interactions taking place in the compartmentalised structure of the living cell, are usually classified as follows:

- Transformation, complex formation and dissociation rules:

  (1) $[\, a \,]_l \rightarrow [\, b \,]_l$
  (2) $[\, a \, b \,]_l \rightarrow [\, c \,]_l$
  (3) $[\, a \,]_l \rightarrow [\, b \, c \,]_l$

- Diffusing in and out:

  (4) $[\, a \,]_l \rightarrow a \, [\,]_l$
  (5) $a \, [\,]_l \rightarrow [\, a \,]_l$

- Binding and unbinding rules:
  (6) $a \, [\, b \,]_l \rightarrow [\, c \,]_l$
  (7) $[\, a \,]_l \rightarrow b \, [\, c \,]_l$
- Recruitment and releasing rules:
  (8) $a \, [\, b \,]_l \rightarrow c \, [\,]_l$
  (9) $c \, [\,]_l \rightarrow a \, [\, b \,]_l$

where a, b, c are objects from the working alphabet and l is a membrane label.

An *instantaneous configuration* of a continuous P system Π is a matrix of $\mathcal{A}_{n,m}(\mathbb{R}^+)$ where $a_{i,j}$ (the element in row i and column j) represents the multiplicity of the object c_j in membrane i.

An *evolution* of a continuous P system is a mapping, $E : \mathbb{R}^+ \longrightarrow \mathcal{A}_{n,m}(\mathbb{R}^+)$, which associates each instant $t \in \mathbb{R}^+$ with an instantaneous configuration of the system. The rules are applied during the evolution of the system in a continuous manner according to their rate of application function.

Observe that the effects of the application of the rules are twofold: the multiplicity of objects appearing in the right-hand side of the rules (products) is increased, while at the same time the multiplicity of objects appearing in the left-hand sides (reactants) is decreased.

In order to approximate the evolution of a continuous P systems in a finite set of instants $t_0, \ldots, t_q$ the rectangle rule numerical method to approximate integrals is used. It is supposed that $t_{j+1} - t_j$ for $j = 0, \ldots, q - 1$ is fixed, and small enough to assume that all $\mathcal{K}_r$ remains constant in any interval $[t_j, t_{j+1}]$. With this assumption in mind, the number of times that a rule r is applied during one of those intervals is approximately $(t_{j+1} - t_j) \cdot \mathcal{K}_r(E(t_j))$. Therefore, by doing this approximation the evolution of a continuous P system during a time interval $[t_0, t_q]$ is approximated by the computation of a discrete P system that performs q steps working in a bounded parallel manner.

3 At the Crossroads of Cell Biology and Computation

The title of this section was actually the motto of the Seventh WMC, which was celebrated in 2006 in Leiden (The Netherlands).

After previously described work, in [18, 33, 42], an improved extension of those P systems was presented. This extension considers that the application of rules is not instantaneous, but takes a predefined amount of time.

In literature, each chemical reaction $r : A + B \xrightarrow{c_r} C$ has an associated mesoscopic rate constant c_r. The following type of P systems captures reaction times as waiting times that determine the order in which reactions place. This time will be computed in a deterministic way, for each reaction, in the following way: $\tau_r = \frac{1}{c_r |A||B|}$ where $|A|$ and $|B|$ represent the number of molecules of the two reactants A, B. $\rho_r = c_r |A||B|$ is considered the probability of the rule to be applied in the next step of evolution.

3.1 Deterministic Waiting Times Algorithm

The following algorithm represents the most natural way of defining the evolution of such a P system.

1. Set t as 0.
2. Calculate $WT = \{(\tau_r, r, i)\}$ for all membranes i in the structure μ and for every rule $r \in \mathcal{R}_{l_i}$.
3. Until the time of the simulation t reaches or exceeds a prefixed time T:
   (a) Sort WT according to their waiting time τ.
   (b) Select from WT the tuple with minimal τ, (τ_M, r_M, i_M) (if there are several τ values, then select all).
   (c) Update WT by subtracting τ_M to the τ of all its elements.
   (d) Update t by adding τ_M.
   (e) Apply the selected rules, r_M, in their corresponding membranes, i_M, only once.
   (f) Recalculate the τ only for those rules which are associated with those compartments affected by the applied rules.
   (g) For each of such rules, compare the new τ with its existing τ and update WT as $\min(\tau, WT)$.

This algorithm simulated and translated the signalling cascade of the epidermal growth factor receptor (EGFR). In a similar manner, it was also used over the set of rules describing the Type I and Type II of FAS-induced apoptotic pathway starting with the stimulation of FAS ligand until the activation of the effector Caspase-3 (see [18]).

3.2 Multienvironment P Systems and Multi-compartmental Gillespie Algorithm

Quorum sensing systems in bacteria are fundamental to the control and regulation of cell behaviour. In particular, in order to capture in detail the activation system of a gene regulation system which depends on cell density, the geographical information is very relevant, and this is why it is worth integrating it within the model [8,44].

A *multienvironment P system* is a construct, $ME = (H, \Gamma, G, \mathcal{M}_E, \Pi, k, \mathcal{R}_E)$, where:

1. H is a finite *set of labels* for the environments.
2. $\Gamma = \{o_1, \ldots, o_{m_E}\}$ is a finite alphabet of *objects* (also for chemical substances).
3. $G = (V, S)$ is a graph with n_E nodes, V, that represent the environments (labelled with elements from L) and whose edges, S define how the environments are linked.
4. $\mathcal{M}_E = \{(\mathcal{M}_{E_i}, h_i)\}_{1 \leq i \leq n_E}$ is the *initial configuration* of ME. S associates each environment j in the graph G with a label, $h_i \in H$ and a continuous multiset, $\mathcal{M}_{E_i}$.

5. Π is a continuous P system with $\Gamma \subseteq \Sigma$.
6. $k \in \mathbb{N}$ is the number of copies of the P system Π that are non-deterministically distributed across the different environments in the initial configuration of the system.
7. $\mathcal{R}_E = \{\mathcal{R}_h\}_{h \in H}$ are finite sets of *rules* of one the following forms:
   - $r : (\ u \xrightarrow{p_r} u'\ )_h$ where $u, u' \in \Gamma^*$.
   - $c : (\ v\ )_h \xrightarrow{p_c} (\ v\ )_{h'}$ where $v \in \Gamma^*$ for the case of movement of different substances from one environment to one of its neighbouring environments.
   - $m : (\ \Pi\ )_h \xrightarrow{p_m} (\ \Pi\ )_{h'}$. In addition to the multisets of objects that represent chemical substances, a certain number of copies of P systems are placed inside the environments. These P systems, and all their contents, can move from one environment to another.

Gillespie's algorithm provides an exact method for the stochastic simulation of systems of bio-chemical reactions. The validity of this method has been rigorously proved and successfully used to simulate various biochemical processes. An extension of this algorithm, called Multi-compartmental Gillespie's Algorithm, was introduced in [42]. Unlike the original version, this method considers the existence of multiple disjoint compartments that represent different regions where chemical reactions occur.

Classical Gillespie's Algorithm

Let us consider an enumeration R of all the rules for one of the membranes of the k P systems, including also the environments. Each one of them is considered to be a separate compartment enclosing a volume.

1. Calculate $a_0 = \sum_{r_i \in R} p_{r_i}$
2. Generate two random numbers n_1 and n_2 over the unit interval $(0, 1)$
3. Calculate the waiting time $\tau = \dfrac{1}{a_0} ln(\dfrac{1}{n_1})$
4. Take the index j of the rule such that $\displaystyle\sum_{1 \leq k \leq j-1} p_{r_k} < n_2 \cdot a_0 \leq \sum_{1 \leq k \leq j} p_{r_k}$
5. Return (τ, j)

Multi-compartmental Gillespie's Algorithm

Let us consider an enumeration C of all such compartments.

1. Set t as 0.
2. Calculate $WT = \{(\tau, j, i) : i \in C\}$ using Classical Gillespie's algorithm (as described above) to calculate (τ, j) for each compartment.
3. Until the time of the simulation t reaches or exceeds a prefixed time:
   (a) Sort WT according to τ
   (b) Select from WT the tuple with minimal τ, (τ_M, j_M, i_M)
   (c) Update WT subtracting τ_M to each τ
   (d) Apply r_{j_M} in compartment i_M only once.
   (e) For those compartments i affected by the applied rule
       Recalculate their corresponding (τ, j), using again Classical Gillespie's algorithm, and update WT

4   Sevilla's Ark: Giant Pandas, Bearded Vultures and Zebra Mussels

The origin of the fascinating journey of RGNC across the ocean of computational modelling of ecosystems began in 2008. The first case study focused on an ecosystem related to the *Bearded vulture (Gypaetus barbatus)* in the Pyrenees. In this line, *Probabilistic P systems* were presented in [16,17]. Although the results qualitatively agreed with experimental data, this model was intended to be a preliminary proof of concept. Shortly after, the model was extended and improved in [15], by adding more species and features in order to improve the model's accuracy.

The next upgrade on the modelling framework enabled the modelling of geographical information, yielding the so-called *Multienvironment probabilistic functional extended P systems* [14,22]. This is useful to capture, for instance, scavengers moving along different areas looking for food, featuring different environmental conditions for each area, or the expansion of a disease among a population [20]. In parallel with such refinements of the technical details about the syntax and semantics of the type of P systems that were used, there was another evolution going on the software part. In particular, several simulation algorithms were engineered, implementing in different ways the hybridisation between probabilistic rules and their maximally parallel mode of application. An abstract virtual ecosystem having three trophic levels (grass, herbivorous and carnivorous) was designed, to be used as a scalable case study to perform virtual experiments and compare the characteristics of each algorithm [24,25,29]. On the other hand, after several ad-hoc software developments for simulation tools, including end-user GUIs, the RGNC started to work on a general purpose solution: *MeCoSim (Membrane Computing Simulator)* (see [22,39] and visit [2]).

In line with this general purpose long-term approach, a step-by-step protocol for building computational models was presented in [21], using *Population Dynamics P systems* (PDP systems). This is a generalisation of the syntax of previous frameworks, whose integration in *pLinguaCore v3.0* was announced together with a new simulation algorithm in [28]. A noticeable case study is gene networks (dynamics of logical networks [49], or *Arabidopsis thaliana*'s regulating its circadian rhythms [48]).

4.1   Probabilistic Systems

An extension of multienvironment P systems, encompassing them, was proposed in [16,17] with the following changes:

- Each environment contains exactly one P system. In the initial configuration, the multisets associated with each P system is empty.
- Environments and membranes have no associated labels. Previous models usually used exactly one label for environments and distinguished them as different elements in the set of nodes $V = \{e_1, \ldots, e_{n_E}\}$ of the graph G that defines their interconnections. Since the association between membranes and

labels is bijective, the enumeration of membranes sufficiently identifies each membrane. In this enumeration, 0 is reserved for the skin.

- Movements of substances between environments were reduced to just one substance and were generalised to expand its spread capacity, considering that this capacity could also change during the process:
$$c : (\; x \;)_{e_i} \xrightarrow{\;p_c\;} (\; y_1 \;)_{e_{i_1}} \ldots (\; y_h \;)_{e_{i_h}}$$
- Polarity was added to the set of properties of each membrane at an instant t. Rules associated with each membrane have the ability to change this polarity:
$$u \; [\; v \;]_i^\alpha \xrightarrow{\;p_{r_i, e_j}\;} u' \; [\; v' \;]_i^{\alpha'} \text{ with } \alpha \in \{0, +, -\}.$$
- Constants associated with rules are changed by computable functions that, given an instant time t, return a real number within the interval $[0, 1]$. For these functions, the following restrictions are imposed:
  - For each environment e_i and object x, the sum of functions associated with the rules from $\mathcal{R}_{e_i}$ whose left-hand side is $(\; x \;)_{e_j}$ coincides with the constant function equal to 1. At each transition step, one of the applicable rules is selected for application according to the "probability" assigned by the functions.
  - For each $u, v \in \Sigma$, $i \in \{1, \ldots, n\}$, $\alpha, \alpha' \in \{0, +, -\}$, the sum of functions associated with the rules from $\mathcal{R}_i$ whose left-hand side is $u \; [\; v \;]_i^\alpha$ and their right-hand side have polarisation α' coincides with the constant function equal to 1. As before, these functions determine which of them is applied.
  - In order to apply several rules to the same membrane simultaneously, all of them must have the same polarity on their right-hand side.
  - If $(\; x \;)_{e_i}$ is the left-hand side of a rule from $\mathcal{R}_{e_i}$ then none of the rules of $\mathcal{R}_0$ has a left-hand side of the form $u \; [\; v \;]_0^\alpha$ for any $u \in \Sigma^*$ that has $x \in u$.
  - The initial configurations for each P system located in each environment and the functions described above may vary between one another.

Binomial Block Based Simulation Algorithm

One of the first simulation algorithms for PDP systems was: *Binomial Block Based algorithm* (BBB) [14]. In this first approach the rules that have exactly the same left sides are organised into a single block. The algorithm consists of a random selection of the blocks, selecting a maximum number of applications for each of them (according to that "common" left side). Then, for each block, a multinomial distribution of the applications of its rules is calculated, according to their probabilities.

Although this simulation algorithm proved to be very useful [14, 15], it has some disadvantages as it does not accurately handle the following semantic properties:

- Competition for resources: Rules with partial and not total overlap on their left-hand sides are classified in different blocks, so common objects will not be distributed among them, since selected blocks are executed to the maximum.
- Consistency of rules: It is up to the designer to ensure that there are no inconsistencies.

- The use of probabilistic functions associated with the rules. Only constant probabilities are considered, which will not be the case in future models based on PDP systems.

Direct Non-deterministic Distribution Algorithm with Probabilities (DNDP)

In order to solve these difficulties, two new algorithms have been developed. that accurately capture the dynamics they intend to emulate: the "Direct Non-deterministic Distribution with Probabilities" algorithm (DNDP) [29] and the "Direct distribution based on Consistent Blocks" algorithm (DCBA) [28]. DNDP intends to make a random distribution of rule applications, but this selection process is biased towards the rules that are most likely to be applied. DCBA was conceived to overcome DNDP's accuracy problem by performing a distribution of objects along rule blocks before applying the random distribution process. Although the accuracy achieved by the DCBA is better than that of the DNDP algorithm, the latter is much faster.

In DNDP algorithm the selection is divided into two microphases:

1. A set of consistent applicable rules is calculated. A priori applicable rules (those whose associated probability is greater than 0 in the current configuration) are shuffled. Following this order, a random number of applications is calculated for each rule according to its probability function using a binomial distribution (taking into account, each time, the objects that will be consumed by the applications of the previous rules and that there will be no consistency problems).
2. The multiplicity of some of them is eventually increased to ensure maximum application, thus obtaining a multiset of maximally consistent applicable rules. In order to fairly distribute the objects among the rules, they are iterated in descendant order with respect to the probabilities. Again, each time, one takes into account objects that will be consumed by the applications of the previous rules and consistency problems, but now adding the maximum number of times that they are applicable.

However, the DNDP algorithm still creates some distortion in the distribution of objects between rules with left-hand side overlap. That is, instead of selecting the rules according to their probabilities in a uniform manner, this selection process is biased towards those with the highest probabilities. In addition, the probabilistic distribution of rule executions within blocks will not ultimately follow a multinomial distribution, since competing rules from other blocks may "consume" necessary objects in the selection process.

The DCBA Algorithm

This is where the latest algorithm comes into play. The main idea behind DCBA is to carry out a proportional distribution of objects between consistent blocks of rules (a concept similar, but not identical, to the blocks in BBB as they take into account polarity change), while dealing probabilities.

In this case, the selection stage consists of three phases: Phase 1 distributes objects to the blocks in a certain proportional way, Phase 2 assures the maximality by checking the maximal number of applications of each block, and Phase 3 translates block applications to rule applications by calculating random numbers using the multinomial distribution.

4.2 Probabilistic Guarded P Systems

Probabilistic Guarded P systems [27] can be considered as an evolution of Population Dynamics P Systems specifically oriented for ecological processes. In this context, PGP systems propose a modelling framework for ecology where inconsistency (that is, having two applicable rules such that they cannot be applied simultaneously, because each of them sets a different polarisation on the right side) is managed by the framework itself, instead of delegating to the designer and the simulation algorithms. In addition, by replacing concepts that are foreign to biology (such as electrical polarizations and internal compartment hierarchies) by state variables known as *flags* that are more natural to the experts, thus simplifying communication between expert and designer.

Although PGP systems provide a simplified alternative to PDP systems, some constraints to the supported models are imposed: only models without object competition are allowed.

In order to assist in the definition, analysis, simulation and validation of PDP-based models related to different real-world ecosystems, MeCoSim (a general purpose application to model, design, simulate, analyse and verify different types of models based on P systems), which uses pLinguaCore as its inference engine, has then been used. Also speed-up of the implemented algorithms by using parallel platforms based on GPUs are addressed.

5   Ongoing and Upcoming Modelling Works

We are currently engaged on the research project *Bio-inspired machines on High Performance Computing platforms: a multidisciplinary approach* (TIN2017-89842-P), funded by the Spanish Government. One of the goals is to bridge the gap between HPC platforms architectures and the specifications of a new type of P systems, trying to gain a significant speed-up in simulations. In particular, one of the specific goals is to investigate the invasion of zebra mussel species in Andalusia (along the Guadalquivir river and its surrounding irrigation network), starting from the model which has been already validated for the Ribarroja reservoir [23]. This is a particularly relevant case study due to its ecological and economic impact.

We are also engaged in the research project *Modeling principles of membrane computing models for giant pandas ecosystems*, supported by the National Natural Science Foundation of China (Grant No. 61672437). We are working in collaboration with the Giant Panda Breeding Base, in Chengdu (China), using the controlled environment (in captivity) as a starting point. The most challenging and exciting goal is to eventually extend the model to individuals living in the wild.

Acknowledgement. The authors are very grateful to Mario de Jesús Pérez-Jiménez for his unconditional support, unlimited generosity, patience and enthusiasm, and particularly for his skillful advising and guiding as their "scientific father".

The authors also acknowledge the support from research project TIN2017-89842-P, co-financed by Ministerio de Economía, Industria y Competitividad (MINECO) of Spain, through the Agencia Estatal de Investigación (AEI), and by Fondo Europeo de Desarrollo Regional (FEDER) of the European Union.

References

1. Bulletin of the International Membrane Computing Society. http://membranecomputing.net/IMCSBulletin/
2. MeCoSim Web. http://www.p-lingua.org/mecosim/
3. P Systems Web Page. http://ppage.psystems.eu/
4. Ardelean, I.I., Besozzi, D.: Mechanosensitive channels, a hot topic in (micro)biology: any excitement for P systems? In: Cavaliere, M., Martin-Vide, C., Păun, G. (eds.) Brainstorming Week on Membrane Computing, pp. 32–36 (2003). Rovira i Virgili University, Technical report 26
5. Ardelean, I.I., Cavaliere, M.: Modelling biological processes by using a probabilistic P system software. Nat. Comput. **2**, 173–197 (2003)
6. Ardelean, I.I., Cavaliere, M.: Playing with a probabilistic P system simulator: mathematical and biological problems. In: Cavaliere, M., Martin-Vide, C., Păun, G. (eds.) Brainstorming Week on Membrane Computing, pp. 37–45 (2003). Rovira i Virgili University, Technical report 26
7. Banâtre, J.-P., Fradet, P., Le Métayer, D.: Gamma and the chemical reaction model: fifteen years after. In: Calude, C.S., Păun, G., Rozenberg, G., Salomaa, A. (eds.) WMC 2000. LNCS, vol. 2235, pp. 17–44. Springer, Heidelberg (2001). https://doi.org/10.1007/3-540-45523-X_2
8. Bernardini, F., Gheorghe, M., Krasnogor, N., Muniyandi, R.C., Pérez-Jímenez, M.J., Romero-Campero, F.J.: On P Systems as a modelling tool for biological systems. In: Freund, R., Păun, G., Rozenberg, G., Salomaa, A. (eds.) WMC 2005. LNCS, vol. 3850, pp. 114–133. Springer, Heidelberg (2006). https://doi.org/10.1007/11603047_8
9. Bernardini, F., Manca, V.: Dynamical aspects of P systems. Biosystems **70**, 85–93 (2003)
10. Bernardini, F., Manca, V.: P systems with boundary rules. In: Păun, G., Rozenberg, G., Salomaa, A., Zandron, C. (eds.) WMC 2002. LNCS, vol. 2597, pp. 107–118. Springer, Heidelberg (2003). https://doi.org/10.1007/3-540-36490-0_8
11. Besozzi, D.: Computational and modelling power of P systems. Ph.D. thesis, Universitá degli Studi di Milano-Bicocca, Italy (2004)
12. Besozzi, D., Ardelean, I.I., Mauri, G.: The potential of P systems for modelling the activity of mechanosensitive channels in E. coli. In: Alhazov, A., Martin-Vide, C., Păun, G. (eds.) Workshop on Membrane Computing, WMC-2003, pp. 84–102, 2003. Rovira i Virgili University, Technical report 28

13. Pescini, D., Besozzi, D., Zandron, C., Mauri, G.: Analysis and simulation of dynamics in probabilistic P systems. In: Carbone, A., Pierce, N.A. (eds.) DNA 2005. LNCS, vol. 3892, pp. 236–247. Springer, Heidelberg (2006). https://doi.org/10.1007/11753681_19

14. Cardona, M., et al.: A computational modeling for real ecosystems based on P systems. Nat. Comput. **10**, 39–53 (2011)

15. Cardona, M., Colomer, M.A., Margalida, A., Pérez-Hurtado, I., Pérez-Jiménez, M.J., Sanuy, D.: A P system based model of an ecosystem of some scavenger birds. In: Păun, G., Pérez-Jiménez, M.J., Riscos-Núñez, A., Rozenberg, G., Salomaa, A. (eds.) WMC 2009. LNCS, vol. 5957, pp. 182–195. Springer, Heidelberg (2010). https://doi.org/10.1007/978-3-642-11467-0_14

16. Cardona, M., Colomer, M.A., Pérez-Jiménez, M.J., Sanuy, D., Margalida, A.: A P system modeling an ecosystem related to the bearded vulture. In: 6th Brainstorming Week on Membrane Computing, vol. 6, pp. 51–66 (2008)

17. Cardona, M., Colomer, M.A., Pérez-Jiménez, M.J., Sanuy, D., Margalida, A.: Modeling ecosystems using P systems: the bearded vulture, a case study. In: Corne, D.W., Frisco, P., Păun, G., Rozenberg, G., Salomaa, A. (eds.) WMC 2008. LNCS, vol. 5391, pp. 137–156. Springer, Heidelberg (2009). https://doi.org/10.1007/978-3-540-95885-7_11

18. Cheruku, S., Păun, A., Romero-Campero, F.J., Pérez-Jiménez, M.J., Ibarra, O.: Simulating FAS-induced apoptosis by using P systems. Prog. Nat. Sci. **17**, 424–431 (2007)

19. Ciobanu, G., Pérez-Jiménez, M.J., Păun, G. (eds.): Applications of Membrane Computing. Springer, Berlín (2006). https://doi.org/10.1007/3-540-29937-8

20. Colomer, M.A., et al.: Modeling population growth of Pyrenean Chamois (Rupicapra p. pyrenaica) by using P-systems. In: Gheorghe, M., Hinze, T., Păun, G., Rozenberg, G., Salomaa, A. (eds.) CMC 2010. LNCS, vol. 6501, pp. 144–159. Springer, Heidelberg (2010). https://doi.org/10.1007/978-3-642-18123-8_13

21. Colomer, M.A., Margalida, A., Pérez-Jiménez, M.J.: Population dynamics P system (PDP) models: a standardized protocol for describing and applying novel bio-inspired computing tools. PLOS One **4**, 1–13 (2013)

22. Colomer, M.A., Margalida, A., Sanuy, D., Pérez-Jiménez, M.J.: A bio-inspired computing model as a new tool for modeling ecosystems: the avian scavengers as a case study. Ecol. Model. **222**, 33–47 (2011)

23. Colomer, M.A., Margalida, A., Valencia-Cabrera, L., Palau, A.: Application of a computational model for complex fluvial ecosystems: the population dynamics of zebra mussel Dreissena polymorpha as a case study. Ecol. Complex. **20**, 116–126 (2014)

24. Colomer, M.A., Pérez-Hurtado, I., Pérez-Jiménez, M.J., Riscos-Núñez, A.: Simulating tritrophic interactions by means of P systems. In: Nagar, A., Thamburaj, R., Li, K., Tang, Z., Li, R. (eds.) IEEE Fifth International Conference on Bio-inpired Computing: Theories and Applications (BIC-TA 2010), Liverpool, UK, vol. 2, pp. 1621–1628. IEEE Press, September 2010

25. Colomer, M.A., Pérez-Hurtado, I., Riscos-Núñez, A., Pérez-Jiménez, M.J.: Comparing simulation algorithms for multienvironment probabilistic P system over a standard virtual ecosystem. Nat. Comput. **11**, 369–379 (2011)

26. Frisco, P., Gheorghe, M., Pérez-Jiménez, M.J. (eds.): Applications of Membrane Computing in Systems and Synthetic Biology. ECC, vol. 7. Springer, Cham (2014). https://doi.org/10.1007/978-3-319-03191-0

27. García-Quismondo, M., Martínez-del Amor, M.A., Pérez-Jiménez, M.J.: Probabilistic guarded P systems, a formal definition. In: Twelfth Brainstorming Week on Membrane Computing (BWMC2014), pp. 183–206 (2014)

28. Martínez-del Amor, M.A., et al.: DCBA: simulating population dynamics P systems with proportional object distribution. In: Tenth Brainstorming Week on Membrane Computing, vol. II, pp. 27–56, February 2012

29. Martínez-del Amor, M.A., Pérez-Hurtado, I., Pérez-Jiménez, M.J., Riscos-Núñez, A., Colomer, M.A.: A new simulation algorithm for multienvironment probabilistic P systems. In: Li, K., Tang, Z., Li, R., Nagar, A., Thamburaj, R. (eds.) IEEE Fifth International Conference on Bio-inpired Computing: Theories and Applications (BIC-TA 2010), Changsha, China, vol. 1, pp. 59–68. IEEE Press, September 2010

30. Milazzo, P., Pérez-Jiménez, M.J.: Proceedings First Workshop on Applications of Membrane Computing, Concurrency and Agent-Based Modelling in Population Biology. Electronic Proceedings in Theoretical Computer Science, vol. 33 (2010)

31. Yasunobu Nishida, T.: Multiset and K-subset transforming systems. In: Calude, C.S., Păun, G., Rozenberg, G., Salomaa, A. (eds.) WMC 2000. LNCS, vol. 2235, pp. 255–265. Springer, Heidelberg (2001). https://doi.org/10.1007/3-540-45523-X_13

32. Nishida, T.Y.: Simulations of photosynthesis by a k-subset transforming system with membrane. Fundam. Inform. **49**, 249–259 (2002)

33. Păun, A., Pérez-Jiménez, M.J., Romero-Campero, F.J.: Modeling signal transduction using P systems. In: Hoogeboom, H.J., Păun, G., Rozenberg, G., Salomaa, A. (eds.) WMC 2006. LNCS, vol. 4361, pp. 100–122. Springer, Heidelberg (2006). https://doi.org/10.1007/11963516_7

34. Păun, G.: P systems with active membranes: attacking NP-complete problems. CDMTCS Research Report Series (1999)

35. Păun, G.: Computing with membranes. J. Comput. Syst. Sci. **61**, 108–143 (2000). Prelim. Version in Turku Center for Computer Science-TUCS Report No. 208 (1998). www.tucs.fi

36. Păun, G.: Membrane Computing. An Introduction. Springer, Berlin (2002). https://doi.org/10.1007/978-3-642-56196-2

37. Păun, G., Pérez-Jiménez, M.J.: Membrane computing: brief introduction, recent results and applications. BioSystems **85**, 11–22 (2006)

38. Păun, G., Romero-Campero, F.J.: Membrane computing as a modeling framework. Cellular systems case studies. In: Bernardo, M., Degano, P., Zavattaro, G. (eds.) SFM 2008. LNCS, vol. 5016, pp. 168–214. Springer, Heidelberg (2008). https://doi.org/10.1007/978-3-540-68894-5_6

39. Pérez-Hurtado, I., Valencia-Cabrera, L., Pérez-Jiménez, M.J., Colomer, M.A., Riscos-Núñez, A.: MeCoSim: a general purpose software tool for simulating biological phenomena by means of P systems. In: Li, K., Tang, Z., Li, R., Nagar, A., Thamburaj, R. (eds.) IEEE Fifth International Conference on Bio-inpired Computing: Theories and Applications (BIC-TA 2010), vol. I, pp. 637–643. IEEE Inc., Changsha (2010)

40. Pérez-Jiménez, M.J., Romero-Campero, F.J.: Modelling EGFR signalling network using continuous membrane systems. In: Third International Workshop on Computational Methods in Systems Biology, CMSB 2005, pp. 118–129, 3–5 April 2005

41. Pérez-Jiménez, M.J., Romero-Campero, F.J.: A study of the robustness of the EGFR signalling cascade using continuous membrane systems. In: Mira, J., Álvarez, J.R. (eds.) IWINAC 2005. LNCS, vol. 3561, pp. 268–278. Springer, Heidelberg (2005). https://doi.org/10.1007/11499220_28

42. Pérez-Jiménez, M.J., Romero-Campero, F.J.: P systems, a new computational modelling tool for systems biology. In: Priami, C., Plotkin, G. (eds.) Transactions on Computational Systems Biology VI. LNCS, vol. 4220, pp. 176–197. Springer, Heidelberg (2006). https://doi.org/10.1007/11880646_8

43. Regev, A., Shapiro, E.: Cellular abstractions: cells as computations. Nature **419**(6905), 343 (2002)

44. Romero-Campero, F.J., Pérez-Jiménez, M.J.: A model of the quorum sensing system in Vibrio fischeri using P systems. Artif. Life **14**, 95–109 (2008)

45. Suzuki, Y., Fujiwara, Y., Takabayashi, J., Tanaka, H.: Artificial life applications of a class of P systems: abstract rewriting systems on multisets. In: Calude, C.S., Păun, G., Rozenberg, G., Salomaa, A. (eds.) WMC 2000. LNCS, vol. 2235, pp. 299–346. Springer, Heidelberg (2001). https://doi.org/10.1007/3-540-45523-X_16

46. Suzuki, Y., Ogishima, S., Tanaka, H.: Modeling the p53 signaling network by using P systems. In: Alhazov, A., Martin-Vide, C., Păun, G. (eds.) Workshop on Membrane Computing, WMC-2003, pp. 449–454, 2003. Rovira i Virgili University, Technical report 28

47. Suzuki, Y., Tanaka, H.: Abstract rewriting systems on multisets and their application for modelling complex behaviours. In: Cavaliere, M., Martin-Vide, C., Păun, G. (eds.) Brainstorming Week on Membrane Computing, pp. 313–331 (2003). Rovira i Virgili University, Technical report 26

48. Valencia-Cabrera, L., García-Quismondo, M., Pérez-Jiménez, M.J., Su, Y., Yu, H., Pan, L.: Analysing gene networks with PDP systems. Arabidopsis thaliana, a case study. In: Eleventh Brainstorming Week on Membrane Computing (11 BWMC), pp. 257–272, August 2013

49. Valencia-Cabrera, L., García-Quismondo, M., Pérez-Jiménez, M.J., Su, Y., Yu, H., Pan, L.: Modeling logic gene networks by means of probabilistic dynamic P systems. Int. J. Unconv. Comput. **9**(5–6), 445–464 (2013)

50. Zhang, G., Pérez-Jiménez, M.J., Gheorghe, M.: Real-Life Applications with Membrane Computing. ECC, vol. 25. Springer, Cham (2017). https://doi.org/10.1007/978-3-319-55989-6

Identifiable Kernel P Systems

Marian Gheorghe[1(✉)] and Florentin Ipate[2]

[1] School of Electrical Engineering and Computer Science, University of Bradford, Bradford BD7 1DP, UK
m.gheorghe@bradford.ac.uk
[2] Department of Computer Science, Faculty of Mathematics and Computer Science and ICUB, University of Bucharest, Str. Academiei 14, 010014 Bucharest, Romania
florentin.ipate@ifsoft.ro

Abstract. This paper introduces the concept of *identifiability* for kernel P systems and establishes a fundamental set of properties for identifiable kernel P systems.

1 Introduction

Inspired by the structure and functioning of living cells, *membrane computing*, the research field initiated by Păun [15], has been intensively investigated in the last fifteen years. Its main research themes addressed so far refer to the computational power of different variants of membrane systems (also *called P systems*), hierarchies of languages or multiset classes produced by these devices, their capability to solve hard problems, decidability and complexity aspects [16]. There have also been significant developments in using the P systems paradigm to model various systems [2]. More recently, variants of P systems have been introduced in connection with modelling problems in various areas, e.g., systems and synthetic biology [5], information in biotic systems [13], synchronisation of distributed systems [3], grid algorithms [14], parallel algorithms utilised in 3D graphics [11].

Since P systems have been extensively used in various applications, it is a natural question to ask whether these applications and their implementations are correct and error-free. As *testing* is an essential part of software development and in many cases consumes large percentages of project efforts and budgets (test generation, in particular), it has been recently considered in the context of P systems applications. Some widely used testing approaches, such as mutation testing or transition cover have been considered [12] or adapted (rule coverage [6]) for P systems specifications. Recently a class of generic P systems, called identifiable P systems, have been introduced and studied in connection with testing [9].

More recently, P systems have been used to model and simulate systems and problems from various areas. This has led to a multitude of P system variants. The newly introduced concept of *kernel P systems (kP systems, for short)* [7,8] combines various features of P systems in a coherent manner, allowing to model complex applications and analyse these models.

© Springer Nature Switzerland AG 2018
C. Graciani et al. (Eds.): Pérez-Jiménez Festschrift, LNCS 11270, pp. 130–141, 2018.
https://doi.org/10.1007/978-3-030-00265-7_11

The kP system model is supported by a modelling language, called kP-Lingua, capable of mapping a kP system specification into a machine readable representation. Furthermore, kP systems are supported by a software framework, kPWORKBENCH [10], which integrates a set of related simulation and verification methods and tools.

In this paper, we present the concept of identifiability for kP systems, continuing the research introduced in [9]. Our contribution has the following significant components:

- *Definition of identifiable kP systems,* a non-trivial extension of identifiable P systems.
- *A reformulation of some previous results regarding identifiable P systems in the context of kP systems.* In order to be self-contained some results regarding identifiable P systems have been slightly changed and presented in this paper. Some results are new, showing the capabilities of the kP systems.

The paper is structured as follows. Section 2 introduces basic concepts related to kP systems. Section 3 investigates the issue of identifiability in the context of the kP system model. Section 3 presents the main results, with complete proofs of the results introduced.

2   Preliminaries

Before proceeding, we introduce the notations used in the paper. For a finite alphabet $A = \{a_1, ..., a_p\}$, A^* denotes the set of all strings (sequences) over A. The empty string is denoted by λ and $A^+ = A \backslash \{\lambda\}$ denotes the set of non-empty strings. For a string $u \in A^*$, $|u|_a$ denotes the number of occurrences of a in u, where $a \in A$. For a subset $S \subseteq A$, $|u|_S$ denotes the number of occurrences of the symbols from S in u. The length of a string u is given by $\sum_{a_i \in A} |u|_{a_i}$. The length of the empty string is 0, i.e. $|\lambda| = 0$. A multiset over A is a mapping $f : A \to \mathbb{N}$. Considering only the elements from the support of f (where $f(a_{i_j}) > 0$, for some j, $1 \leq j \leq p$), the multiset is represented as a string $a_{i_1}^{f(a_{i_1})} \ldots a_{i_p}^{f(a_{i_p})}$, where the order is not important. In the sequel multisets will be represented by such strings.

2.1   Kernel P System Basic Definitions

We start by introducing the concept of a *compartment type* utilised later in defining the compartments of a kP system.

Definition 1. *A set of compartment types, t is a set $T = \{t_1, \ldots, t_s\}$, where $t_i = (R_i, \sigma_i)$, $1 \leq i \leq s$, consists of a set of rules, R_i, and an execution strategy, σ_i, defined over $Lab(R_i)$, the labels of the rules of R_i.*

The compartments that appear in the definition of the kP systems will be constructed using compartment types introduced by Definition 1. A compartment C, is defined by a tuple (t, w), where $t \in T$ is the type of the compartment and w the initial multiset of it. The types of rules and the execution strategies occurring in the compartment types will be introduced and discussed later.

Definition 2. *A* kP *system of degree n is a tuple*

$$k\Pi = (A, \mu, C_1, \ldots, C_n, i_0),$$

where A *is a non-empty finite set, its elements are called* objects; μ *defines the* initial membrane structure, *which is a graph,* (V, E), *where* V *is the set of vertices indicating compartments of the* kP *system, and* E *is the set of edges;* $C_i = (t_i, w_i), 1 \le i \le n$, *is a compartment of the* kP *system, as presented above;* $i_0, \ 1 \le i_0 \le n$, *is the label of the* output *compartment, where the result is obtained.*

2.2   Kernel P System Rules

Each rule occurring in a kP system definition has the form $r : t \ \{g\}$, where r identifies the rule, is its **label**, t is the **rule** itself and g is its **guard**. The part t is also called the **body** of the rule, denoted also $b(r)$.

The guards are constructed using multisets over A, as operands, and relational or Boolean operators. We start with some notations.

Let us denote $Rel = \{<, \le, =, \ne, \ge, >\}$, the set of relational operators, $\gamma \in Rel$, a relational operator, and a^n a multiset, consisting of n copies of a. We first introduce an *abstract relational expression*.

Definition 3. *If* g *is the* abstract relational expression *denoting* γa^n *and* w *a multiset, then the guard* g *applied to* w *denotes the* relational expression $|w|_a \gamma n$.

The abstract relational expression g is true for the multiset w, if $|w|_a \gamma n$ is true.

We consider now the following Boolean operators $\neg$ (negation), $\wedge$ (conjunction) and $\vee$ (disjunction). An *abstract Boolean expression* is defined by one of the following conditions:

- any abstract relational expression is an abstract Boolean expression;
- if g and h are abstract Boolean expressions then $\neg g$, $g \wedge h$ and $g \vee h$ are abstract Boolean expressions.

The concept of a guard, introduced here, is a generalisation of the promoter and inhibitor concepts utilised by some variants of P systems.

Definition 4. *If* g *is an* abstract Boolean expression *containing* g_i, $1 \le i \le q$, *abstract relational expressions and* w *a multiset, then* g *applied to* w *means the* Boolean expression *obtained from* g *by applying* g_i *to* w *for any* $i, 1 \le i \le q$.

As in the case of an abstract relational expression, the guard g is true with respect to the multiset w, if the abstract Boolean expression g applied to w is true.

Example 1. If g is the guard defined by the abstract Boolean expression $\geq a^5 \wedge <$ $b^3 \vee \neg > c$ and w a multiset, then g applied to w is true if it has at least 5 a's and no more than 2 b's or no more than one c.

In this paper we will use a simplified version of kP systems, called *simple kP systems*, using only rewriting and communication rules. In what follows these will be called simply kP systems.

We say that a rule $r : x \rightarrow y$ $\{g\}$ is applicable to a multiset w iff $x \subseteq w$ and g is true for w.

Definition 5. *Any rule from a compartment $C_{l_i} = (t_{l_i}, w_{l_i})$ will be a* **rewriting and communication** *rule: $x \rightarrow y$ $\{g\}$, where $x \in A^+$ and y has the form $y = (a_1, t_1) \ldots (a_h, t_h)$, $h \geq 0$, $a_j \in A$ and t_j, $1 \leq j \leq h$, indicates a compartment type from T (see Definition 1) associated with a compartment linked to the current one; t_j might also indicate the type of the current compartment, $C_{t_{l_i}}$; if a link does not exist (i.e., there is no link between the two compartments in E) then the rule is not applied; if a target, t_j, refers to a compartment type that appears in more than one compartments connected to C_{l_i}, then one of them will be non-deterministically chosen.*

2.3   Kernel P System Execution Strategies

In kP systems the way in which rules are executed is defined for each compartment type t from T – see Definition 1. As in Definition 1, $Lab(R)$ is the set of labels of the rules of R.

Definition 6. *For a compartment type $t = (R, \sigma)$ from T and $r \in Lab(R)$, $r_1, \ldots, r_s \in Lab(R)$, the execution strategy, σ, is defined by the following*

- $\sigma = \lambda$, *means no rule from the current compartment will be executed;*
- $\sigma = \{r\}$ – *the rule r is executed;*
- $\sigma = \{r_1, \ldots, r_s\}$ – *one of the rules labelled $r_1, \ldots, r_s$ will be non-deterministically chosen and executed; if none is applicable then nothing is executed; this is called* alternative *or* choice;
- $\sigma = \{r_1, \ldots, r_s\}^*$ – *the rules are applied an arbitrary number of times (arbitrary parallelism);*
- $\sigma = \{r_1, \ldots, r_s\}^\top$ – *the rules are executed according to the* maximal parallelism *strategy;*
- $\sigma = \sigma_1 \& \ldots \& \sigma_s$ – *this means executing sequentially $\sigma_1, \ldots, \sigma_s$, where σ_i, $1 \leq i \leq s$, describes any of the above cases; if one of σ_i fails to be executed then the rest is no longer executed.*

Definition 7. *A* configuration *of a kP system, $k\Pi$, with n compartments, is a tuple $c = (c_1, \ldots, c_n)$, where $c_i \in A^*$, $1 \leq i \leq n$, is the multiset from compartment i. The initial configuration is $(w_1, \ldots, w_n)$, where $w_i \in A^*$ is the initial multiset of the compartment i, $1 \leq i \leq n$.*

A *transition* (or *computation step*), introduced by the next definition, is the process of passing from one configuration to another.

Definition 8. *Given two configurations $c = (c_1, \ldots, c_n)$ and $c' = (c'_1, \ldots, c'_n)$ of a kP system, $k\Pi$, with n compartments, where for any $i, 1 \leq i \leq n$, $u_i \in A^*$, and a multiset of rules $M_i = r_{1,i}^{n_{1,i}} \ldots r_{k_i,i}^{n_{k_i,i}}$, $n_{j,i} \geq 0$, $1 \leq j \leq k_i, k_i \geq 0$, a transition or a* computation step *is the process of obtaining c' from c by using the multisets of rules M_i, $1 \leq i \leq n$, denoted by $c \Longrightarrow^{(M_1, \ldots, M_n)} c'$, such that for each i, $1 \leq i \leq n$, c'_i is the multiset obtained from c_i by first extracting all the objects that are in the left-hand side of each rule of M_i from c_i and then adding all the objects a that are in the right-hand side of each rule of M_i represented as (a, t_i) and all the objects b that are in the right-hand side of each rule of M_j, $j \neq i$, such that b is represented as (b, t_i) and an appropriate link between compartments exists.*

In the theory of kP systems, each compartment might have its own execution strategy. In the sequel we will consider that all the compartments will use the same execution strategy and the focus will be on three such execution strategies, namely maximal parallelism, arbitray parallelism (also called asynchronous execution) and sequential execution. These will be denoted by $max, async$ and seq, respectively. When in a transition from c to c' using $(M_1, \ldots, M_n)$ we intend to refer to a specific transition mode tm, $tm \in \{max, async, seq\}$, this will be denoted by $c \Longrightarrow_{tm}^{(M_1, \ldots, M_n)} c'$.

A *computation* in a kP system is a sequence of transitions (computation steps).

A configuration is called *final configuration* if no rule can be applied to it. In a final configuration the computation stops.

As usual in P systems, we only consider terminal computations, i.e., those arriving in a final configuration and using one of the above mentioned transition modes. We are now ready to define the result of a computation.

Definition 9. *For a kP system $k\Pi$ using the transition mode tm, $tm \in \{max, async, seq\}$, in each compartment, we denote by $N_{tm}(k\Pi)$ the number of objects appearing in the output compartment of any final configuration.*

Two kP systems $k\Pi$ and $k\Pi'$ are called *equivalent* with respect to the transition mode tm, $tm \in \{max, async, seq\}$, if $N_{tm}(k\Pi) = N_{tm}(k\Pi')$.

In this paper we will only deal with kP systems having *one single compartment* as this does not affect the general method introduced here and makes the presentation easier to follow. Indeed, limiting the investigation to one compartment kP systems does not affect the generality of the results due to the fact that there are ways of flattening an arbitrary P system, including the kP system discussed in this paper, into a P system with one single compartment. For details regarding the flattening of a P system we refer mainly to [4], but similar approaches are also presented in other papers [1,17]. Such a kP system will be denoted $k\Pi = (A, \mu_1, C_1, 1)$, where μ_1 denotes the graph with one node. On the right-hand side of the rules there will simply be multisets over A, as in the case of one single compartment there is no need to indicate where objects are sent to.

We now introduce the key concept we aim to investigate in this paper, namely *identifiability* of kP systems. This concept has been studied for generic P systems and is now investigated for kP systems where some additional constraints appear. The identifiability concept is first introduced for simple rules and then is generalised for multisets of rules.

Definition 10. *Two rules $r_1 : x_1 \rightarrow y_1 \{g_1\}$ and $r_2 : x_2 \rightarrow y_2 \{g_2\}$ from R_1, are said to be* identifiable *in configuration c if (i) they are applicable to c and (ii) if $c \Longrightarrow^{r_1} c'$ and $c \Longrightarrow^{r_2} c'$ then $b(r_1) = b(r_2)$. Otherwise the rules are said to be non identifiable.*

According to the above definition, the rules r_1 and r_2 are identifiable in c if whenever the result of applying them to c is the same, their bodies, $x_1 \rightarrow y_1$ and $x_2 \rightarrow y_2$, are identical.

A multiset $M = r_1^{n_1} \dots r_k^{n_k}, M \in R_1^*$, where $r_i : x_i \rightarrow y_i \{g_i\}, 1 \le i \le k$, is applicable to the multiset c iff $x_1^{n_1} \dots x_k^{n_k} \subseteq c$ and g_i is true in c for any i, $1 \le i \le k$.

Notation. Given a multiset $M = r_1^{n_1} \dots r_k^{n_k}$, where $r_i : x_i \rightarrow y_i \{g_i\}, 1 \le i \le k$, we denote by r_M the rule $x_1^{n_1} \dots x_k^{n_k} \rightarrow y_1^{n_1} \dots y_k^{n_k} \{g_1 \wedge \cdots \wedge g_k\}$, i.e., the concatenation of all the rules in M.

Definition 11. *The multisets of rules $M', M'' \in R_1^*$, are said to be* identifiable, *if there is a configuration c where M' and M'' are applicable and if $c \Longrightarrow^{M'} c'$ and $c \Longrightarrow^{M''} c'$ then $b(r_{M'}) = b(r_{M''})$.*

Definition 12. *We say that a kP system $k\Pi$ has identifiable rules if any two multisets of rules, $M', M'' \in R_1^*$, are identifiable.*

3 Identifiable Transitions in kP Systems

In this section we investigate the property of identifiability for kP system rules and multisets of rules. We start by introducing a notation utilised in this section.

One can observe, based on Definition 11, that the applicability of the multiset of rules M to a certain configuration is equivalent to the applicability of the rule r_M to that configuration. It follows that one can study first the usage of simple rules.

Remark 1. For any two rules $r_i : x_i \rightarrow y_i \{g_i\}, 1 \le i \le 2$, when we check whether they are identifiable or not one can write them as $r_i : uv_i \rightarrow wz_i \{g_i\}$, $1 \le i \le 2$, where for any $a \in A$, a appears in at most one of the v_1 or v_2, i.e., all the common symbols on the left-hand side of the rules are in u.

We first show that the identifiability of two rules does not depend on the configurations in which they are applicable. For the two rules introduced in Remark 1 let us denote by c_{r_1,r_2}, the configuration uv_1v_2. Obviously this is the smallest configuration in which r_1 and r_2 are applicable, given that g_1 and g_2 are true in uv_1v_2.

Remark 2. If $r_i : x_i \to y_i \{g_i\}$, $1 \leq i \leq 2$, are applicable in a configuration c and $c \subseteq c'$ then they are not always applicable to c'. They are applicable to c' when all g_i, $1 \leq i \leq 2$, are true in c'.

Remark 3. If the rules r_1, r_2 are not applicable to c_{r_1, r_2} then there must be minimal configurations c where the rules are applicable and they are minimal, i.e., there is no c_1, $c_1 \subset c$, where the rules are applicable. Such minimal configurations where r_1, r_2 are applicable are of the form $t c_{r_1, r_2}$, where $t \in A^*$, $t \neq \lambda$.

Lemma 1. *Two rules which are identifiable in a configuration c are identifiable in any configuration containing c in which they are applicable.*

Proof. Applying the two identifiable rules, $r_1 : x_1 \to y_1 \{g_1\}$ and $r_2 : x_2 \to y_2 \{g_2\}$, to the configuration c, one gets c' and c'' and $c' \neq c''$. If the rules are applicable to another configuration c_1 bigger than c, i.e., $c_1 = ct$, then $x_1, x_2 \subseteq c_1$ and g_1 and g_2 are true for c_1. In this case the results are $c_1' = c't$ and $c_1'' = c''t$ and obviously $c_1' \neq c_1''$, hence r_1 and r_2 are identifiable in c_1.

Lemma 2. *Two rules which are identifiable in a minimal configuration c are identifiable in any other minimal configuration c' in which they are applicable.*

Proof. According to Remark 3, the configurations c, c' can be written as $c = t_1 c_{r_1, r_2}$ and $c' = t_2 c_{r_1, r_2}$, where $t_1, t_2 \in A^*$, and $c \neq c'$ iff $t_1 \neq t_2$. According to Remark 1 the two rules can be written as $r_i : uv_i \to wz_i \{g_i\}$, $1 \leq i \leq 2$, where for any $a \in A$, a appears in at most one of the v_1 or v_2. The two rules are identifiable in $t_1 c = t_1 uv_1 v_2$, i.e., $t_1 wz_1 v_2 \neq t_1 wv_1 z_2$. This is true iff $z_1 v_2 \neq v_1 z_2$. The rules are applicable in $c' = t_2 uv_1 v_2$, i.e., $uv_i \subseteq c'$ and g_i is true in c', $1 \leq i \leq 2$. Given that $z_1 v_2 \neq v_1 z_2$, it follows that $t_2 wz_1 v_2 \neq t_2 wv_1 z_2$. This means that the two rules are identifiable in $c' = t_2 uv_1 v_2 = t_2 c_{r_1, r_2}$.

Corollary 1. *Two rules r_1 and r_2 identifiable in a minimal configuration $t c_{r_1, r_2}, t \in A^*$, are identifiable in any configuration in which they are applicable.*

Proof. The result is an immediate consequence of Lemmas 1 and 2, and Remarks 1, 2 and 3.

One can formulate a similar result for two multisets of rules.

Corollary 2. *Two multisets of rules M_1 and M_2 identifiable in $t c_{r_{M_1}, r_{M_2}}, t \in A^*$, are identifiable in any configuration in which they are applicable.*

Proof. The result is an immediate consequence of Corollary 1 and Notation above.

From now on, we will always verify the identifiability (or non identifiability) only for the smallest configurations associated with rules or multisets of rules and will not mention these configurations anymore in the results to follow.

The applicability of two rules (multisets of rules) to a certain configuration depends not only on the fact that their left hand sides (the concatenation of the left hand sides) must be contained in the configuration and the guards must be true, but takes into account the execution strategy.

Remark 4. For the *async* transition mode two multisets of rules (and two rules) applicable in a configuration are also applicable in any other bigger configuration, when the corresponding guards are true. For the *seq* mode this is true only for multisets with one single element and obviously for simple rules. In the case of the *max* mode the applicability of the multisets of rules (or rules) to various configurations depends on the contents of the configurations and other available rules. For instance if we consider a kP system containing the rules $r_1 : a \rightarrow a \ \{\geq a\}; r_2 : ab \rightarrow abb \ \{\leq b^{100}\}; r_3 : bb \rightarrow c \ \{\geq b^2\}$ and the configuration $c = ab$ then in c only r_1 and r_2 are applicable and identifiable, but in $c_1 = abb$, containing c, r_1 is no longer applicable, but instead we have r_2 and the multiset $r_1 r_3$ applicable. In ab^{101} r_2 and any multiset containing it are not applicable due to the guard being false; also r_1 is no longer applicable, but $r_1 r_3^{55}$ is now applicable, due to maximal parallelism.

Remark 5. In the following results whenever we refer to arbitrary rules or multisets of rules they are always meant to be applicable with respect to the transition mode.

We now provide a characterisation of the two rules to be (non) identifiable.

Theorem 1. *The rules* $r_1 : x_1 \rightarrow y_1 \ \{g_1\}$ *and* $r_2 : x_2 \rightarrow y_2 \ \{g_2\}$, *are not identifiable if and only if they have the form* $r_1 : uv_1 \rightarrow wv_1 \ \{g_1\}$ *and* $r_2 : uv_2 \rightarrow wv_2 \ \{g_2\}$ *and for any* $a \in A$, *a appears in at most one of* v_1 *or* v_2.

Proof. Let us start with this implication "$\Longrightarrow$". As we have already discussed one can use the rules as $r_1 : uv_1 \rightarrow y_1 \ \{g_1\}$ and $r_2 : uv_2 \rightarrow y_2 \ \{g_2\}$ and for any $a \in A$, a appears in at most one of v_1 or v_2; and one can consider one of the smallest configurations where they are applicable, $tc_{r_1,r_2} = tuv_1v_2$, where $t \in A^*$. Applying these rules to tc_{r_1,r_2}, the following computations are obtained:

$$tc_{r_1,r_2} \Longrightarrow^{r_1} ty_1v_2; tc_{r_1,r_2} \Longrightarrow^{r_2} ty_2v_1.$$

As these rules are not identifiable it turns out that the results of the two computations are the same, i.e., $ty_1v_2 = ty_2v_1$ and this is true iff $y_1v_2 = y_2v_1$. Given that for any $a \in A$, a appears in at most one of v_1 or v_2, it follows that y_1 contains v_1 and y_2 contains v_2, i.e., $y_1 = w_1v_1$ and $y_2 = w_2v_2$. From the equality of the results of the computations it follows that $w_1 = w_2 = w$ and this proves the result.

Let us consider the opposite "$\Longleftarrow$". In this case the rules are $r_1 : uv_1 \rightarrow wv_1 \ \{g_1\}$, $r_2 : uv_2 \rightarrow wv_2 \ \{g_2\}$ and for any $a \in A$, a appears in at most one of v_1 or v_2. We consider again one of the smallest configurations where the rules are applicable, $tc_{r_1,r_2} = uv_1v_2, t \in A^*$, and apply the two rules; then one can obtain:

$$tc_{r_1,r_2} \Longrightarrow^{r_1} twv_1v_2; tc_{r_1,r_2} \Longrightarrow^{r_2} tv_1wv_2.$$

Hence, r_1 and r_2 are not identifiable.

The above proof assumes that v_1 and v_2 are not empty multisets. The result remains true when one of them or both are empty. In the latter case we have the same body of the rules, which might have the right-hand side λ.

Based on the result provided by Theorem 1 one can state when two rules are identifiable.

Corollary 3. *The rules $r_1 : uv_1 \to wz_1 \{g_1\}$ and $r_2 : uv_2 \to wz_2 \{g_2\}$, such that for any $a \in A$, a appears in at most one of v_1 or v_2, are identifiable if and only if $v_1 \neq z_1$ or $v_2 \neq z_2$.*

With the results obtained so far one can determine, for a kP system, whether any two rules are identifiable or not. In various transition modes utilised in kP systems – maximal parallelism or asynchronous mode – in any computation step either single rules or multisets of rules are involved. It is therefore important to determine whether the identifiability of single rules can be lifted to multisets of rules. More precisely, we want to know whether it is true that the identifiability of any pair of simple rules is inherited by the multisets of rules. Unfortunately, this is not true in general, as it is shown by the next example.

Example 2. Let us consider a P system with the following four rules: $r_1 : a \to b \{\geq a\}$, $r_2 : b \to a \{\geq b\}$, $r_3 : c \to d \{\geq c\}$, $r_4 : d \to c \{\geq d\}$. According to Corollary 3, any two rules are identifiable, but $M_1 = r_1 r_2$ and $M_2 = r_3 r_4$ are not, as $r_{M_1} : ab \to ab \{\geq a \wedge \geq b\}$ and $r_{M_2} : cd \to cd \{\geq c \wedge \geq d\}$ are identity rules and according to Theorem 1 they are not identifiable.

However, one can show that some particular multisets of rules are identifiable when their components are. More precisely, we have the following result.

Theorem 2. *If r_1 and r_2 are identifiable then r_1^n and r_2^n are identifiable, for any $n \geq 1$.*

Proof. According to Corollary 3 the rules can be written $r_1 : uv_1 \to wz_1 \{g_1\}$ and $r_2 : uv_2 \to wz_2 \{g_2\}$, such that for any $a \in A$, a appears in at most one of v_1 or v_2, and $v_1 \neq z_1$ or $v_2 \neq z_2$. This implies that $v_1^n \neq z_1^n$ or $v_2^n \neq z_2^n$, for any $n \geq 1$, i.e., r_1^n and r_2^n are identifiable.

One can show that identifiability of any two multisets of rules can be achieved in some special circumstances. More precisely, we show that for any kP system one can construct an equivalent kP system, in which the rules are slightly modified and an additional one introduced, and the later has any multiset of rules identifiable (according to Definition 12).

We first make a notation based on some simple observations. Given a rule $r : x \to y \{g\}$, this is applicable in a configuration w iff $x \subseteq w$ and g is true in w. It follows that the rule is not applicable in w iff $x \not\subseteq w$ or g is not true in w. If $x = a_1^{n_1}...a_h^{n_h}$ and g_x denotes the abstract Boolean expression, $\geq a_1^{n_1}...a_h^{n_h}$, then $x \subseteq w$ iff g_x is true in w and $x \not\subseteq w$ when g_x is false in w.

One can now formulate a result similar with Theorems 2 and 3 in [9], but stronger than those given the context provided by the kP systems model.

Theorem 3. *For any kP system $k\Pi$ there is a kP system $k\Pi_L$ such that (i) $N_{tm}(k\Pi) = N_{tm}(k\Pi_L)$, for any of the transition modes tm, $tm \in \{max, async, seq\}$, and (ii) $k\Pi_L$ has identifiable rules.*

Proof. (i) Let us consider a kP system $k\Pi = (A, \mu_1, C_1, 1)$, as introduced in Definition 2. The compartment $C_1 = (t_1, w_1)$ consists of $t_1 = (R_1, tm)$, $tm \in \{max, async, seq\}$.

We build the following kP system

$$k\Pi_L = (A', \mu_1, C'_1, 1)$$

where $A' = A \cup Lab(R_1) \cup \{\#\}$, with $Lab(R_1) = \{r \mid r : x \to y \{g\} \in R_1\}$ and $\#$ a new symbol. $C'_1 = (t'_1, w_1)$ and $t'_1 = (R'_1, tm)$. In order to define R'_1 we make a few notations.

Let us consider R_1 denoting the set of rules $\{r_1 : x_1 \to y_1 \{g_1\}, \ldots, r_p : x_p \to y_p \{g_p\}\}$. For each rule $r_i : x_i \to y_i \{g_i\}$, we consider the abstract Boolean expression, g_{x_i}, introduced above for the left-hand side of the rule r_i, $1 \le i \le p$. We now denote g_{R_1} the abstract Boolean expression $(g_{x_1} \wedge g_1) \vee \cdots \vee (g_{x_p} \wedge g_p)$. One can observe that g_{R_1} ($\neg g_{R_1}$) is true (false) in a multiset w iff at least a rule (none of the rules) of R_1 is applicable to w.

The multiset R'_1 contains the following rules

(1) $r'_i : x_i \to y_i r_i \{g_i \wedge < \#\}$, $r''_i : x_i \to y_i r_i \# \{g_i \wedge < \#\}$, for $r_i : x_i \to y_i r_i \{g_i\} \in R_1$, $1 \le i \le p$.
(2) $r'''_i : r_i \to \lambda \{\ge \#\}$, $1 \le i \le p$.
(3) $r'_{p+1} : \# \to \lambda \{\neg g_{R_1}\}$.
(4) $r'_{p+2} : \# \to \# \{g_{R_1}\}$.

In order to show that $k\Pi$ and $k\Pi_L$ are equivalent for the transition mode tm, $tm \in \{max, async, seq\}$, one can observe that for any terminal computation in $k\Pi$

$$u_0 = w_1 \Longrightarrow_{tm}^{M_1} u_1 \ldots u_{n-1} \Longrightarrow_{tm}^{M_n} u_n$$

there is a terminal computation in $k\Pi_L$ and vice versa. Firstly, one can obtain

$$u'_0 = w_1 \Longrightarrow_{tm}^{M'_1} u'_1 = u_1 Lab(M_1) \ldots u'_{n-1} = u_{n-1} Lab(M_1) \ldots Lab(M_{n-1})$$
$$\Longrightarrow_{tm}^{M'_n} u'_n = u_n Lab(M_1) \ldots Lab(M_{n-1}) Lab(M_n) \#^h,$$

where $Lab(M)$ denote the multiset of labels of rules occurring in M. M'_i, $1 \le i \le n-1$, is obtained from M_i, $1 \le i \le n-1$, by replacing each rule $r \in R_1$ by its corresponding $r' \in R'_1$; M'_n is obtained from M_n, with r' rules and h r'' rules ($h \ge 1$) introducing $\#^h$. Then we have the following cases

- $tm = max$, implies $u'_n = u_n Lab(M_1) \ldots Lab(M_{n-1}) Lab(M_n) \#^h \Longrightarrow_{tm}^{M'_{n+1}} u'_{n+1} = u_n$, where the multiset of rules M'_{n+1} includes rules of type (2) that remove the labels of the rules $Lab(M_1) \ldots Lab(M_n)$ and rule (3) erasing $\#^h$.
- when $tm = async$, the rules of the multiset M'_{n+1} may be applied in more than a step leading to the same result, u_n.
- for $tm = seq$, we have $h = 1$ and as only one rule is applied in a step, u_n is obtained after a number of step given by the cardinal of M'_{n+1}.

One can observe that in any computation in $k\Pi_L$ in the first steps only rules $r'_i, 1 \leq i \leq p$ of type (1) are applicable. When at least a rule $r''_i, 1 \leq i \leq p$ of type (1) is applied, a symbol $\#$ is introduced. In the next step the rules of type (2) are applicable. The rule (3) is used only when none of the rules of type (1) are applicable, i.e., a computation simulating a terminal computation in $k\Pi$. Otherwise, a rule of type (4) is applicable, leading to an infinite computation.

(ii) Let us consider two multisets of rules, M_1 and M_2, applicable to a configuration in given transition mode. Using a notation introduced earlier, one can obtain the rules, r_{M_1} and r_{M_2}, associated with the multisets of rules, and Remark 1 for providing the following format of them:

- $r_{M_i} : uv_i \rightarrow wz_i Lab(M_i) \{g_i\}, 1 \leq i \leq 2$, when rules of type (1) are used; and
- $r_{M_i} : uv_i \rightarrow wz_i \{g_i\}, 1 \leq i \leq 2$, otherwise.

Obviously, $v_i \neq z_i Lab(M_i), 1 \leq i \leq 2$, in the first case, and $v_i \neq z_i, 1 \leq i \leq 2$, in the last one. According to Corollary 3 the rules are identifiable and consequently the multisets of rules, M_1 and M_2, are identifiable.

4   Conclusions

This paper extends the concept of identifiability, previously introduced in the context of cell-like P systems, to kernel P systems and establishes a fundamental set of properties for identifiable kP systems. Future work will aim at developing a testing approach for kernel P systems. This will be based on automata and X-machine theory and will be able to determine that, under certain, well defined conditions, the implementation conforms to the specification.

Acknowledgements. This work is supported by a grant of the Romanian National Authority for Scientific Research, CNCS-UEFISCDI, project number PN-III-P4-ID-PCE-2016-0210.

References

1. Agrigoroaiei, O., Ciobanu, G.: Flattening the transition P systems with dissolution. In: Gheorghe, M., Hinze, T., Păun, G., Rozenberg, G., Salomaa, A. (eds.) CMC 2010. LNCS, vol. 6501, pp. 53–64. Springer, Heidelberg (2010). https://doi.org/10.1007/978-3-642-18123-8_7
2. Ciobanu, G., Pérez-Jiménez, M.J., Păun, Gh.: Applications of Membrane Computing (Natural Computing Series). Springer, Heidelberg (2005). https://doi.org/10.1007/3-540-29937-8
3. Dinneen, M.J., Yun-Bum, K., Nicolescu, R.: Faster synchronization in P systems. Nat. Comput. **11**(4), 637–651 (2012)
4. Freund, R., Leporati, A., Mauri, G., Porreca, A.E., Verlan, S., Zandron, C.: Flattening in (tissue) P systems. In: Alhazov, A., Cojocaru, S., Gheorghe, M., Rogozhin, Y., Rozenberg, G., Salomaa, A. (eds.) CMC 2013. LNCS, vol. 8340, pp. 173–188. Springer, Heidelberg (2014). https://doi.org/10.1007/978-3-642-54239-8_13

5. Frisco, P., Gheorghe, M., Pérez-Jiménez, M.J. (eds.): Applications of Membrane Computing in Systems and Synthetic Biology. ECC, vol. 7. Springer, Cham (2014). https://doi.org/10.1007/978-3-319-03191-0

6. Gheorghe, M., Ipate, F.: On testing P systems. In: Corne, D.W., Frisco, P., Păun, G., Rozenberg, G., Salomaa, A. (eds.) WMC 2008. LNCS, vol. 5391, pp. 204–216. Springer, Heidelberg (2009). https://doi.org/10.1007/978-3-540-95885-7_15

7. Gheorghe, M., Ipate, F., Dragomir, C.: Kernel P systems. In: Pre-Proceedings of the 10th Brainstorming Week on Membrane Computing, BWMC10, pp. 153–170. Fénix Editora, Universidad de Sevilla (2012)

8. Gheorghe, M., et al.: Kernel P systems - version 1. In: Pre-Proceedings of the 11th Brainstorming Week on Membrane Computing, BWMC11, pp. 97–124. Fenix Editora, Universidad de Sevilla (2013)

9. Gheorghe, M., Ipate, F., Konur, S.: Testing based on identifiable P systems using cover automata and X-machines. Inf. Sci. **372**, 565–578 (2016)

10. Gheorghe, M., Konur, S., Ipate, F., Mierla, L., Bakir, M.E., Stannett, M.: An Integrated model checking toolset for kernel P systems. In: Rozenberg, G., Salomaa, A., Sempere, J.M., Zandron, C. (eds.) CMC 2015. LNCS, vol. 9504, pp. 153–170. Springer, Cham (2015). https://doi.org/10.1007/978-3-319-28475-0_11

11. Gimel'farb, G.L., Nicolescu, R., Ragavan, S.: P system implementation of dynamic programming stereo. J. Math. Imaging Vis. **47**(1–2), 13–26 (2013)

12. Ipate, F., Gheorghe, M.: Mutation based testing of P systems. Int. J. Comput. Commun. Control **4**(3), 253–262 (2009)

13. Manca, V.: Infobiotics. ECC, vol. 3. Springer, Heidelberg (2013). https://doi.org/10.1007/978-3-642-36223-1

14. Nicolescu, R.: Structured grid algorithms modelled with complex objects. In: Rozenberg, G., Salomaa, A., Sempere, J.M., Zandron, C. (eds.) CMC 2015. LNCS, vol. 9504, pp. 321–337. Springer, Cham (2015). https://doi.org/10.1007/978-3-319-28475-0_22

15. Păun, Gh.: Computing with membranes. J. Comput. Syst. Sci. **61**(1), 108–143 (2000)

16. Păun, Gh., Rozenberg, G., Salomaa, A. (eds.): The Oxford Handbook of Membrane Computing. Oxford University Press, Inc., Oxford (2010)

17. Verlan, S.: Using the formal framework for P systems. In: Alhazov, A., Cojocaru, S., Gheorghe, M., Rogozhin, Y., Rozenberg, G., Salomaa, A. (eds.) CMC 2013. LNCS, vol. 8340, pp. 56–79. Springer, Heidelberg (2014). https://doi.org/10.1007/978-3-642-54239-8_6

Other Buds in Membrane Computing

Miguel A. Gutiérrez-Naranjo[✉]

Department of Computer Science and Artificial Intelligence, University of Seville,
Seville, Spain
magutier@us.es

Abstract. It is well-known the huge Mario's contribution to the development of Membrane Computing. Many researchers may relate his name to the theory of complexity classes in P systems, the research of frontiers of the tractability or the application of Membrane Computing to model real-life situations as the Quorum Sensing System in *Vibrio fischeri* or the Bearded Vulture ecosystem. Beyond these research areas, in the last years Mario has presented many new research lines which can be considered as *buds* in the robust Membrane Computing tree. Many of them were the origin of new research branches, but some others are still waiting to be developed. This paper revisits some of these *buds*.

1 Introduction

Mario has contributed to the development of Membrane Computing in many research lines (see, e.g., [16,24,57]). From his early works on the formalization of transition P systems [53] or the links between P systems and diophantine sets [61], Mario has published dozens of papers on Membrane Computing. His contributions cover many different areas of the P systems research, from theoretical ones to real-life case studies applications, together with the development of different simulators or the proposal of many different P systems models. Many young researchers may relate his name to the theory of complexity classes in P systems [51], the research of frontiers of the tractability [46] or to the application of Membrane Computing to model real-life situations as the Quorum Sensing System in *Vibrio fischeri* [59] or the Bearded Vulture ecosystem [9], but Mario's contributions go deeper in many other areas.

Beyond these strong branches in the robust Membrane Computing tree, there are many other research lines in Membrane Computing where Mario also has made a pioneer contribution. Some of these ideas were shortly developed in a few papers and others only appear in the paper where they were presented. I call *buds* these ideas. In this paper, I revisit some of these *buds* which are waiting for young researchers to be studied in depth.

The paper is organized as follows: In Sect. 2, some papers where Mario explored the links between Membrane Computing and Artificial Intelligence are revisited. They cover aspects related to sorting and searching algorithms and machine learning. Section 3 recalls other contributions bridging P systems with

© Springer Nature Switzerland AG 2018
C. Graciani et al. (Eds.): Pérez-Jiménez Festschrift, LNCS 11270, pp. 142–154, 2018.
https://doi.org/10.1007/978-3-030-00265-7_12

other aspects of Computer Science, as metrics defined on configurations of P systems, properties of Markov chains or the possibility of computing backwards. Later, Sect. 4 revisits some papers related to the graphical representation of P systems and Sect. 5 some other papers not included in the previous sections. Finally, some conclusions are drawn.

2 Artificial Intelligence

Mario is a full professor at the Department of Computer Science and Artificial Intelligence in the University of Seville, and both disciplines, Computer Science and Artificial Intelligence, have been present in Mario's research. We revisit some of these contributions.

2.1 Sorting

Sorting sequences of items according to specified criteria is on the basis on many computational processes and this is a recurrent problem in Membrane Computing (see, e.g. [1,2]). In the case of parallel algorithms, the problem is especially interesting, since it requires an appropriate combination of computation and communication.

In [14], two models for sorting sequences of numbers were presented. They were based on bitonic sorting networks. The key idea is the use of *bitonic merge-sort* which is a parallel algorithm for sorting introduced by Batcher [3]. The first of the models consists on N membranes, each of them storing two numbers; one number is an element of the sequence, and the other one is an auxiliary register used to route values. A number is encoded as the multiplicity of a symbol a in each membrane. Moreover, membranes are disposed on a $2D$-mesh, where only communication between neighboring membranes on the mesh is permitted. This model uses a variant of P systems called *P systems with dynamic communication graphs* [11], which is closely related to the implementation of the bitonic sort on the $2D$-mesh[1]. The second model presented in [14] consisted of only one membrane, where all the N numbers were encoded as occurrences of N different symbols. Restrictions on communication were no longer imposed, as if the underlying communication graph was the complete graph. Later, a new model which takes ideas from both models has been presented in [15].

2.2 Searching

The design of solutions for **NP**-complete problems in Membrane Computing usually trades time against space in order to solve these problems in polynomial (even linear) time with respect to the size of the input data [51]. The cost is the

---

[1] Such model of *P systems with dynamic communication graphs* is another of the many *buds* which is waiting to be explored. It follows the same lines as the one presented in [12,13].

number of resources, mainly the number of membranes, which grows exponentially. The usual idea of such brute force algorithms is to encode each feasible solution in one membrane. The number of candidate solutions is exponential in the input size, but the coding and checking process can be done in polynomial time. In spite of the theoretical success, such approaches are far from being applicable to real-world problems and other research lines must be explored. In this context, Mario has also made contributions by applying into the Membrane Computing framework some ideas from searching methods studied in Artificial Intelligence.

In [34], the problem of solving the N-queens puzzle with P systems was studied by considering a depth-first search strategy. Depth-first search is a well-known algorithm for exploring tree or graph data structures. One starts at the root (selecting some arbitrary node as the root in the case of a graph) and explores as far as possible along each branch before backtracking. In the paper, the authors explore the possibilities of introducing such search strategy in the framework of Membrane Computing. The case study was the N-queens puzzle. This is an old well-known problem. It is a generalization of the 8-queens problem which consists of placing N chess queens on an $N \times N$ board. In [30], a first solution to the N-queens problem in Membrane Computing had been shown, but the solution was based on an appropriate encoding of the problem in a SAT formula and the use of a modified solution for the SAT problem with P systems. The same problem of N-queens also was considered in [35] where some ideas from local search were studied in the framework of Membrane Computing. In this paper, from an initial $N \times N$ chessboard with N queens, different movements of the queens are performed in order to *improve* the position. Such improvements are evaluated by using the notion of *collision* [63]: *The number of collisions on a diagonal line is one less than the number of queens on the line, if the line is not empty, and zero if the line is empty. The sum of collisions on all diagonal lines is the total number of collisions between queens.* The target of the computation is to move from a board to another, with the corresponding encoding, by decreasing the number of *collisions*. Figure 1, borrowed from [35], illustrates the process.

2.3   Machine Learning

Mario has also made contributions by linking Membrane Computing to Machine Learning. In this section, two of them are revisited. The first one takes ideas form *supervised learning* and the second one from *unsupervised learning*.

Spiking neural P systems (SN P systems) were introduced in 2006 (see [42]) with the aim of incorporating in Membrane Computing ideas specific to spike-based neural networks. Only two years later, a first model for Hebbian learning with spiking neural P systems was presented [32]. The target of this paper was to explore the applicability of ideas from the artificial neural networks into the SN P systems. Artificial neural networks [40] is one of the most powerful tools in Machine Learning and the most extended learning algorithm for such networks, backpropagation [62], can be roughly described as the iterative refinement of the weights associated to the synapses among neurons in order to minimize a

Fig. 1. Starting from a configuration C_0 with 4 collisions (up-left) we can reach C_1 with 3 collisions (up-right) and then C_2 with 2 collisions (bottom-left) and finally C_3 with 0 collisions (bottom-right), which is a solution to the 5-queens problem. Figure borrowed from [35].

loss function. Such change in the weights is inspired in Donald Hebb's works [41] and all the learning processes based on these principles are called *Hebbian Learning*. In [32], a first approach to Hebbian learning in the framework of Membrane Computing was presented. In this paper, a new feature coming from alive neurons was added to the SN P systems: the *decay*. Such decay of the electric potential inside an alive neuron along time was codified by endowing the rules with a finite non-increasing sequence of natural numbers called the decaying sequence. Besides these sequences, the learning model is structured in *Hebbian SN P system units*, which consider weights associated to the synapses between neurons. According to the learning process inspired by Hebb's work, the weights change along time according to the concept of *efficacy* introduced in the paper. In this way, the efficacy of the synapses with a high contribution to reach the spiking threshold is increased and, on the other hand, if the synapses has no contribution (or it is low) the efficacy is decreased.

The second *bud* revisited in this section is related to the data clustering problem. In the paper [32] discussed above, Mario made an exploration by bridging Membrane Computing with supervised learning. The proposal in [50] links P systems with unsupervised learning. The clustering algorithm presented in this paper is based on a tissue-like P system with a loop structure of cells. The objects of the cells express the candidate cluster centers and are evolved by the evolution rules. Based on the loop membrane structure, the communication rules realize a local neighborhood topology, which helps the co-evolution of the objects and improves the diversity of objects in the system. The tissue-like P system can effectively search for the optimal clustering partition with the help of its parallel computing advantage. The proposed clustering algorithm is evaluated on four artificial data sets and six real-life data sets. Experimental results show that the proposed clustering algorithm is superior or competitive to classical k-means algorithm and other evolutionary clustering algorithms.

3   Other Areas of Computer Science

Besides Artificial Intelligence, Mario has also contributed to bridge Membrane Computing with many other areas in Computer Science.

As a first example, we can consider the study of metrics on configurations presented in [19]. In this paper, two different (weak) metrics were presented. The first one was based on the distance between regions. The distance between two regions was defined as the cardinality of the symmetrical difference of their associated multisets. This definition was used to measure the distance between two occurrences of the same membrane in two different configurations and the difference between configurations is the sum of the differences between their regions. For the definition of the second weak metric, a new auxiliary concept called *dependency graph* was defined. This concept has been widely used for studying frontiers on complexity classes (see, e.g., [38]), but it was firstly defined in this paper for studying the proximity between configurations. The distance between two nodes of the dependency graph is the basis of the study of proximity between configurations.

Other remarkable Mario's contribution which is still a *bud* in the Membrane Computing tree is related to the link between P systems and Markov chains. In [10], the authors propose a first approach to the problem of computing the natural powers of the transition matrix of a finite and homogeneous Markov chain. Such computation allows to estimate its limit in the case that it is convergent, and therefore, to know the stationary distribution of the process. This subject has been treated with other bio-inspired techniques in [7] where two algorithms based on DNA were described. The proposed cellular computing solution provides an exact solution in a time which is linear in the order of the power and it is independent of the number of states of the Markov chain. Such Markov chains were also considered later in [8]. In this paper, the aperiodicity of irreducible Markov chains was characterized by using P systems.

A different question was studied in [33], where the problem of computing backwards with P systems was considered. The starting point for this study was to look for the previous state of a given one in a computational model where the time is considered in a discrete way. In this study, the authors consider a variant of the dependency graphs [18] for introducing a representation of the computation of a P system based on matrices. This matrix representation opens a door for the study of algebraic properties of cell-like and tissue-like P systems and represents one of the most promising *buds* waiting to be explored. Mario has also contributed to the study of the matrix representation of spiking neural P systems [66] which is the basis of the efficient simulation of such devices [5].

4   Graphics

Many P system models allow to change their membrane structure by adding new membranes (e.g., by the application of *creation* or *division* rules [52]) or removing membranes (by the application of *dissolution* rules [39]). This evolution in time of the membrane structure of a P system is the starting point for studying the evolution of graphical structures.

The first approach for linking the computation of P systems with the evolution of graphical structures was presented in [25, 26]. In these papers, P systems were used to simulate the growth and development of living plants. This approach mixes L systems [23, 45] and P systems. A different approach was presented in [60]. In this paper, the growth of branching structures was studied by using exclusively P systems. The key idea is the use of a cell-like P system model with evolution and creation rules. The membrane structure of a cell-like model is a tree-like graph which is easily visualized as a branching structure. The geometrical properties of the associated picture can be obtained by the association of a *meaning* to the objects in the multisets in the different membranes. For example, each membrane represents a segment in the corresponding picture and the length of the drawn segment depends on the multiplicity of a *length-unit* object. These ideas were also considered in [58], where a specific software for this graphical representation was developed. Some examples of polygons, spirals, friezes and plants can be found in this paper. Figure 2 shows some of them.

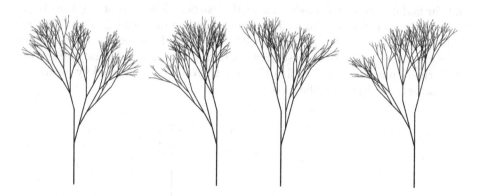

Fig. 2. Graphical representation of four configurations of a P system. Images borrowed from [58].

A different approach was presented in [31]. It is also related to the graphical representation of P systems, but it explores the possibility of Membrane Computing devices for representing fractals. The starting point here is that a fractal can be considered, roughly speaking, as a self-similar geometrical structure which can be generated by the application of (infinitely repeated) fixed rules. In this way, the generation of fractals can be associated, on the one hand, to the evolution of P systems by using creation rules for obtaining a new (and more precise) stage in the generation of the fractal and, on the other hand, to the *interpretation* of the symbols inside the membranes for representing the *geometrical information* of the fractal. The paper presents a pair of classic fractals, the Koch curve [43,44] and the middle third Cantor set [6], in the framework of P systems. Besides this mathematical objects, the paper also points out the possibility of using the non-determinism of P systems for studying random fractals, which can be considered as the formal representation of many real-life objects with fractal dimension[2].

5   Other Buds

The contributions made by Mario cover many different areas, some of them by bridging Membrane Computing with other unexpected research fields. One of these *rara avis* can be found in [28] where a Membrane Computing model for ballistic depositions was presented. The starting point in this study is the evolution of *rough interfaces* between different media. The propagation of forest fires [17] or the growth of a colony of bacteria [4] are examples showing such interfaces, although all surfaces in Nature can be seen as rough surfaces, since the concept of roughness is associated to the scale and all the natural surfaces are rough at an appropriate scale. The evolution of a surface can be modelled by the concepts of *erosion*, where some elements are removed, or *deposition*, where new elements are placed. Ballistic Deposition was proposed by Vold [65] and Sutherland [64] as a model where the particle follows a straight vertical trajectory until it reaches the surface, whereupon it sticks (see Fig. 3). In [28] the problem was modelled by a tissue-like P system model with a linear membrane structure where each cell represents a column of the aggregate and the pieces of information needed for encoding the growth process are encoded by means of the multisets of objects in the cells.

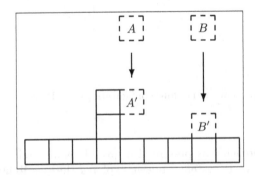

Fig. 3. Ballistic Deposition. Figure borrowed from [28].

---

[2] These ideas were also considered in [37], but it is still one of the most promising *buds* waiting to be developed.

A further exploration looking for links between Membrane Computing and other research areas was presented in [54]. In this case, the target was to bridge P systems and *reaction systems*. Reaction systems, also known as *R systems*, is a bio-inspired computation model [21,22] which shares with P systems some features as the use of populations of reactants (molecules) which evolve by means of reactions. This paper compares the two computation models, and further results can be found in [56].

Another theoretical *bud* can be found in [36]. In this paper, the degree of parallelism in P systems is investigated. The starting point is to study different tools for comparing the designs of P systems able to perform the same task. Two designs can be compared according to many different criteria. In this paper, the authors focus the attention on the parallelism. In this way, a *bad* design of a P system consists of a P system which does not exploit its parallelism, that is, it works as a sequential machine: in each step only one object evolve in one membrane whereas the remaining objects do not evolve. On the other hand, a *good* design consists of a P system in which a huge amount of objects are evolving simultaneously in all membranes. If both P systems perform the same task, it is obvious that the second one is a better design than the first one.

6   Conclusions

Mario's contribution to the development of Membrane Computing has been enormous and in the last years he has been one of the pillars of the Membrane Computing community[3]. The research lines opened by him cover all the research fields in Membrane Computing. Many of his proposals have been studied in depth, but some of them are still waiting for research efforts. In this paper, we have revisited some of them but many others have not been cited in the previous sections. I encourage the young researchers to read Mario's contributions cited in this paper, but not only them. Many other papers not cited here contain seminal ideas which are waiting for young and enthusiastic researchers who can help these *buds* develop and become new strong branches in the Membrane Computing tree.

References

1. Alhazov, A., Sburlan, D.: Static sorting P systems. In: Ciobanu et al. [16], pp. 215–252. https://doi.org/10.1007/3-540-29937-8_8
2. Ardelean, I.I., Ceterchi, R., Tomescu, A.I.: Sorting with P systems: a biological perspective. Rom. J. Inf. Sci. Technol. 11(3), 243–252 (2008). http://www.imt.ro/romjist/Volum11/Number11_3/pdf/03-Ardelean.pdf

---

[3] At the moment of writing this paper (April 2018), according to Scopus, Mario has published in collaboration with 150 co-authors. This fact can give an idea of Mario's role as an *engine* of the P systems community.

3. Batcher, K.E.: Sorting networks and their applications. In: American Federation of Information Processing Societies: AFIPS Conference Proceedings: 1968 Spring Joint Computer Conference, Atlantic City, NJ, USA, vol. 32, pp. 307–314. Thomson Book Company, Washington D.C. http://doi.acm.org/10.1145/1468075.1468121

4. Ben-Jacob, E., Schochet, O., Tenenbaum, A., Cohen, I., Czirok, A., Vicsek, T.: Generic modelling of cooperative growth patterns in bacterial colonies. Nature **368**(6466), 46–49 (1994). https://www.nature.com/articles/368046a0

5. Cabarle, F.G.C., Adorna, H., Martínez, M.A.: A spiking neural P system simulator based on CUDA. In: Gheorghe, M., Păun, G., Rozenberg, G., Salomaa, A., Verlan, S. (eds.) CMC 2011. LNCS, vol. 7184, pp. 87–103. Springer, Heidelberg (2012). https://doi.org/10.1007/978-3-642-28024-5_8

6. Cantor, G.: Über unendliche, lineare punktmannichfaltigkeiten v. Math. Ann. **21**, 545–591 (1883). https://doi.org/10.1007/BF01446819

7. Cardona, M., Colomer, M., Conde, J., Miret, J., Miró, J., Zaragoza, A.: Markov chains: computing limit existence and approximations with DNA. Biosystems **81**(3), 261–266 (2005). http://www.sciencedirect.com/science/article/pii/S0303264705000663

8. Cardona, M., Colomer, M.A., Pérez-Jiménez, M.J.: Characterizing the aperiodicity of irreducible Markov chains by using P systems. In: Gutiérrez-Escudero et al. [29], pp. 81–95, https://idus.us.es/xmlui/handle/11441/38857

9. Cardona, M., Colomer, M.A., Pérez-Jiménez, M.J., Sanuy, D., Margalida, A.: Modeling ecosystems using P systems: the bearded vulture, a case study. In: Corne, D.W., Frisco, P., Păun, G., Rozenberg, G., Salomaa, A. (eds.) WMC 2008. LNCS, vol. 5391, pp. 137–156. Springer, Heidelberg (2009). https://doi.org/10.1007/978-3-540-95885-7_11

10. Cardona, M., Colomer, M.Á., Pérez-Jiménez, M.J., Zaragoza, A.: Handling Markov chains with membrane computing. In: Gutiérrez-Naranjo, M.A., et al. (eds.) Fourth Brainstorming Week on Membrane Computing, vol. I, pp. 99–111. Fénix Editora, Sevilla (2006). https://idus.us.es/xmlui/handle/11441/36996

11. Ceterchi, R., Pérez-Jiménez, M.J.: On two-dimensional mesh networks and their simulation with P systems. In: Mauri et al. [49], pp. 259–277. https://doi.org/10.1007/978-3-540-31837-8_15

12. Ceterchi, R., Pérez-Jiménez, M.J.: A perfect shuffle algorithm for reduction processes and its simulation with P systems. In: International Conference on Computers and Communications, pp. 92–97 (2004). http://www.cs.us.es/~marper/investigacion/oradea.pdf

13. Ceterchi, R., Pérez-Jiménez, M.J.: Simulating shuffle-exchange networks with P systems. In: Păun et al. [55], pp. 117–129. https://idus.us.es/xmlui/handle/11441/34641

14. Ceterchi, R., Pérez-Jiménez, M.J., Tomescu, A.I.: Simulating the bitonic sort using P systems. In: Eleftherakis, G., Kefalas, P., Păun, G., Rozenberg, G., Salomaa, A. (eds.) WMC 2007. LNCS, vol. 4860, pp. 172–192. Springer, Heidelberg (2007). https://doi.org/10.1007/978-3-540-77312-2_11

15. Ceterchi, R., Pérez-Jiménez, M.J., Tomescu, A.I.: Sorting omega networks simulated with P systems: optimal data layouts. In: Díaz-Pernil et al. [20], pp. 79–92. https://idus.us.es/xmlui/bitstream/handle/11441/68018/dl-ps-4a.pdf

16. Ciobanu, G., Pérez-Jiménez, M.J., Păun, Gh. (eds.): Applications of Membrane Computing. Natural Computing. Springer, Heidelberg (2006). https://doi.org/10.1007/3-540-29937-8

17. Clar, S., Drossel, B., Schwabl, F.: Forest fires and other examples of self-organized criticality. J. Phys.: Condens. Matter **8**(37), 6803 (1996). http://stacks.iop.org/0953-8984/8/i=37/a=004

18. Cordón-Franco, A., Gutiérrez-Naranjo, M.A., Pérez-Jiménez, M.J., Riscos-Núñez, A.: Exploring computation trees associated with P systems. In: Mauri et al. [49], pp. 278–286. https://doi.org/10.1007/978-3-540-31837-8_16

19. Cordón-Franco, A., Gutiérrez-Naranjo, M.A., Pérez-Jiménez, M.J., Riscos-Núñez, A.: Weak metrics on configurations of a P system. In: Păun et al. [55], pp. 139–151. https://idus.us.es/xmlui/handle/11441/34641

20. Díaz-Pernil, D., Graciani, C., Gutiérrez-Naranjo, M.A., Păun, Gh., Pérez-Hurtado, I., Riscos-Núñez, A. (eds.): Sixth Brainstorming Week on Membrane Computing. Fénix Editora, Sevilla (2008)

21. Ehrenfeucht, A., Rozenberg, G.: Basic notions of reaction systems. In: Calude, C.S., Calude, E., Dinneen, M.J. (eds.) DLT 2004. LNCS, vol. 3340, pp. 27–29. Springer, Heidelberg (2004). https://doi.org/10.1007/978-3-540-30550-7_3

22. Ehrenfeucht, A., Rozenberg, G.: Reaction systems. Fundam. Inform. **75**(1–4), 263–280 (2007). http://content.iospress.com/articles/fundamenta-informaticae/fi75-1-4-15

23. Frijters, D., Lindenmayer, A.: A model for the growth and flowering of aster novae-angliae on the basis of table $<1,0>$ L-systems. In: Rozenberg, G., Salomaa, A. (eds.) L Systems. LNCS, vol. 15, pp. 24–52. Springer, Heidelberg (1974). https://doi.org/10.1007/3-540-06867-8_2

24. Frisco, P., Gheorghe, M., Pérez-Jiménez, M.J.: Applications of Membrane Computing in Systems and Synthetic Biology. Springer, Cham (2014). https://doi.org/10.1007/978-3-319-03191-0

25. Georgiou, A., Gheorghe, M.: Generative devices used in graphics. In: Alhazov, A., Martín-Vide, C., Păun, Gh. (eds.) Preproceedings of the Workshop on Membrane Computing. Technical report, vol. 28/03, pp. 266–272. Research Group on Mathematical Linguistics, Universitat Rovira i Virgili, Tarragona (2003)

26. Georgiou, A., Gheorghe, M., Bernardini, F.: Membrane-based devices used in computer graphics. In: Ciobanu, G., Păun, Gh., Pérez-Jiménez, M.J. (eds.) Applications of Membrane Computing. Natural Computing, pp. 253–281. Springer, Heidelberg (2006). https://doi.org/10.1007/3-540-29937-8_9

27. Graciani, C., Păun, Gh., Romero-Jiménez, A., Sancho-Caparrini, F. (eds.): Fourth Brainstorming Week on Membrane Computing, vol. II. Fénix Editora, Sevilla (2006)

28. Graciani-Díaz, C., Gutiérrez-Naranjo, M.A., Pérez-Jiménez, M.J.: A membrane computing model for ballistic depositions. In: Gutiérrez-Naranjo, M.A. et al. (eds.) Fifth Brainstorming Week on Membrane Computing, pp. 179–197. Fénix Editora, Sevilla (2007). https://idus.us.es/xmlui/handle/11441/38583

29. Gutiérrez-Escudero, R., Gutiérrez-Naranjo, M.A., Păun, Gh., Pérez-Hurtado, I., Riscos-Núñez, A. (eds.): Seventh Brainstorming Week on Membrane Computing, vol. I. Fénix Editora, Sevilla (2009)

30. Gutiérrez-Naranjo, M.A., Martínez-del-Amor, M.A., Pérez-Hurtado, I., Pérez-Jiménez, M.J.: Solving the N-queens puzzle with P systems. In: Gutiérrez-Escudero et al. [29], pp. 199–210. https://idus.us.es/xmlui/handle/11441/38865

31. Gutiérrez-Naranjo, M.A., Pérez-Jiménez, M.J.: Fractals and P systems. In: Graciani et al. [27], pp. 65–86. https://idus.us.es/xmlui/handle/11441/38328

32. Gutiérrez-Naranjo, M.A., Pérez-Jiménez, M.J.: A first model for Hebbian learning with spiking neural P systems. In: Díaz-Pernil et al. [20], pp. 211–233. https://idus.us.es/xmlui/handle/11441/38778

33. Gutiérrez-Naranjo, M.A., Pérez-Jiménez, M.J.: Computing backwards with P systems. In: Gutiérrez-Escudero et al. [29], pp. 211–226. https://idus.us.es/xmlui/handle/11441/38866

34. Gutiérrez-Naranjo, M.A., Pérez-Jiménez, M.J.: Membrane computing meets artificial intelligence: a case study. In: Martínez del Amor et al. [47], pp. 133–144. https://idus.us.es/xmlui/handle/11441/39004

35. Gutiérrez-Naranjo, M.A., Pérez-Jiménez, M.J.: Implementing local search with membrane computing. In: Martínez del Amor et al. [48], pp. 159–168. https://idus.us.es/xmlui/handle/11441/39476

36. Gutiérrez-Naranjo, M.A., Pérez-Jiménez, M.J., Riscos-Núñez, A.: An approach to the degree of parallelism in P systems. In: Graciani-Díaz et al. [27], pp. 87–104. https://idus.us.es/xmlui/handle/11441/38335

37. Gutiérrez-Naranjo, M.A., Pérez-Jiménez, M.J., Riscos-Núñez, A., Romero-Campero, F.J.: How to express tumours using membrane systems. Prog. Nat. Sci. **17**(4), 449–457 (2007). http://www.tandfonline.com/doi/abs/10.1080/10020070708541022

38. Gutiérrez–Naranjo, M.A., Pérez–Jiménez, M.J., Riscos–Núñez, A., Romero–Campero, F.J.: On the power of dissolution in P systems with active membranes. In: Freund, R., Păun, G., Rozenberg, G., Salomaa, A. (eds.) WMC 2005. LNCS, vol. 3850, pp. 224–240. Springer, Heidelberg (2006). https://doi.org/10.1007/11603047_16

39. Gutiérrez-Naranjo, M.A., Pérez-Jiménez, M.J., Riscos-Núñez, A., Romero-Campero, F.J.: Computational efficiency of dissolution rules in membrane systems. Int. J. Comput. Math. **83**(7), 593–611 (2006). https://doi.org/10.1080/00207160601065413

40. Haykin, S.S.: Neural Networks and Learning Machines, 3rd edn. Pearson Education, Upper Saddle River (2009)

41. Hebb, D.O.: The Organization of Behavior: A Neuropsychological Theory. Wiley, New York (1949)

42. Ionescu, M., Păun, Gh., Yokomori, T.: Spiking neural P systems. Fundam. Inform. **71**(2–3), 279–308 (2006). http://content.iospress.com/articles/fundamenta-informaticae/fi71-2-3-08

43. Koch, H.v.: Sur une courbe continue sans tangente, obtenue par une construction géométrique élémentaire. Arkiv för Matematik, Astronomi och Fysik **1**, 681–704 (1904)

44. von Koch, H.: Une méthode géometrique élémentaire pour l'étude de certaines questions de la théorie des courbes planes. Acta Math. **30**, 145–174 (1906). https://doi.org/10.1007/BF02418570

45. Lindenmayer, A.: Developmental systems without cellular interactions, their languages and grammars. J. Theor. Biol. **30**(3), 455–484 (1971)

46. Macías-Ramos, L.F., Martínez-del-Amor, M.A., Pérez-Jiménez, M.J., Riscos-Núñez, A., Valencia-Cabrera, L.: Unconventional approaches to tackle the P Versus NP problem. In: Păun, Gh., Rozenberg, G., Salomaa, A. (eds.) Discrete Mathematics and Computer Science. Memoriam Alexandru Mateescu (1952–2005), pp. 223–237. The Publishing House of the Romanian Academy (2014)

47. Martínez del Amor, M.A., Păun, Gh., Pérez Hurtado, I., Riscos-Núñez, A. (eds.): Eighth Brainstorming Week on Membrane Computing. Fénix Editora, Sevilla (2010)

48. Martínez del Amor, M.A., Păun, Gh., Pérez Hurtado, I., Romero Campero, F.J., Valencia-Cabrera, L. (eds.): Ninth Brainstorming Week on Membrane Computing. Fénix Editora, Sevilla (2011)

49. Mauri, G., Păun, Gh., Pérez-Jiménez, M.J., Rozenberg, G., Salomaa, A. (eds.): WMC 2004. LNCS, vol. 3365. Springer, Heidelberg (2005). https://doi.org/10.1007/b106721

50. Peng, H., Zhang, J., Wang, J., Wang, T., Pérez-Jiménez, M.J., Riscos-Núñez, A.: Membrane clustering: a novel clustering algorithm under membrane computing. In: Macías-Ramos, L.F. et al. (eds.) Twelfth Brainstorming Week on Membrane Computing, pp. 311–327. Fénix Editora, Sevilla (2014). https://idus.us.es/xmlui/handle/11441/33577

51. Pérez–Jiménez, M.J.: A computational complexity theory in membrane computing. In: Păun, Gh., Pérez-Jiménez, M.J., Riscos-Núñez, A., Rozenberg, G., Salomaa, A. (eds.) WMC 2009. LNCS, vol. 5957, pp. 125–148. Springer, Heidelberg (2010). https://doi.org/10.1007/978-3-642-11467-0_10

52. Pérez-Jiménez, M.J., Riscos-Núñez, A., Romero-Jiménez, A., Woods, D.: Complexity - membrane division, membrane creation. In: Păun et al. [57], pp. 302–336

53. Pérez-Jiménez, M.J., Sancho-Caparrini, F.: A formalization of transition P systems. Fundam. Inform. 49(1–3), 261–272 (2002). http://content.iospress.com/articles/fundamenta-informaticae/fi49-1-3-20

54. Păun, Gh., Pérez-Jiménez, M.J.: Towards bridging two cell-inspired models: P systems and R systems. In: Martínez del Amor et al. [48], pp. 305–316. https://idus.us.es/xmlui/handle/11441/39575

55. Păun, Gh., Riscos-Núñez, A., Romero-Jiménez, Á., Sancho-Caparrini, F. (eds.): Second Brainstorming Week on Membrane Computing. Fénix Editora, Sevilla (2004)

56. Păun, Gh., Pérez-Jiménez, M.J., Rozenberg, G.: Bridging membrane and reaction systems – Further results and research topics. In: Valencia-Cabrera, L., et al. (eds.) Eleventh Brainstorming Week on Membrane Computing, pp. 243–256. Fénix Editora, Sevilla, February 2013. https://idus.us.es/xmlui/handle/11441/33819

57. Păun, Gh., Rozenberg, G., Salomaa, A. (eds.): The Oxford Handbook of Membrane Computing. Oxford University Press, Oxford (2010)

58. Rivero-Gil, E., Gutiérrez-Naranjo, M.A., Pérez-Jiménez, M.J.: Graphics and P systems: experiments with JPLANT. In: Díaz-Pernil et al. [20], pp. 241–253. https://idus.us.es/xmlui/handle/11441/38787

59. Romero-Campero, F.J., Pérez-Jiménez, M.J.: A model of the quorum sensing system in Vibrio fischeri using P systems. Artif. Life 14(1), 95–109 (2008). https://doi.org/10.1162/artl.2008.14.1.95

60. Romero-Jiménez, A., Gutiérrez-Naranjo, M.A., Pérez-Jiménez, M.J.: The growth of branching structures with P systems. In: Graciani et al. [27], pp. 253–265. http://www.gcn.us.es/4BWMC/vol2/thegrowth.pdf

61. Jiménez, Á.R., Pérez Jiménez, M.J.: Generation of diophantine sets by computing P systems with external output. In: Calude, C.S., Dinneen, M.J., Peper, F. (eds.) UMC 2002. LNCS, vol. 2509, pp. 176–190. Springer, Heidelberg (2002). https://doi.org/10.1007/3-540-45833-6_15

62. Rumelhart, D.E., Hinton, G.E., Williams, R.J.: Learning representations by back-propagating errors. Nature 323, 533–536 (1986)

63. Sosic, R., Gu, J.: Efficient local search with conflict minimization: a case study of the N-queens problem. IEEE Trans. Knowl. Data Eng. 6(5), 661–668 (1994)

64. Sutherland, D.: Comments on Vold's simulation of floc formation. J. Colloid Interface Sci. 22(3), 300–302 (1966). http://www.sciencedirect.com/science/article/pii/0021979766900373

65. Vold, M.J.: A numerical approach to the problem of sediment volume. J. Colloid Sci. **14**(2), 168–174 (1959). http://www.sciencedirect.com/science/article/pii/0095852259900418
66. Zeng, X., Adorna, H., Martínez-del-Amor, M.Á., Pan, L., Pérez-Jiménez, M.J.: Matrix representation of spiking neural P systems. In: Gheorghe, M., Hinze, T., Păun, G., Rozenberg, G., Salomaa, A. (eds.) CMC 2010. LNCS, vol. 6501, pp. 377–391. Springer, Heidelberg (2010). https://doi.org/10.1007/978-3-642-18123-8_29

The Java Environment for Nature-Inspired Approaches (JENA): A Workbench for BioComputing and BioModelling Enthusiasts

Thomas Hinze[✉]

Department of Bioinformatics, Friedrich Schiller University Jena,
Ernst-Abbe-Platz 2, 07743 Jena, Germany
thomas.hinze@uni-jena.de

Abstract. The term *biocomputing* subsumes a growing variety of effective concepts, strategies, and algorithmic techniques adopted from facets of biological information processing. In an highly interdisciplinary manner, underlying principles succeed in getting identified, understood, and transferred into the practice of computer science. Resulting models and simulation systems widely differ in their level of abstraction from almost realistic up to strongly idealised. Corresponding implementations have been categorised into microscale, mesoscale, and macroscale, but an interscale approach able to bridge existing gaps in between is still missing. Within an ongoing long-term project we are going to incorporate modelling components and descriptive instruments from different scales into a common programming workbench making the process of *abstraction* and *concretion* visible when elucidating a problem solution strategy throughout the scales. For instance, a DNA strand might be simply captured by a name, more detailed by a sequence of bits, eventually by its primary and secondary structure mentioning all involved nucleotides and nucleotide pairs, and finally by its tertiary structure expressing the spatial positions of all atoms bonded to each other. Analogously, chemical reactions and physical processes can be specified at various levels of abstraction. Our workbench has been designed as an experimental system open for successive extension along with student's contributions by integration of more and more issues from biocomputing. We present the current status of the project together with its underlying software design concept implemented in Java. A case scenario addressing double-stranded DNA and separation of DNA pools by length using gel electrophoresis demonstrates the practicability of the workbench.

1 Introduction

Computer science and engineering sustainably benefit from principles of biological information processing and from problem solutions found in living organisms. Nowadays, technical implementations of *neural networks* outperform the world's

© Springer Nature Switzerland AG 2018
C. Graciani et al. (Eds.): Pérez-Jiménez Festschrift, LNCS 11270, pp. 155–169, 2018.
https://doi.org/10.1007/978-3-030-00265-7_13

best players in chess and Go [3,19]. *Cognitive systems* are capable of autonomous vehicle driving [12], smartphone computers can reliably identify persons by looking at their face [25]. The shape of wings in modern airplanes resembles its biological counterpart from storks and cranes [13]. Surface structures of leaves give an example for making outer walls of buildings resistant against pollution [21]. Spam detection for emails exhibits best results when organised like an *artificial immune system* [14]. *Evolutionary computing* has been successively employed to generate unconventional ideas and even entire algorithms able to solve computationally hard problems efficiently in sufficient approximation [2,9]. Molecules of *deoxyribonucleic acid* (DNA) turn out to be an excellent, compact, and durable storage medium for data [1]. Energy consumption of biological organisms commonly constitutes a small fraction of those necessary for technical devices to fulfill the same task [17]. No doubt, computer scientists and engineers can learn a lot from biology.

Discovery and exploration of biological principles not seldom represents a hard challenge to tackle. Exhaustive studies, endless observations, extreme patience, experience, finest measurement equipment and last but not least a huge portion of fortune are important prerequisites for researchers to find new empirical knowledge in nature. The process of *understanding* comes along with the ability of *abstraction* in order to detect the relevant facts and finally extract these findings from negligible information. Building a *model* is the common method of first choice to separate relevant facts and their interplay. Using a model, a simplified description of the underlying system under study can be found keeping its main properties of interest. Particularly, *formal* models feature by a high expressivity which in turn enables computer-based simulations on the one hand and continuative evaluation by means of mathematical tools on the other. It is no surprise that formal models tend to become the most popular and highly favourite instrument for scientists in numerous disciplines.

When witnessing the emergence of biocomputing as a research area for more than two decades, there is some evidence for the impression that formal models in biocomputing compete by their mathematical elegance. Particularly, this becomes apparent in formal descriptions of biological processes and chemical reactions interpreted as operations from a theoretical perspective. Aimed by the inspiration of mathematical elegance, the formulation of corresponding operators often results in compact algebraic expressions with a high level of abstraction. The more models in biocomputing get used and modified from a theoretical perspective, the more its level of abstraction increases. In order to employ diverse mathematical tools and for conduction of proofs, the level of abstraction typically gets higher and higher while the relation to "real" biology diminishes. Let us illustrate this thought by a simple example. We assume that molecules are captured by characters like a or b. The presence of molecules within a reaction system is expressed by a set of molecules like $T = \{a, b, d, e\}$. For the output of a biocomputing system Π, an alphabet Σ consisting of selected characters has been specified. For extraction of system's output $L(\Pi)$ from the rest of molecules, the intersection is commonly used like $L(\Pi) = T \cap \Sigma$. Unequivocally,

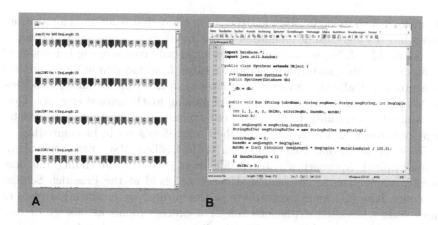

Fig. 1. JENA simulation of DNA oligonucleotide synthesis including occurring side effects. (A) $1,000$ single stranded copies of the 20mer nucleotide sequence 5'-ACCTAGCAGGTATTCGCCAT-3' have been desired. Around 5% of the nucleotides are damaged because of point mutations, another 5% of nucleotides are left out due to deletions. These side effects reduce the number of correctly synthesised strands to 906. A total number of 94 incorrect strands persist in the test tube. They can affect further actions. (B) Section of Java source code describing the process of oligonucleotide synthesis with consideration of parameterised side effects. Although cumbersome and bulky, it is close to the outcome by real chemistry.

this is elegant from a theoretical point of view but it is far away from a single real process in biology. Although there are some molecular filters like ion channels or specific receptors, they need additional features to function. For instance, molecules need to be transported by special transport proteins, by diffusion, or by electrical charge to reach and to pass a filter. Moreover, biological filters are commonly less specific than expected. Sometimes, undesired molecules are allowed to pass while proper exemplars might get rejected. What stands out is that a majority of models in biocomputing convinces by a high degree of mathematical elegance in concert with a high level of abstraction loosing the direct relation to the real world of biology and biochemistry. For some *in-silico* applications this does not matter. When striving for simulations close to its archetype, the situation becomes much more complicated.

The aforementioned scenario was the starting point to think about an alternative approach to cope with the implications of abstraction in models of biocomputing. In terms of a bottom-up strategy, we begin the modelling part with a low abstraction level close to the "real world". Molecules and processes are described based on empirical studies, on natural laws, and on observations like sequences of microscopic images. Resulting models implemented in a programming language like Java turn out to be cumbersome and bulky, see Fig. 1. They contain lots of estimated parameters, much dead weight, and a certain portion of redundancy. Now, we start to simplify the model by successive abstraction, for instance we replace chemical structures of molecules by names or characters. In this stage, we can treat the input and output in a way that is common for abstract models but the algorithmic emulation of the processes to carry out still remains at a detailed level. So, we are able to experimentally compare the behaviour of our model with its counterpart candidates taken from biocomputing theoretical literature. Especially the deviance is of interest in this context since it discloses the "costs" (loss of closeness to reality) of gaining mathematical elegance. Getting a notable sensibility to that is in our opinion an important milestone for young researchers at the beginning of their scientific career in biocomputing.

To do so, we initiated the long-term project called "Java Environment for Nature-inspired Approaches", JENA for short. Students attending the one-semester master course "Molecular Algorithms" held at the Friedrich Schiller University Jena (Germany) contribute to this project by producing a piece of source code addressing a phenomenon or a process found in biology or biochemistry. Accompanied by an exhaustive literature search, the phenomenon or process gets described at a low level of abstraction. To this end, suitable data structures and data types need to be created in order to capture all details of interest. Furthermore, we make use of parameters for control of randomised or predetermined effects that might occur. Parameters can also include probability distributions based on empirical studies or derived from natural laws. Attention is paid to the objective that as many effects as possible have been integrated into the corresponding Java source code. Simultaneously, another group of students is searching for abstract models of biocomputing reflecting the phenomenon or process under study. So, the Java source code can be complemented by one or more formal representations. In consequence, we successively obtain a collection of varying implementations, all dedicated to the same phenomenon or process but widely spread in their level of abstraction. We are aware of the fact that our JENA system primarily serves as an experimental workbench directed to "play" with models and implementations and to learn about their advantages and disadvantages which facilitates an evaluation from a practical perspective.

Our JENA workbench is not intended to compete with existing software available for simulation or analysis of biocomputing models. During the last two decades, a variety of high-quality software has been provided like *Amber* [15], *CellDesigner* [5], *COPASI* [10], *MGS* [22], *P-Lingua* [6], *metaPlab* [4], *NetLogo* [20,23], *SRSim* [7], and many others. Each of these valuable tools is highly specialised to certain aspects of modelling scale, selection of operators, and behaviour of the configured system. The tools have in common that each of them focuses on one modelling paradigm it is made for. We plan to keep our workbench open for interdisciplinary use. For instance, the DNA toolbox might be employed for a genetic algorithm in evolutionary computing.

In the following section, we familiarise the reader with the technical implementation of our JENA workbench at its current status. We introduce the hierarchy of Java classes and their interplay. A subsequent section is dedicated to an introductory example addressing the process of gel electrophoresis utilised for separation of DNA double strands by length. Final conclusions summarise achievements and challenges for future work.

2   JENA Software Source Code Design

Object-oriented programming as a popular paradigm comes with numerous advantages when planning large software development projects in a team. For modelling of all constituents we need, the organisation of classes and their relations to each other offers a perfect technical infrastructure. Among the pool of object-oriented programming languages, *Java* has a clear preference due to its syntactical maturation in concert with concepts like generic data types, type variables, and a class library which includes strong easy-to-use engines *swing* and *awt* for generation of graphical user interfaces. Moreover, Java is independent of platforms and operating systems since its runtime environment handles many aspects of memory and resources management automatically. Students enroled at the Friedrich Schiller University Jena in curricula of computer science or bioinformatics attend a two-semester course "Introduction to Programming" in which Java is addressed and a practical training passed. Since our JENA project is driven by students, the decision for Java meets and refreshes their knowledge, and last but not least they commonly enjoy becoming a part of the project as a first step into science.

We decided to structure the software in several *packages*, each of them collecting several *classes* providing data structures and methods for related topics. In the current stage, there are eight packages available in total called `Algebra`, `Molecules`, `Processes`, `Membranes`, `Organism`, `Population`, `Simulation`, and `Visualisation`. Hereafter, we give a brief overview of the packages.

Package `Algebra`

For incorporation of biocomputing models at a high level of abstraction, we need a toolbox of data types and operators reflecting algebraic instruments.

The class `Set` is able to manage a finite number of distinguishable elements of an arbitrary type. An object might start with an empty set capable of addition of new elements and removal of existing ones. Alternatively, sets can be specified via finite enumeration of countable elements like $S = \{n \mid n = 1, \ldots, 100\}$ and implicitly via common properties of the elements like $T = \{n \mid (n = 1, \ldots, 10) \wedge (n \cdot n + 5 \in \{14, 21\})\}$. Set operations $\cup$, $\cap$, $\backslash$, card, $\wp$ (power set), and $\Box$ with respect to a given finite basic set are defined, furthermore the tests $\in$ (presence of an element), $\subset$, $=$, and `isEmpty`. Technically, a set has been managed dynamically by a list of unique entities.

`Multiset` is the name of a class in which each element is stored together with the number of occurrences. A new object induces an empty multiset whose elements might be explicitly added or removed. Multisets must be finite with respect to both, number of unique elements and multiplicity of elements. Elements are allowed to be of an arbitrary type. When handling countable elements, multisets can be specified by finite enumeration or implicitly by common properties of the elements. The class provides multiset operations $\cup$, $\uplus$ (multiset sum), $\cap$, $\backslash$, supp, card, $\wp$ (power set) complemented by the tests $\in$, $\subset$, $=$, and `isEmpty`.

A multiset object results in a dynamical list of pairs (unique element, multiplicity) whereas elements with multiplicity of 0 get automatically eliminated.

For utilisation of tuples, we have introduced a collection of classes reflecting relations. At the current state of implementation, there exists a variety of classes corresponding to the arity of tuples under study. We distinguish ordered pairs (binary relations), triples, quadruples, and quintuples, each of them forming a class on their own. All classes have in common the Cartesian product which generates all tuples from the elements of the underlying finite sets. Hence, the number of tuples remains finite as well. A relation might also be specified explicitly by enumeration of its elements. In addition, methods for projection allow extraction of individual components from tuples. Relations can be compared to each other with respect to $=$ and $\subset$. The $\in$ operator checks whether or not a given tuple is element of a relation. Since relations extend the class `Set`, the set operations $\cup$, $\cap$, $\setminus$, card, and $\wp$ (power set) are available for relations. Particularly for binary relations, we offer tests for reflexivity, symmetry, antisymmetry, and transitivity. Implicit generation of relations by specification of common properties among its elements is still planned for future versions.

Complementing the toolboxes for sets, multisets, and relations, dedicated classes for handling of numbers and characters along with algebraic operators have become a part of the `Algebra` package. To this end, we adopt the predefined classes and wrappers `String`, `Integer`, and `Double` from the Java Standard Edition class library. Since fractions need to be handled as well without loss of numerical precision, we add the class `Fraction` together with the operations addition, subtraction, multiplication, and division, and tests $=$, $<$, $>$. Fractions get automatically cancelled using Euclid's algorithm.

Package Molecules

Molecules stand for a variety of constituents acting within chemical reactions or physical processes. The package `Molecules` contains a collection of hierarchically organised classes aiming at capturing specific instruments subject to the sort of molecules. As the most general class, we have defined `Particle`. A particle object can be equipped with a name, its geometrical coordinates, and an encoding given by an arbitrary string. Further attributes formulate properties like mass, volume, speed vector, colour (for visualisation), and some others. Based on that, the class `Molecule` refines properties of relevance in chemistry and physics like molecular formula, electrical charge, reactivity, half-life, and others.

The `DNA` class exhibits a prototype of classes addressing special sorts of molecules whose inner structure is of interest and opens a selection of methods able to operate on these structures. In our `DNA` class at its current state of implementation, linear DNA single or double strands can be managed together with strand end labels. A sequential list of nucleotides (A, C, G, T) and nucleotide pairs (A/T, T/A, C/G, G/C) represents the structural information. Since a DNA double strand is composed of two or more single strands annealed to each other, each single strand component possesses two strand ends (5' and 3') along with molecular labels (like phosphate, hydroxyl group, biotin, or fluorescence markers). Based on the DNA strand data structure, we provide a collection of methods. Here, a DNA strand can be decomposed into its single stranded components analogously to melting (denaturation). Another method tests whether or not two DNA double strands can ligate (stick) to each other taking into account the compatibility of their outer ends and labels. The `equals` method checks the equality of either DNA double strands including strand end labels taking into consideration that a DNA double strand might have different representations. Further methods calculate the mass of the DNA strand, its length (in base pairs), and its melting temperature. From a technical point of view, some auxiliary methods for serialisation (conversion into a character string) and visualisation complement the `DNA` class. We plan to prepare additional classes dedicated to proteins (at the level of their binding sites), messengers (hormones), and sugars for future versions.

Package `Processes`

The `Processes` package has been developed in order to manage molecular interactions at different levels of abstraction. Here, the class `GeneralReaction` contains all required instruments to conduct a chemical reaction in terms of replacement of symbols. Each molecule needs to be identified by a name without consideration of any inner structure. The major part of the class is formed by the parser capable of analysing the reaction equation under study. The parser identifies the multisets of substrates (educts) and products. Stoichiometric factors expressed by positive integers are allowed. In addition, a priority value is assigned to each reaction to cope with situations in which several reactions compete against each other with the substrates. In a simple way, the substrate molecules get removed and the product molecules have been added to conduct the application of a reaction rule. Applied in an iterative manner, the effect of a reaction can be emulated. It terminates as soon as the need of substrates fails to be satisfied. This implementation of a reaction turns out to be rather abstract and far from any real chemistry but it is common in some models of membrane systems.

In a more detailed approach, the class `ReactionWithKinetics` permits employment of reaction kinetics in refinement of a general reaction. To this end, each reaction comes with a kinetic function complementing the reaction equation. We equipped the class with the most popular kinetic terms (mass-action, Michaelis-Menten, and Hill) together with corresponding parameters. Evaluation of a reaction kinetics formula enables a more precise determination of the number of molecules treated as substrates within a time step of the reaction.

Since DNA implies a specific pool of chemical reactions and physical processes, we implemented the class `DNAProcesses`. Currently, this class contains oligonucleotide synthesis, annealing (hybridisation), melting (denaturation), strand end labelling, ligation, and gel electrophoresis among linear DNA strands. Each process model incorporates side effect parameters based on empirical data. For instance, generation of DNA single strands using oligonucleotide synthesis induces point mutations (specified by its rate) and deletions (specified by its rate and average length). Typically, side effect parameters characterise a distribution which in turn affects the execution of the corresponding process on DNA. In addition to its primary and secondary structure, a DNA strand is also specified by a name, so it can act in general reactions and reactions with kinetics as well. In this way, interactions of DNA with other molecules might be described.

We are going to make available the class `BilliardModel` in which the molecules are assumed to move within a three-dimensional space having individual speed and direction of move in conformance with the Maxwell-Boltzmann distribution. Whenever two or more molecules collide and their kinetic energy exceeds the required activation energy, the reaction happens if defined.

Package `Membranes`

Molecules and process models need to come together in order to exhibit notable effects. Classes incorporated into the package `Membranes` fulfill this task. They have been conceived for definition of a reaction space. At the moment, the class `Membrane` is the only representative in this package. A membrane object comprises numerous attributes, most of them objects from other classes. A membrane might contain arbitrary multisets of particles, molecules, and/or DNA strands. Moreover, general reaction, reactions with kinetics, and/or processes on DNA can be made available. Further attributes address the membrane volume and auxiliary information for visualisation.

Since membranes are allowed to be arranged within a nested tree-like structure, a membrane may incorporate other (inner) membranes dynamically organised in a tree. A membrane structure implies a mechanism for molecules to enter an inner membrane or to leave its hosting membrane. To this end, we define a multiplicity of receptors attached to a membrane. A receptor is specified by its unique name. This name can be utilised in reaction equations to bind a molecule to the receptor. A reaction defined within the corresponding inner membrane formulates release of the molecule. Ion channels can be modelled by a membrane on their own.

The JENA workbench should be able to cope with active membranes. At the moment, we are in the preparation process to implement this feature. It will result in a class of processes responsible for modification of the membrane structure. So, an inner membrane might be eliminated (dissolution). A membrane can enter a hosting membrane (endocytosis), a membrane can leave its hosting membrane (exocytosis), and a membrane can be created together with a set of processes. Division of a membrane still need to be implemented [16]. Please note that the `Membranes` package exclusively manages a nested membrane structure.

Package `Organism`

We assume that an organism or tissue is composed of membranes adjacent to each other. For this purpose, we provide a collection of classes to arrange membranes in a graph-based structure forming the package `Organism`. Here, the class `GraphOfMembranes` provides a basic functionality to dynamically create an undirected graph of membranes. Exchange of molecules among neighboured membranes is done via receptors. An extension of the class `GraphOfMembranes` is given by the class `GraphOfMembranesWithChannels`. It makes available direct channels between adjacent membranes in a way that molecules can directly pass. A channel is defined by its capacity (maximum number of residing molecules), the time span necessary for passage and a filter pattern for molecules. The filter pattern consists of a list of names to identify molecules with permission to pass. We plan to equip this filter with wildcards and regular expressions for the future.

Package `Population`

Within an organism, membranes are connected to each other forming a graph. In contrast, a population consists of a loose collection of individuals able to move and to interact with each other or with the environment. The JENA workbench supports this aspect by the package `Population`. Its central class is called `Individuals` capable of managing arbitrary collections of particles, molecules, DNA strands, membranes, and organisms in an unordered manner. Each individual has a geometrical position within the habitat of the population. Individuals might be enriched by a scheme of movement within the habitat. In case of colliding individuals, a selection of interactions is available. It ranges from "do nothing" via "turn and escape" to "feed". The feed action requires definition of a predator-and-prey order. For instance, particles are fed by membranes which in turn are fed by organisms. In addition, the feed action must be configured regarding the exposure to the prey. When fed, the prey might simply disappear but it can also become a part of the predator in some cases.

Packages `Simulation` and `Visualisation`

The packages `Simulation` and `Visualisation` subsume all technical components of the software necessary for the interaction with the user via menu bars, pop-up and dialogue windows, for the control of simulation loops corresponding to the processes available in the system under study, and for a graphical or text-based output. At the moment, the sequence of processes is manually controlled by the user. As an example, let an empty membrane be initially defined. The process "oligonucleotide synthesis" activated by the user will create a multiset of DNA single strands. Afterwards, the user might execute the process "annealing" to build double strands from the DNA pool. Finally, using "run reactions", the DNA strands will be identified by their names (without consideration of their inner structure) and underlying reaction rules have been iteratively carried out for a number of steps. This leads to a list of molecular abundance (multiplicity of molecules) for each membrane after each time step. For processes on DNA, a graphical visualisation of the outcome is available. Emergence of membrane structures within an organism results in a corresponding bracketed text string unless finalisation of a graphical representation. The same holds for populations.

3   Example: Gel Electrophoresis on DNA

Electrophoresis subsumes a physical technique able to spatially separate electrically charged molecules by their weights [11]. Particularly, DNA (negatively charged) and many naturally originated proteins (twisted and folded chains of amino acids whose electrical charge is mainly determined by outer amino acid side chains) are beneficial candidates for widespread applications in molecular biology and chemical analysis [24].

Mostly, electrophoresis takes place within a special physical medium like a *gel* which carries and steers the molecules during the separation process. To do so, the gel is prepared in a way to be equipped with numerous *pores* forming woven channels or tunnels sufficiently sized to allow passage of charged sample molecules. For instance, *agarose* is commonly used to compose a gel suitable for electrophoresis on DNA. The fibre structure of agarose enables pores whose diameter usually varies between 150 and 500 nanometres while a DNA strand (in biologically prevalent B-DNA conformation) diametrally consumes merely 2 nanometres but its length can reach several hundred nanometres [8]. The ready-made gel, typically between 10 and 30 centimetres in length or width and up to 5 millimetres thick, is embedded in a gel *chamber* filled up with a buffer solution in order to adjust an appropriate pH environment. The gel chamber comes with two electrodes, a negative one and a positive one, placed at the opposite boundaries of the gel, see Fig. 2.

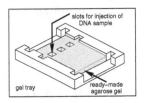 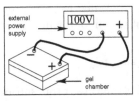 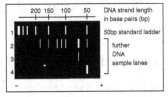

Fig. 2. Sketching technical instruments and outcome of agarose gel electrophoresis.

Subsequently, the sample mixture of DNA strands to be separated becomes injected into the gel close to the negative electrode. Now, an electrical direct-current (DC) voltage, provided by an external power supply and mostly chosen between 80 and 120 volts, is applied to the electrodes. Driven by the electrical force, the negatively charged molecules begin to run towards the positive electrode along a lane through the pores of the gel. In order to mobilise, each molecule has to overcome its friction notable in both forms, with the gel on the one hand and inherently on the other. Interestingly, the resulting velocity of movement strongly depends on the mass (weight) of the individual molecules. Since small and light molecules induce a low friction, they run faster than heavier exemplars. This distinction finally effects the resulting spatial separation according to the weights of involved charged molecules. The process of electrophoresis is stopped by switching off the voltage shortly before the smallest molecules have reached the opposite end of the gel. For an easier visualisation of this process, the molecular mixture initially becomes enriched by a weakly binding dye whose velocity converges in compliance with the smallest sample molecules [24].

In addition, the DNA sample molecules had been stained using a fluorescence marker like *ethidium bromide* [18]. This substance loosely binds to the hydrogen bonds of double-stranded DNA and persists at the DNA during the electrophoresis run. Ethidium bromide attached to DNA fluoresces under ultra violet (UV) light making the DNA visible inside the gel. Typically, the DNA after electrophoresis is arranged in so-called *bands* (sustained bar-shaped blots) along the underlying lane. Normally, these bands appear in light-grey up to white colours on a dark gel background. The colours intensity gives a raw information on the absolute number of molecules of almost the same mass accumulated within each band. In a first and mostly sufficient approximation, gel electrophoresis can be modelled by an obvious equation. The electrical force F_E needs to overcome the friction F_R. Movement of charged molecules starts up if and only if both forces equal to each other:

$$F_E = F_R$$

Now, we can resolve both forces by formulating its strength using a couple of dedicated parameters. The electrical force is defined as the product of the molecular electrical charge q with the electrical field E which in turn can be expressed by the quotient of the voltage U and the distance h between the electrodes: $F_E = q \cdot E = q \cdot \frac{U}{h}$. In contrast, the friction in accordance with *Stokes' law* reads: $F_R = 6 \cdot \pi \cdot \eta \cdot r \cdot v$ assuming movement of a sphere where r denotes the radius, v symbolises its velocity, and η stands for the viscosity of the medium, mainly reflecting the average size of the pores. The velocity can be assumed to remain almost constant after a short acceleration phase in conjunction with switching on the electrical voltage. Putting everything together reveals:

$$v = \frac{q \cdot E}{6 \cdot \pi \cdot \eta \cdot r}$$

The only indetermined parameter is the radius r of the anticipated sphere representing the moving charged molecule. In order to cope with that, we can imagine that the volume $V_{molecule}$ of the charged molecule resembles the volume V_{sphere} of the anticipated sphere. Having this in mind, we can write $V_{molecule} = \frac{m}{\rho}$ with m denoting the mass (weight) of the molecule and ρ its density. Moreover, $V_{sphere} = \frac{4}{3} \cdot \pi \cdot r^3$. From that, we obtain:

$$r = \left(\frac{3}{4 \cdot \pi} \cdot \frac{m}{\rho} \right)^{\frac{1}{3}}$$

Let us now compose a resulting function s : $\mathbb{R}^2 \longrightarrow \mathbb{R}$ which describes the distance moved by a charged molecule with mass m after an elapsed time t:

$$s(m,t) = v \cdot t$$

$$= \frac{q \cdot E}{6 \cdot \pi \cdot \eta \left(\frac{3 \cdot m}{4 \cdot \pi \cdot \rho}\right)^{\frac{1}{3}}} \cdot t$$

$$= \underbrace{\frac{q}{6 \cdot \pi \cdot \left(\frac{3}{4 \cdot \pi \cdot \rho}\right)^{\frac{1}{3}}}}_{\text{taken as global parameter } G} \cdot \frac{E}{\eta} \cdot \frac{1}{m^{\frac{1}{3}}} \cdot t$$

$$= G \cdot \frac{E}{\eta} \cdot \frac{1}{m^{\frac{1}{3}}} \cdot t$$

For DNA agarose gel electrophoresis, the electrical field E frequently constitutes between $400\frac{V}{m}$ and $500\frac{V}{m}$ while the viscosity commonly differs from $0.001\frac{kg}{m \cdot s}$ (consistency like water in large-pored gels) up to $0.02\frac{kg}{m \cdot s}$ in small-meshed gels enhancing the friction along with producing heat. From empirical studies, we fitted a constant average value of approx. $6.794 \cdot 10^{-4}\frac{A \cdot s \cdot kg^{\frac{1}{3}}}{m}$ for G in agarose gel electrophoresis on double-stranded non-denaturing DNA. When employing the molecule mass m in kg along with elapsed time t in s and remembering that $1VAs = 1\frac{kg \cdot m^2}{s^3}$, the final value of the function is returned in metres.

In order to disclose the relation between mass of a DNA double strand and its length in base pairs, we need to consider the average mass of a nucleotide. Indeed, there are slight mass deviations between single nucleotides A (Adenine, $\approx 5.467 \cdot 10^{-25}$kg), C (Cytosine, $\approx 5.234 \cdot 10^{-25}$kg), G (Guanine, $\approx 5.732 \cdot 10^{-25}$kg), and T (Thymine, $\approx 5.301 \cdot 10^{-25}$kg). Each nucleotide mass comprises the chemical base together with its section of the sugar-phosphate backbone. In average, we obtain $\approx 5.4335 \cdot 10^{-25}$kg per nucleotide or $\approx 1.0867 \cdot 10^{-24}$kg per base pair. Marginal influences of dye and ethidium bromide are neglected.

Having the formalisation of gel electrophoresis in terms of a parameterised process on a pool of DNA strands at hand, we can implement corresponding methods to be incorporated into the class DNAProcesses complemented by a visualisation scheme and a dialogue in order to receive all parameter values from the user. Gel electrophoresis utilises user-defined values for the electrical field E and viscosity η. In addition, a number of lanes and a membrane attached to each lane have to be specified. All DNA strands residing in the underlying membrane are involved in the gel electrophoresis simulation which successively runs over time to see the formation of DNA bands and their movement through the virtual gel. The simulation might be terminated at any point in time. The intensity of DNA bands reflects the density of DNA and hence indicates the number of DNA strands with same or similar mass, see Fig. 3, right part. As an additional feature, a section of a lane can be marked to excise the DNA inside this region. A new membrane gets created, and all excised DNA strands are placed there for further examination.

When observing gel electrophoresis on DNA in practise, we witness the occurrence of undesired side effects resulting in misplaced DNA strands. It might happen that short DNA strands run slower than expected due to its supercoiled

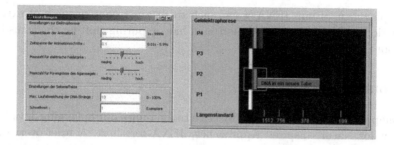

Fig. 3. JENA simulation of gel electrophoresis on DNA within four lanes P1, ..., P4. Each lane processes all DNA strands from a dedicated membrane. Intensity of DNA bands corresponds to the density of DNA inside the virtual gel and hence indicates the number of DNA strands with same or similar mass. Side effects of gel electrophoresis imply a slight fuzziness among masses of DNA strands.

spatial structure which increases the friction. Several DNA strands of different mass can be spatially interwoven in a way that the electrical force used to move the strands does not suffice to ungarble the DNA cluster. What stands out is a certain fuzziness regarding the masses of DNA strands enriched in the same band. We accomodate this phenomenon by introduction of a parameterised side effect into the process model of gel electrophoresis. To do so, we fuzzificate the individual mass of each DNA strand by addition of a randomly generated Gauss variable. Its value represents an influence quantity to slow down a DNA strand. We restrict ourselves to positive values since an acceleration of DNA strands in comparison to their expected speed has not been found so far.

Our process model of gel electrophoresis on DNA has been verified by experimental wetlab studies conducted with diverse DNA ladders using agarose with varying pore size. DNA ladders comprise a mixture of double stranded DNA with standardised lengths and mass typically obtained from cleaved plasmids. The number of strand copies collected in a band equals to each other. So, band's width rawly indicates the deviation of DNA when running in the gel subject to its desired (optimal) position which gives evidence for estimation of the side effect parameter value.

Please note that in our JENA workbench, a DNA strand is also identified by its name and by its encoding which can be a sequence of bits for example. After excision of a virtual DNA band and extraction of the incorporated DNA strands into a new membrane, we can simply shift to the abstraction level of bit sequences. Interestingly, in many cases the influence of side effects results in some additional undesired shorter bit sequences among the ideal pool of bitstrings with uniform length. Here, we disclose a difference of the behaviour taking into account an idealised abstract model of DNA computation based on bitstrings on the one hand and the outcome derived by a more realistic process simulation with subsequent conversion of DNA structures into bitstrings on the other. Obviously, either process models are not confluent although using the same output encoding of DNA strands by bitstrings. The gel electrophoresis illustrates one example for the employment of our JENA workbench to discover consequences of extreme abstraction and highly idealised models in biocomputing shifting the focus back on a more realistic perspective.

4   Conclusions

This chapter is motivated by the objective to announce our upcoming Java Environment for Nature-inspired Approaches, JENA for short. A brief overview of the software, its underlying main ideas and the concept as a long-term project driven by students was given. The source code along with implemented features successively grows but it is still away from finalisation. We are going to treat the JENA system in terms of an open source project making all source files available to the public after the first release. We consider the JENA project to be a platform for students to do their first contact with scientific research in the field of biocomputing. That's why we emphasise an open-minded atmosphere for extensions and refinement taking care that all pieces of the software harmonise to each other. Currently, the toolset of operations on DNA has the most significant progress. Its Java source code package is available upon request. External honorary collaborators, constructive hints, and feedback are welcome. From time to time we will present an information update and news about the JENA workbench.

References

1. Adleman, L.M.: Molecular computation of solutions to combinatorial problems. Science **266**(5187), 1021–1024 (1994)
2. Baeck, T., Fogel, D.B., Michalewicz, Z.: Evolutionary Computation. Basic Algorithms and Operators. Taylor & Francis, Milton Park (2000)
3. Campbell, M., Hoane Jr., A.J., Hsu, F.: Deep blue. Artif. Intell. **134**(1–2), 57–83 (2002)
4. Castellini, A., Manca, V.: MetaPlab: a computational framework for metabolic P systems. In: Corne, D.W., Frisco, P., Păun, G., Rozenberg, G., Salomaa, A. (eds.) WMC 2008. LNCS, vol. 5391, pp. 157–168. Springer, Heidelberg (2009). https://doi.org/10.1007/978-3-540-95885-7_12
5. Funahashi, A., Matsuoka, Y., Jouraku, A., Morohashi, M., Kikuchi, N., Kitano, H.: Cell designer 3.5: a versatile modeling tool for biochemical networks. Proc. IEEE **96**(8), 1254–1265 (2008)
6. García-Quismondo, M., Gutiérrez-Escudero, R., Pérez-Hurtado, I., Pérez-Jiménez, M.J., Riscos-Núñez, A.: An overview of P-lingua 2.0. In: Păun, G., Pérez-Jiménez, M.J., Riscos-Núñez, A., Rozenberg, G., Salomaa, A. (eds.) WMC 2009. LNCS, vol. 5957, pp. 264–288. Springer, Heidelberg (2010). https://doi.org/10.1007/978-3-642-11467-0_20
7. Gruenert, G., Ibrahim, B., Lenser, T., Lohel, M., Hinze, T., Dittrich, P.: Rule-based spatial modeling with diffusing, geometrically constrained molecules. BMC Bioinform. **11**, 307 (2010)
8. Hames, D., Hooper, N.: Biochemistry, 3rd edn. Taylor & Francis, Milton Park (2005)

9. Hinze, T., Weber, L.L., Hatnik, U.: Walking membranes: grid-exploring P systems with artificial evolution for multi-purpose topological optimisation of cascaded processes. In: Leporati, A., Rozenberg, G., Salomaa, A., Zandron, C. (eds.) CMC 2016. LNCS, vol. 10105, pp. 251–271. Springer, Cham (2017). https://doi.org/10.1007/978-3-319-54072-6_16

10. Hoops, S., et al.: COPASI - a COmplex PAthway simulator. Bioinformatics **22**(24), 3067–3074 (2006)

11. Johannson, B.G.: Agarose gel electrophoresis. Scand. J. Clin. Lab. Invest. **29**(s124), 7–19 (1972)

12. Maurer, M., Gerdes, J.C., Lenz, B., Winner, H. (eds.): Autonomous Driving. Technical, Legal and Social Aspects. Springer, Heidelberg (2015). https://doi.org/10.1007/978-3-662-48847-8

13. Mueller, T.J. (ed.): Fixed and Flapping Wing Aerodynamics for Micro Air Vehicle Applications. Progress in Astronautics and Aeronautics, vol. 195. American Institute of Aeronautics and Astronautics (2001)

14. Oda, T., White, T.: Immunity from spam: an analysis of an artificial immune system for junk email detection. In: Jacob, C., Pilat, M.L., Bentley, P.J., Timmis, J.I. (eds.) ICARIS 2005. LNCS, vol. 3627, pp. 276–289. Springer, Heidelberg (2005). https://doi.org/10.1007/11536444_21

15. Pearlman, D.A., et al.: AMBER, a package of computer programs for applying molecular mechanics, normal mode analysis, molecular dynamics and free energy calculations to simulate the structural and energetic properties of molecules. Comput. Phys. Commun. **91**(1–3), 1–41 (1995)

16. Pérez-Jimenez, M.J., Romero-Jiménez, A., Sancho-Caparrini, F.: A polynomial complexity class in P systems using membrane division. J. Automata Lang. Comb. **11**(4), 423–434 (2006)

17. Purdon, A.D., Rosenberger, T.A., Shetty, H.U., Rapoport, S.I.: Energy consumption by phospholipid metabolism in mammalian brain. Neurochem. Res. **27**(12), 1641–1647 (2002)

18. Sabnis, R.W.: Handbook of Biological Dyes and Stains: Synthesis and Industrial Application. Wiley-VCH, Weinheim (2010)

19. Silver, D., et al.: Mastering the game of Go with deep neural networks and tree search. Nature **529**, 484–489 (2016)

20. Sklar, E.: NetLogo, a multi-agent simulation environment. Artif. Life **13**(3), 303–311 (2007)

21. Solga, A., Cerman, Z., Striffler, B.F., Spaeth, M., Barthlott, W.: The dream of staying clean: lotus and biomimetic surfaces. Bioinspiration Biomim. **2**(4), s126 (2007)

22. Spicher, A., Michel, O., Giavitto, J.-L.: A topological framework for the specification and the simulation of discrete dynamical systems. In: Sloot, P.M.A., Chopard, B., Hoekstra, A.G. (eds.) ACRI 2004. LNCS, vol. 3305, pp. 238–247. Springer, Heidelberg (2004). https://doi.org/10.1007/978-3-540-30479-1_25

23. Tisue, S., Wilensky, U.: NetLogo: a simple environment for modeling complexity. In: Proceedings International Conference on Complex Systems, Nothwestern University (2004)

24. Westermeier, R.: Electrophoresis in Practice. Wiley-VCH, Weinheim (2005)

25. Wright, J., Yang, A.Y., Ganesh, A., Sastry, S.S., Ma, Y.: Robust face recognition via sparse representation. IEEE Trans. Pattern Anal. Mach. Intell. **31**(2), 210–227 (2009)

WEBRSIM: A Web-Based Reaction Systems Simulator

Sergiu Ivanov[1], Vladimir Rogojin[2,3], Sepinoud Azimi[2,3], and Ion Petre[2,3,4(✉)]

[1] IBISC, Université Évry, Université Paris-Saclay, Évry, France
`sergiu.ivanov@univ-evry.fr`
[2] Computational Biomodeling Laboratory, Turku Centre for Computer Science, Turku, Finland
[3] Department of Information Technologies, Åbo Akademi University, Agora, Domkyrkotorget 3, Turku 20500, Finland
`{vrogojin,sazimi,ipetre}@abo.fi`
[4] National Institute for Research and Development in Biological Sciences, Bucharest, Romania

Abstract. We introduce WEBRSIM, the first web-based simulator for reaction systems. The simulator has an easy-to-use interface where the input is a reaction system and four functionalities: the computation of the interactive process driven by a given context sequence, the behaviour graph of the reaction system, its conservation dependency graph, and all its conserved sets. WEBRSIM comes with a browser-based friendly interface and offers a fast software to support computational modeling with reaction systems.

1 Introduction

Reaction systems, first introduced in [12], are a qualitative framework inspired by two cellular regulation mechanisms, *facilitation* and *inhibition*, which control the interaction between biochemical reactions. Intuitively (and on a high level of abstraction), a biochemical reaction is enabled when all the components needed to facilitate the reaction are present and all the components that inhibit it are absent from the environment. Based on this intuition a reaction in the reaction systems formalism is defined as a triplet $a = (R_a, I_a, P_a)$ where R_a represents the set of reactants, I_a the set of inhibitors and P_a the set of products corresponding to reaction a. As a result of being triggered, the reaction transforms its set of reactants into the corresponding set of products.

The two main assumptions considered in the reaction systems framework are the following:

- *Threshold assumption*: an element is either abundantly present in the environment or it is absent from it. This implies that the cardinality of elements is either 0 or 1 in reaction systems framework.
- *No permanency assumption*: an element vanishes from the environment if no reaction is triggered to produce it back. This principle is supported by

© Springer Nature Switzerland AG 2018
C. Graciani et al. (Eds.): Pérez-Jiménez Festschrift, LNCS 11270, pp. 170–181, 2018.
https://doi.org/10.1007/978-3-030-00265-7_14

abstract biochemical considerations that maintaining an element in the environment is the result of an active (and energy-consuming) process. In the absence of such an explicit mechanism to maintain it, an element disappears from the environment.

Research done in the field of reaction systems has been very diverse, see for example [4,6,7,9,11,13,19] for several recent contributions. The simple, yet expressive nature of this framework has attracted researchers from both theoretical and practical areas of science to focus on studying and analysing reaction systems. One of the main lines of such efforts focuses on modelling real world problems through reaction systems' framework. Such applications vary from biological modelling to number theory to quantum computing, see for example [4,5,8,15,19]. To study the properties of such models, especially the bio-inspired ones, a series of studies was initiated to formalise several properties of central interest in biomodeling and to study the computational complexity of deciding those properties, such as mass conservation, invariants, steady states, multistability, stationary processes, elementary fluxes, and periodicity: [1–3,5].

The dynamics of a reaction system model can be observed through *interactive processes*. Intuitively, interactive processes describe the step-by-step evolution of a reaction system's model from one state to the next driven by external environment interventions. Many of the above mentioned properties of a reaction system's model can be captured through its interactive processes. Reaction systems models corresponding to real world processes get quickly highly complex. That is why, even though it is straightforward to write an interactive process of a reaction system, doing this manually can very easily become tedious and highly error-prone. In this paper we introduce a reaction system simulator, WEBRSIM that automates the process of calculating states of a reaction system's model for a corresponding interactive process to overcome this issue. The simulator also provides the conserved sets of a given reaction system's model. The basic simulation engine behind WEBRSIM, brsim, was discussed in passing in [2].

Other software supporting modeling with reaction system exist. The one closest to WEBRSIM was introduced in [17] in the form of a CPU- and GPU-based simulator for reaction systems: HERESY. The basic approach to simulating reaction systems is similar in HERESY and WEBRSIM, with the added feature of HERESY to parallelise the computation on Graphics Processing Units (GPU). The comparison done in [17] between HERESY and brsim shows that the running time in brsim is only marginally slower than the highly parallelised GPU-version of HERESY and much faster than its CPU version. WEBRSIM is highly user friendly as it comes with a web-based version that may be used through a standard browser, whereas HERESY requires some knowledge of Python programming to invoke its graphical user interface. As WEBRSIM comes with the open source code [21] (as does HERESY), it also provides the possibility of tweaking the code to the need of more expert users. Where both HERESY and WEBRSIM provide interactive processes simulation for reaction systems, WEBRSIM takes one step further and implements an algorithm to compute the behaviour graph, the conserved sets and the dependency graph.

Another useful software for modeling with reaction systems is introduced in [16], that offers the possibility to do model checking of temporal properties, a feature not offered by WEBRSIM.

2   Preliminaries

In this section, we recall the notion of a reaction system, as well as some related concepts. For more details we refer to [10, 12].

Definition 1 ([12]). *Let S be a finite set. A reaction a in S is a triplet of finite nonempty sets $a = (R_a, I_a, P_a)$, where $R_a, I_a, P_a \subseteq S$ and $R_a \cap I_a = \varnothing$. We say that R_a, I_a, and P_a are the sets of reactants, inhibitors, and products of a, respectively. The set of all reactions in S is denoted by $\mathrm{rac}(S)$.*

A reaction system (in short, RS) is an ordered pair $\mathcal{A} = (S, A)$, where S is a finite set of symbols (also called sometimes elements, species, or entities) and $A \subseteq \mathrm{rac}(S)$. The set S is called the background *(set) of A.*

We use the following notations:

$$\mathcal{R} = \bigcup_{a \in A} R_a, \quad \mathcal{P} = \bigcup_{a \in A} P_a, \quad \text{and} \quad \mathrm{supp}(\mathcal{A}) = \mathcal{R} \cup \mathcal{P}.$$

The set $\mathrm{supp}(\mathcal{A})$ will be called the support set *of $\mathcal{A}$.*

The following definition introduces the notion of interactive processes in reaction systems.

Definition 2 ([12]). *Let $\mathcal{A} = (S, A)$ be a reaction system, $T \subseteq S$, and $a \in A$. We say that a is* enabled *by T, denoted by $\mathrm{en}_a(T)$, if $R_a \subseteq T$ and $I_a \cap T = \varnothing$.*

(1) The result of a on T is defined as follows:

$$\mathrm{res}_a(T) = \begin{cases} P_a, & \text{if } \mathrm{en}_a(T), \\ \varnothing, & \text{otherwise.} \end{cases}$$

(2) The result of $\mathcal{A}$ on T is defined as follows:

$$\mathrm{res}_\mathcal{A}(T) = \bigcup_{a \in A} P_a.$$

(3) An interactive process in $\mathcal{A}$ is a pair $\pi = (\gamma, \delta)$, where $\gamma = (C_0, C_1, ..., C_n)$ and $\delta = (D_1, D_2, ..., D_n)$, $n \geq 1$, are sequences of subsets of S with $D_1 = \mathrm{res}_\mathcal{A}(C_0)$ and, for each $1 < i \leq n$, $D_i = \mathrm{res}_\mathcal{A}(C_{i-1} \cup D_{i-1})$.

2.1   Running Example

The heat shock response is one of the highly conserved cellular defence mechanisms among eukaryotes against environmental stressors such as high temperatures, toxins, bacterial infection, etc. In this paper we consider a simplified model of the heat shock response of [18]. This model's set of reactions is in Table 1 and the model was proposed in [3].

When a cell is exposed to stress, proteins misfold (reaction (7) in Table 1) into complexes that disable certain cell functions which can eventually lead to cell death (necrosis). To address such effects, the number of a special family of molecular chaperones, called heat shock proteins (hsp's), increases. These molecular chaperones bind to misfolded proteins and facilitate their correct refolding (reactions (8), (9) in Table 1).

Table 1. The molecular model of the eukaryotic heat shock response proposed in [18].

No.	Reaction
(1)	$3\,\text{hsf} \rightleftarrows \text{hsf}_3$
(2)	$\text{hsf}_3 + \text{hse} \rightleftarrows \text{hsf}_3\colon \text{hse}$
(3)	$\text{hsf}_3\colon \text{hse} \rightarrow \text{hsf}_3\colon \text{hse} + \text{hsp}$
(4)	$\text{hsp} + \text{hsf} \rightleftarrows \text{hsp}\colon \text{hsf}$
(5)	$\text{hsp} + \text{hsf}_3 \rightarrow \text{hsp}\colon \text{hsf} + 2\,\text{hsf}$
(6)	$\text{hsp} + \text{hsf}_3\colon \text{hse} \rightarrow \text{hsp}\colon \text{hsf} + 2\,\text{hsf} + \text{hse}$
(7)	$\text{prot} \rightarrow \text{mfp}$
(8)	$\text{hsp} + \text{mfp} \rightleftarrows \text{hsp}\colon \text{mfp}$
(9)	$\text{hsp}\colon \text{mfp} \rightarrow \text{hsp} + \text{prot}$

A family of proteins called heat shock transcription factors (hsf's) regulates the expression of hsp's. In a trimeric state (hsf_3) they bind to heat shock elements (hse's - the hsp-encoding gene promoter regions) and activate the transcription of hsp's (reactions (1)–(3) in Table 1). By binding to the hsf_3: hse's, hsf_3's, and hsf's and breaking down the complexes, the hsp's downregulate their expression which leads to stopping the expression activity (reactions (4)–(6)).

We use the reaction system model corresponding to the heat shock response model of Table 1 as the running example in this paper. This reaction system was first introduced in [3]. The reaction system model for the heat shock response is presented in Table 2. As discussed in [3], this RS-based model for the heat shock response is satisfactory in that its conserved sets (see below) correspond exactly to the mass conservation relations of the quantitative model of [18].

We now recall the definition of conserved sets for reaction systems models, as proposed in [1].

Table 2. Reaction system for heat shock response

No.	Reaction
1	$(\{hsf\}, \{hsp\}, \{hsf_3\})$
2	$(\{hsp, hsf\}, \{mfp\}, \{hsp\!:\!hsf\})$
3	$(\{hsf, hsp, mfp\}, \{d_l\}, \{hsf_3\})$
4	$(\{hsf_3\}, \{hse, hsp\}, \{hsf\})$
5	$(\{hsp, hsf_3\}, \{mfp\}, \{hsp\!:\!hsf, hsf\})$
6	$(\{hsf_3, hsp, mfp\}, \{hse\}, \{hsf\})$
7	$(\{hsf_3, hse\}, \{hsp\}, \{hsf_3\!:\!hse\})$
8	$(\{hse, hsf_3, hsp\}, \{mfp\}, \{hse\})$
9	$(\{hsf_3, hse, hsp, mfp\}, \{d_l\}, \{hsf_3\!:\!hse\})$
10	$(\{hsf_3\!:\!hse\}, \{hsp\}, \{hsf_3\!:\!hse, hsp\})$
11	$(\{hsp, hsf_3\!:\!hse\}, \{mfp\}, \{hsp\!:\!hsf, hse\})$
12	$(\{hsf_3\!:\!hse, hsp, mfp\}, \{d_l\}, \{hsf_3\!:\!hse, hsp\})$
13	$(\{hse\}, \{hsf_3\}, \{hse\})$
14	$(\{hsp\!:\!hsf, stress\}, \{nostress\}, \{hsp, hsf\})$
15	$(\{hsp\!:\!hsf, nostress\}, \{stress\}, \{hsp\!:\!hsf\})$
16	$(\{prot, stress\}, \{nostress\}, \{prot, mfp\})$
17	$(\{prot, nostress\}, \{stress\}, \{prot\})$
18	$(\{hsp, mfp\}, \{d_l\}, \{hsp\!:\!mfp\})$
19	$(\{mfp\}, \{hsp\}, \{mfp\})$
20	$(\{hsp\!:\!mfp\}, \{d_l\}, \{hsp, prot\})$

Definition 3 (Conserved sets, [1]). *Let* $\mathcal{A} = (S, A)$ *be a reaction system. We say that a set* $M \subseteq \operatorname{supp}(\mathcal{A})$ *is* conserved *if for any* $W \subseteq \operatorname{supp}(\mathcal{A})$, $M \cap W \neq \varnothing$ *if and only if* $M \cap \operatorname{res}_{\mathcal{A}}(W) \neq \varnothing$.

For our running example, a conserved set is $M = \{hse, hsf_3\!:\!hse\}$. For an arbitrary set $W \subseteq \operatorname{supp}(\mathcal{A})$, let us suppose $hse \in W \cap M$. We claim that at least one of the reactions (7), (8), (9), or (13) is enabled by W:

- if $hsf_3 \notin W$, then reaction (13) is enabled,
- if $hsf_3 \in W$ and $hsp \notin W$, then reaction (7) is enabled,
- if $\{hsf_3, hsp\} \subseteq W$ and $mfp \notin W$, then reaction (8) is enabled, and
- if $\{hsf_3, hsp, mfp\} \subseteq W$, then reaction (9) is enabled.

The product sets of these reactions contain either hse or $hsf_3\!:\!hse$, so $\operatorname{res}_{\mathcal{A}}(W) \cap M \neq \varnothing$. Similarly we can argue that if $hsf_3\!:\!hse \in W \cap M$, then either of the reactions (10), (11), and (12) are enabled and therefore $\operatorname{res}_{\mathcal{A}}(W) \cap M \neq \varnothing$ as well. As a result we can conclude that whenever $\operatorname{res}_{\mathcal{A}}(W) \cap M \neq \varnothing$, then $W \cap M \neq \varnothing$. Consequently, $W \cap M \neq \varnothing$ if and only if $\operatorname{res}_{\mathcal{A}}(W) \cap M \neq \varnothing$, i.e., M is a conserved set.

3   The Back-End of WEBRSIM

In this section we will recall the algorithms behind WEBRSIM, briefly discuss its design and Haskell-based implementation brsim, and show an example of how a concrete reaction system can be analysed with brsim.

3.1   Direct Simulation

The principal goal of brsim is automating the execution of reaction systems to avoid error-prone manual analysis. Due to the fact that, technically, reaction systems are a particular case of set rewriting, their simulation is straightforward. The worst-case time complexity of the simulation can be bounded in the following way:

1. Checking that a reaction $a = (R_a, I_a, P_a)$ is enabled on a set W can be done in $O(m \log |W|)$, where $m = \max(|R_a|, |I_a|)$ (e.g., see the documentation of the module Data.Set [20] for details and sharper bounds).
2. Filtering a set of reactions A to only keep the ones enabled on the set W can be done in $O(|A| \cdot m \log |W|)$, where $m = \max\{|R_a|, |I_a| : a = (R_a, I_a, P_a) \in A\}$ (extension of the definition from the previous paragraph).
3. Applying a set of enabled reactions A to a set W essentially consists in putting together all the product sets in A; the complexity of this operation does not depend on the size of W. Taking the union of all product sets in A can be done in $O(|A| \cdot k \log k)$, where $k = \max\{|P_a| : a = (R_a, I_a, P_a) \in A\}$ is the maximal size of a product set in A.
4. Finally, running the whole set of reactions A for t steps can be done in $O(t|A| \cdot (m \log |S| + k \log k))$, where k and m are defined as in points 2 and 3, and S is the universe of species.

Thus, a rougher but easier to read upper bound on the worst-case complexity of a t-step simulation of a reaction system (S, A) is $O(t|A| \cdot |S| \log |S|)$.

3.2   Mass Conservation Analysis

Besides directly simulating reaction systems, brsim can also list all conserved sets. As mentioned in [1], deciding whether a set M is conserved in a given reaction system is coNP-complete. It turns out that, in case one needs to enumerate *all* sets conserved by a given reaction system, it is possible to do better than just going through every possible set of species and checking whether it is conserved [2].

We will now briefly recall the central ideas of the algorithm for listing all conserved sets, presented in detail in [2]. The main steps are as follows:

1. *Build the behaviour graph* G_b: The behaviour graph of a reaction system (S, A) is the graph whose nodes are all subsets of S and which contains the edge (W, W') iff $res_A(W) = W'$.

2. *Build the conservation dependency graph* G_{cd}: The conservation dependency graph of a reaction system (S, A) is a graph whose vertices are species from S, and which contains the edge (x, y) if y appears in at least one of the sets of the connected component of G_b which also contains the singleton set $\{x\}$. The graph G_{cd} has an important property: if it contains the edge (x, y), then every conserved set that contains y must also contain x.
3. *Build the condensation* $\widetilde{G}_{cd}$ *of* G_{cd}: The condensation of a directed graph is the directed acyclic graph of its strongly connected components.
4. *Enumerate the source sets of* $\widetilde{G}_{cd}$: Given a directed acyclic graph $G = (V, E)$, a subset of its nodes $X \subseteq V$ is a source set if all edges in E involving a node $x \in X$ have x as the source node.
5. *Check which source sets are also conserved sets*: As shown in [2, Proposition 3.3], any set conserved by a given reaction system must be a source set of $\widetilde{G}_{cd}$. The reverse implication is not necessarily true, meaning that one still needs to check conservation directly, but for a reduced number of candidates.

Subsection 4.2 of [2] showcases the performance of this algorithm on multiple examples, showing situations in which the number of candidates is considerably reduced, as well as situations in which all subsets of species must eventually be analysed.

Our simulator `brsim` includes an exact implementation of the algorithm, including the optimisations further reducing the number of candidates. Moreover, `brsim` can output the behaviour graph and the conservation dependency graph of a given reaction system.

3.3 Overview of the Implementation

`brsim` is written in Haskell and is distributed under GPLv3 [14]. The source code is freely available in an online Git repository [21].

`brsim` is a stand-alone command line application. It is principally intended to be run in batch mode, in which it reads the description of a reaction system and the context sequence from a file and outputs the sequence of states the reaction system traverses (the result sequence). `brsim` can be also run in interactive mode, in which it prompts the user to input the next context at every simulation step. Finally, `brsim` can be told to output the behaviour graph or the conservation dependency graph of the reaction system. Further technical details can be found on the project page [21], as well as by running `brsim help`.

Haskell was chosen as the implementation language for `brsim` mainly because it is a strictly typed, functional programming language, implying easy transposition of formal definitions into runnable code, as well as verifying some properties of the software at compile time via type checking. Moreover, Haskell has a rich ecosystem including libraries for graph manipulation and quick development of user interfaces. Finally, an overwhelming majority of Haskell's ecosystem is distributed under free or open-source software licences, meaning that `brsim` can be freely reused (provided the terms of the license are respected).

Table 3. The input file `example.rs` describing the reaction system from the running example.

```
hsf , hsp , hsf3
hsf hsp mfp, dI , hsf3
hsf3 , hse hsp , hsf
hsf3 hsp mfp, hse , hsf
hsf3 hse , hsp , hsf3 : hse
hsf3 hse hsp mfp, dI , hsf3 : hse
hse , hsf3 , hse
hse hsf3 hsp , mfp, hse
hsf3 : hse , hsp , hsf3 : hse hsp
hsf3 : hse hsp mfp, dI , hsf3 : hse hsp

hsp hsf , mfp, hsp : hsf
hsp : hsf stress , nostress , hsp hsf
hsp : hsf nostress , stress , hsp : hsf
hsp hsf3 , mfp, hsp : hsf
hsp hsf3 : hse , mfp, hsp : hsf hse
prot stress , nostress , prot mfp
prot nostress , stress , prot
hsp mfp, dI , hsp : mfp
mfp, hsp , mfp
hsp : mfp, dI , hsp prot
```

3.4 Example of Usage

In this section we will briefly show how `brsim` can be used to analyse the reaction system from our running example.

To run a reaction system, `brsim` needs its list of reactions. The input format is very close to the typical way in which reactions are written. For example, the reaction $(\{a,b\}, \{e,f\}, \{c,d\})$ will be transcribed as follows: `a b, e f, c d`. Table 3 shows how to transcribe the reaction system from the running example.

A similar syntax is used to supply `brsim` with a context sequence to drive the activity of the reaction system. Table 4 shows how do transcribe the context sequence from the running example.

Table 4. The input file `example.ctx` describing the context sequence from the running example.

```
hsf prot hse nostress
nostress
nostress
nostress
nostress
nostress
```

We can now run the simulator using the following command:

```
brsim run example.rs --context=example.ctx
```

The output of this command is shown in Table 5.

Table 5. The output of `brsim run example.rs --context=example.ctx`.

hse	hsf3	prot
hsf3 : hse	prot	
hsf3 : hse	hsp	prot
hse	hsp : hsf	prot
hse	hsp : hsf	prot
hse	hsp : hsf	prot

To see which sets are conserved by the reaction system from the running example, the following command should be issued to `brsim`:

```
brsim show conserved-sets example.rs
```

The output produced for the reaction system from the running example is

```
 .
hse  hsf3 : hse
```

The dot in the first line of the listing stands for the empty set (which is always trivially conserved).

Finally, `brsim` can be told to show the behaviour graph and the conservation dependency graph of the reaction system from the running example using the following respective commands:

```
brsim show behaviour-graph example.rs
brsim show cons-dep-graph example.rs
```

Figure 1 shows the conservation dependency graph of the reaction system from the running example as output by `brsim` and rendered using a circular layout filter. We do not show the behaviour graph here for reasons of space: it contains 2048 nodes (since the reaction system has 11 species).

4   The Web-Service

From the very beginning, we developed `brsim` with portability and ease of use in mind. To improve user experience even further, we decided to also deploy an online version, which is freely available here [22]. This page includes two examples giving some typical usage patterns.

The online version of `brsim` covers an essential subset of the functionality: simulating reaction systems, enumerating all conserved sets, and showing the behaviour and the conservation dependency graphs. As before, reactions are described in a format close to how they are usually written. For example, `hse hsf3 hsp, mfp, hse` would stand for the reaction $(\{hse, hsf_3, hsp\}, \{mfp\}, \{hse\})$. To run a simulation, the reactions and the context sequence should be given in the two text fields available on the page. The context sequence is not required for enumerating the conserved sets or for showing the conservation dependency graph. Obviously, since the behaviour graph's

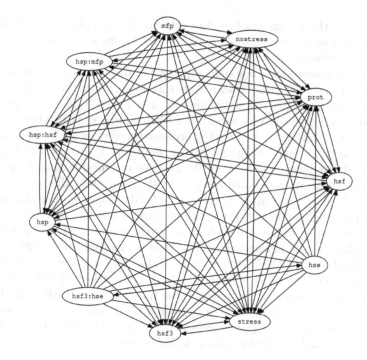

Fig. 1. The conservation dependency graph of the reaction system from the running example as constructed by `brsim` and rendered using a circular layout filter.

size is exponential in the size of the background set, its calculation is only possible for modest-sized models.

The implementation of the online instance of the simulator is straightforward: when the user clicks on one of the four buttons "Simulate", "Behaviour graph", "Conservation dependency graph", or "Conserved sets", the web server executes the corresponding command of `brsim`. The result, when ready, is rendered on the page. The online interface was mainly written in basic PHP and JavaScript.

5   Discussion

Reaction systems is the latest addition to the burgeoning field of computational modelling frameworks for complex systems. It is a binary framework focusing on the cause-effects of various events in a given system: a reaction can only be triggered once its reactants were produced (by other reactions) and none of its inhibitors are present in the environment. In particular, it gives the modeller the ability to trace explicitly why a certain event (reaction) was eventually triggered. Its two main principles, the non-permanency assumption and the threshold assumption, distinguish it from other modelling frameworks (e.g., ODE-based, or Petri net-based, Boolean networks). In our experience, see [3–5], the modeller is forced in reaction systems to be explicit about the nature of all interactions in the system, rather than rely on the interplay between numerical parameters of the system, which necessarily brings a plus of clarity in the model's assumptions.

Having an easy-to-use computer support for reaction systems is a crucial ingredient in developing the research on this topic, both the theoretical line exploring their mathematical properties, as well as the applied one exploring their modelling expressivity in various domains. This is exactly where WEBRSIM contributes, by offering a user-friendly, browser-based software for reaction systems. The software takes a simple textual input and it gives a simple output directly in the browser. It hides from the user the technical details of the implementation through its web-based service. At the same time, the source code of the back-end engine is openly available at [21] for developers to experiment with.

WEBRSIM is highly efficient, even with its current hosting on a standard web server. For example, we ran the simulation for the reaction system model of the Erbb signalling as the benchmark of [17]. This model comprised 6720 reactions and the simulation in WEBRSIM was successfully performed in less than three seconds. Detailed experiments done in [17] show that in fact WEBRSIM's computational efficiency is only marginally less than that of a highly parallelised version of HERESY [17], running on a dedicated GPU hardware with thousands of processors. WEBRSIM thus gives access to the standard user to a highly efficient simulation and analysis platform for reaction systems.

References

1. Azimi, S., Gratie, C., Ivanov, S., Manzoni, L., Petre, I., Porreca, A.E.: Complexity of model checking for reaction systems. Theor. Comput. Sci. **623**, 103–113 (2016)
2. Azimi, S., Gratie, C., Ivanov, S., Petre, I.: Dependency graphs and mass conservation in reaction systems. Theor. Comput. Sci. **598**, 23–39 (2015)
3. Azimi, S., Iancu, B., Petre, I.: Reaction system models for the heat shock response. Fundam. Inform. **131**(3–4), 299–312 (2014)
4. Azimi, S., Panchal, C., Czeizler, E., Petre, I.: Reaction systems models for the self-assembly of intermediate filaments. Ann. Univ. Buchar. **62**(2), 9–24 (2015)
5. Azimi, S., Panchal, C., Mizera, A., Petre, I.: Multi-stability, limit cycles, and period-doubling bifurcation with reaction systems. Int. J. Found. Comput. Sci. **28**(08), 1007–1020 (2017)
6. Brijder, R., Ehrenfeucht, A., Rozenberg, G.: A note on causalities in reaction systems. Electron. Commun. EASST **30**, 1–10 (2010)
7. Brijder, R., Ehrenfeucht, A., Rozenberg, G.: Reaction systems with duration. In: Kelemen, J., Kelemenová, A. (eds.) Computation, Cooperation, and Life. LNCS, vol. 6610, pp. 191–202. Springer, Heidelberg (2011). https://doi.org/10.1007/978-3-642-20000-7_16
8. Corolli, L., Maj, C., Marini, F., Besozzi, D., Mauri, G.: An excursion in reaction systems: from computer science to biology. Theor. Comput. Sci. **454**, 95–108 (2012)
9. Ehrenfeucht, A., Main, M., Rozenberg, G.: Combinatorics of life and death for reaction systems. Int. J. Found. Comput. Sci. **21**(03), 345–356 (2010)
10. Ehrenfeucht, A., Petre, I., Rozenberg, G.: Reaction systems: a model of computation inspired by the functioning of the living cell, pp. 1–32. World Scientific, 01 July 2018 (2016)

11. Ehrenfeucht, A., Rozenberg, G.: Events and modules in reaction systems. Theor. Comput. Sci. **376**(1), 3–16 (2007)
12. Ehrenfeucht, A., Rozenberg, G.: Reaction systems. Fundam. Inform. **75**(1), 263–280 (2007)
13. Ehrenfeucht, A., Rozenberg, G.: Introducing time in reaction systems. Theor. Comput. Sci. **410**(4), 310–322 (2009)
14. Free Software Foundation. GNU General Public License. http://www.gnu.org/licenses/gpl.html
15. Hirvensalo, M.: Quantum computing. In: Runehov, A.L.C., Oviedo, L. (eds.) Encyclopedia of Sciences and Religions, pp. 1922–1926. Springer, Dordrecht (2013). https://doi.org/10.1007/978-1-4020-8265-8
16. Meski, A., Penczek, W., Rozenberg, G.: Model checking temporal properties of reaction systems. Inf. Sci. **313**, 24–42 (2015)
17. Marco, S.: Efficient simulation of reaction systems on graphics processing units. Fundam. Inform. **154**(1–4), 307–321 (2017)
18. Petre, I., et al.: A simple mass-action model for the eukaryotic heat shock response and its mathematical validation. Natural Comput. **10**(1), 595–612 (2011)
19. Salomaa, A.: Applications of the Chinese remainder theorem to reaction systems with duration. Theor. Comput. Sci. **598**, 15–22 (2015)
20. Documentation of `Data.Set`. http://hackage.haskell.org/package/containers-0.5.11.0/docs/Data-Set.html
21. GitHub – scolobb/brsim: A Basic Reaction System Simulator. https://github.com/scolobb/brsim
22. Web interface for Basic Reaction System Simulator. http://combio.abo.fi/research/reaction-systems/reaction-system-simulator/

Open Problems in Membrane Computing and How Not to Solve Them

Alberto Leporati[(✉)], Luca Manzoni, Giancarlo Mauri, Antonio E. Porreca, and Claudio Zandron

Dipartimento di Informatica, Sistemistica e Comunicazione, Università degli Studi di Milano-Bicocca, Viale Sarca 336/14, 20126 Milano, Italy
{leporati,luca.manzoni,mauri,porreca,zandron}@disco.unimib.it

Abstract. We present some high-level open problems in the complexity theory of membrane systems, related to the actual computing power of confluence vs determinism, semi-uniformity vs uniformity, deep vs shallow membrane structures, membrane division vs internal evolution of membranes. For each of these problems we present some reasonable approaches that are, however, unable to be employed "as-is" to provide a complete solution. This will hopefully sparkle new ideas that will allow tackling these open problems.

1 Introduction

It is common in most of the literature, not only of P systems but of science in general, to highlight the successful approaches, not only the ones that gave positive results, but also the ones that were successful in proving the negative ones. It is considerably rarer to write about the unsuccessful ideas, the roads that, while initially promising, were unable to give a full and satisfactory answer to a research question under examination. Unfortunately, this leads multiple people to follow the same path multiple times without the insight that might have been gained by sharing previous failed attempts. Here we want to take the opportunity to share some problems that we consider of particular interest for the membrane computing community but, since they are still open problems, we are not able to share a solution to them. What we want to share is, instead, a collection of promising attempts that were ultimately unsuccessful in solving these open problems. While unsuccessful, those attempts were far from useless: we were able to gain a deeper understanding of the problems and to solve some special cases. We think that, by sharing our non-working approaches we might be able to help the community in gaining a better understanding of these open problems and, hopefully, produce inspiration on how to solve them.

2 Confluence vs Determinism

P systems solving decision problems (*recogniser P systems* [16]) are usually required to be *confluent* [16] rather than strictly deterministic. That is, they

ⓒ Springer Nature Switzerland AG 2018
C. Graciani et al. (Eds.): Pérez-Jiménez Festschrift, LNCS 11270, pp. 182–191, 2018.
https://doi.org/10.1007/978-3-030-00265-7_15

are allowed to result in multiple computations, as long as all of them agree on the final result, which is acceptance or rejection.

This sometimes simplifies the presentation of some algorithms. For instance, a classic membrane computing technique [14, 22] consists in generating all 2^n truth assignments of n variables by using membrane division rules of the form $[x_i]_h \rightarrow [t_i]_h [f_i]_h$, with $1 \leq i \leq n$. The membrane division is triggered separately in each membrane with label h by one of the objects x_i, nondeterministically chosen at each computation step. Irrespective of all such nondeterministic choices, the final result is invariably a set of 2^n membranes, each containing a different truth assignment.

Notice, however, that this kind of nondeterminism can be completely avoided by serialising the generation of truth assignments for each variable: first all instances of x_1 trigger the division, then all instances of x_2, and so on. This can be achieved by adding an extra subscript to each object, which counts down to zero and only then starts the division process.

It is often the case that confluent nondeterminism can be avoided in a similar way, although this is usually proved by exhibiting a deterministic algorithm, rather than showing how to remove the nondeterminism from existing algorithms. It is then natural to ask whether this is indeed always the case, or if there exists a variant of P systems where confluent nondeterminism is strictly stronger than determinism.

For powerful enough P systems (e.g., able to efficiently simulate deterministic Turing machines, or stronger than that) we feel that the existence of such a variant would be very surprising, although there do exist confluent nondeterministic algorithms with no known deterministic version. For instance, the currently known proof of efficient universality (i.e., the ability to simulate any Turing machine with a polynomial slowdown) of P systems with active membranes using elementary membrane division [1] relies on a massive amount of nondeterministic choices performed at each simulated step; these are due to the fact that send-in communication rules cannot differentiate among membranes having the same label and electrical charges.

2.1 Simulation of Priorities

To better examine the problem given by nondeterminism, even in the case of confluence, we will use a simple example. Consider the following two rules:

$$[a]_h^+ \rightarrow [\,]_h^0 \, b \tag{1}$$
$$[a \rightarrow w']_h^+ \tag{2}$$

When an instance of an object a is present inside a membrane with label h and positive charge, both rule (1) and rule (2) are applicable and, in a nondeterministic system, a nondeterministic choice is performed. If the P system is confluent, then the actual outcome of this choice is immaterial. However, if we know that the P system is a *deterministic* one then we can also infer a stronger condition: there will never be any instance of objects of type a inside any membrane with label h with charge $+$ in the only computation starting from the initial configuration. Otherwise, there would be two different computations generated by the presence of a, contradicting the assumption that the P system is deterministic.

If we want to simulate a confluent system by means of a deterministic one in a somewhat direct way, then we must take care of situations like the one above. How can we simulate a situation that a deterministic P system cannot even reach? One such approach is the introduction of rule priorities. As shown in [10], for P systems with active membranes with charges the introduction of rule priorities *does not* change the computational power of confluent systems when the bound on computation time is at least polynomial.

Why It Might Work. Rule priorities provide a way of addressing the problem of the example above and the more general problem of conflicts among rules. Suppose that in the previous example rule (1) has higher priority than rule (2). Then, there is no conflict between the two rules: the first one will always be applied if no other blocking rule with higher priority has already been applied, and the second one will be applied to all remaining copies of a. In fact, once a total ordering has been provided among all rules then no further conflict can happen: among two rules one will always have higher priority than the other. Therefore, now in a deterministic system we can have objects of type a inside a membrane with label h and positive charge, since their presence will not generate two distinct computations anymore.

Why It Does Not Work. If with rule priorities it is never possible to obtain two distinct computations due to a conflict between rules, since there are no conflicts anymore, then have we found a way to have one single computation starting from the initial configuration? Have we found a way to obtain determinism from confluence? The answer is, unfortunately, negative. The main problem is given by *send-in* communication rules. Consider, for example, the following rule:

$$a\,[\,]_h^+ \rightarrow [b]_h^- \tag{3}$$

Furthermore, suppose that there are two membranes with label h and positive charge inside the membrane where a is located. If there is a single instance of a then rule (3) can send in a in either of the two membranes in a nondeterministic way. If the contents of the two membranes differ, then two computations are actually generated. In a confluent system this is not a problem, but for a deterministic system the application of a send-in rule is valid in only two situations:

- There are enough instances of object a to be sent-in inside all the membranes where rule (3) was applicable;
- The contents of all the membranes where rule (3) is applicable were actually the same.

This problem cannot be solved by rule priorities; in fact, there is no rule conflict in the example that we just presented. This is the main difference between the nondeterminism introduced by send-in rules and the one introduced by rule conflicts. This remains the main obstacle in showing that confluence and determinism give, for powerful enough systems, the same computational power.

3   Semi-uniformity vs Uniformity

Recogniser P systems usually appear in families $\Pi = \{\Pi_x : x \in \Sigma^*\}$, where each member of the family is associated to a string x and accepts if and only if x belongs to a given language.

A family of P systems is usually required to be at least *semi-uniform*, that is, to have an associated Turing machine M with some suitable resource bound (usually, polynomial time) such that M on input x outputs a suitable encoding of Π_x [11,16].

A more restrictive condition on families of P systems is full-fledged *uniformity* [11,16]: there exist *two* Turing machines F and E (again, usually with polynomial runtime) such that F on input $n = |x|$ constructs a P system "skeleton" Π_n, valid for all strings of length n, and E on input x produces a multiset w encoding x, which is then placed inside the input region of Π_n, giving the P system Π_x that computes the answer.

It is known [12] that, for restrictive enough resource bounds, uniformity is weaker than semi-uniformity. However, when polynomial-time semi-uniform solutions to problems sometimes appear in the literature first, polynomial-time uniform solutions usually follow.

We conjecture that polynomial-time uniformity and semi-uniformity do indeed coincide for powerful enough P systems, such as standard P systems with active membranes [14]. The idea here is that a semi-uniform family could be made uniform by simulating the "semi-uniform portion" of the construction, depending on the actual symbols of $x \in \Sigma^n$, with the P system constructed for all strings of length n.

3.1   Building and Filling the Membrane Structure at Runtime

Given a semi-uniform family of P systems Π constructed by a machine M we want to build two machines E and F that define a uniform family of P systems that solves the same problems that are solved by the systems in Π.

One of the possible ideas to prove the equivalence of uniformity and semi-uniformity, at least for powerful enough kinds of P systems, is to capture the power of machine E of the uniformity condition, i.e., the one that has access to the entire input and not only to its length. While that machine does not have the ability to construct the membrane structure of the P system or even to put objects inside membranes different from the input ones, it can perform the same operations of machine M of the semi-uniformity condition, therefore obtaining a "copy" of the initial membrane structure of the P system. Can we make use of such knowledge to overcome the limitation of uniformity and show that we can, in fact, simulate semi-uniformity?

Why It Might Work. With the knowledge of the initial membrane structure and the content it is quite easy to build, for each object type a new types of objects of the form a_p where p is a path inside the membrane structure. It is usually not hard to write rules "consuming" the path p while moving the objects around following the directions stored in p. Therefore, in polynomial time it is possible to move objects around the membrane structure. Since the objects in the initial system built by M on input x might depend on the input, we can delegate the creation of all the initial objects to machine E. The multiset produced as output of E on input x will contain all the objects present in the initial membrane structure built by M. However, that objects will be subscripted by a path as shown before. In this way they will be able to reach the correct position before starting to act like the objects in the system built by M.

Why It Does Not Work. A larger problem than the one tackled above is the fact that there is no assurance that the membrane structure generated by machine M will be the same on two different inputs x and y even when they are of the same length. We might think that machine F of the uniformity condition might be able to build a membrane structure that is the "sum" of all possible membrane structures that machine M can generate for inputs of a certain length. By looking at the literature it is possible to observe that this is an effective method to convert semi-uniform families to uniform ones. This method, however, will not work in general. A combinatorial analysis shows that the membrane structures that can be generated by machine M are too many to obtain a polynomially-sized membrane structure that contains all of them as substructures. The sharp contrast between the efficacy of this method in practice and its viability as a formal tool to prove the equivalence of uniformity and semi-uniformity leaves us with the following question: is a super-polynomial number of different membrane structures for inputs of the same length actually useful? Can we prove that this is never the case?

4   Membrane Division vs Internal Evolution

The computing power of a *single* membrane (for cell-like P systems) or cell (for tissue-like P systems) working in polynomial time usually has a **P** upper bound, as already proved by the "Milano theorem" [22]; the only way to exceed this bound would be to include *really overly powerful* rules (e.g., rules able to perform an **NP**-complete task in a single step). The **P** upper bound can actually be achieved by having cooperative rewriting rules (even minimal cooperation [20,21] suffices) or rules able to simulate them indirectly (e.g., active membrane rules with membrane charges [10]). Several techniques for simulating polynomial-time Turing machines using a single membrane are known [9].

Any additional power beyond **P** of models presented in the literature is due to membrane division, first exploited in order to solve **NP**-complete problems in polynomial time [14]. Membrane division enables us to create exponentially many processing units working in parallel; by using communication rules, these can synchronise and exchange information (this is the famous space-for-time trade-off in membrane computing).

It is reasonable to expect that P system variants where the power of a single membrane working in polynomial time coincides with **P** can be standardised in a "Turing machine normal form": each membrane performs a Turing machine simulation[1], and the communication and division rules implement a network, whose shape can be exploited to simulate nondeterminism, alternation, or oracle queries [9].

Notice that what previously described does not necessarily carry over to variants of P systems with weaker rules internal to the membranes, such as "P conjecture systems" [15, Problem F] (active membranes without charges), which do not seem able to simulate cooperation [2], or with communication restricted to a single direction, either send-out [6,7,19] or send-in only [18].

4.1   Putting a Turing Machine Inside a Membrane

One approach that is at first glance promising to solve the problem of characterising the computational power of a single membrane is to simply substitute the content of a membrane with a Turing machine simulated by that membrane, that makes its behaviour indistinguishable from the one of the original membrane. For an example, we will use P systems with more than three charges, like the ones in [10].

Let M be a Turing machine with set of states Q, alphabet Σ, transition function δ, and working in space n. Then it can be simulated by a single membrane M_h with the following kinds of rules:

$$[a_i \to b_i \, r_d]_{M_h}^{q_i} \qquad \text{for } q, r \in Q, \, a, b \in \Sigma, \, 1 \le i \le n, \text{ and } \delta(q, a) = (r, b, d)$$
$$[r_d]_{M_h}^{q_i} \to [\,]_{M_h}^{r_{i+d}} \, \# \qquad \text{for } q, r \in Q, \, r \in \{-1, 1\}, \text{ and } 1 \le i \le n$$

The main idea is that in the objects inside the membrane it is possible to store the tape of the machine and the state and position of the tape head are stored in the charge of M_h. By alternating evolution rules (to rewrite the tape) and send-outs (to update the state and position of the tape head) it is possible to simulate an entire Turing machine inside a single membrane. How can we use this to replace the entire inner working of a membrane?

Why It Might Work. If we consider an isolated membrane and we investigate its behaviour from the outside we are only interested in what is sent out and what is sent in. That is, if we are unable to distinguish a membrane h and a membrane simulating machine M that simulates h then the computational power of a single membrane cannot be greater than the one of machine M and, if M is a deterministic machine working in polynomial time then all the power of a P system comprised of such membranes must reside in the ability of the

---

[1] This can be trivially implemented by having each membrane simulate a Turing machine which, in turn, simulates the original membrane via the Milano theorem.

membranes to divide. Since most variants of P systems when limited to a single membrane are subjected to the Milano theorem, we can think that, with a careful enough "interfacing" with the objects sent in from the environment (which, when they enter, are not part of the machine tape and must be "incorporated" into it by other rules) we might be able to replicate (with a polynomial slowdown) the entire behaviour of a membrane h with the machine M simulated inside another membrane. And, in fact we can. So, why this does not prove that we can replace all the "inner working" of a membrane with a Turing machine?

Why It Does Not Work. When considering a membrane in isolation we can easily replace it with a Turing machine - and we can replace the Turing machine with a membrane simulating it. There is, however, one major problem. Consider the following membrane structure:

$$\underbrace{[[\,]_k \cdots [\,]_k]_h}_{2^n}$$

If we replace the "inner working" of membrane h with the simulation performed by a Turing machine, then at the moment when the membranes with label k send out – all at the same time – 2^n instances of the same object a then the simulation inside h is not sufficient anymore. It is not possible to write all the objects (either one at time or all together) on the Turing machine tape for reasons either of space (the tape is not long enough) or time (writing them one at a time requires exponentially many time steps). We would like to write, instead, the number of objects of type a that have entered membrane h by send-out. This, however, requires the power to count or, more precisely, the power to convert from unary to binary the number of objects. While this is possible with cooperative rewriting rules, it is unclear if for P systems with charges this is a task feasible for a single membrane.

5   Deep vs Shallow Membrane Structures

Let us now consider cell-like P systems with membrane division, for instance P systems with active membranes [14]. It has already been shown that the nesting depth of membranes (more specifically, the nesting depth of membranes with associated division rules, which we might call *division depth*) is one of the most influential variables when establishing the efficiency of these P systems.

Indeed, P systems without membrane division (i.e., with division depth 0) are known to characterise the complexity class **P** in polynomial time [22]. At the other end of the spectrum, we have P systems with active membranes with elementary and non-elementary division rules (i.e., with polynomial division depth), which characterise **PSPACE** in polynomial time.

When only elementary membrane division is allowed (i.e., division depth 1), then the intermediate complexity class $\mathbf{P}^{\#\mathbf{P}}$ is characterised in polynomial time [3,7]. This class contains all decision problems solved by deterministic polynomial-time Turing machines with oracles for counting problems in the class #**P** [13].

It has been proved that moving from any constant division depth d to division depth $d+1$ allows the P systems to simulate Turing machines with more powerful oracles [4]. We conjecture that this is in fact a proper hierarchy. This result would require proving the upper bounds corresponding to the known lower bounds.

It also remains open to characterise the computing power of polynomial-time P systems with other division depths, such as $O(\log n)$.

More Profound Reasons for the Split. The reason for this split between shallow and deep membrane structures seems to be related to the way confluent systems perform a "simulation" of non-determinism by means of parallel computations inside different membranes. Shallow membrane structures can perform exponentially many computations (and each computation can perform the same work of a polynomial-time Turing machine) inside exponentially many elementary membranes; the results of the different computations are then collected inside the outermost membrane. P systems with a deep membrane structure can also perform the same number of computations, but the main difference is that they can combine the results in a more structured way: the results are, in some sense, organized hierarchically. When non-confluence is allowed, the importance of the membrane structure seems to fade away: it is known that shallow membrane structures are able to achieve the full power of **PSPACE** [8]. It is therefore natural to ask what is the relation between the power granted by non-confluence and the one obtained by having a deep membrane structure.

It seems that the problem of the computational power that depth gives to P systems is a more profound question related to the computational power that automata (or limited-resources Turing machines) can gain with different communication topologies. For example, with a polynomial time limit, automata on a grid are usually limited to the power of a deterministic Turing machine working in polynomial time. Similar results also hold for tissue P systems embedded in the Euclidean space [5], showing another point of contact with the more general problem. This approach linking complexity and communication topologies is quite new [17] and we think that it might be able to give us a better understanding of the link between membrane depth and computational power in P systems.

References

1. Alhazov, A., Leporati, A., Mauri, G., Porreca, A.E., Zandron, C.: Space complexity equivalence of P systems with active membranes and Turing machines. Theor. Comput. Sci. **529**, 69–81 (2014)
2. Gutiérrez–Naranjo, M.A., Pérez–Jiménez, M.J., Riscos–Núñez, A., Romero–Campero, F.J.: On the power of dissolution in P systems with active membranes. In: Freund, R., Păun, G., Rozenberg, G., Salomaa, A. (eds.) WMC 2005. LNCS, vol. 3850, pp. 224–240. Springer, Heidelberg (2006). https://doi.org/10.1007/11603047_16

3. Leporati, A., Manzoni, L., Mauri, G., Porreca, A.E., Zandron, C.: Simulating elementary active membranes, with an application to the P conjecture. In: Gheorghe, M., Rozenberg, G., Salomaa, A., Sosík, P., Zandron, C. (eds.) CMC 2014. LNCS, vol. 8961, pp. 284–299. Springer, Cham (2014). https://doi.org/10.1007/978-3-319-14370-5_18

4. Leporati, A., Manzoni, L., Mauri, G., Porreca, A.E., Zandron, C.: Membrane division, oracles, and the counting hierarchy. Fundam. Inform. **138**(1–2), 97–111 (2015)

5. Leporati, A., Manzoni, L., Mauri, G., Porreca, A.E., Zandron, C.: Tissue P systems in the Euclidean space. In: Gheorghe, M., Petre, I., Pérez-Jiménez, M.J., Rozenberg, G., Salomaa, A. (eds.) Multidisciplinary Creativity: Homage to Gheorghe Păun on His 65th Birthday, pp. 118–128. Editura Spandugino (2015)

6. Leporati, A., Manzoni, L., Mauri, G., Porreca, A.E., Zandron, C.: Monodirectional P systems. Nat. Comput. **15**(4), 551–564 (2016)

7. Leporati, A., Manzoni, L., Mauri, G., Porreca, A.E., Zandron, C.: The counting power of P systems with antimatter. Theor. Comput. Sci. **701**, 161–173 (2017)

8. Leporati, A., Manzoni, L., Mauri, G., Porreca, A.E., Zandron, C.: Shallow nonconfluent P systems. In: Leporati, A., Rozenberg, G., Salomaa, A., Zandron, C. (eds.) CMC 2016. LNCS, vol. 10105, pp. 307–316. Springer, Cham (2017). https://doi.org/10.1007/978-3-319-54072-6_19

9. Leporati, A., Manzoni, L., Mauri, G., Porreca, A.E., Zandron, C.: Subroutines in P systems and closure properties of their complexity classes. In: Graciani, C., Păun, G., Riscos-Núñez, A., Valencia-Cabrera, L. (eds.) 15th Brainstorming Week on Membrane Computing, pp. 115–128, No. 1/2017 in RGNC Reports. Fénix Editora (2017)

10. Leporati, A., Manzoni, L., Mauri, G., Porreca, A.E., Zandron, C.: A toolbox for simpler active membrane algorithms. Theor. Comput. Sci. **673**, 42–57 (2017)

11. Murphy, N., Woods, D.: The computational power of membrane systems under tight uniformity conditions. Nat. Comput. **10**(1), 613–632 (2011)

12. Murphy, N., Woods, D.: Uniformity is weaker than semi-uniformity for some membrane systems. Fundam. Inform. **134**(1–2), 129–152 (2014)

13. Papadimitriou, C.H.: Computational Complexity. Addison-Wesley, Boston (1993)

14. Păun, G.: P systems with active membranes: attacking NP-complete problems. J. Autom. Lang. Comb. **6**(1), 75–90 (2001)

15. Păun, G.: Further twenty six open problems in membrane computing. In: Gutíerrez-Naranjo, M.A., Riscos-Nuñez, A., Romero-Campero, F.J., Sburlan, D. (eds.) Proceedings of the Third Brainstorming Week on Membrane Computing, pp. 249–262. Fénix Editora (2005)

16. Pérez-Jiménez, M.J., Romero-Jiménez, A., Sancho-Caparrini, F.: Complexity classes in models of cellular computing with membranes. Nat. Comput. **2**(3), 265–284 (2003)

17. Porreca, A.E.: Communication topologies in natural computing, Seminar of the CANA research group, Laboratoire d'Informatique et Systèmes (LIS), UMR 7020, Aix-Marseille Université, CNRS, Université de Toulon, France (2018). https://aeporreca.org/talks/

18. Valencia-Cabrera, L., Orellana-Martín, D., Martínez-del Amor, M.A., Riscos-Núñez, A., Pérez-Jiménez, M.J.: Restricted polarizationless P systems with active membranes: minimal cooperation only inwards. In: Graciani, C., Păun, G., Riscos-Núñez, A., Valencia-Cabrera, L. (eds.) 15th Brainstorming Week on Membrane Computing, pp. 215–252, No. 1/2017 in RGNC Reports. Fénix Editora (2017)

19. Valencia-Cabrera, L., Orellana-Martín, D., Martínez-del Amor, M.A., Riscos-Núñez, A., Pérez-Jiménez, M.J.: Restricted polarizationless P systems with active membranes: Minimal cooperation only outwards. In: Graciani, C., Păun, G., Riscos-Núñez, A., Valencia-Cabrera, L. (eds.) 15th Brainstorming Week on Membrane Computing, pp. 253–290. No. 1/2017 in RGNC Reports. Fénix Editora (2017)

20. Valencia-Cabrera, L., Orellana-Martín, D., Martínez-del-Amor, M.A., Riscos-Núñez, A., Pérez-Jiménez, M.J.: Computational efficiency of minimal cooperation and distribution in polarizationless P systems with active membranes. Fundam. Inf. **153**(1–2), 147–172 (2017)

21. Valencia-Cabrera, L., Orellana-Martín, D., Martínez-del-Amor, M.A., Riscos-Núñez, A., Pérez-Jiménez, M.J.: Reaching efficiency through collaboration in membrane systems: dissolution, polarization and cooperation. Theor. Comput. Sci. **701**, 226–234 (2017)

22. Zandron, C., Ferretti, C., Mauri, G.: Solving NP-complete problems using P systems with active membranes. In: Antoniou, I., Calude, C.S., Dinneen, M.J. (eds.) Unconventional Models of Computation, UMC'2K, pp. 289–301. Springer, Heidelberg (2001). https://doi.org/10.1007/978-1-4471-0313-4_21

A Note on the Entropy of Computation

Vincenzo Manca[✉]

Department of Computer Science, Center for BioMedical Computing,
University of Verona, Verona, Italy
vincenzo.manca@univr.it

Abstract. In this note a computation is considered as a special dynamics in a space of events (sets of possible states). In this perspective, it turns out that computations are anti-entropic processes. This point of view is compared with well-known results about the energetic aspects of computations, by discussing perspectives that could be of interest and relevance in many models of natural computing.

1 Shannon's Entropy and Thermodynamic Entropy

Shannon founded Information Theory [10,13,27] on the notion of Information Source, that is, a pair (X, p_X) of a variable X and a probability distribution p_X assigning to every value of X its probability of occurring. In this framework he defined a measure of information quantity to the event $X = a$ (X assumes the value a):

$$Inf(X = a) = -\lg_2 p_X(a).$$

The intuitive motivation for the equation above is due to the fact that the information quantity associated to an event is inversely proportional to the probability of the event, and moreover, the information quantity has to be additive for pair of independent events (for which $p(a_1, a_2) = p(a_1)p(a_2)$):

$$Inf(E_1, E_2) = Inf(E_1) + Inf(E_2).$$

On the basis of Inf definition, if $\widehat{X}$ denotes the range of variable X, the entropy of the information source (X, p_X) is defined by:

$$H(X, p_X) = \sum_{a \in \widehat{X}} p_X(a) Inf(X = a) = -\sum_{a \in \widehat{X}} p_X(a) \lg_2 p_X(a).$$

Therefore, the entropy of an information source is the mean (in probabilistic sense) of the information quantity of the events generated by the information source (X, p_X).

One crucial result about entropy is the **Equipartition Property** (proved by Shannon in an appendix to its paper): in the class of information sources over the same variable X, entropy reaches its maximum value for a source (X, q_X) where q_X is the uniform probability distribution (all the values of variable X are assumed with the same probability).

© Springer Nature Switzerland AG 2018
C. Graciani et al. (Eds.): Pérez-Jiménez Festschrift, LNCS 11270, pp. 192–203, 2018.
https://doi.org/10.1007/978-3-030-00265-7_16

This notion of entropy is strongly related to the thermodynamic entropy S that emerged in physics since Carnot analysis of heat-work conversion [11] and was named by Clausius "entropy" (from a Greek root "en-tropos" meaning "internal verse"). Entropy is subjected to a famous inequality stating the second principle of Thermodynamics for isolated systems (systems that do not exchange energy with their environment), where $\Delta S = S_{t'} - S_t, t' > t$:

$$\Delta S \geq 0.$$

In years 1870's, Ludvig Boltzmann started a rigorous mathematical analysis of a thermodynamic system consisting of an ideal gas within a volume, aimed at explaining the apparent contradiction of the inequality above with respect to the equations of Newtonian mechanics underlying the microscopic reality on which heat phenomena are based on. Boltzmann question was: "From where the inequality comes from, if molecules colliding in a gas follow mechanics equational laws with no intrinsic time arrow?"

Boltzmann introduced, in a systematic way, a probability perspective in the analysis of physical phenomena that for its importance transcends the particular field of his investigation. In fact, after Boltzmann probability [8,14,15,31] became a crucial aspect of any theory in modern physics. He defined a function H, which in discrete terms can be expressed by:

$$H = \sum_{i=1,m} n_i \lg_2 n_i$$

where n_i are the number of gas molecules having velocities in the i-class of velocities (velocities are partitioned in m disjoint classes).

By simple algebraic passages it turns out that H function coincides, apart a multiplicative positive constant, and the negative sign, with Shannon's entropy (Shannon quotes Boltzmann's work). On the basis of H function Boltzmann proved the microscopic representation of Clausius entropy S [19]:

$$S = k \log_e W \tag{1}$$

where W is the number of distinguishable micro-states associated to the thermodynamic macro-state of the system, and k is the so-called Boltzmann constant (two micro-states are associated to the same macro-state if they have the same velocity distribution, even if realized by different velocities of single molecules).

However, despite this remarkable result, Boltzmann was not able to deduce that $\Delta S \geq 0$, by using H function. The so-called Theorem H stating $H_{t+1} \leq H_t$, or $\Delta H \leq 0$, was never proved by him in a satisfactory way (from $\Delta H \leq 0$ inequality $\Delta S \geq 0$ follows as an easy consequence of the above equation, where the opposite verses of inequalities are related to the different sign between Boltzmann's H and Shannon's H) [6,9,11,22,29,30].

Let us shortly outline, mainly in discrete terms, the argument underlying Boltzmann's microscopic representation of thermodynamic entropy. In an ideal gas the volume × pressure product equals the product of gas constant R, absolute temperature and the number of gas moles:

$$PV = NRT. \tag{2}$$

If we replace the number N of gas moles by n/A where n is the number of molecules and A is the Avogadro constant, we get an equivalent formulation, where $k = R/A$ is called the Boltzmann constant:

$$PV = nkT. \tag{3}$$

If the gas expands from a volume V_1 to a volume V, by taking a heat quantity Q and leaving unchanged the value of T, we have:

$$Q = \int_{V_1}^{V} P dv \tag{4}$$

and, according to Eq. (2), we get:

$$Q = \int_{V_1}^{V} nkT/V \, dv = nkT \int_{V_1}^{V} 1/V \, dv = nkT(\ln V - \ln V_1). \tag{5}$$

Finally, assuming $V_1 = 1$, we obtain:

$$Q/T = nk \ln V \tag{6}$$

but the ratio Q/T, is by definition the difference of the gas entropy in passing from V_1 to V, therefore:

$$S = nk \ln V \tag{7}$$

that is:

$$S = k \ln V^n \tag{8}$$

where V^n represents the number of possible arrangements of n molecules in V volume cells. The gas is spatially homogeneously distributed and molecules with the same speed are indiscernible. Let us discretize speed values in m intervals: $v_1 \pm \Delta, v_2 \pm \Delta, \ldots, v_m \pm \Delta$ therefore, the possible allocations of molecules in the volume is, apart multiplicative constants, the number W of different ways in which n molecules can be distributed into m different velocity classes, where W corresponds to number of micro-states associated to the thermodynamic macro-state. Whence, the famous Boltzmann's equation follows:

$$S = k \ln W. \tag{9}$$

but the number W is given by the following multinomial expression (Boltzmann's "Wahrscheinlichkeit" Principle):

$$W = \frac{n!}{n_1! n_2! \ldots n_m!} \tag{10}$$

therefore:

$$S = k \ln \frac{n!}{n_1! n_2! \ldots n_m!} \tag{11}$$

from which, by assuming asymptotically $\ln n! = n \ln n$, as a consequence of Stirling approximation $n! \approx \sqrt{2\pi n}\, n^n/e^n$ [14], we can derive:

$$S = kn \ln n - k(n_1 \ln n_1 + n_2 \ln n_2 + \ldots n_m \ln n_m)$$

if, for $i = 1, \ldots m$, we express n_i by means of $p_i = n_i/n$, that is, $n_i = np_i$, then we get $(p_1 + p_2 + \ldots + p_m = 1)$:

$$S = kn \ln n - k(np_1 \ln np_1 + np_2 \ln np_2 + \ldots + np_m \ln np_m)$$

$$S = kn \ln n - kn[p_1(\ln n + \ln p_1) + p_2(\ln n + \ln p_2) + \ldots + p_m(\ln n + \ln p_m)]$$

$$S = kn \ln n - kn \ln n[p_1 + p_2 - + \ldots + p_m] - kn(p_1 \ln p_1 + p_2 \ln p_2 + \ldots + p_m \ln p_m)$$

$$S = -kn \sum_{i=1}^{m} p_i \ln p_i \text{ (Shannon Entropy apart fron the constant } kn).$$

The microscopic interpretation of thermodynamic entropy given by Boltzmann has a very general nature and it essentially provides a proof of the following principle ECP (Entropy Circularity Principle) that expresses Boltzmann's "Wahrscheinlichkeit" Principle in terms of Shannon information sources. In other words, the entropy of a source (X, p) is proportional to the logarithm of the number W of different sources over X with the same probabilities $\{p(x) | x \in \widehat{X}\}$, that is, the entropy of a given source is proportional to the number of sources having that entropy.

Entropy Circularity Principle (ECP)

$$H(X, p_X) = c \lg_2 |\mathbb{X}|$$

for some constant c, where:

$$\mathbb{X} = \{(X, q) \mid \{q(x) | x \in \widehat{X}\} = \{p(x) | x \in \widehat{X}\}\}.$$

From this principle emerges an interesting link between probabilistic and digital aspects of information. In fact, it can be proved that $\lg_2 n$ corresponds essentially to the minimum average number of binary digits necessary for encoding n different values (the exact value $digit_2(n)$ is bounded by: $(\lfloor lg_2(n) \rfloor - 2) < digit_2(n) < n(\lfloor lg_2(n) \rfloor))$. Therefore, entropy corresponds (apart multiplicative constants) to the average length of codewords encoding all the sources with the same entropy. This digital reading of the entropy relates also to the First Shannon Theorem stating that $H(X, p_X)$ is a lower bound for the (probabilistic) mean of yes-no questions necessary to guess a value $a \in \widehat{X}$ by asking $a \leq b?$, for suitable b in $\widehat{X}$. This explains in a very intuitive manner the meaning of $H(X, p)$ as average uncertainty of the source.

ECP principle points out a subtle aspect of entropy. It is, at same time, the average uncertainty of the events generated by a source, and the average uncertainty to identify the source in the class of those with the same probabilities, that is, the uncertainty of its *internal* space of events, but also the uncertainty of its *external* space.

Coming back to Boltzmann's analysis, information sources (X, p) correspond to the micro-states of the given gas volume (p is the velocity distribution normalized as probability distribution), whereas a macro-state of the considered thermodynamic system is completely identified by the pressure, volume and temperature of the gas. In this perspective, the ECP principle unveils the intrinsic *circularity* of entropy, because $H(X, p_X)$ is completely determined by p_X but, at same time, corresponds to the (logarithm of the) number of ways the probabilities of p_X can be distributed among the values of X.

The reason of Boltzmann failure in correctly proving H theorem is due to the fact that this theorem is, in its essence, an information Theory theorem (see [19, 22] for proofs of H theorem). In fact, in simple words, the irreversible increasing of entropy in time, results from a collective effect of a huge number of reversible elementary events, according to the large number of molecules and to the casual nature of their collisions. Molecules that collide, exchanging information, produce in time an increasing uniformity of molecule velocities. The global energy does not change (collision are elastic), but differences between velocities decrease, in the average, and this provides, in time, a greater value of the entropy, according to the entropy equipartition property.

2   Entropy and Computation

Shannon's Entropy entropy is related to physics and time is related to physical entropy. In computation the informational and physical components are intertwined, because any computational device is based on a physical process, where states, symbols, or configurations are transformed along a dynamics that starts by some initial configurations ending eventually, if computation reaches a result, with a final configuration (the initial one encodes some input data, the final one encodes the corresponding output data).

A computation is a trajectory in space of events, where events can be conceived as suitable sets of states (according to micro-state/macro-state Boltzmann's distinction, events are macro-states each of them consisting of a collection of micro-states). In this perspective, the entropy of a computation configuration is given by the number of different states belonging to the configuration. On the other side, if computation is a process intended to acquire information, this representation suggests that the configurations along a computation have to reduce the number of internal micro-states. In fact, the uncertainty of a configuration corresponds with the number of states it contains, and a computation tends to reduce the initial uncertainty by reaching certain configurations satisfying the constraints of a given problem. In terms of entropy, if the number of states of configurations reduce along a computation, consequently, the entropy $\lg W$

(W number of states) reduce along computation. In conclusion, a computation results to be an anti-entropic process. For this reason, from a physical point of view, a computation is a dissipative process releasing energy (heat) in the environment. A computational device is comparable with a living organism who increases the environment entropy for keeping its functions (maintaining his low internal entropy) [30], whereas a computational device increases the environment entropy for proceeding in the computation and for providing a final result (reaching a lower entropy for computation configurations).

A very intuitive way for realizing that "information is physical" is a simple device called *Centrifugal Governor*, invented by James Watt in 1788 for controlling his steam engine. The principle on which it is based is that of "conical pendulum". The axis of a rotating engine is supplied with an attached rigid arm terminating with a mass that can assume an angle with respect to the axis (two symmetrical arms in Watt's formulation, the masses at arms are negligible). When the axis is rotating, in proportion with the rotation speed, the mass at end of the arm is subjected to a centrifugal force rising the arm (see Fig. 1). This rising opens a valve, in proportion to the vertical rising of the arm, that diminishes a physical parameter related to the speed (a pressure in the case of a steam engine), and consequently, decreases the rotation speed. This phenomenon is a negative feedback that, according to the length of the arm, stabilizes the rotation speed to a fixed velocity (negative means that control acts in the opposite verse of the controlled action). It realizes a kind homeostasis (keeping some variables within a fixed sub-range of variability), a property that is crucial for any complex systems and thus is typical of living organisms.

The term "cybernetics" introduced by Wiener [35] comes from a Greek root expressing the action of guiding or controlling, and is essentially based on the image of Centrifugal Governor, where the arm length encodes the information capable of controlling the rotation speed (Wiener's book title is: Cybernetics, or Control and Communication in the Animal and the Machine). Information directs processes, but it is realized by a physical process too. And in the centrifugal governor mgh is the energetic cost of the control exerted by the arm on the rotation (see Fig. 1: m is the mass at the end of the arm, g the gravity acceleration, and h is the vertical rising of the arm with respect to its lowest position). We remark that from equation $mv^2/2 = mgh$ (kinetic energy = potential energy) it follows that rising $h = v^2/2g$ does not depend on the value of the mass, but only on the speed (if the mass is negligible in affecting the speed), and on the arm length. The value of the mass needs to be only sufficient to exert a centrifugal force.

The investigation about the relationship between information and physics has a long history, going back to the famous Maxwell demon, where the great physicist posed the problem of how an intelligent agent can interfere with physical principles (his demon was apparently violating the second principle of thermodynamics, by his ability of getting information about the molecules velocity). A very intensive and active line a research was developed in this regard (see [3] for a historical account of these researches) and continues to be developed

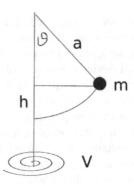

Fig. 1. The schema of the centrifugal governor.

even in recent years, especially under the pressure of the new results in quantum information and in quantum computing that show how much the informational perspective is essential for a deep analysis of quantum phenomena [25].

It is becoming always more evident that any mathematical model of physical phenomena is based on the acquisition of data coming from information sources generated by measurement processes. This fact is not of secondary relevance with respect to the construction of the model, especially when the data acquisition processes are very sophisticated and cannot ingenuously be considered as mirrors of reality, rather, the only reality on which reconstructions can be based on are just the information sources resulting from the interactions between the observer and the observed phenomena.

In a celebrated paper [16] Landauer asserts the *Erasure Principle*, according to which the erasure of a bit during a computation has an energetic cost of $kT \ln 2$ (k Boltzmann constant, T absolute temperature) [5,17,18]. This means that, if the computation entropy diminishes (for the reduction of computation configuration states), then the environment entropy has to compensate this decrease by increasing at least of an amount S and a corresponding quantity of energy ST has to be released in the environment, if T is its Kelvin temperature. The logic of this argument follows from our previous analysis of a computation process, when also the environment is considered and the second principle of thermodynamic is applied. The erasure principle is nothing else than a direct derivation of Boltzmann Eq. 1 when from two possible state one of them is chosen, by passing from $W = 2$ to $W = 1$. It is a lower bound, implicitly assuming that physical states that do not correspond to data do not change in number. However, it is important to remark that "erasing" has to be considered in the wide sense of decreasing states of a computation configuration, as indicated in Fig. 2 (the term erasure could be misleading, because it means erasing information, as uncertainty, that could correspond to writing a symbol on a Turing machine tape).

A continuation of Landauer's research has been developed by Bennet et al. [1–4] (in [3] a historical account of the theory of reversible computation is given).

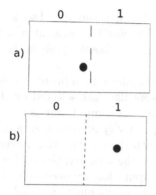

Fig. 2. Landauer's minimal erasure as a compression of the state space: in (a) the ball can be located in any of the two parts 0, 1 of the volume; in (b) it is confined in part 1, therefore in (b) the state space is reduced from two possibilities to only one of them.

Computation steps can be reversible and irreversible. The first kind of steps arise when information is not lost after the step and it is possible go back by returning to the data previously available. The irreversible steps are those that do not satisfy the condition of reversibility, because some data are lost after the step. In this framework it is shown that any computation can be performed in a reversible way, by using suitable strategies, where all the steps of a computation ending in a given configurations are copied in a suitable zone of a memory such that from the final state it is possible to go back in the reverse way. Of course, in this way computation is reversible, but I am perplexed about the effective meaning of this result. In fact, if information is gained by reducing the set of states of the initial configuration, then in the case of a reversible computation no new information is obtained at end of computation. This would require a different way of considering computations, where the evaluation of the amount of the gained information at the end of computation has to be defined in terms of some other mechanism of evaluation. Otherwise, if a computation does not generates information, for what reason it is performed? What is the advantage of obtaining a result when computation halts? If a result is not new information, what means result? The theory of reversible computation, even if correct, is surely incomplete, as far as it does not answer these open natural questions that it raises.

Any data configuration corresponds to a physical configuration, but the opposite is not true, therefore a data anti-entropic process does not necessarily imply a physical anti-entropic process. This means that data-reversible operations do not necessarily correspond to physically reversible transformations. In particular, copying operations are surely data-reversible, but this cannot always imply that the corresponding physical process of copying are reversible. In fact, consider a copy of a prefix of the tape content of a Turing machine [24]. This copy is realized at the opposite end of the tape (on the right of which only blank symbols are written). In this case, firstly the head of machine has to move along all the non-blank content of the tape, and at end some blank symbol are replaced by the prefix to be copied, but any replacement of a blank by a non-blank, in a Turing machine with many non-blank symbols, is an erasure in Landauer's sense.

Physical states representing data are a proper subset of all physical states of a system. Those that represent data are selected by the observer of the system who is using it for computing, but computation is not only a physical activity, it is mainly a coding-decoding activity according to a code chosen by a processor (another system) coupled with the computation memory device according to a mechanism that is not only in the memory, but is also internal to the processor. This means that in any computation we need to distinguish a passive and an active component. Forgetting this coupling and analyzing computations only on the side of the operations applied to the memory can be useful, but does not tell the whole story of the computing process. This partiality is, in my opinion, the source of some wrong conclusions drawn in the theory of reversible computation. If even all the logical gates are reversible, the internal states of the processor where the "interpreter" of the rules of computation process are located (which operation activate at each step) could require forgetting some information along the computation. Of course, this can be simulated by a new program where a trace of erased information is saved, but then the problem is only moved to the new interpreter. I am not sure about the continuation of this story, but is not so obvious that you can always get rid of erasing operations, when also the memory of the process and not only data transformations are taken into account. In any case I think that a general proof of it is so far missing.

In 1956 [28] Shannon found a universal Turing machine [24, 32] working with only two symbols, say $1, B$ (the symbol B for blank). In this case during computation symbol 1 can be replaced by symbol B, and *viceversa*, then we can deduce that any computation can be performed without Landauer's erasing, because replacing one symbol with the other one does not necessarily change the number of states of the computation configurations. This would imply that Shannon computations could escape from the Landauer's bound. Of course, this fact puts in evidence a subtle point in physical analysis of computation, according to which Landauer's bound evaluation needs to be integrated with other important aspects enlarging the computation states in order to include other physical parameter inherent to the internal state of the computation agent. Otherwise, Shannon's universal computations would suffer the same criticism addressed above to reversible computations, that is, the possibility of computations giving results with no gain of information.

The hidden trap, in analyzing an irreversible computation that is transformed into a reversible one, is that, even if the reversible computation steps do not change the entropy of data, the "program" managing the transformation has to be memorized at beginning of the computation. This means that, in the obtained data-reversible computation, the "internal" states of the computation agent executing the program surely changes and no reason can exclude that the related dynamics is irreversible. In any case, it has to be taken into account in the entropic/energetic evaluation of the computation.

In reversible computation theory a recurrent comparison is presented with the RNA Polymerase transcription from DNA to RNA, by arguing that this copy phenomenon is reversible, but in this comparison no mention is done about the anti-entropic character of RNA Polymerase that in order to be maintained "alive" requires some corresponding anti-entropic processes.

In conclusion, the theory of reversible computation is surely of a great interest for the new perspectives introduced in the analysis of computations, by disclosing subtle relations among time, space, and energy in computation [3], however, even if this theory is well-founded about the "logical reversibility", its extension to "physical reversibility" presents, in my opinion, several controversial aspects that need further clarifications and experiments.

3 Conclusions

Wheeler, a famous physicist of the last century coined the expression [34]: "It from bit", for expressing the fundamental role that information plays in Physics. The recent developments in quantum information and quantum physics seem to confirm this viewpoint [25] and clearly suggest the necessity of more general frameworks where informational concepts will be the main part of new physical theories. Natural computing, in a wider sense, could provide contexts suitable for developing specific analyses about entropy and computation (see, for example [7,12,19–21,23,26,33]). In a sense, models of reversible computation (brownian, billiard, electro-mechanical, nano-mechanical, enzymatic) are computation models in the field of natural computing, because they are mainly based on processes occurring in natural contexts and at different levels of complexity and miniaturization. Therefore, integrated perspectives of computation where physical informational aspects are jointly evaluated in their dynamical interplay are surely the most "natural" way of considering natural computing.

References

1. Bennett, C.H.: Logical reversibility of computation. IBM J. Res. Dev. **17**, 525–532 (1973)
2. Bennett, C.H.: Notes on the history of reversible computation. IBM J. Res. Dev. **32**(1), 16–23 (1988)
3. Bennett, C.H.: Time/space trade-offs for reversible computation. SIAM J. Comput. **18**, 766–776 (1989)
4. Bennett, C.H.: Notes on Landauer's principle, reversible computation, and Maxwell's Demon. Stud. Hist. Philos. Mod. Phys. **34**, 501–510 (2003)
5. Bérut, A.: Experimental verification of Landauer's principle linking information and thermodynamics. Nature **483**, 187–189 (2012)
6. Boltzmann, L., Weitere Studien uber das Wärmegleichgewicht unter Gasmolekulen, Sitzungsber. Kais. Akad. Wiss. Wien Math. Naturwiss. Classe **66**, 275–370 (1872)

7. Bonnici, V., Manca, V.: Informational laws of genome structures. Sci. Rep. **6** (2016). Article no. 28840. http://www.nature.com/articles/srep28840

8. Brillouin, L.: Scienze and Information Theory. Academic Press Inc., New York (1956)

9. Brush, S.G., Hall, N.S. (eds.): The Kinetic Theory of Gases. An Anthology of Classical Papers with Historical Commentary. Imperial College Press, London (2003)

10. Calude, C.S.: Information and Randomness: An algorithmic Perspective. Monographs in Theoretical Computer Science. An EATCS Series. Springer, Heidelberg (1994). https://doi.org/10.1007/978-3-662-03049-3

11. Carnot, S.: Reflections on the Motive Power of Heat (English Translation from French Edition of 1824, with Introduction by Lord Kelvin). Wiley, New York (1890)

12. Ciobanu, G., Păun, G., Pérez-Jiménez, M.J.: Applications of Membrane Computing. Springer, Heidelberg (2006). https://doi.org/10.1007/3-540-29937-8

13. Cover, T., Thomas, C.: Information Theory. Wiley, New York (1991)

14. Feller, W.: An Introduction to Probability Theory and Its Applications. Wiley, New York (1968)

15. Jaynes, E.T.: Information theory and statistical mechanics. Phys. Rev. **33**(5), 620–630 (1957)

16. Landauer, R.: Irreversibility and heat generation in the computing process. IBM J. Res. Dev. **5**, 183–191 (1961)

17. Landauer, R.: Dissipation and noise immunity in computation and communication. Nature **335**, 779–784 (1988)

18. Lloyd, S.: Ultimate physical limits to computation. Nature **406**, 1047–1054 (2000)

19. Manca, V.: Infobiotics: Information in Biotic Systems. Springer, Heidelberg (2013). https://doi.org/10.1007/978-3-642-36223-1

20. Manca, V.: Grammars for discrete dynamics. In: Holzinger, A. (ed.) Machine Learning for Health Informatics: State-of-the-Art and Future Challenges. LNCS (LNAI), vol. 9605, pp. 37–58. Springer, Cham (2016). https://doi.org/10.1007/978-3-319-50478-0_3

21. Manca, V.: The principles of informational genomics. Theor. Comput. Sci. **701**, 190–202 (2017)

22. Manca, V.: An informational proof of H-theorem. Open Access Libr. (Mod. Phys.) **4**, e3396 (2017)

23. Martínez-del-Amor, M.A., Riscos-Núñez, A., Pérez-Jiménez, M.J.: A survey of parallel simulation of P systems with GPUs. Bull. Int. Membr. Comput. Soc. **3**, 55–67 (2017)

24. Minsky, M.L.: Computation: Finite and Infinite Machines. Prentice-Hall Inc., Englewood Cliffs (1967)

25. Nielsen, M.A., Chuang, I.L.: Quantum Computation and Quantum Information. Cambridge University Press, Cambridge (2000)

26. Păun, G., Rozenberg, G., Salomaa, A. (eds.): The Oxford Handbook of Membrane Computing. Oxford University Press, Oxford (2010)

27. Shannon, C.E.: A mathematical theory of communication. Bell Syst. Tech. J. **27**, 623–656 (1948)

28. Shannon, C.E.: A universal turing machine with two internal states. In: Automata Studies, Annals of Mathematics Studies, vol. 34, pp. 157–165, Princeton University Press (1956)

29. Sharp, K., Matschinsky, F.: Translation of Ludwig Boltzmann's paper "on the relationship between the second fundamental theorem of the mechanical theory of heat and probability calculations regarding the conditions for thermal equilibrium". Entropy **17**, 1971–2009 (2015)

30. Schrödinger, E.: What Is Life? The Physical Aspect of the Living Cell and Mind. Cambridge University Press, Cambridge (1944)
31. Schervish, M.J.: Theory of Statistics. Springer, New York (1995). https://doi.org/10.1007/978-1-4612-4250-5
32. Turing, A.M.: On computable numbers, with an application to the Entscheidungsproblem. Proc. London Math. Soc. **42**(1), 230–265 (1936)
33. Valencia-Cabrera, L., Orellana-Martín, D., Martínez-del-Amor, M.A., Riscos-Núñez, A., Pérez-Jiménez, M.J.: Cooperation in transport of chemical substances: a complexity approach within membrane computing. Fundam. Inform. **154**, 373–385 (2017)
34. Wheeler, J.A.: Information, physics, quantum: the search for links. In: Zurek, W.H. (ed.) Complexity, Entropy, and the Physics of Information. Addison-Wesley, Redwood City (1990)
35. Wiener, N.: Cybernetics or Control and Communication in the Animal and the Machine. Hermann, Paris (1948)

An Introduction to cP Systems

Radu Nicolescu[✉] and Alec Henderson

The University of Auckland, Auckland, New Zealand
r.nicolescu@auckland.ac.nz, ahen386@aucklanduni.ac.nz

Abstract. We overview the current state of cP systems and illustrate it with a series of old and new examples, intentionally simple, but fundamental in their areas. cP systems – i.e. P systems with compound terms – share the fundamental features of traditional cell-like (tree-based) and tissue (graph-based) P systems: unlimited space and computing power, cells, nested cells, multisets, messages, rewriting rules, possibly running in maximal parallel modes. In contrast to traditional P systems, inner nested cells do not have their own rulesets. However, this restriction is usually more than compensated by their significant extensions: compound Prolog-like terms, high-level rules, control on incoming messages. Additionally, the same rulesets can run in either synchronous or asynchronous mode, without any syntactic change. cP systems have been successfully used to model quite a few fundamental and real-life problems, e.g. in NP complexity, data structures, graph theory, distributed algorithms, image processing. As trademark, cP models use fixed sized alphabets and crisp rulesets, independent of the problem size. The samples cover a wide variety of areas, such as arithmetic, list structures, summary statistics and sorting, asynchronous communications, μ-recursive functions.

1 Introduction

As noted in Cooper and Nicolescu [1], cP systems share the fundamental features of traditional cell-like (tree-based) and tissue (graph-based) P systems [10,11]: unlimited space and computing power, top-cells are organised in graph/digraph networks, top-cells contain nested (and labelled) sub-cells, the evolution is governed by multiset rewriting rules, possibly running in maximal parallel modes. Top-cell represent nodes in a distributed computation, and interact by messages (aka inter-cell parallelism). Subcells represent local data that can be processed either sequentially or in the max-parallel mode (aka intra-cell parallelism). Although not strictly necessary – but also shared with other versions of the traditional P systems – our typical rulesets are state based and run in a weak priority mode.

cP systems are based on five fundamental innovations, one restriction and four extensions: (0) no rules for inner (nested) subcells, which are just labelled nested multisets; (1) compound terms, similar to Prolog compound terms, but based on multisets; (2) high-level rewriting rules, that work on nested multisets;

© Springer Nature Switzerland AG 2018
C. Graciani et al. (Eds.): Pérez-Jiménez Festschrift, LNCS 11270, pp. 204–227, 2018.
https://doi.org/10.1007/978-3-030-00265-7_17

(3) Actor-like control on incoming messages; (4) no syntactic difference between synchronous and asynchronous communication models.

First, unlike in traditional cell-like P systems, sub-cells do NOT have their own rules. Basically, sub-cells are just nested passive repositories of other sub-cells or atomic symbols; briefly, these are labelled nested multisets.

This sounds like a severe limitation. However, it is more than compensated by the provision of higher level rules, which extend the classical multiset rewriting rules with concepts borrowed from logic programming, namely Prolog unification, with optional constraints, introduced by promoters and inhibitors. In other words, cP systems may also be seen as evolving the classical Prolog unification from structured terms to multiset-based terms – which again is a novel feature.

However, unlike traditional Prolog, where rules are applied in a backward-chaining mode, with possible backtracks, cP rules work in a forward mode, like all known P system rules. This seems to allow better parallelism capabilities than the past and actual parallel versions of concurrent Prolog – but this topic will not be further followed here.

Outgoing messages are terms that appear in right-hand-side of the rules and are suffixed by the '!' symbol. Acceptable incoming messages are terms that appear in the left-hand-side of the rules and are suffixed by the '?' symbol. Syntactically, this notation is inspired by process calculi, but here has an Actor model semantics [2,3]. Roughly, the '?' symbol correspond to Receive and Scan operations used in F#, or receive and stash operations used in Akka. Thus, like in Actor models, each top-level cell can control its incoming messages, by deciding when to accept incoming data and of what format. Not yet accepted messages remain in implicit message queues, without affecting the cell's behaviour.

Additionally, the same rulesets can run in either synchronous or asynchronous mode, without any syntactic change. Obviously, the results are generally different, but the choice between these two modes only affects the evolution, thus it can be delayed as a "runtime" decision. Essentially, a synchronous cP evolution will look as expected in traditional P systems. However, the asynchronous evolution is based on a different base, in fact it closely matches the classical asynchronous model in the field of distributed algorithms [6,12].

To the best of our knowledge, this is the only P system version that uses an asynchronicity definition aligned to the definition used in distributed algorithms. This may have a significant effect on the modelling capacity or related concepts such as fairness.

The net result is a powerful system that can crisply and efficiently solve many complex problems, with small fixed-size alphabets and small, fast fixed-size rulesets. In particular, cP systems enable a reasonably straightforward creation and manipulation of high-level data structures typical of high-level languages, such as: numbers, lists, trees, relations (graphs), associative arrays, strings.

In this sense, cP systems have been successfully used to develop parallel and distributed models in a large variety of domains, such as NP complete problems, data structures, graph theory, distributed algorithms, image processing (e.g. see [1]).

In this paper, we overview the current state of cP systems and we showcase
their features on a wide range of fundamental tasks, such as arithmetic, list processing, efficient sorting and summary statistics, asynchronous communications,
μ-recursivity. The first sections, from Sect. 2 to Sect. 4, are revised versions of
definitions which have appeared in our earlier papers, such as [1], with one major
addition: provision for Actor-like input control. Readers may digest the sections
in the given order; but can also temporary skip the more arid definitions and
start with the examples, e.g. Sect. 5, referring to the definitions as needed. Unless
otherwise specified, samples assume one single top-level cell.

2   P Systems with Compound Terms

As suggested by Fig. 1, P systems with compound terms, – *cP systems* for brief
– share and extend some of the fundamental features of both traditional cell-like
(tree-based) and tissue (graph-based) P systems:

- Top-level cells are organised in digraph networks and are usually differentiated
  by unique IDs. Top-level cells represent nodes in a distributed computation
  (aka inter-cell parallelism).
- Each arc represents an unidirectional communication channel and has two
  labels: one label at the source cell and another at the target cell (these two
  labels may, but need not, be different). Where graphs are used, each edge is
  considered a pair of opposite arcs.
- Top-level cells contain nested (and labelled) sub-cells. Subcells represent local
  data that can be processed either sequentially or in the max-parallel mode
  (aka intra-cell parallelism).
- The evolution is governed by multiset rewriting+communication rules, running in exactly-once or max-parallel modes.
- Only top-level cells have evolution rules – nested subcells are just passive
  data repositories. This seems a severe limitation; however, it is more than
  compensated by the provision of powerful higher-level rules.
- In a synchronous evolution, each internal step takes zero time units (sic!), and
  each message takes exactly one time unit to transit from source to target. This
  model is equivalent to the traditional model, where internal steps take one
  time unit and messages are instantaneous.

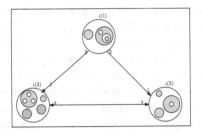

Fig. 1. Bird's eye view of a sample cP system, with top-level cells and subcells.

- In an asynchronous evolution, each message may take any finite real time (in $\mathcal{R}_{\geq 0}$) to transit from source to target. This model closely matches the standard runtime model of asynchronous distributed algorithms, and includes the synchronous model as a particular case.
- Top-level cells send messages – via the right-hand-side of rewriting rules, using symbol '!' – over outgoing arcs, to their structural neighbours.
- Top-level cells receive messages – via the left-hand-side of rewriting rules, using symbol '?' – over incoming arcs, from their structural neighbours.
- Messages which arrive at the target cell are not immediately inserted among the target's contents; instead, these messages are conceptually "enqueued" and there is one message "queue" – read "multiset" – for each incoming arc.
- Receiving cells have full control over the time and format of messages accepted from the message "queues". This model matches similar facilities of Actor models, such as Receive/Scan (F#) and receive/stash (Akka).
- Messages not yet accepted remain in their message "queues".

Note: although not strictly necessary – but also shared with other versions of the traditional P systems – our typical rulesets are state based and run in a weak priority mode.

Note: *subcells* – aka *compound terms* – play the roles of cellular micro-compartments or substructures, such as organelles, vesicles or cytoophidium assemblies ("snakes"), which are embedded in cells or travel between cells, but without having the full processing power of a complete cell. In our proposal, *subcells* represent nested labelled data compartments which have no own processing power: they are acted upon by the rules of their enclosing cells.

3 cP Terms Grammar and Unification

Our basic vocabulary consists of *atoms* and *variables*, collectively known as *simple terms*, plus a dedicated symbol, '1', and a few delimiters: '(', ')', '[', ']', '|'.

Compound terms are similar to Prolog-like *first-order terms*, but recursively built from *multisets* of atoms and variables. Roughly, our compound terms play the role of hierarchically nested subcells in traditional P systems. *Numbers* and *lists* are now explicit in this new extended grammar, although they are ad-hoc derivable as compound terms, by the other rules (as also shown below).

Together, simple terms, compound terms, numbers, and lists are collectively called *terms* and can be defined by the formal grammar in Fig. 2, where '...' denote arbitrary *multiset* repetitions, including zero times.

Symbol λ is an emphatic designation of the empty multiset. *Numbers* are represented in base 1, with 1 as unity symbol. *Atoms* are typically denoted by lower case letters, such as a, b, c. *Variables* are typically denoted by uppercase letters, such as X, Y, Z. If useful, atoms and variables may include subscripts or primes. *Functors* are subcell *labels*, not necessarily distinct; here functors can only be atoms (not variables).

```
<term> ::= <simple-term> | <compound-term>
          | <number> | <list>
<simple-term> ::= <atom> | <variable>
<compound-term> ::= <functor> '(' <argument> ')'
<functor> ::= <atom>
<argument> ::= <term>...
<number> ::= 1...
<list> ::= '[]' | '[' <head> '|' <list> ']'
<head> ::= <term>...
```

Fig. 2. Term grammar

For improved readability, we also consider *anonymous variables*, which are denoted by underscores ('_'). Each underscore occurrence represents a *new* unnamed variable and indicates that something, in which we are not interested, must fill that slot.

Terms that do *not* contain variables are called *ground*, e.g.:

- Ground terms: a, $a() = a(\lambda)$, $a(b)$, $a(bc)$, $a(b^2c)$, $a(b(c))$, $a(bc(\lambda))$, $a(b(c)d(e))$, $a(b(c)d(e))$, $a(b(c)d(e(\lambda)))$, $a(bc^2d)$.
- Terms which are not ground: X, $a(X)$, $a(bX)$, $a(b(X))$, $a(XY)$, $a(X^2)$, $a(XdY)$, $a(Xc())$, $a(b(X)d(e))$, $a(b(c)d(Y))$, $a(b(X^2)d(e(Xf^2)))$; also, using anonymous variables: $\_$, $a(b\_)$, $a(X\_)$, $a(b(X)d(e(\_)))$.
- This term-like construct which starts with a variable is not a term (this grammar defines first-order terms only): $X(aY)$.

In *concrete* models, *cells* may contain *ground* terms only (no variables). Rules may however contain *any* kind of terms, atoms, variables and terms (whether ground and not).

Unification. All terms which appear in rules (ground or not) can be (asymmetrically) *matched* against *ground* terms, using an ad-hoc version of *pattern matching*, more precisely, a *one-way first-order syntactic unification* (one-way, because cells may not contain variables). An atom can only match another copy of itself, but a variable can match any multiset of ground terms (including λ). This may create a combinatorial *non-determinism*, when a combination of two or more variables are matched against the same multiset, in which case an arbitrary matching is chosen. For example:

- Matching $a(b(X)fY) = a(b(cd(e))f^2g)$ deterministically creates a single set of unifiers: $X, Y = cd(e), fg$.
- Matching $a(XY^2) = a(de^2f)$ deterministically creates a single set of unifiers: $X, Y = df, e$.
- Matching $a(b(X)c(1X)) = a(b(1^2)c(1^3))$ deterministically creates one single unifier: $X = 1^2$.

- Matching $a(b(X)c(1\,X)) = a(b(1^2)c(1^2))$ fails.
- Matching $a(XY) = a(df)$ non-deterministically creates one of the following four sets of unifiers: $X, Y = \lambda, df$; $X, Y = df, \lambda$; $X, Y = d, f$; $X, Y = f, d$.

Performance Note. If the rules avoid any matching non-determinism, then this proposal should not affect the performance of P simulators running on existing machines. Assuming that multisets are efficiently represented, e.g. via hash-tables, our proposed unification probably adds an almost linear factor. Let us recall that, in similar contexts (no occurs check needed), Prolog unification algorithms can run in $O(ng(n))$ steps, where g is the inverse Ackermann function. Our conjecture must be proven though, as the novel presence of multisets may affect the performance.

4   cP Rules Grammar

Typically, our rewriting rules use *states* and are applied top-down, in the so-called *weak priority* order.

Pattern Matching. Rewriting rules are matched against cell contents using the above discussed *pattern matching*, which involves the rule's left-hand side, promoters and inhibitors. Generally, variables have *global rule scope*; these are assumed to be introduced by *existential* quantifiers preceding the rule – with the exception of inhibitors, which may introduce *local variables*, as further discussed below.

Intuitively, the matching is *valid* only if, after substituting variables by their values, the rule's right-hand side contains ground terms only (so *no* free variables are injected in the cell or sent to its neighbours), as illustrated by the following sample scenario:

- The cell's *current content* includes the *ground term*:
  $n(a\,\phi(b\,\phi(c)\,\psi(d))\,\psi(e))$
- The following (state-less) *rewriting rule fragment* is considered:
  $n(X\,\phi(Y\,\phi(Y_1)\,\psi(Y_2))\,\psi(Z)) \;\rightarrow\; v(X)\,n(Y\,\phi(Y_2)\,\psi(Y_1))\,v(Z)$
- Our pattern matching determines the following *unifiers*:
  $X = a,\; Y = b,\; Y_1 = c,\; Y_2 = d,\; Z = e.$
- This is a *valid* matching and, after *substitutions*, the rule's *right-hand* side gives the *new content*:
  $v(a)\,n(b\,\phi(d)\,\psi(c))\,v(e)$

Generic Rules Format. More precisely, the rewriting rules are defined by the formal grammar in Fig. 3, where '...' denote arbitrary repetitions (including zero times). We call this format generic, because it actually defines templates involving variables.

The rewriting rule is unified according to the following rules; ensuring that all states and cell contents are ground:

```
<rule>   ::= <lhs>  →α <rhs> <promoters> <inhibitors>
<lhs>    ::= <state> (<loc−term> | {<in−term>}?δ)...
<rhs>    ::= <state> (<loc−term> | {<out−term>}!δ)...
<state>  ::= <compound−term>
<promoters>  ::= (| <term−or−eq>)...
<inhibitors> ::= (¬ <term−or−eq>)...
<state>  ::= <atom> | <compound−term>
<loc−term>  ::= <term>      // local term
<in−term>   ::= <term>      // input term
<out−term>  ::= <term>      // output term
<term−or−eq> ::= <loc−term>
             | '('<loc−term> '=' <loc−term>')'
```

Fig. 3. Rule grammar (Here we use the standard abbreviations: lhs = left-hand-side, rhs = right-hand-side.)

- Lhs local terms must be unifiable to the cell's ground contents.
- Promoter local terms must be unifiable to the cell's ground contents; but inhibitors must *not* be unifiable to the cell's ground contents; see also note below.
- Lhs local terms are consumed as in traditional P systems.
- Lhs input terms designated by the receive symbol, '$?_\delta$', are received over incoming arcs (from cell's structural neighbours):
  - δ is the label of an incoming arc, a set of such labels, or a variable (including the '_' wildcard).
  - $(a)?_i$ indicates that a is received over incoming arc i;
  - $(a)?_{i,j}$ indicates that a is received over incoming arc i *or* j;
  - $(a)!_X$ indicates that a is received over an arbitrary incoming arc, whose label will be unified with X;
  - Any queued messages that do not match the template 'a' are not accepted in the cell, but kept in the corresponding queue.
- Rhs must contain only ground terms!
- Rhs local terms become available after the end of the current step only, as in traditional P systems (we can also imagine that these are sent via an ad-hoc fast *loopback* arc).
- Rhs output terms designated by the send symbol, '$!_\delta$', are sent over outgoing arcs (to cell's structural neighbours):
  - δ is the label of an outgoing arc, a set of such labels, a variable, or the special symbol ∀.
  - $(a)!_i$ indicates that a is sent over outgoing arc i (unicast);
  - $(a)!_{i,j}$ indicates that a is sent over outgoing arcs i and j (multicast);
  - $(a)!_\forall$ indicates that a is sent over all outgoing arcs (broadcast).
- Application mode $\alpha \in \{1, +\}$, indicates the *exactly-once* (aka *min*) or *max-parallel* mode, as further discussed below.

- All terms sent out to the same destination and in the same step form one single *message* and travel together as one single block (regardless of the application modes used).

Application Modes: Exactly-Once and Max-Parallel. To explain our two rule application modes, *exactly-once* and *max-parallel*, let us consider a cell, σ, containing three counter-like compound terms, $c(1^2)$, $c(1^2)$, $c(1^3)$, and the two possible application modes of the following high-level "decrementing" rule:

$$S_1\ c(1\ X) \rightarrow_\alpha S_2\ c(X), \text{where } \alpha \in \{1, +\}. \tag{ρ_α}$$

The left-hand side of rule ρ_α, $c(1\ X)$, can be unified in three different ways, to each one of the three c terms extant in cell σ. Conceptually, we instantiate this rule in three different ways, each one tied and applicable to a distinct term:

$$
\begin{aligned}
S_1\ c(1^2) &\rightarrow S_2\ c(1), & (\rho_1) \\
S_1\ c(1^2) &\rightarrow S_2\ c(1), & (\rho_2) \\
S_1\ c(1^3) &\rightarrow S_2\ c(1^2). & (\rho_3)
\end{aligned}
$$

1. If $\alpha = 1$, rule ρ_1 non-deterministically selects and applies *exactly one* of these virtual rules ρ_1, ρ_2, ρ_3. Using ρ_1 or ρ_2, cell σ ends with counters $c(1)$, $c(1^2)$, $c(1^3)$. Using ρ_3, cell σ ends with counters $c(1^2)$, $c(1^2)$, $c(1^2)$.

2. If $\alpha = +$, rule ρ_+ applies all these virtual rules ρ_1, ρ_2, ρ_3, in *max-parallel* mode. Cell σ ends with counters $c(1)$, $c(1)$, $c(1^2)$.

Semantically, the max-parallel mode is equivalent to a virtual sequential "while" loop around the same rule in the exactly-once mode, which would be then repeated until it is no more applicable.

Special Cases. Simple scenarios involving generic rules are sometimes semantically equivalent to sets of non-generic rules defined via bounded loops. For example, consider the rule

$$S_1\ a(x(I)\ y(J)) \rightarrow_+ S_2\ b(I)\ c(J),$$

where the cell's contents guarantee that I and J only match integers in ranges $[1, n]$ and $[1, m]$, respectively. Under these assumptions, this rule is essentially equivalent to the following set of $n \times m$ non-generic rules:

$$S_1\ a_{i,j} \rightarrow S_2\ b_i\ c_j,\ \forall i \in [1, n], j \in [1, m].$$

However, unification is a much more powerful concept, which cannot be generally reduced to simple bounded loops.

Promoters and Inhibitors. To expressively define additional useful matchings, our promoters and inhibitors may also use virtual "equality" terms, written in infix format, with the '$=$' operator. For example, including the term $(ab = XY)$ indicates the following additional matching constraints on variables X and Y: either $X, Y = ab, \lambda$; or $X, Y = a, b$; or $X, Y = b, a$; or $X, Y = \lambda, ab$.

To usefully define inhibitors as full logical negations, variables which only appear in the scope of an inhibitor are assumed to have *local scope*. These variables are assumed to be defined by *existential* quantifiers, immediately after the negation. Semantically, this is equivalent as introducing these variables at the global rule level, but by *universal* quantifiers, after all other global variables, which are introduced by *existential* quantifiers.

As an illustration, consider a cell containing two terms, $a(1)\ a(111)$, and contrast the following two sample rule fragments (for brevity, other rule details are here omitted).

... $\mid\ a(1XY)\ \neg\ a(X)$	(1)
... $\mid\ a(1Z)\ \neg\ (Z = XY)\ \mid\ a(X)$	(2)

These two rules appear quite similar and their inhibitor tests seem to model the same intuitive expression: *no* $a(X)$ must be present in the cell. In fact, these rule fragments could be explicited with the following quantifiers:

$\exists X, Y:$	... $\mid\ a(1XY),\ \neg a(X)$	(1)
$\exists Z:$	... $\mid\ a(1Z),\ \neg(\exists X, Y,\ (Z = XY),\ a(X))$	(2)
$\exists Z, \forall X, Y:$	... $\mid\ a(1Z),\ (Z = XY)\ \Rightarrow\ \neg a(X)$	(2')

Rule (1) uses two global variables, X and Y, that can be matched in four different ways: (*i*) $X, Y = \lambda, \lambda$; (*ii*) $X, Y = 11, \lambda$; (*iii*) $X, Y = \lambda, 11$; (*iv*) $X, Y = 1, 1$. The first three unifications, (*i-iii*), pass the inhibitor test, as there are *no* terms $a()$, $a(11)$, $a()$, respectively. However, unification (*iv*) fails the inhibitor test, because there *is* one cell term $a(1)$.

Rules (2, 2') use one global variable, Z, and two local inhibitor variables, X and Y. Variable Z can be matched in two different ways: (*i*) $Z = \lambda$; (*ii*) $Z = 11$. Unification (*i*) passes the inhibitor test, because it only checks one unification, $X, Y = \lambda, \lambda$, and there is *no* cell term $a()$. However, unification (*ii*) fails the inhibitor test, because it checks three local unifications: $X, Y = 11, \lambda$; $X, Y = \lambda, 11$; $X, Y = 1, 1$; and the last check fails, because of extant term $a(1)$.

The pattern of rule (2) has been further used, in [1], to define a one-step minimum finding ruleset.

Benefits. This type of generic rules allow algorithm descriptions with *fixed-size alphabets* and *fixed-sized rulesets*, independent of the size of the problem and number of cells in the system (often *impossible* with only atomic terms).

5   cP Numbers

Natural numbers can be represented via *multisets* containing repeated occurrences of the *same* atom. The extended cP terms grammar has a built-in symbol, 1, for the unary digit. Thus, the following compound terms can be used to describe the contents of an integer container a: (i) $a() = a(\lambda) \equiv$ the value of a is 0; (ii) $a(1^3) \equiv$ the value of a is 3.

For concise expressions, we may alias multisets of 1 by their corresponding multiplicity, e.g. $a() \equiv a(0), b(1^3) \equiv b(3)$. Nicolescu et al. [9] show how the basic arithmetic operations can be efficiently modelled by P systems with compound terms.

Figure 4 shows a few simple arithmetic assignments, expressions, and comparisons. Note that "strictly less than" $(<)$ requires the extra 1, because Y can match on λ. Figure 5 shows a simple multiplication by repeated additions and Fig. 6 shows a simple division by repeated subtractions. In this approach, multiplication and division are performed sequentially. Multiplications and divisions could also run in parallel, by allowing a restricted reuse of symbols generated in the same step, but we do not discuss such possible extensions here.

$$
\begin{aligned}
&x = 0 \;\equiv\; x(\lambda) \\
&x = 1 \;\equiv\; x(1) \\
&x = 2 \;\equiv\; x(11) \\
&x = n \;\equiv\; x(1^n)
\end{aligned}
$$

$$x := y + z \;\equiv\; y(Y)\,z(Z) \;\rightarrow_1\; x(YZ) \qquad\qquad \text{destructive add}$$

$$
\begin{aligned}
&x := y + z \;\equiv\; \rightarrow_1\; x(YZ) \mid y(Y)\,z(Z) &&\text{preserving add} \\
&x := y - z \;\equiv\; \rightarrow_1\; x(X) \mid y(XZ)\,z(Z) &&\text{preserving subtract, } \textbf{if } y \geq z
\end{aligned}
$$

$$
\begin{aligned}
&x = y \;\equiv\; x(X)\,y(X) &&\text{equality} \\
&x \leq y \;\equiv\; x(X)\,y(XY) &&\text{less than or equal to} \\
&x < y \;\equiv\; x(X)\,y(XY1) &&\text{strictly less than}
\end{aligned}
$$

$$
\begin{aligned}
&x\%2 = 0 \;\equiv\; x(XX) &&\text{even} \\
&x\%2 = 1 \;\equiv\; x(XX1) &&\text{odd}
\end{aligned}
$$

$$
\begin{aligned}
x := \max(0, y - z) \;\equiv\; && \text{preserving subtract (two rules)}\\
&\rightarrow_1\; x(X) \mid y(XZ)\,z(Z) \\
&\rightarrow_1\; x() \mid y(Y)\,z(YZ)
\end{aligned}
$$

Fig. 4. Numbers: simple assignments, expressions, and comparisons

$$
\begin{aligned}
x := y \times z \;\equiv\; S_0 \;&\rightarrow_1\; S_2\,x() \mid z() \\
S_0 \;&\rightarrow_1\; S_1\,x()\,y'(Y) \mid y(Y) \\
S_1\,x(X)\,y'() \;&\rightarrow_1\; S_2\,x(X) \\
S_1\,x(X)\,y'(Y1) \;&\rightarrow_1\; S_1\,x(XZ)\,y'(Y) \mid z(Z)
\end{aligned}
$$

Fig. 5. Numbers: multiplication by repeated addition

$$x := y \div z \equiv \begin{array}{ll} S_0 \rightarrow_1 & S_2 \; x(\infty) \mid z() \\ S_0 \rightarrow_1 & S_1 \; x() \; y'(Y) \mid y(Y) \\ S_1 \; x(X) \; y'(Y) \rightarrow_1 & S_2 \; x(X) \mid z(YZ1) \\ S_1 \; x(X) \; y'(YZ) \rightarrow_1 & S_1 \; x(X1) \; y'(Y) \mid z(Z) \end{array}$$

Fig. 6. Numbers: division by repeated subtraction

6   cP Lists

Consider the *list* y, containing the following sequence of values: $[u, v, w]$ (using a standard programming notation). List $[u, v, w]$ can be represented as a compound term: $.(u \; .(v \; .(w \; .())))$, where the ad-hoc functor '.' represents the standard list constructor *cons* and '.()' the empty list. However, to avoid ambiguities, different lists may need to use different *cons* functors.

To simplify list processing, the new extended grammar has an unambiguous built-in list, starting with the empty list '[]', and using operator | to separate the head and the tail of a non-empty list.

Thus, list $.(u \; .(v \; .(w \; .())))$ can now be represented as $[u \mid [v \mid [w \mid []]]]$. As a notational convenience, we can also use the standard list notation, $[u, v, w]$. Our named list y can be now be represented as a compound term, $y([u, v, w])$, and, as the round parentheses are now redundant, directly as $y[u, v, w]$.

Our lists work as lists in functional programming, i.e. essentially as *stacks*. Figure 7 shows rule fragments for a few simple list/stack operations.

$\rightarrow_1 \; y[]$	creating empty list y
$a \; y[Y] \rightarrow_1 \; y[a \mid Y]$	pushing a on list y
$a(X) \; y[Y] \rightarrow_1 \; y[X \mid Y]$	pushing contents of a on list y
$y[X \mid Y] \rightarrow_1 \; b(X) \; y[Y]$	popping the top of list y to contents of b

Fig. 7. Lists: stack operations

Operations that require a complete list traversal are possible, but are performed sequentially. Also, resulting list appear in reverse order, so a reversal function may be required. Figure 8 shows rule fragments for a few typical list monad operations. These operations destroy the initial list, so copies need to be made if this is not desired. Associative arrays, cf. Sect. 7, may be a better choice when fast parallel operations are required.

A pair of lists/stacks, say x and y, can efficiently emulate a *queue*, using known functional programming "tricks". In the simplest scenario, enqueue means push on stack x and dequeue means pop from stack y; popping from an empty y will first trigger a reversal of x onto y. Despite some appearances, this construct has an dequeue complexity $\mathcal{O}(1)$.

```
unit:: y := List.unit a
S₀ a →₁ S₁ y[a]


reverse:: y := List.reverse x
S₀ →₁ S₁ y[]
S₁ x[] →₁ S₂
S₁ x[H|X] y[Y] →₁ S₁ x[X] y[H|Y]


map:: y := List.map (h → hh) x
S₀ →₁ S₁ y[]
S₁ x[] →₁ S₂
S₁ x[H|X] y[Y] →₁ S₁ x[X] y[HH|Y]
if order is important, then y needs now to be reversed


sum:: y := List.sum x
S₀ →₁ S₁ y()
S₁ x[] →₁ S₂
S₁ x[H|X] y(Y) →₁ S₁ x[X] y(HY)
```

Fig. 8. Lists: a few basic monad operations

7   cP Associative arrays

Consider the *associative array* y, containing the following key/value pairs: $[a \to 1, b \to 3, c \to 5]$. Essentially, an associative array is a fast computable mapping from keys to values (e.g. a hash-based structure). To maintain the fast access and ensure that it is parallelisable, an associative array can be represented as a multiset of similarly shaped key value pairs. For example, the above associative array y can be represented as the multiset $y(\kappa(a)\,\nu(1))\ y(\kappa(a)\,\nu(3))\ y(\kappa(c)\,\nu(5))$. If functors κ and ν are assumed, then we can also use the more intuitive list-like notation $y[a \to 1, b \to 3, c \to 5]$.

Figure 9 shows rule fragments for a few monad operations, in the distructive mode. Note that map-like operations are highly parallelisable.

```
unit:: y := Array.unit (a → t)
S₀ a'(T) →₁ S₁ y[a → T]

map:: y := Array.map (t → tt) x
S₀ →₁ S₁ y[]
S₁ x[] →₁ S₂
S₁ x[K → V|X] y[Y] →₊ S₁ x[X] y[K → VV|Y]
```

Fig. 9. Associative arrays: a few basic monad operations

8   cP Asynchronous Evaluation

In our models, we do not make any *syntactic* difference between the synchronous and asynchronous scenarios; this is strictly a *runtime* behaviour [7]. Any model is able to run on both the synchronous and asynchronous runtime "engines", albeit the results may differ.

To the best of our knowledge, in all other P systems versions, asynchronicity appears from the internal evaluation of the rulesets, *not* from the communication. For example, such a *discrete* internal asynchronicity could be introduced when a rule, which is n times applicable, is applied m times only, where m is an arbitrary number in the integer interval $[1, n]$.

Such approaches *reverse* the standard definition used in distributed algorithms [6,12], where all internal processes take very small or even negligible *real* time, and the message transit times make the main or even the only contribution to the runtime complexity. This may create modelling issues, by the need for additional asynchronous/delaying artifacts. Also, this may preclude or make more difficult theoretical considerations on runtime complexity and fairness.

Our asynchronous model matches closely the standard definition for asynchronicity used in distributed algorithms, which considers that any internal step takes zero time, while messages may take any *real* time to transit, but are nevertheless *guaranteed* to arrive. To get more useful figures, transit times are normalised, to $[0, 1]$, by the dividing them to the longest transit time.

Then the runtime complexity (worst-case) of a distributed algorithm is the *supremum* over all possible normalised executions [12]. If a finer estimation is required, we can of course add a transit time between internal states, i.e. for internal processing [6]), but this should be small compared with actual message transit times – probably au par with the smallest message transit time. Following examples will illustrate this; for simplicity, here we ignore the possible contribution of the internal evaluation steps.

8.1   Distributed Echo Algorithm – Synchronous vs. Asynchrnous

Echo [12] is a simple but fundamental algorithm in distributed computing, which serves as the base for several other more complex and useful algorithms. Echo creates a spanning tree over the reachable network; it is a diffuse algorithm, starting from a single initiator and gradually encompassing the whole network.

The basic algorithm starts when the initiator sends a broadcast (fan-out) token to all its neighbours. The initiator then waits until its receives convergecast (fan-in) confirmation tokens from all its neighbours. This will complete the algorithm.

Each receiver starts by waiting to receive a token. Once it receives the first token, the receiver marks that sender as its spanning tree parent. Then it further sends the broadcast token to all its neighbours, minus its accepted parent. The receiver then waits until it receives tokens from all its neighbours, minus its accepted parent; these tokens can be either broadcast tokens or convergecast tokens. When this occurs, the receiver sends its own confirmation token back to its parent.

As an illustration, let's run the given rulesets on exactly the same network, in two scenarios: (1) synchronously and (2) asynchronously. Figure 10 summarises a completed synchronous run, while Fig. 11 summarises a completed asynchronous run. The thick arrows indicate the resulting spanning tree. The numbers besides the short arrows indicate transit times. Ignoring internal state transitions, the runtime complexities of the two scenarios are different:

- The synchronous case. Here, time = 4 = 2D time units, where D is the graph diameter. However, asymptotically, the time complexity is $\mathcal{O}(D)$.
- The asynchronous case. Here, time ≈ 3 = N − 1, where N is the number or nodes in graph. However, asymptotically, the time complexity is $\mathcal{O}(N)$ (i.e. usually larger or much larger).

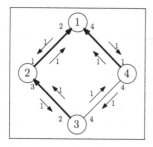
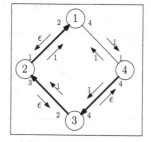

Fig. 10. Echo sync – possible end configuration. Total messaging time = 4 = 2D = $\mathcal{O}(D)$ time units.

Fig. 11. Echo async – possible end configuration. Total messaging time ≈ 3 = N − 1 = $\mathcal{O}(N)$ time units. Here ϵ is very small number.

Generally, the synchronous case, when all messages travel in exactly one time unit, is just one of the possible cases in the asynchronous scenario, when each message travels independently and arbitrarily in any time in the interval $[0, 1]$ (normalised case). Thus, the asymptotic synchronous time complexity is always less or equal to the asymptotic asynchronous time complexity.

This shows that, even if there are no syntactical differences, networks may perform widely different in the two scenarios, synchronous vs. asynchronous. In fact, many important synchronous algorithms will not work at all in asynchronous networks, or only after substantial changes.

Figures 12 and 13 show the cP rulesets of the Echo initiator top-cell and of an Echo receiver top-cell, respectively. We assume that each cell contains a multiset with functor $\bar{\pi}$ that identifies its neighbours. As result of the algorithm, each receiver cell will contain a term with functor ρ, indicating its determined spanning tree parent; the initiator cell starts with an already included empty ρ term, indicating that it is the root. Figure 14 shows the initial states of our sample four cells; Figs. 15 and 16 show their final states, in the synchronous and asynchronous scenarios, respectively.

$$
\begin{array}{llll}
S_0 & & \rightarrow_+ & S_1 \ !_X\{\theta\} \ \pi(X) \mid \bar{\pi}(X) & (0) \\
S_1 \ ?_Y\{\theta\} \ \pi(Y) & & \rightarrow_+ & S_1 & (1) \\
S_1 & & \rightarrow_1 & S_2 \ \neg \ \pi(X) & (2)
\end{array}
$$

Fig. 12. Echo initiator ruleset.

$$
\begin{array}{llll}
S_0 \ ?_Z\{\theta\} & & \rightarrow_1 & S_1 \ \rho(Z) & (0) \\
S_1 & & \rightarrow_+ & S_2 \ !_X\{\theta\} \ \pi(X) \mid \bar{\pi}(X) \ \neg \ \rho(X) & (1) \\
S_2 \ ?_Y\{\theta\} \ \pi(Y) & & \rightarrow_+ & S_2 & (2) \\
S_2 & & \rightarrow_1 & S_3 \ !_Z\{\theta\} \mid \rho(Z) \ \neg \ \pi(X) & (3)
\end{array}
$$

Fig. 13. Echo receiver ruleset.

Node	State	Cell contents		
1	S_0	$\rho()$	$\bar{\pi}(2) \ \bar{\pi}(4)$	$\bar{\mu}(1)$
2	S_0		$\bar{\pi}(1) \ \bar{\pi}(3)$	$\bar{\mu}(2)$
3	S_0		$\bar{\pi}(2) \ \bar{\pi}(4)$	$\bar{\mu}(3)$
4	S_0		$\bar{\pi}(1) \ \bar{\pi}(3)$	$\bar{\mu}(4)$

Fig. 14. Echo initial state – synchronous and asynchronous

Node	State	Cell contents		
1	S_2	$\rho()$	$\bar{\pi}(2) \ \bar{\pi}(4)$	$\bar{\mu}(1)$
2	S_3	$\rho(1)$	$\bar{\pi}(1) \ \bar{\pi}(3)$	$\bar{\mu}(2)$
3	S_3	$\rho(2)$	$\bar{\pi}(2) \ \bar{\pi}(4)$	$\bar{\mu}(3)$
4	S_3	$\rho(1)$	$\bar{\pi}(1) \ \bar{\pi}(3)$	$\bar{\mu}(4)$

Fig. 15. Echo final state – possible synchronous scenario

Node	State	Cell contents		
1	S_2	$\rho()$	$\bar{\pi}(2) \ \bar{\pi}(4)$	$\bar{\mu}(1)$
2	S_3	$\rho(1)$	$\bar{\pi}(1) \ \bar{\pi}(3)$	$\bar{\mu}(2)$
3	S_3	$\rho(2)$	$\bar{\pi}(2) \ \bar{\pi}(4)$	$\bar{\mu}(3)$
4	S_3	$\rho(3)$	$\bar{\pi}(1) \ \bar{\pi}(3)$	$\bar{\mu}(4)$

Fig. 16. Echo final state – possible asynchronous scenario

8.2 Fairness and Unbounded Non-determinism

As a brief illustration, consider a network consisting of two interconnected top-cells, #0 and #1. Cell #1 represents a counter actor, which loops by sending self-addressed messages and incrementing an internal counter, ι. Cell #0 represents a main actor, which sends a query token message to #1, expecting back a natural number. The expectations are quite high and strict: cell #1 should be able to return *any natural number* and its response should be *deterministically guaranteed* to arrive. A probability one will NOT be enough in this case; the whole process must deterministically terminate.

Running this two cell system asynchronously will satisfy all these constraints. The query message from #0 to #1 may take *any arbitrary time*, but is *guaranteed* to arrive. By the time it is accepted, #1's counter ι could have incremented to *any natural number*, which will be sent back to #0.

This scenario illustrates the problem of *unbounded non-determinism* [2], also closely related to the concept of *fairness* in distributed computations [6, 12]. This behaviour is possible in the theoretical actor model, and – as far as we know – cP systems seems to be the first P system version which supports this. Figures 17 and 18 show the cP rules of such counter and main actors, respectively.

$$
\begin{array}{llll}
S_0 & & \to_1 S_0 \ !_1\{1\} \ \iota() \ \neg \ \iota(X) & (0) \\
S_0 \ ?_1\{1\} \ \iota(X) & \to_1 S_0 \ !_1\{1\} \ \iota(X1) & (1) \\
S_0 \ ?_0\{1\} \ \iota(X) & \to_1 S_1 \ !_0\{X\} & (2)
\end{array}
$$

Fig. 17. Cell #1, the counter actor.

$$
\begin{array}{lll}
S_0 & \to_1 S_1 \ !_1\{1\} & (0) \\
S_1 \ ?_1\{X\} \to_1 S_2 \ \dots & & (1)
\end{array}
$$

Fig. 18. Cell #0, the main actor

9 cP Miscellanea

9.1 Efficient Summary Statistics

This section is reproduced from Cooper and Nicolescu [1]. Consider an unstructured multiset $A \subseteq \mathbb{N}$ of size n. It is well known that (1) any sequential algorithm that finds its minimum needs at least n steps, and (2) any parallel algorithm that finds its minimum needs at least $\log n$ parallel steps.

Without loss of generality, consider a cP system cell, in state S_1, where multiset A is given via functor a; e.g., multiset $A = \{1, 2, 2, 5\}$ is represented as $a(1) \, a(2) \, a(2) \, a(5)$. The following rulesets implement various versions of a cP system minimum finding algorithm. All these rulesets transit to state S_2 and construct a term with functor b, containing $\min A$. Some of these are destructive processes; if otherwise desired, one could first make a copy of the initial multiset A.

The following destructive ruleset is an emulation of the classical sequential minimum finding algorithm, which takes n steps:

$$
\begin{array}{lll}
S_1 & a(X) \rightarrow_1 S_2 \ b(X) & \\
S_2 & a(XY) \ b(X) \rightarrow_1 S_2 \ b(X) & a \geq b \\
S_2 & a(X) \ b(XY1) \rightarrow_1 S_2 \ b(X) & a < b
\end{array}
$$

The following destructive ruleset is an emulation of the classical parallel minimum finding algorithm, which takes $\log n$ steps. As long as there are more than one term a, the ruleset loops in state S_1, keeping minima between pairs. When only one a remains (containing the minimum value), the ruleset transits to state S_2 and tags the minimum.

$$
\begin{array}{l}
S_1 \ a(XY) \ a(X) \rightarrow_+ S_1 \ a(X) \\
S_1 \ a(X) \rightarrow_1 S_2 \ b(X)
\end{array}
$$

However, using the full associative power of cP systems, we can find a non-destructive version with two rules, which works in *just two steps* (regardless of the set cardinality). This is a substantial improvement over existing classical algorithms (both sequential and parallel). It starts by making a full copy of a as b, in one max-parallel step, and then deletes all non-minimal b values in another max-parallel step.

$$
\begin{array}{l}
S_1 \rightarrow_+ S_1' \ b(X) \mid a(X) \\
S_1' \ b(XY1) \rightarrow_+ S_2 \mid a(X)
\end{array}
$$

Note that, if the minimum value appears several times in multiset A, then we will end with the same multiplicity of b's, each one containing the same value, $\min A$. If this is required, there are several ways to select only one copy and delete the rest – but we do not further deal with this issue here.

Moreover, using the full power of cP inhibitors (as logical negations, with local variables), we can even non-destructively solve the problem in just *one single step*, with one or two rules. This version is implemented by the following ruleset:

$$
\begin{array}{l}
S_1 \rightarrow_1 S_2 \ b() \mid a() \\
S_1 \rightarrow_1 S_2 \ b(Z1) \mid a(Z1) \ \neg \ (Z = XY) \ a(X)
\end{array}
$$

If A contains zero, then there is a term $a()$, and: (1) the first rule applies, constructing $b()$; (2) the second rule is not applicable. Otherwise (if there is no zero in A): (1) the first rule is not applicable; (2) the second rule constructs $b(Z1)$, a value which exists among a's, as $a(Z1)$, but there is NO other a containing a strictly lesser value, such as $a(X)$, where X is a sub-multiset of Z, $X \subseteq Z$. In the end, the newly constructed b will contain one copy of the minimum value of multiset A.

If multiset A does not contain zero values, i.e. $A \subseteq \mathbb{N}^+$, then the first rule can be safely omitted (as it will never be applicable).

The above rules are non-deterministic, but confluent. Similar rulesets can be devised for finding other summary statistics, such as the maximum of a given set of natural numbers.

9.2   Efficient Sorting

This section is based on ideas presented in Nicolescu [8]. In cP systems, like in most P systems, the basic data structure is the unordered multiset; more complex cP data structures are recursively built by nesting labellel multisets. In this scenario, we need to start by first defining what we mean by sorting a given multiset. There are two rather staightforward options: (1) create a list (cf. Sect. 6) containing ordered values; or (2) output ordered values via a designated output arc. Note that, regardless which option we chose, (1) or (2), arranging or sending values in order are sequential processes.

In this section, we take the second approach. We propose and use a *dynamic* version of the classical *pigeonhole algorithm*, where – metaphorically – pigeon-holes are only opened one at a time, instantly attracting objects with matching values.

Consider a top-level cell containing a multiset of numbers, defined by functor a (cf. Sect. 5), e.g. $a(2)\,a(4)\,a(2)\,a(1)$. Functor b defines our pigeonhole. The ruleset of Fig. 19 sends an ordered sequence of a's via arc 1. Figure 20 traces the contents of the considered cell. In the worst case scenario, when all elements are distinct, this ruleset needs $\mathcal{O}(N)$ steps, where N is the size of the multiset, here $N = 4$.

$$S_0 \;\to_1\; S_2\; b() \;\mid\; a() \tag{1}$$
$$S_0 \;\to_1\; S_1\; b() \tag{2}$$

$$S_1\; b(X) \;\to_1\; S_3\; \neg\, a(XY1) \tag{3}$$
$$S_1\; b(X) \;\to_1\; S_2\; b(XY1) \;\mid\; a(XY1) \,\neg\, (Y = ZZ')\, a(XZ) \tag{4}$$

$$S_2 \;\to_+\; S_1\; \{a(X)\}!_1 \;\mid\; b(X) \tag{5}$$

Fig. 19. Sorting ruleset.

10   cP μ-recursion

In this section we provide a straightforward cP construction for μ-recursive functions, defined here in Figs. 24 and 25. Being an extension of more traditional P systems [10,11], cP systems are automatically Turing complete, so this construction does not prove anything new on this issue. However, it is – to the

$S_0 \; a(2) \, a(4) \, a(2) \, a(1)$ rule (2)
$S_1 \; a(2) \, a(4) \, a(2) \, a(1) \, b()$ rule (4)
$S_2 \; a(2) \, a(4) \, a(2) \, a(1) \, b(1)$ rule (5) sends $a(1)$
$S_1 \; a(2) \, a(4) \, a(2) \, a(1) \, b(1)$ rule (4)
$S_2 \; a(2) \, a(4) \, a(2) \, a(1) \, b(2)$ rule (5) sends $a(2) \, a(2)$
$S_1 \; a(2) \, a(4) \, a(2) \, a(1) \, b(2)$ rule (4)
$S_2 \; a(2) \, a(4) \, a(2) \, a(1) \, b(4)$ rule (5) sends $a(4)$
$S_1 \; a(2) \, a(4) \, a(2) \, a(1) \, b(4)$ rule (3)
$S_3 \; a(2) \, a(4) \, a(2) \, a(1)$ final idle state

Fig. 20. Sorting trace.

best of our knowledge – the first effective construction which directly models the construction of μ-recursive functions. As such, it could enable us to effectively construct an universal function for a family of P systems; again, to the best of our knowledge, no such construction was yet presented.

Our construction follows the standard Kleene definition for μ-recursive functions [4,5]. Here, we build a network of top-level cells. However, a mirror construction is possible using one single top-level cell and subcells.

In our cP systems, we can use lists, such as $[x_1, x_2, \ldots, x_n]$, to represent vectors, such as $\mathbf{x} = (x_1, x_2, \ldots, x_n)$. As shown in the shaded cells of Fig. 21, our basic building block is a top-level cell with: (i) one incoming arc #1; (ii) one outgoing arc #2; (iii) one incoming arc #3; (iv) one outgoing arc #4.

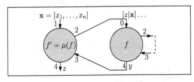

Fig. 22. Minimisation 'μ'

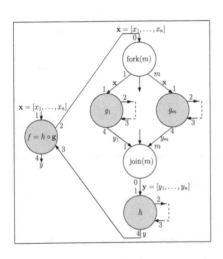

Fig. 21. Composition '$\circ$'

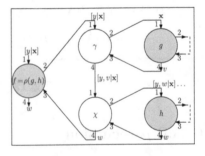

Fig. 23. Primitive recursion 'ρ'

The function arguments are given via a list of n numbers, expected on the incoming arc #1. The function result is sent, when available, on the outgoing arc #4.

If needed, the outgoing arc #2 is used to send arguments to previously built auxiliary functions and their result is expected to come on input arc #3. The rulesets start on state S_0 and return to a clean state S_0 after the result is sent out.

The rules corresponding to the basic μ functions are straightforward, see Fig. 26.

Figure 21 illustrates the composition, $f = h \circ \mathbf{g}$, and Fig. 27 shows its rulesets. We use two generic auxiliary cells: fork(m) and join(m). Fork(m) takes one list of m values, on input arc 0, and broadcasts it, on m output arcs, $1, 2, \ldots, m$. Join(m) takes m separate values, on input arcs, $1, 2, \ldots, m$, and outputs a list composed of these elements, on output arc 0.

Constant function

$f(x_1, x_2, \ldots, x_n) = k$

Successor function

$S(x_1) = x_1 + 1$

Projection function

$P_i^n(x_1, x_2, \ldots, x_n) = x_i$

Fig. 24. Basic μ-recursive functions.

Composition operator $\circ$: $f = h \circ \mathbf{g}$

$f(x_1, x_2, \ldots, x_n) = h(g_1(x_1, x_2, \ldots, x_n), \ldots, g_m(x_1, x_2, \ldots, x_n))$

Primitive recursion operator ρ: $f = \rho(g, h)$

$f(0, x_1, x_2, \ldots, x_n) = g(x_1, x_2, \ldots, x_n)$
$f(y + 1, x_1, x_2, \ldots, x_n) = h(y, f(y, x_1, x_2, \ldots, x_n), x_1, x_2, \ldots, x_n)$

Minimisation operator μ: $f' = \mu(f)$

$\mu(f)(x_1, x_2, \ldots, x_n) = z \Longleftrightarrow$
$\quad f(z, x_1, x_2, \ldots, x_n) = 0$
$\quad f(y, x_1, x_2, \ldots, x_n) \neq 0, \forall y \in [0, z - 1]$

Fig. 25. Operators for constructing μ-recursive functions.

Constant function: $f(x_1, x_2, \ldots, x_n) = k$

$S_0 \ \{X\}?_1 \ \rightarrow_1 \ S_0 \ \{k\}!_4 \ | \ \kappa(k)$

The cell is configured with an immutable term $\kappa(k)$, containing the out value.

Successor function: $S(x_1) = x_1 + 1$

$S_0 \ \{[X]\}?_1 \ \rightarrow_1 \ S_0 \ \{X1\}!_4$

Receives a singleton list and sends out the incremented value.

Projection function: $P_i^n(x_1, x_2, \ldots, x_n) = x_i$

$S_0 \ \{X\}?_1 \ \rightarrow_1 \ S_1 \ \pi(X) \ \xi(I) \ | \ \iota(I1)$
$S_1 \ \pi[X|Y] \ \xi(0) \ \rightarrow_1 \ S_0 \ \{X\}!_4$
$S_1 \ \pi[X|Y] \ \xi(I1) \ \rightarrow_1 \ S_1 \ \pi(Y) \ \xi(I)$

The cell is configured with an immutable term $\iota(i)$. The received list is successively popped until the element at the required index i comes on top and then is sent out.

Fig. 26. Rules for the basic μ functions.

Figure 22 illustrates the μ-minimisation, $f' = \mu(f)$, and Fig. 28 shows its ruleset.

Figure 23 illustrates the primitive recursion, $f = \rho(g, h)$, where the main top-cell uses two ad-hoc helper cells: (i) γ, a wrapper for g; and (ii) χ, a wrapper for h. The three rulesets are shown in Fig. 29.

11   Evaluations and Conclusions

We have overviewed the current state of cP systems and illustrated it with a series of old and new examples, intentionally simple, but fundamental in their areas. The current definitions have been gradually evolved bottom-up, by attempting to apply more traditional P systems to a wider range of applications.

We have included here two previous samples for efficient sorting and summary statistics, and highlighted several fundamental issues surrounding asynchronous communications, unbounded non-determinism, and fairness.

Also, we have proved that cP systems are Turing complete via a novel high-level "textbook" construction, in the spirit of Kleene's definition for μ-recursive functions. All rulesets have been small, with up to four rules; no inhibitors have been used, and promoters have been used for convenience only.

Composition – main cell

$$S_0 \{X\}?_1 \ \rightarrow_1 \ S_1 \{X\}!_2$$
$$S_1 \{Y\}?_3 \ \rightarrow_1 \ S_0 \{Y\}!4$$

The received list **x** is forked to cells $g_m, g_{m-1}, \ldots, g_1$. Their results are collected into a list sent to cell h, which returns the result of composition f.

Composition – helper cell fork(m)

$$S_0 \{X\}?_0 \ \rightarrow_1 \ S_1 \ \pi(X) \ \xi(M) \mid \iota(M)$$
$$S_1 \ \xi(M) \ \rightarrow_1 \ S_1 \{X\}!_M \ \xi(M') \mid \pi(X) \mid (M = M'1)$$
$$S_1 \ \xi(0) \ \pi(X) \ \rightarrow_1 \ S_0$$

The cell starts configured with an immutable term $\iota(m)$. The received value is successively sent over arcs $m, m-1, \ldots, 1$.

Composition – helper cell join(m)

$$S_0 \ \rightarrow_1 \ S_1 \ \pi[] \ \xi(M) \mid \iota(M)$$
$$S_1 \{X\}?_M \ \xi(M) \ \pi(Y) \ \rightarrow_1 \ S_1 \ \pi[X|Y] \ \xi(M') \mid (M = M'1)$$
$$S_1 \ \xi(0) \ \pi(X) \ \rightarrow_1 \ S_0 \{X\}!_0$$

The cell starts configured with an immutable term $\iota(m)$. The requested list is built by successively stacking values received from arcs $m, m-1, \ldots, 1$.

Fig. 27. Rules for composition, cf. Fig. 21.

μ-minimisation

$$S_0 \{X\}?_1 \ \rightarrow_1 \ S_1 \{[0|X]\}!_2 \ z(0) \ \pi(X)$$
$$S_1 \{Y\}?_3 \ \rightarrow_1 \ S_2 \ y(Y)$$
$$S_2 \ z(Z) \ y(0) \ \pi(X) \ \rightarrow_1 \ S_0 \{Z\}!4$$
$$S_2 \ z(Z) \ y(Y) \ \rightarrow_1 \ S_1 \{[Z1|X]\}!_2 \ z(Z1) \mid \pi(X)$$

Receives list **x**. Then, extended lists $[z|\mathbf{x}]$ are successively sent to cell f, in increasing order of $z = 0, 1, 2, \ldots$, until f returns a value $y = 0$ (possibly never). When this ever happens, the last z becomes the result of the minimisation.

Fig. 28. Rules for μ-minimisation, cf. Fig. 22.

Primitive recursion – main cell

$S_0 \{[Y|X]\}?_1 \rightarrow_1 S_1 \{[Y|X]\}!_2$
$S_1 \{W\}?_3 \rightarrow_1 S_0 \{W\}!_4$

Sends received $[y, \mathbf{x}]$ to helper cell γ, which wraps g, and outputs value w received from helper cell χ, which wraps h.

Primitive recursion – helper cell γ

$S_0 \{[Y|X]\}?_1 \rightarrow_1 S_1 \{X\}!_2 \, y(Y) \, \pi(X)$
$S_1 \{V\}?_3 \, y(Y) \, \pi(X) \rightarrow_1 S_0 \{[Y, V|X]\}!_4$

Receives $[y, \mathbf{x}]$, sends $\mathbf{x}$ to wrapped cell g, picks its result v, and outputs $[y, v|\mathbf{x}]$.

Primitive recursion – helper cell χ

$S_0 \{[Y, V|X]\}?_1 \rightarrow_1 S_1 \{[0, V|X]\}!_2 \, z(0) \, \pi(X) \, y(Y)$
$S_1 \{W\}?_3 \rightarrow_1 S_2 \, h(W)$
$S_2 \, z(Y) \, h(W) \, \pi(X) \, y(Y) \rightarrow_1 S_0 \{W\}_4$
$S_2 \, z(Z) \, h(W) \rightarrow_1 S_1 \{[Z1, W|X]\}!_2 \, z(Z1) \mid \pi(X)$

Receives $[y, v|\mathbf{x}]$, then sends, to wrapped cell h, the sequence $[z, w|\mathbf{x}]$, $z = 0, 1, 2, \ldots, y$, where first $w = v$ and each other successive w is the result of h on the preceding item. The output value w is the result of the last sent item.

Fig. 29. Rules for primitive recursion, cf. Fig. 23.

This novel construction suggests further theoretical work, such as: (i) extending this construction to cover the Gödel-Herbrand definitions of recursive functions (more closely related to recursive functions in programming); (ii) constructing universal cP systems and universal reversible cP systems; and (iii) studying the rule hierarchy defined by an alternation of promoters and inhibitors.

More generally, future research should also consider (i) cP systems specific verification tools, and (ii) efficient algorithms for our multiset-based unification with optional constraints – this could pave the way for practical interpreters or compilers.

References

1. Cooper, J., Nicolescu, R.: The travelling salesman problem in cP systems. In: Zhang, G., Wang, J., Pan, L., Qiang, Zeng, Y. (eds.) Asian Conference on Membrane Computing, pp. 9–21 (2017)
2. Hewitt, C.: What is computation? Actor model versus Turing's model. In: A Computable Universe: Understanding and Exploring Nature as Computation, pp. 159–185. World Scientific (2013)

3. Hewitt, C., Bishop, P., Steiger, R.: Session 8 formalisms for artificial intelligence a universal modular actor formalism for artificial intelligence. In: Advance Papers of the Conference, vol. 3, p. 235. Stanford Research Institute (1973)

4. Kleene, S.C.: General recursive functions of natural numbers. Math. Ann. **112**(1), 727–742 (1936)

5. Kleene, S.C.: Introduction to Metamathematics. Bibl. Matematica. North-Holland, Amsterdam (1952)

6. Lynch, N.A.: Distributed Algorithms. Morgan Kaufmann Publishers Inc., San Francisco (1996)

7. Nicolescu, R.: Parallel and distributed algorithms in P systems. In: Gheorghe, M., Păun, G., Rozenberg, G., Salomaa, A., Verlan, S. (eds.) CMC 2011. LNCS, vol. 7184, pp. 35–50. Springer, Heidelberg (2012). https://doi.org/10.1007/978-3-642-28024-5_4

8. Nicolescu, R.: Most common words – A cP systems solution. In: Gheorghe, M., Rozenberg, G., Salomaa, A., Zandron, C. (eds.) CMC 2017. LNCS, vol. 10725, pp. 214–229. Springer, Cham (2018). https://doi.org/10.1007/978-3-319-73359-3_14

9. Nicolescu, R., Wu, H.: Complex objects for complex applications. Rom. J. Inf. Sci. Technol. **17**(1), 46–62 (2014)

10. Păun, G.: A quick introduction to membrane computing. J. Log. Algebr. Program. **79**(6), 291–294 (2010)

11. Păun, G., Rozenberg, G.: An introduction to and an overview of membrane computing, Chap. 1. In: The Oxford Handbook of Membrane Computing, pp. 1–27. Oxford University Press, New York (2009)

12. Tel, G.: Introduction to Distributed Algorithms. Cambridge University Press, Cambridge (2000)

A Look at the Descriptional Complexity of SNQ P Systems

Andrei Păun[1,2(⊠)] and Florin-Daniel Bîlbîe[1]

[1] University of Bucharest, 14 Academiei St., District 1, 010014 Bucharest, Romania
apaun@fmi.fmi.unibuc.ro, florin-daniel.bilbie@my.fmi.unibuc.ro
[2] National Institute of Research and Development for Biological Sciences,
296 Independenței Bd., District 6, 060031 Bucharest, Romania

Abstract. We present the known results pertaining to the recently introduced spiking neural P Systems with communication on request (SNQ P Systems). Aside from showing the properties of these systems working with multiple types of spikes (as defined originally) we also give the results obtained by our group in the area of SNQ P Systems using only one type of spikes. All the results are given from the perspective of descriptional complexity, taking into account the number of neurons needed in the universal systems. Several open problems and ideas for improvements of the results are also presented.

Keywords: P Systems · Universality · Descriptional complexity
Register machines · Spiking neural networks

1 Introduction

Neural networks are extensively researched due to their capacity to learn and compute various problems in the area of artificial intelligence, like pattern recognition, computer vision, game theory, machine learning etc. But capacity to learn is not the only drive for research on neural networks. The computational power and potential of solving combinatorial problems is another important direction of investigation for neural networks.

Spiking neural P Systems [6] (in short SN P Systems) incorporate the idea of spiking neural networks in the field of membrane computing. A SN P System can be imagined as a directed graph, where the nodes represent the neurons and the edges represent the synapses. The neurons send electrical signals, called spikes, along the synapses through spiking rules, which are of the form $E/a^c \rightarrow a$, where E is a regular expression, c is the number of spikes consumed by the rule. A rule is applied only if the content of the neuron, denoted by the number n of spikes in the neuron, is "covered" by the regular expression E (formally, $a^n \in L(E)$, where $L(E)$ is the language generated by E). SN P Systems were intensely studied by researchers, such as M.J. Pérez-Jiménez and his followers, from two perspective: universal computational devices [2,3,7,12,18,21,24] and NP-complete problem solving [9,17,23].

© Springer Nature Switzerland AG 2018
C. Graciani et al. (Eds.): Pérez-Jiménez Festschrift, LNCS 11270, pp. 228–236, 2018.
https://doi.org/10.1007/978-3-030-00265-7_18

In this paper, we focus our attention on spiking neural P Systems with communication on request [11] (in short SNQ P Systems). The main difference between SNQ P Systems and SN P Systems is the spike exchange pattern. In SN P Systems the communication is done by command, in the sense that the emitting neuron has the initiative of the communication. SNQ P Systems work in a request pattern, meaning that the receiving neuron is making a query to request spikes from one or more neighboring neurons. The request communication pattern is inspired by the request-response communication between components in parallel-cooperating grammar systems [4, 16].

SNQ P Systems, while still recently introduced, have evolved pretty fast since the introduction paper from the perspective of descriptional complexity. Hence, the main talking point of this work is the descriptional complexity of SNQ P Systems. Specifically, we will analyze the existing literature for these devices and discuss some further research ideas, that may or may not improve the descriptional complexity of SNQ P Systems.

The reminder of the paper is structured as follows. In Sect. 2 we present SNQ P Systems so that the reader understands the model discussed. In Sect. 3 we go over existing results on SNQ P Systems and analyze what aspects were improved. In Sect. 4 we describe some research ideas that may produce improvements over the current results. Finally, in Sect. 5 we present some conclusions of the current work.

2 SNQ P Systems - Definitions and Generalities

In this section we present the definition of SNQ P Systems [11] and rule semantics. The reader is assumed to be familiar with notions from formal language and automata theory, especially regular expressions, and membrane computing. For details about formal language and automata theory and membrane computing we refer the reader to [15, 19].

2.1 SNQ P Systems

A SNQ P Systems is a tuple

$$\Pi = (O, \sigma_1, \dots, \sigma_m, a_{i_0}, out)$$

where:

- $O = \{a_1, a_2, \dots, a_k\}$ is an alphabet (a_i is called a type of spike), $k \geq 1$.
- $\sigma_1, \dots, \sigma_m$ are neurons, of the form $\sigma_i = (a_1^{n_1} a_2^{n_2} \dots a_k^{n_k}, R_i)$, $1 \leq i \leq m$, $n_t \geq 0$, $1 \leq t \leq k$, where:
  1. n_t is the initial number of spikes of type a_t, contained by σ_i
  2. R_i is a finite set of rule of form E/Qw, being E a regular expression over O and w a finite non-empty list of queries;
- a_{i_0}, $1 \leq i_0 \leq k$ is the output spike and $out \in \{1, 2, \dots, m\}$ indicates the output neuron.

As seen in the definition, the neurons of a SNQ P Systems are denoted by using σ_l, where l is the label of the neuron. If the context allows it, we may refer to neuron σ_l by its label (i.e. neuron l).

Let σ_i and σ_j denote two neurons and let $r = E/Qw$ be a rule of σ_i. The queries present in w have two possible forms: 1. (a_t^p, j) and 2. (a_t^∞, j). In the first case, the query (a_t^p, j) is interpreted as requesting p spikes neurons of type a_t from neuron σ_j. We call a query of this type satisfiable if neuron σ_j can satisfy the query (i.e. σ_j has at least p spikes of type a_t). The second type of query refers to a degenerative case, in which σ_i asks for all spikes of type a_t from σ_j. This type of queries are always satisfiable.

If one or more neurons ask for the same amount p of spike a_t from σ_j, then neuron j will lose only p spikes of type a_t and will multiply the requested spikes as many times as necessary to satisfy all queries (e.g. if 3 neurons request x spikes a_t from σ_j, then σ_j loses x spikes a_t, multiply the removed spikes by 3 and sends the spikes to each neuron which made a query). On the contrary, two queries (a^p, j) and (a^q, j) are conflicting queries if $p \neq q$. In this scenario only one query is satisfied, nondeterministically chosen.

A rule, of the form E/Qw, can be applied if and only if: (i) the content of the querying neuron is a word in the language generated the by the regular expression E and (ii) all queries specified in w are satisfiable. If one of the previous conditions is not met, then the rule is not applicable. Another case when a rule is not applicable is when two or more queries are in conflict with each other.

It is possible to have two or more rules that are enabled at the same time. Like in the case of conflicting queries, only one rule is applied, chosen in a nondeterministic manner.

Starting from the initial configuration, denoted by the number of spikes in each neuron, a SNQ P System begins the computation by applying at each step the available rule in each neuron. A computation ends when no rule is applicable. The result of a computation is represented by the number of spikes of type a_{i_0} from output neuron out.

SNQ P Systems are massively parallel computational devices, meaning that, at each computational step, all neurons that can apply a rule, will apply rules in parallel. For more details about SNQ P Systems, the reader is referred to [11].

2.2 Register Machines

In this subsection we will provide a short description of register machines. While there are not parts that rely heavily on register machines and their characteristics, we will mention them a few times. It is worth to note that register machines play a heavy part into proving the universality of a SN P System.

Informally speaking, a register machine consists of a specified number of registers (counters) which can hold any natural number, and which are handled according to a program consisting of labeled instructions; the registers can be increased or decreased by 1 – the decreasing being possible only if a register holds a number greater than or equal to 1 (we say that it is non-empty) –, and checked whether they are non-empty.

Formally, a (non-deterministic) *register machine* is a device M of the form $M = (m, B, l_0, l_h, R)$, where $m \geq 1$ is the number of counters, B is the (finite) set of instruction labels, l_0 is the initial label, l_h is the halting label, and R is the finite set of instructions labeled (hence uniquely identified) by elements from B (R is also called the *program* of the machine). The labeled instructions are of the following forms:

- $l_i : (\text{ADD}(r), l_j, l_k), 1 \leq r \leq m$ (add 1 to register r and go nondeterministically to one of the instructions with labels l_j, l_k),
- $l_i : (\text{SUB}(\mathbf{r}), l_j, l_k), 1 \leq r \leq m$ (if register r is not empty, then subtract 1 from it and go to the instruction with label l_j, otherwise go to the instruction with label l_k),
- $l_h : \text{HALT}$ (the halt instruction, which can only have the label l_h).

A register machine generates a natural number in the following manner: we start computing with all m registers being empty, with the instruction labeled by l_0; if the computation reaches the instruction $l_h : \text{HALT}$ (we say that it halts), then the value of register 1 is the number generated by the computation. The set of numbers computed by M in this way is denoted by $N(M)$. It is known (see [10]) that non-deterministic register machines as defined above generate exactly the family NRE, of Turing computable sets of numbers. Further, register machines with only three registers, one of them being non-decreasing, are universal.

We refer the interested reader to [10] for the universality proof of the register machines and to [20] p. 2 as well as [10] pp. 170–174 for the universality of register machines with 3 registers.

3   The State of the Art for SNQ P Systems

In the current section we will analyze the current literature on SNQ P Systems and we will discuss the complexity aspects. We will not present full proofs, but will present key aspects that made each proof correct. The results are not presented in chronological order – we group the results by correlating the aspects addressed in them.

3.1   SNQ P Systems with Two Spikes

When introduced in [11], the SNQ P Systems were able to achieve Turing universality, but not without a great toll. Only SNQ P Systems with two types of spikes were proven to be equivalent to Turing Machines. The universality was achieved by simulating a register machine. For each instruction of the register machine, the SNQ P System had a "module" (a group of neurons) which, by cleverly moving the spikes around the neurons composing the module, was able to simulate each instruction in 2 or 3 computational steps.

Each counter of the register machine was simulated by neuron, which was storing the value as spikes – n spikes for value n in a the counter. The two types of spikes, a and b, were necessary to be able to simulate the operations on register (type a), but at the same time to keep inactive the neurons that were not components of the module that was simulating the current instruction (type b). The spikes needed for ADD instructions were generated by a group of three neurons.

The SNQ P System from [11] halts when the register machine reaches the HALT instruction. At that time the result of the computation is present in the neuron simulating the first counter of the register machine, denoted by the number of spikes of type a.

$$l_0 : (SUB(1), l_1, l_2);$$
$$l_2 : (ADD(6), l_3);$$
$$l_4 : (SUB(6), l_5, l_3);$$
$$l_6 : (SUB(7), l_7, l_8);$$
$$l_8 : (SUB(6), l_9, l_0);$$
$$l_{10} : (SUB(4), l_0, l_{11});$$
$$l_{12} : (SUB(5), l_{14}, l_{15});$$
$$l_{14} : (SUB(5), l_{16}, l_{17});$$
$$l_{16} : (ADD(4), l_{11});$$
$$l_{18} : (SUB(4), l_0, l_h);$$
$$l_{20} : (ADD(0), l_0)$$
$$l_h : HALT$$

$$l_1 : (ADD(7), l_0);$$
$$l_3 : (SUB(5), l_2, l_4);$$
$$l_5 : (ADD(5), l_6);$$
$$l_7 : (ADD(1), l_4);$$
$$l_9 : (ADD(6), l_{10});$$
$$l_{11} : (SUB(5), l_{12}, l_{13});$$
$$l_{13} : (SUB(2), l_{18}, l_{19});$$
$$l_{15} : (SUB(3), l_{18}, l_{20});$$
$$l_{17} : (ADD(2), l_{21});$$
$$l_{19} : (SUB(0), l_0, l_{18});$$
$$l_{21} : (ADD(2), l_{18});$$

Fig. 1. The M_{23} register machine from [8].

Besides first universality proof for SNQ P Systems, in [11] was present an upper bound of the numbers of neurons needed to achieve universality for function computation. The SNQ P System had 49 neurons and was built by simulating the M_{23} register machine from [8], Fig. 1.

Despite the fact that a neuron working with two types of spikes is not biologically motivated, the SNQ P Systems used to compute functions had further reductions on the number of neurons needed to achieve universality. In [13] a new universal spiking system was presented. It had only 14 neurons and it was able to simulate the register machine M_{23} in a quite ingenious way.

Instead of constructing a module to simulate each instruction, only two neurons were used to simulate all instructions. By moving spikes between these two neurons, the right instruction was simulating at the right time. Eight more neurons were used to simulate the counters and four additional neurons were used to generate spikes used to increment the number of spikes in neurons during simulation of ADD instructions.

The SNQ P System from [13] has a tiny problem: it does not stop when the simulation of the register machine stops. This issue is created by the four neurons that generate spikes. Since they need to work all to type to provide spikes for the ADD instructions, the halting simulation should also stop these neurons from working. This is not a massive error that is making the proof wrong, and the correction can be achieve easily achieved.

For further details on these results we refer the reader to [11,13].

3.2   SNQ P Systems with only One Type of Spikes

As mentioned in previously, SNQ P Systems with two types of spikes are not biologically motivated. That is because spikes are identical electrical impulses. Hence, in order to lay the ground for a practical implementation of such devices, the number of types of spikes needed to achieve universality should be reduced to 1. There are three proofs for this result.

First proof of universality for SNQ P Systems with one type of spikes was presented in [1], but with small change in the semantic of rules: instead of demanding that all queries of a rule to be satisfied, in order to apply it, it is applicable if at least one query is satisfied. This change is not as restrictive as the original semantic [11] and might prove more practical, as far as the implementation of this devices go.

Like the universal SNQ P System from [11], in [1] the proof is done by simulating register machines in the same way: construct a module that will simulate the instruction l_i and simulate each register with a neuron. The problem solved by having two spikes was solved by encoding each operation in a number of spikes. The neurons were simulating the registers by holding $4(n + 1)$ spikes, where n is the number from the simulated register; $4n + 3$ encodes the ADD operation on the register and $4n + 2$ encodes the SUB operations on the register.

To properly simulate the register machine, a decode phase was necessary after the simulation reached the HALT instruction. That is because the values in the neurons simulating register was encoded. Here, like in [11,13], new spikes needed were added by a three neurons group.

As function computer, the construction from [1] results into a SNQ P System with 61 neurons, by simulating the register machine M_{23}.

The second proof of universality [14] was made on SNQ P Systems which work within the original rule semantic (i.e. all queries must be satisfied in order to make the rule applicable). The proof idea follows the same direction from [1]. The main change is on modules that simulates SUB operations, where an additional neuron is required to check if the operation is applied correctly. Here, the universal SNQ P System that computes functions requires 74 neurons.

The third proof of universality [22] for SNQ P Systems with one type of spikes is done in a different direction. No spike encodings are required here. Instead, the accent is put on query satisfiability: neurons are not kept inactive because the regular expression of a rule does match the neuron content, but rather because queries are not satisfiable. Also, instead of loading neurons with rules, enabled by distinct regular expressions, each neuron has at most 3 rules (except the neuron used to collect "waste" spikes). This change is best captured into the number of neurons needed to create a universal SNQ P System that computes function: 181.

In [22] is also discussed the number of unbounded neurons (neurons for which the number of spikes is unbounded) needed to achieve universality. Here, the lowest number is 4 for SNQ P Systems working in generating mode and 9 for SNQ P Systems that compute functions.

These three proofs capture one important aspect of the complexity of computational devices: the tradeoff between the number of components and the complexity of each component. For more details on these proofs we refer the reader to [1,14,22].

4   Further Improvements Ideas on SNQ P Systems

In this section we discuss some ideas that may result in improvements on SNQ P Systems, from the perspective of descriptional complexity. As far as we know, the following ideas are yet to be discussed in any paper.

If we compare the SN P Systems with the SNQ P Systems, despite the evident communication pattern difference, the rule of a SNQ P System do not consume any spikes from the neuron, when applied, and do not have delays. Furthermore, the SNQ P Systems do not have forgetting rule. The only way a SNQ P System will "lose" spikes is by responding to a query. It will be interesting to see if any of these modeling changes will result into simplified SNQ P Systems that are still universal. Another important aspect is if adding delays, forgetting rules and/or spike consuming will make spiking neural P Systems with communication on request to lose the Turing equivalence.

Another idea worth exploring is to find how small a universal SNQ P System can get. The smallest SNQ P Systems have 14 neurons for 2 types of spikes and 61 neurons for one type of spikes. We believe the current numbers could be reduced.

One way to reduce the number of neurons is to increase the number of types of spikes used. In this way, we make some processing with spikes instead of neurons. Our investigation is making us to believe that with 5 neurons we can obtain a universal SNQ P Systems (the number of spikes needed depends on the register machine simulated). While this yields impressive potential results, it is not a biologically motivated. It is more of an exploratory quest to find what can be done when there are no restrictions.

Another way to reduce the number of spikes is to efficiently use the available neurons. If we take a closer look at the register machine M_{23}, it is easy to see that some instructions are always executed in the same order (e.g. l_7 is always executed after the subtraction from l_6 is successful). By aggregating instructions into groups, we can build modules that simulate two or more instructions. We believe that an approach similar to this one may yield at least from a 10% to a 15% of reduction in number of neurons needed to build the SNQ P System.

A similar approach to [13] on SNQ P Systems with one type of spikes is also worth considering. If successful, it may result in a greater reduction of the number of neurons than the overspecialization on the format of a register machine. Our assumption is that it has very few chances to work.

One last idea we believe that has great potential is how SNQ P Systems change when they are working into a sequential manner. Despite the fact that spiking systems are massively parallel, in reality things are not working like this. From a group of neurons that may be able to spike at a given moment, usually only one of them spikes. That neuron is the one that "dominates" the group. The ideas of sequential SN P System based on min and max spiking from [5] may work on SNQ P Systems too. Intuitively, the min spiking seems to be compatible with SNQ P Systems, because of spike losing effect of satisfying queries.

5 Conclusions

In this paper we put in retrospective the current literature on spiking neural P Systems with communication on request. We discuss each important result and detail some insights on how each result was achieved.

We have seen how universal SNQ P Systems with two types of spikes evolved into universal SNQ P Systems with one type of spikes. In this evolution we observed how variations into rule complexity result into huge differences in number of neurons needed to build the system.

We have also given in Sect. 4 several open problems and ideas for improving and continuing the work in this area. The most promising ones are the M_{23} and the max-spiking ones.

We believe that the SNQ P Systems are one of the most interesting SN P Systems variations and are worth further study due to their features and properties that differentiate them from the other such biologically-inspired computational models.

References

1. Bîlbîe, F.-D., Păun, A.: Universality of SNQ P systems using one type of spikes. In: Proceedings of the 18th International Conference on Membrane Computing (CMC 2017), Bradford, UK, 25–28 July 2017
2. Carbarle, F.G.C., Adorna, H.N., Pérez-Jiménez, M.J.: Sequential spiking neural P systems with structural plasticity based on max/min spike number. Neural Comput. Appl. 27(5), 1337–1347 (2016)
3. Chen, H., Freund, R., Ionescu, M., Păun, G., Pérez-Jiménez, M.J.: On string languages generated by spiking neural P systems. Fundam. Inform. 18(6), 1371–1382 (2007)
4. Csuhaj-Varju, E.: Grammar Systems: A Grammatical Approach to Distribution and Cooperation. Gordon and Breach, London (1994)
5. Ibarra, O.H., Păun, A., Rodríguez-Patón, A.: Sequential SNP systems based on min/max spike number. Theor. Comput. Sci. 410, 2982–2991 (2009)
6. Ionescu, M., Păun, G., Yokomori, T.: Spiking neural P systems. Fundam. Inform. 71(2–3), 279–308 (2006)

7. Ionescu, M., Păun, A., Păun, G., Pérez-Jiménez, M.J.: Computing with spiking neural P systems: traces and small universal systems. In: Mao, C., Yokomori, T. (eds.) DNA 2006. LNCS, vol. 4287, pp. 1–16. Springer, Heidelberg (2006). https://doi.org/10.1007/11925903_1

8. Korec, I.: Small universal register machines. Theor. Comput. Sci. **168**, 267–301 (1996)

9. Leporati, A., Mauri, G., Zandron, C., Păun, G., Pérez-Jiménez, M.J.: Uniform solutions to SAT and Subset Sum by spiking neural P systems. Nat. Comput. **8**(4), 681–702 (2009)

10. Minsky, M.: Computation - Finite and Infinite Machines. Prentice Hall, Englewood Cliffs (1967)

11. Pan, L., Păun, G., Zhang, G., Neri, F.: Spiking neural P systems with communication on request. Int. J. Neural Syst. **28**(08), 1750042 (2017)

12. Pan, L., Păun, G., Pérez-Jiménez, M.J.: Spiking neural P systems with neuron division and budding. Sci. China Inf. Sci. **54**(8), 1596–1607 (2011)

13. Pan, T., Shi, X., Zhang, Z., Xu, F.: A small universal spiking neural P system with communication on request. Neurocomputing **275**, 1622–1628 (2018)

14. Păun, A., Bîlbîe, F.-D.: Universality of SNQ P systems using one type of spikes and restrictive rule application. Int. J. Comput. Sci. (2018, accepted)

15. Păun, G.: Membrane Computing - An Introduction. Springer, Berlin (2002). https://doi.org/10.1007/978-3-642-56196-2

16. Păun, G.: Grammar systems: a grammatical approach to distribution and cooperation. In: Fülöp, Z., Gécseg, F. (eds.) ICALP 1995. LNCS, vol. 944, pp. 429–443. Springer, Heidelberg (1995). https://doi.org/10.1007/3-540-60084-1_94

17. Păun, G., Pérez-Jiménez, M.J., Rozenberg, G.: Computing morphisms by spiking neural P systems. Int. J. Comput. Sci. **18**(6), 1371–1382 (2007)

18. Păun, G., Pérez-Jiménez, M.J., Rozenberg, G.: Spike trains in spiking neural P systems. Int. J. Found. Comput. Sci. **17**(04), 975–1002 (2006)

19. Rozenberg, G., Salomaa, A. (eds.): Handbook of Formal Languages, vol. 3. Springer, Berlin (1997). https://doi.org/10.1007/978-3-642-59126-6

20. Schroeppel, R.: A two counter machine cannot calculate 2^N. Technical report AIM-257, A. I. Laboratory, Massachusetts Institute of Technology, Cambridge, MA, 1–31 May 1972. ftp://publications.ai.mit.edu/ai-publications/pdf/AIM-257.pdf. Accessed 14 Oct 2015

21. Wang, J., Hoogeboom, H.J., Pan, L., Păun, G., Pérez-Jiménez, M.J.: Spiking neural P systems with weights. Neural Comput. **22**(10), 1615–2646 (2010)

22. Wu, T., Bîlbîe, F.-D., Păun, A., Pan, L., Neri, F.: Simplified and yet Turing universal spiking neural P systems with communication on request. Int. J. Neural Syst. (2018, accepted)

23. Zhang, G., Rong, H., Neri, F., Pérez-Jiménez, M.J.: An optimization spiking neural P system for approximately solving combinatorial optimization problems. Int. J. Neural Syst. **24**(5), 1440006 (2014)

24. Zeng, X., Pan, L., Pérez-Jiménez, M.J.: Small universal simple spiking neural P systems with weights. Sci. China Inf. Sci. **57**(9), 1–11 (2014)

Design Patterns for Efficient Solutions to NP-Complete Problems in Membrane Computing

Álvaro Romero-Jiménez$^{(\boxtimes)}$ and David Orellana-Martín

Research Group on Natural Computing,
Department of Computer Science and Artificial Intelligence, Universidad de Sevilla,
Avda. Reina Mercedes s/n, 41012 Sevilla, Spain
{romero.alvaro,dorellana}@us.es

Abstract. Many variants of P systems have the ability to generate an exponential number of membranes in linear time. This feature has been exploited to elaborate (theoretical) efficient solutions to **NP**-complete, or even harder, problems. A thorough review of the existent solutions shows the utilization of common techniques and procedures. The abstraction of the latter into design patterns can serve to ease and accelerate the construction of efficient solutions to new hard problems.

Keywords: Membrane computing · NP-complete problems
Efficient solutions · Design patterns · SAT problem

1 Introduction

All of us have seen ourselves, at one time or another of our lives, in the need to solve a "hard problem", whatever this may mean. Computational complexity is a branch of the theory of computation that makes this concept precise by defining in mathematical terms the notions of (decision) problems and of the amount of resources required for any mechanical procedure (algorithm) to solve them. For example, **NP**-complete problems are most of the time regarded to be hard (at least, for those who believe that $\mathbf{P} \neq \mathbf{NP}$). A historical review of many of the ideas from this theory can be found in [1].

Membrane computing is a branch of the natural computing field aiming to abstract computing models, called P systems, from the structure and the functioning of the living cell. It was initiated by Gh. Păun in 1998 [2] and it has quickly become a vigorous scientific discipline, as [3,4] testify.

P systems provide highly parallel and distributed devices. As **NP**-complete problems are intuitively those problems for which checking, but not finding, a solution can be done in feasible time, it was soon realized that (theoretical) efficient solutions to them could be accomplished by several variants of P systems [5]. The main feature of these variants is their ability to construct an exponential space in linear time. This is usually exploited to implement a brute

© Springer Nature Switzerland AG 2018
C. Graciani et al. (Eds.): Pérez-Jiménez Festschrift, LNCS 11270, pp. 237–255, 2018.
https://doi.org/10.1007/978-3-030-00265-7_19

force search in which first all possible solutions to the problem are generated, and then all of them are verified in parallel at the same time.

The flourish of efficient solutions to **NP**-complete, or even harder, problems has led to the development of a rich computational complexity theory for membrane computing [6,7]. The purpose of this theory is to rigorously define what a solution to a decision problem is in the membrane computing domain, how to measure the resources spent by those solutions and when they can be said to be efficient.

In this theory the following key concepts are defined:

1. Solutions are families of recognizer P systems. These are systems verifying the following properties: there are two special objects, yes and no, in the working alphabet; all the computations must supply their result by sending out to the output region only one of these two objects; at the precise moment that this happens, the computation must stop.
2. The solutions can be uniform or semi-uniform. In the former case, the systems of the family own an input membrane, and each of them is able to solve all the instances of the problem of a specific "size" (as determined by a polynomial-time computable function s) when an encoding of the instance (computed by a polynomial-time computable function cod) is introduced in its input membrane. In the latter case, each instance of the problem is associated with a system of the family, that solves it without requiring additional information because the instance is directly encoded within its objects and rules.
3. A decision problem is said to be solvable in polynomial time by a family of recognizer P systems if the family: can be constructed in polynomial time (by a Turing machine); is polynomially bounded, meaning that there exists a polynomial on the size of the instances of the problem that bounds the number of steps performed by any computation of any of the systems of the family; is sound and complete with respect to the problem, meaning that for each instance of the problem an object yes is provided as the result of a computation if and only if the answer to the instance is positive.

The task of setting up an efficient solution to a hard problem is not an easy one. A judicious way to tackle it is to base ourselves on what others have already proved to work. In fact, in software engineering it is recommended practice to make use of the so-called design patterns to improve and speed up software development. Quoting Wikipedia:[1]

> A software design pattern is a general, reusable solution to a commonly occurring problem within a given context in software design. It is not a finished design that can be transformed directly into source or machine code. It is a description or template for how to solve a problem that can be used in many different situations. Design patterns are formalized best practices that the programmer can use to solve common problems when designing an application or system.

---

[1] Software design pattern, https://en.wikipedia.org/w/index.php?title=Software_design_pattern\&oldid=834346932 (last visited May 10, 2018).

A detailed analysis of many existent efficient solutions to hard problems that can be found in the membrane computing literature shows indeed that similar techniques and constructions have been utilized. This paper is devoted to describe some of those common patterns, with the aim of serving as a starting point for the non-experts to develope their own solutions.

The paper is organized as follows: in Sect. 2 some design patterns for membrane computing are described, namely the *exponential space* (Subsect. 2.1), the *all present* (Subsect. 2.2) and the *no if not yes* (Subsect. 2.3) patterns. It is also demonstrated how to implement them with different ingredients. Section 3 exemplifies the use of these design patterns by constructing distinct solutions to the SAT problem, namely one using polarizations and membrane division (Subsect. 3.1), one using dissolution and membrane creation (Subsect. 3.2), one using polarizations and membrane separation (Subsect. 3.3) and one using membrane division and minimal cooperation (Subsect. 3.4). The paper ends with some concluding remarks.

2   Design Patterns for Membrane Computing

One of the peculiarities of many of the variants of P systems considered so far in the literature is their ability to trade time for space. By this we mean that they are able to build an exponential space in polynomial, often linear, time. Although for objects it is pretty obvious, since a simple rewriting rule of the form $a \rightarrow a^2$ allows to double the number of objects a in one step, we are more interested in obtaining an exponential number of membranes. Exploiting this feature and the inherent parallelism of P systems, many **NP**-complete problems have been solved in polynomial time following a brute force approach: first, generate an exponential number of membranes each one containing a bunch of objects representing a potential solution to the problem; next, check in a parallel way if any of those is indeed a real solution; finally, provide an answer according to the results obtained.

The analysis of this scheme for the solutions discovers the use of these three patterns: the *exponential space* pattern, to generate an exponential number of membranes; the *all present* pattern, to test if all of the objects from a specific set are present in a membrane; and the *no if not yes* pattern, to be able to provide a negative answer when only the positive one can be checked.

In the next subsections, we describe each of these design patterns and show how to implement them with several features that can be found in P systems with active membranes. We will make use of the following types of rules:

1. Evolution rules $[a \rightarrow u]_l^c$, for changing the object a into the multiset u in a membrane with label l and, optionally, a charge c.
2. Communication rules $a_1[\ ]_l^{c_1} \rightarrow [a_2]_l^{c_2}$ and $[a_1]_l^{c_1} \rightarrow [\ ]_l^{c_2} a_2$, to send an object a_1 into or out from a membrane with label l. The object is rewritten to a_2 and the possible charge c_1 of the membrane changed to c_2.

3. Dissolution rules $[a_1]_l^c \to a_2$, to dissolve a membrane with label l that contains an object a_1 and, optionally, has a charge c. All the objects of the membrane goes to its parent membrane, object a_1 rewritten to a_2.

4. Membrane division rules $[a_1]_l^{c_1} \to [a_2]_l^{c_2}[a_3]_l^{c_3}$, to divide a membrane with label l and that contains an object a_1 and, optionally, has a charge c_1. The membrane divides in two new membranes each of them containing a copy of all its objects, with a_1 rewritten to a_2 and a_3, respectively, and the charge changed to c_2 and c_3, respectively.

5. Membrane creation rules $[a \to [u]_{l_2}^{c_2}]_{l_1}^{c_1}$, to create a membrane with label l_2, contents u and possible charge c_2 from an object a in a membrane with label l_1 and possible charge c_1. The objects from the latter membrane are not replicated into the membrane being created. To simplify the description of the patterns, we will omit the surrounding brackets when the membrane they are referring to is clear from the context.

6. Membrane separation rules $[a]_l^{c_1} \to [\Gamma_0]_l^{c_2}[\Gamma_1]_l^{c_3}$, to separate in two a membrane with label l and possible charge c_1. This separation is triggered by object a and sends all the other objects to one of the new membranes if they belong to Γ_0 and to the other membrane if they belong to Γ_1 (Γ_0 and Γ_1 must be a partition of the working alphabet). The new membranes have, optionally, charges c_2 and c_3, respectively.

2.1 The *Exponential Space* Pattern

The *exponential space* pattern allows to generate an exponential number of membranes in a linear number of steps. If we focus specifically on P systems with active membranes, the usual mechanism is to make use of a collection of objects, each of them triggering a rule that duplicates a membrane. If we arrange those objects in such a way that they appear sequentially in the membranes being created, the number of those membranes is doubled in each step. The final result is that after n steps we get 2^n membranes.

The *Exponential Space* Pattern with Membrane Division. To implement the *exponential space* pattern for P systems with active membranes we will make use of a sequence of objects to repeatedly divide the membranes in two. Each time that any of these objects has performed its task, it is changed into the next object in the sequence and put within both new membranes.

In order to write the pattern rules in an homogeneous way, it is customary to identify with subscripts the objects in the sequence. Thus, using objects $a_0, \ldots, a_n$, we can produce 2^n membranes with label l in n steps as follows:

Initial setup: $[a_0]_l$

Rules: $[a_i]_l \to [a_{i+1}]_l[a_{i+1}]_l, \quad 0 \le i < n$

It is important to note that the semantics itself of the division rule imposes that all the objects other than the one triggering the rule have to be replicated into the new membranes. This eases the design of the subsequent operations, which are usually required to be performed in parallel within each membrane. Compare it with the pattern for membrane separation, where we do not have this facility.

On the other hand, the fact that rules of the rewriting type are allowed to be run alongside division rules enables us to intercalate other operations with that of constructing the exponential space. This can even be boosted with the use of polarizations for the membranes, since they provide a mechanism to hold up the divisions of the membranes until the intercalated task has finished.

The *Exponential Space* Pattern with Membrane Creation. When dealing with P systems with membrane creation, in order to obtain an exponential space in linear time we face with the difficulty of being able to create only one membrane from the object triggering the rule. To circumvent this obstacle an exponential number of objects from which to create the membranes could be generated (for example, by rewriting rules of the form $a \rightarrow a^2$). But this solution has the disadvantage of making harder to set up the scenarios for other operations.

A better alternative is to exploit the semantics of membrane creation rules. Since when creating a membrane any number of objects can be placed within it, the number of objects can be doubled and distributed at the same time. Thus, with the help of objects $a_0, a'_0, \ldots, a_n, a'_n$, we can create 2^n membranes with label l in n steps as follows:

$$\begin{aligned}
\text{Initial setup:} \quad & a_0 a'_0 \\
\text{Rules:} \quad & a_i \rightarrow [a_{i+1} a'_{i+1}]_l, \quad 0 \leq i < n \\
& a'_i \rightarrow [a_{i+1} a'_{i+1}]_l, \quad 0 \leq i < n
\end{aligned}$$

Note that the result of the previous pattern is the creation, inside of the wrapping membrane that contains the initial setup, of a nested membrane structure whose depth is increased and whose number of most inner membranes is doubled with each application of the rules. If we are allowed to dissolve membranes, it is possible to obtain a flat membrane structure in the following manner:

$$\begin{aligned}
\text{Initial setup:} \quad & a_0 a'_0 \\
\text{Rules:} \quad & a_i \rightarrow [a_{i+1} a'_{i+1} d]_l, \quad 0 \leq i < n - 1 \\
& a'_i \rightarrow [a_{i+1} a'_{i+1} d]_l, \quad 0 \leq i < n - 1 \\
& [d]_l \rightarrow \lambda \\
& a_{n-1} \rightarrow [a_n a'_n]_l \\
& a'_{n-1} \rightarrow [a_n a'_n]_l
\end{aligned}$$

Again, by means of rewriting rules other operations can be performed at the same time as the exponential space is created. Also, the creation of the new membranes can be delayed with the aid of different techniques, such as the use of charges or the rotation of objects (for example, $a_{i,0} \rightarrow a_{i,1} \rightarrow \cdots \rightarrow a_{i,m} \rightarrow [a_{i+1,0} a'_{i+1,0}]_l$).

Finally, the objects required by the succeeding operations to be within the membranes with label l can be effortlessly put inside them by the last creation rules applied (the pattern above puts the objects a_n and a'_n, but this is only for simplicity of the description).

The *Exponential Space* Pattern with Membrane Separation. Separation rules, like division rules, provide two membranes from an initial one. This is the essential property allowing an efficient exponential space generation. However, the key difference is that, unlike with division rules, with separation rules no new objects are created, but the already existing ones are distributed into the new membranes. This means that the number of membranes that could be obtained is limited by the number of objects present in the P system at the beginning.

To overcome this restriction, membrane separation has to be combined with another mechanism, such as evolution rules, providing a way to generate an exponential number of objects in linear time. Also, to accommodate the separation, the pattern uses pairs of objects with identical role. Thus, we need objects $a_0, a'_0, \tilde{a}_0, \tilde{a}'_0, \ldots, a_n, a'_n, \tilde{a}_n, \tilde{a}'_n$ to create 2^n membranes with label l in n steps:

$$
\begin{aligned}
&\text{Initial setup:} \quad && [a_0 \tilde{a}_0]_l \\
&\text{Rules:} \quad && [\tilde{a}_i \to a_{i+1} a'_{i+1} \tilde{a}_{i+1} \tilde{a}'_{i+1}]_l, \quad 0 \le i < n \\
& && [\tilde{a}'_i \to a_{i+1} a'_{i+1} \tilde{a}_{i+1} \tilde{a}'_{i+1}]_l, \quad 0 \le i < n \\
& && [a_i]_l \to [\Gamma_0]_l [\Gamma_1]_l, \quad 0 \le i < n \\
& && [a'_i]_l \to [\Gamma_0]_l [\Gamma_1]_l, \quad 0 \le i < n
\end{aligned}
$$

where $a_i, \tilde{a}_i \in \Gamma_0$ and $a'_i, \tilde{a}'_i \in \Gamma_1$.

If we would like a specific object, say for example b, to remain within all the created membranes, the same duplication technique as for objects a_i could be employed:

$$
\begin{aligned}
&\text{Initial setup:} \quad && [a_0 \tilde{a}_0 b]_l \\
&\text{Rules:} \quad && [\tilde{a}_i \to a_{i+1} a'_{i+1} \tilde{a}_{i+1} \tilde{a}'_{i+1}]_l, \quad 0 \le i < n \\
& && [\tilde{a}'_i \to a_{i+1} a'_{i+1} \tilde{a}_{i+1} \tilde{a}'_{i+1}]_l, \quad 0 \le i < n \\
& && [b \to bb']_l \\
& && [b' \to bb']_l \\
& && [a_i]_l \to [\Gamma_0]_l [\Gamma_1]_l, \quad 0 \le i < n \\
& && [a'_i]_l \to [\Gamma_0]_l [\Gamma_1]_l, \quad 0 \le i < n
\end{aligned}
$$

where $a_i, \tilde{a}_i, b \in \Gamma_0$ and $a'_i, \tilde{a}'_i, b' \in \Gamma_1$.

2.2   The *All Present* Pattern

Almost all of the efficient solutions to hard problems found in the membrane computing bibliography follow a brute force approach. They first generate all the possible solutions to the problem and then check if any of them is indeed a solution. For this it is usually demanded that certain requirements are met.

The *all present* pattern arises in this context to confirm the fulfillment of all of these requirements. For that it assumes that the accomplishment of the i-th requirement is signaled by the presence of an object r_i in a certain membrane. It then takes care of verifying that for all of the requirements there is at least one associated object in that membrane.

The *All Present* Pattern with Polarizations. Let us suppose that we want to confirm if in a certain membrane with label l there is at least one copy of all the objects $r_1, \ldots, r_n$. When membrane charges are available, the alternation of two of them provides a control mechanism to iterate a two step process: when the membrane is, for example, positively charged, the presence of the object r_1 is checked; conversely, when the membrane is negatively charged, the subscripts of the objects r_i are decreased by one and a certain counter is increased by one. The absence of the object r_1 prevents the charge of the membrane to change to negative and so the counter gets stalled.

By representing the counter by the objects $c_0, \ldots, c_n$, the pattern takes the following form:

Initial setup: $[c_0 r_{i_1} \ldots r_{i_k}]_l^+$

Rules: $[r_1]_l^+ \to [\ ]_l^- r_1$

$[r_i \to r_{i-1}]_l^-, \quad 1 \le i \le n$

$[c_i \to c_{i+1}]_l^-, \quad 0 \le i < n$

$r_1[\ ]_l^- \to [r_0]_l^+$

$[c_n]_l^+ \to [\ ]_l^+ \text{yes}$

Just as it is described above, the pattern sends out of the membrane an object **yes** to acknowledge the presence of all the objects r_i. This answer can be obviously changed to another one more suitable for the purpose of the P system being designed.

The *All Present* Pattern with Membrane Creation. When working with polarizationless P systems it is necessary to look for another mechanisms allowing the two step process of checking for the presence of the objects and increasing the counter when they are detected. Membrane creation provides one of them, given place to the following pattern:

Initial setup: $[c_0 r_{i_1} \ldots r_{i_k}]_l$

Rules: $r_i \to [\ ]_i, \quad 1 \le i \le n$

$c_{i-1}[\ ]_i \to [c_i]_i, \quad 1 \le i \le n$

$[c_i]_i \to [\ ]_i c_i, \quad 1 \le i \le n$

$[c_n]_l \to [\ ]_l \text{yes}$

This pattern acknowledges the presence of an object r_i by creating a membrane with label i. The counter traverses these membranes in order, simply by entering and immediately exiting them. If any object r_i is missing, no membrane with label i is created and the counter gets stalled.

Again the final answer **yes** when all the objects are present is arbitrary and can be changed to another more suitable one.

The *All Present* Pattern with Cooperation. When objects can cooperate in evolution rules, verifying that all objects r_i are within the target membrane is a triviality.

$$\begin{aligned}
&\text{Initial setup:} &&[c_0 r_{i_1} \dots r_{i_k}]_l \\
&\text{Rules:} &&[c_0\, r_1 \dots r_n \to c_n]_l \\
& &&[c_n]_l \to [\,]_l\textbf{yes}
\end{aligned}$$

Since complete cooperation is so powerful, we often restrict to minimal cooperation, where the left-hand side of an evolution rule is restricted to length at most two. In this case it is also easy to build an *all present* pattern:

$$\begin{aligned}
&\text{Initial setup:} &&[c_0 r_{i_1} \dots r_{i_k}]_l \\
&\text{Rules:} &&[c_i r_{i+1} \to c_{i+1}]_l, \quad 0 \le i < n \\
& &&[c_n]_l \to [\,]_l\textbf{yes}
\end{aligned}$$

2.3   The *No If Not Yes* Pattern

To solve a decision problem means to provide, for any of its instances, either the answer *yes* or the answer *no*. When designing a solution to a hard problem by means of a brute force search, it usually happens that the P system is able to signal the true solutions from the candidate ones that have been produced. Thus, since those signals can be effortlessly detected, it is easy to manage the positive instances of the problem. The difficulty arises with the negative instances, for which we have to guarantee that no signal will be generated, meaning that all candidate solutions have been discarded.

The *no if not yes* pattern comes to the rescue. The idea is very simple: we assume that the exact computation step when the signal would be detected can be figured out, what is almost always true. The pattern handles a counter that is increased at each step of the computation. If a signal is detected, the object **yes** is sent out to the environment and the computation is halted, which includes, of course, stopping the counter. Otherwise, the counter will go beyond the step where the signals should have been detected, so we can safely send the object **no** out to the environment and halt the computation.

The *No If Not Yes* Pattern with Polarizations. To provide a plain implementation of this pattern in P systems with polarizations, we will presuppose that the signal objects are collected within the skin membrane and that the charge of this membrane is initially neutral.

$$\begin{aligned}
&\text{Initial setup:} &&[c_0]^0_{skin} \\
& &&\text{signal objects } s \text{ appear in the skin at step } n
\end{aligned}$$

Rules:
$$[c_i \rightarrow c_{i+1}]^0_{skin}, \quad 0 \le i \le n$$
$$[s]^0_{skin} \rightarrow [\ ]^+_{skin} \textbf{yes}$$
$$[c_{n+1}]^0_{skin} \rightarrow [\ ]^0_{skin} \textbf{no}$$

Therefore, the computation is supposed to stop after step $n+2$. Any solution to the instance of the problem makes an object s to enter the skin membrane at step n. This, in turn, makes the skin membrane to send an object **yes** out to the environment and to become positively polarized, what blocks the counter. In the case that the instance has no solution, the skin membrane remains neutrally polarized, and with the aid of the counter an object **no** is sent out to the environment.

The *No If Not Yes* Pattern with Dissolution. When instead of polarizations it is dissolution what is available, the impossibility of dissolving the skin membrane compels us to work in an ancillary membrane within it. The pattern is simply translated as follows: the appearance of a signal object s at step n dissolves that membrane, preventing the counter to keep on advancing, and releasing an object **yes** into the skin; if the above does not happen, the counter dissolves the membrane at step $n + 1$, releasing an object **no** into the skin; the latter just has to send out whichever of the answer objects is received, and the computation then stops.

Initial setup: $[[c_0]_l]_{skin}$

signal objects s appear in membrane l at step n

Rules: $[c_i \rightarrow c_{i+1}]_l, \quad 0 \le i \le n$
$$[s]_l \rightarrow \textbf{yes}$$
$$[c_{n+1}]_l \rightarrow \textbf{no}$$
$$[\textbf{yes}]_{skin} \rightarrow [\ ]_{skin} \textbf{yes}$$
$$[\textbf{no}]_{skin} \rightarrow [\ ]_{skin} \textbf{no}$$

The *No If Not Yes* Pattern with Cooperation. With (minimal) cooperation as the control mechanism, the pattern can be implemented by combining an auxiliary object able to react with the signal objects and a counter to account for their absence. The appearance of any of the signal objects at step n removes the auxiliary object, releasing an object **yes** into the skin. Otherwise it remains in the system and cooperate with the counter to release an object **no** into the skin. Whichever the answer object received is sent out to the environment by the skin and the computation then stops.

Initial setup: $[c_0\, c]_{skin}$

signal objects s appear in the skin at step n

Rules: $[c_i \rightarrow c_{i+1}]_{skin}, \quad 0 \le i < n + 1$
$$[cs \rightarrow \textbf{yes}]_{skin}$$
$$[c_{n+1}c \rightarrow \textbf{no}]_{skin}$$

$$[\text{yes}]_{skin} \rightarrow [\ ]_{skin}\text{yes}$$
$$[\text{no}]_{skin} \rightarrow [\ ]_{skin}\text{no}$$

3   Practical Examples

To illustrate the use of the design patterns previously described, in this section we elaborate some solutions to a hard problem, namely the propositional satisfiability problem. The SAT problem was the first one proved to be **NP**-complete [8], and can be stated as follows: *given a Boolean formula in conjunctive normal form (CNF), determine whether or not it is satisfiable, that is, whether there exists an assignment to its variables on which it evaluates to true.*

There are already numerous efficient solutions to SAT in the membrane computing literature, devised in different frameworks, for example, the ones in [6,7,9–12] and many more. Taking inspiration from these solutions, in the subsections coming next we exhibit three new solutions to SAT, with the focus on making apparent how they integrate the design patterns.

These new solutions will be provided within the framework of P systems with active membranes, first introduced by Păun [5] as a type of P systems that, abstracting the process of cell mitosis, provide rules for making the membranes to divide. Along with this kind of operations, these systems can also: make an object evolve within a membrane; send an object into or out of a membrane; dissolve a membrane. Besides, each of the membranes has an associated charge –positive, negative or neutral– subject to changes by the applications of the rules. Finally, rules are triggered by a unique object, disallowing their cooperation.

Since the computational power of this model has been shown to be as high as to be able to efficiently solve hard problems, several variants have been considered in an attempt to determine what borderlines in efficiency provides each of its ingredients. Thus, with respect to the mechanism generating exponential space, membrane creation (abstracting cell autopoiesis) and membrane separation (abstracting cell meiosis) have been studied. The role of polarization, dissolution and cooperation, and even of membrane labels, have also been analyzed. A survey of diverse results that have been obtained can be found in [7]. Our solutions will differ in the ingredients utilized, to show how the design patterns are able to adapt to distinct conditions.

For a better understanding of the solutions, we refer to [7] for the semantics of the variants with membrane division and creation and to [13] for the semantics of the variant with membrane separation. Some details to take into account: the working mode is maximal parallelism, meaning that the rules are applied to all objects and all membranes at the same time in parallel; for active membranes with division or separation rules, the semantics states that each membrane can be affected by at most one rule of the send in, send out, dissolution and division/separation type (all types but evolution); when creation rules are used, the standard semantics is polarizationless and, besides, it only restricts the simultaneous application of dissolution rules; it is assumed that to perform a computation step, the system applies first the evolution rules and then all the others.

The solutions presented here are uniform: for every $m \geq 1$ and every $n \geq 1$ they construct a P system $\Pi(m, n)$ for dealing with any Boolean formula in CNF with m clauses and n variables. The input alphabet of this P system will always be

$$\Sigma(m, n) = \{x_{i,j}, \bar{x}_{i,j} \mid 1 \leq i \leq m, 1 \leq j \leq n\}$$

Given a Boolean formula $\varphi = C_1 \wedge \cdots \wedge C_m$, before starting a computation of $\Pi(m, n)$ an object $x_{i,j}$ (respectively, $\bar{x}_{i,j}$) has to be put inside its input membrane for any clause C_i and any variable x_j such that x_j is in C_i (respectively, $\neg x_j$ is in C_i). The computation will then carry out these operations:

- *Generate* all the possible assignments for φ: the *exponential space* pattern will be useful here.
- *Compute* for each of the assignments which clauses take a true value: this can be done after the previous operation ends, but usually also at the same time, as we will see.
- *Check* for every assignment, in parallel, if all the clauses take a true value: the *all present* pattern is clearly suitable for this task.
- *Decide* if the formula φ is satisfiable or not: the *no if not yes* pattern will be needed for this.

3.1 Solution to SAT Using Polarizations and Membrane Division

Given φ a Boolean formula in CNF with m clauses and n variables, the recognizer P system $\Pi(m, n)$ of the solution that decides if φ is satisfiable or not is constructed in polynomial time from:

- A working alphabet:

$$\Sigma(m, n) \cup \{d_i \mid 0 \leq i \leq 2n\}$$
$$\cup \{r_{i,j} \mid 0 \leq i \leq m, 1 \leq j \leq n+1\}$$
$$\cup \{c_i \mid 0 \leq i \leq 3n + 2m + 3\}$$
$$\cup \{d, \mathsf{yes}, \mathsf{no}\}$$

- A set $\{1, 2\}$ of labels for the membranes.
- An initial membrane structure and contents of the membranes $[c_0 [d\, d_0]_2^0]_1^0$ (the input membrane is the one labelled 2).
- A set of rules *GenerateCompute* $\cup$ *Sync* $\cup$ *Check* $\cup$ *Decide* where:
  - The rules in *GenerateCompute* are:

  1. $[d_i]_2^0 \rightarrow [d_{i+1}]_2^+ [d_{i+1}]_2^-$ $0 \leq i < n$

  2. $[x_{i,1} \rightarrow r_{i,1}]_2^+, \ [\bar{x}_{i,1} \rightarrow \lambda]_2^+$
     $[x_{i,1} \rightarrow \lambda]_2^-, \ [\bar{x}_{i,1} \rightarrow r_{i,1}]_2^-$ $1 \leq i \leq m$

3. $[x_{i,j} \to x_{i,j-1}]_2^+$, $[\bar{x}_{i,j} \to \bar{x}_{i,j-1}]_2^+$ $1 \leq i \leq m, 2 \leq j \leq n$

   $[x_{i,j} \to x_{i,j-1}]_2^-$, $[\bar{x}_{i,j} \to \bar{x}_{i,j-1}]_2^-$

4. $[d \to d^2]_2^0$

   $[d]_2^+ \to [\ ]_2^0 d$, $[d]_2^- \to [\ ]_2^0 d$

- The rules in *Sync* are:

  5. $[r_{i,j} \to r_{i,j+1}]_2^0$ $1 \leq i \leq m, 1 \leq j < n+1$
  6. $[d_i \to d_{i+1}]_2^0$ $n \leq i < 2n-1$
  7. $[d_{2n-1} \to d_{2n} c_0]_2^0$
  8. $[d_{2n}]_2^0 \to [\ ]_2^+ d_{2n}$

- The rules in *Check* are:

  9. $[r_{1,n+1}]_2^+ \to [\ ]_2^- r_{1,n+1}$
  10. $[r_{i,n+1} \to r_{i-1,n+1}]_2^-$ $1 \leq i \leq m$
  11. $[c_i \to c_{i+1}]_2^-$ $0 \leq i < m$
  12. $r_{1,n+1}[\ ]_2^- \to [r_{0,n+1}]_2^+$
  13. $[c_m]_2^+ \to [\ ]_2^+ \text{yes}$

- The rules in *Decide* are:

  14. $[c_i \to c_{i+1}]_1^0$ $0 \leq i < 3n + 2m + 3$
  15. $[\text{yes}]_1^0 \to [\ ]_1^+ \text{yes}$
  16. $[c_{3n+2m+3}]_1^0 \to [\ ]_1^0 \text{no}$

In this P system rules number 1 implement the *exponential space* pattern, with the membranes dividing when neutrally charged. Charges $+$ and $-$ are used to sequentially track the different values assigned to the variables. This way, rules number 2–3 are able to determine, along the process of generating the 2^n membranes representing the different assignments, which clauses are taking the true value. Both membrane division and clause value determination are intercalated by means of rules number 4.

Since only three charges are available and both the *exponential space* and the *all present* pattern make use of them, we need a mechanism preventing the patterns to interfere. A regular technique is to append subscripts to the common objects, allowing them to differentiate. For $\Pi(m,n)$, although all objects $r_{i,j}$ represent that the i-th clause is true, the generation/computation stage works with those with $0 \leq j \leq n$, whereas the checking stage works with those with $j = n+1$. One caveat is that we have to assure that all the objects are the correct ones before letting the checking stage start, and that is the duty of rules number 5–8.

Next, rules number 9–13 carry out the *all present* pattern in each of the 2^n internal membranes, to verify if for their associated assignments all the clauses take the true value and send out a **yes** object to the skin membrane if so. Finally, rules number 14–16 provide the definitive answer by means of a *no if not yes* pattern.

3.2   Solution to **SAT** Using Dissolution and Membrane Creation

Given φ a Boolean formula in CNF with m clauses and n variables, the recognizer P system $\Pi(m, n)$ of the solution that decides if φ is satisfiable or not is constructed in polynomial time from:

- A working alphabet:

$$\Sigma(m, n) \cup \{x_{i,j,l}, \bar{x}_{i,j,l} \mid 1 \leq i \leq m, 1 \leq j \leq n, l = t, f\}$$
$$\cup \{d_{i,t}, d_{i,f} \mid 0 \leq i \leq n\}$$
$$\cup \{r_i, r_{i,l} \mid 1 \leq i \leq m, l = t, f\}$$
$$\cup \{c_i \mid 0 \leq i \leq 3n + 2m + 5\}$$
$$\cup \{\text{yes}, \text{no}\}$$

- A set $\{a, b, c, t, f, 1, \ldots, m\}$ of labels for the membranes.
- An initial membrane structure and contents of the membranes $[[c_0 d_{0,t} d_{0,f}]_b]_a$ (the input membrane is the one labelled b).
- A set of rules $GenerateCompute \cup Link \cup Check \cup Decide$ where:
  - The rules in $GenerateCompute$ are:

  1. $[d_{0,t} \rightarrow [d_{1,t} d_{1,f}]_t]_b$
     $[d_{0,f} \rightarrow [d_{1,t} d_{1,f}]_f]_b$
  2. $[d_{i,t} \rightarrow [d_{i+1,t} d_{i+1,f}]_t]_l$
     $[d_{i,f} \rightarrow [d_{i+1,t} d_{i+1,f}]_f]_l$ $1 \leq i < n, l = t, f$
  3. $x_{i,1}[\,]_t \rightarrow [r_i]_t, \ \bar{x}_{i,1}[\,]_f \rightarrow [r_i]_f$ $1 \leq i \leq m$
  4. $[x_{i,j} \rightarrow x_{i,j,t} x_{i,j,f}]_l$
     $[\bar{x}_{i,j} \rightarrow \bar{x}_{i,j,t} \bar{x}_{i,j,f}]_l$
     $x_{i,j,l}[\,]_l \rightarrow [x_{i,j-1}]_l$ $1 \leq i \leq m, 2 \leq j \leq n, l = t, f$
     $\bar{x}_{i,j,l}[\,]_l \rightarrow [\bar{x}_{i,j-1}]_l$
  5. $[r_i \rightarrow r_{i,t} r_{i,f}]_l$
     $r_{i,l}[\,]_l \rightarrow [r_i]_l$ $1 \leq i \leq m, l = t, f$

  - The rules in $Link$ are:

  6. $[d_{n,t} \rightarrow [c_0]_c]_l$ $l = t, f$
  7. $r_{i,t}[\,]_c \rightarrow [r_i]_c$ $1 \leq i < m$

  - The rules in $Check$ are:

  8. $[r_i \rightarrow [\,]_i]_c$ $1 \leq i \leq m$
  9. $c_{i-1}[\,]_i \rightarrow [c_i]_i$ $1 \leq i \leq m$
  10. $[c_i]_i \rightarrow [\,]_i c_i$ $1 \leq i \leq m$
  11. $[c_m]_c \rightarrow [\,]_c \text{yes}$
  12. $[\text{yes}]_l \rightarrow [\,]_l \text{yes}$ $l = t, f$

  - The rules in $Decide$ are:

  13. $[c_i \rightarrow c_{i+1}]_b$ $0 \leq i < 3n + 2m + 5$

14. $[\text{yes}]_b \to \text{yes}$
15. $[c_{3n+2m+5}]_b \to \text{no}$
16. $[\text{yes}]_a \to [\,]_a \text{yes}$
17. $[\text{no}]_a \to [\,]_a \text{no}$

In this P system rules number 1–2 implement the *exponential space* pattern to create a nested membrane structure, each of whose inner membranes stands for a different assignment to the variables of φ. As this membrane structure is created, but at a slower pace, the objects $x_{i,j}$ that represent this formula traverse it, computing at the same time which of the clauses makes true, which is signified by the objects r_i. Rules number 3–5 are in charge of this, including the use of the object duplication technique to be able to transmit a copy of the objects from each membrane to both of the membranes created inside it.

Rules number 6–7 link the generation/computation stage with the checking one, preventing the latter to start until the whole nested membrane structure has been constructed. They then create inside each of the internal membranes a new membrane where the *all present* pattern, implemented by rules number 8–11, is used to verify if all the clauses are true. Note, however, that objects r_i arrive at different times, but this does not affect the pattern performance. Also, the affirmative answers traverse, by means of rule number 12, the membrane structure back until arriving to membrane b.

Finally, rules number 13–17 use the *no if not yes* pattern to provide the definitive answer. Here, the time needed by the objects $x_{i,j}$ and r_i to travel forward and by the objects **yes** to travel backward through the membrane structure has been taken into account before concluding that the formula is unsatisfiable.

3.3   Solution to SAT Using Polarizations and Membrane Separation

Given φ a Boolean formula in CNF with m clauses and n variables, the recognizer P system $\Pi(m, n)$ of the solution that decides if φ is satisfiable or not is constructed in polynomial time from:

– A working alphabet $\Gamma_1 \cup \Gamma_2$ with:

$$
\begin{aligned}
\Gamma_1 =& \{x_{i,j}, \bar{x}_{i,j} \mid 1 \le i \le m, 1 \le j \le n\} \\
& \cup \{d_i \mid 0 \le i \le 2n + 1\} \\
& \cup \{\tilde{d}_i \mid 0 \le i \le n\} \\
& \cup \{r_{i,j} \mid 1 \le i \le m, 1 \le j \le n + 1\} \\
& \cup \{c_i \mid 0 \le i \le 3n + 2m + 4\} \\
& \cup \{d, \text{yes}, \text{no}\}
\end{aligned}
$$

and

$$
\begin{aligned}
\Gamma_2 =& \{x'_{i,j}, \bar{x}'_{i,j} \mid 1 \le i \le m, 1 \le j \le n\} \\
& \cup \{d'_i \mid 0 \le i \le 2n + 1\}
\end{aligned}
$$

$$\cup \{\tilde{d}'_i \mid 0 \leq i \leq n\}$$
$$\cup \{r'_{i,j} \mid 1 \leq i \leq m, 1 \leq j \leq n+1\}$$
$$\cup \{d'\}$$

- A set $\{1,2\}$ of labels for the membranes.
- An initial membrane structure and contents of the membranes $[c_0[d_0\tilde{d}_0d]^0_2]^0_1$ (the input membrane is the one labelled 2).
- A set of rules *GenerateCompute* $\cup$ *Sync* $\cup$ *Check* $\cup$ *Decide* where:
  • The rules in *GenerateCompute* are:

  1. $[d_i]^0_2 \rightarrow [\Gamma_0]^+_2[\Gamma_1]^-_2$
     $[d'_i]^0_2 \rightarrow [\Gamma_0]^+_2[\Gamma_1]^-_2$ $\quad 0 \leq i < n$
  2. $[\tilde{d}_i \rightarrow d_{i+1}d'_{i+1}\tilde{d}_{i+1}\tilde{d}'_{i+1}]^0_2$
     $[\tilde{d}'_i \rightarrow d_{i+1}d'_{i+1}\tilde{d}_{i+1}\tilde{d}'_{i+1}]^0_2$ $\quad 0 \leq i < n$
  3. $[x_{i,j} \rightarrow x_{i,j}x'_{i,j}]^0_2,\ [x'_{i,j} \rightarrow x_{i,j}x'_{i,j}]^0_2$
     $[\bar{x}_{i,j} \rightarrow \bar{x}_{i,j}\bar{x}'_{i,j}]^0_2,\ [\bar{x}'_{i,j} \rightarrow \bar{x}_{i,j}\bar{x}'_{i,j}]^0_2$ $\quad 1 \leq i \leq m, 1 \leq j \leq n$
     $[r_{i,j} \rightarrow r_{i,j+1}r'_{i,j+1}]^0_2,\ [r'_{i,j} \rightarrow r_{i,j+1}r'_{i,j+1}]^0_2$
  4. $[d \rightarrow d^2d'^2]^0_2,\ [d' \rightarrow d^2d'^2]^0_2$
  5. $[x_{i,1} \rightarrow r_{i,1}]^+_2,\ [\bar{x}_{i,1} \rightarrow \lambda]^+_2$
     $[x'_{i,1} \rightarrow r_{i,1}]^+_2,\ [\bar{x}'_{i,1} \rightarrow \lambda]^+_2$ $\quad 1 \leq i \leq m$
     $[x_{i,1} \rightarrow \lambda]^-_2,\ [\bar{x}_{i,1} \rightarrow r_{i,1}]^-_2$
     $[x'_{i,1} \rightarrow \lambda]^-_2,\ [\bar{x}'_{i,1} \rightarrow r_{i,1}]^-_2$
  6. $[x_{i,j} \rightarrow x_{i,j-1}]^+_2,\ [\bar{x}_{i,j} \rightarrow \bar{x}_{i,j-1}]^+_2$
     $[x'_{i,j} \rightarrow x'_{i,j-1}]^+_2,\ [\bar{x}'_{i,j} \rightarrow \bar{x}'_{i,j-1}]^+_2$ $\quad 1 \leq i \leq m, 2 \leq j \leq n$
     $[x_{i,j} \rightarrow x_{i,j-1}]^-_2,\ [\bar{x}_{i,j} \rightarrow \bar{x}_{i,j-1}]^-_2$
     $[x'_{i,j} \rightarrow x'_{i,j-1}]^-_2,\ [\bar{x}'_{i,j} \rightarrow \bar{x}'_{i,j-1}]^-_2$
  7. $[d]^+_2 \rightarrow [\ ]^0_2d,\ [d]^-_2 \rightarrow [\ ]^0_2d$
     $[d']^+_2 \rightarrow [\ ]^0_2d',\ [d']^-_2 \rightarrow [\ ]^0_2d'$

  • The rules in *Sync* are:

  8. $[r_{i,j} \rightarrow r_{i,j+1}]^0_2,\ [r'_{i,j} \rightarrow r'_{i,j+1}]^0_2$ $\quad 1 \leq i \leq m, 1 \leq j < n+1$
  9. $[r'_{i,n+1} \rightarrow r_{i,n+1}]^0_2$ $\quad 1 \leq i \leq m$
  10. $[d_i \rightarrow d_{i+1}]^0_2,\ [d'_i \rightarrow d'_{i+1}]^0_2$ $\quad n \leq i < 2n$
  11. $[d_{2n} \rightarrow d_{2n+1}c_0]^0_2,\ [d'_{2n} \rightarrow d'_{2n+1}c_0]^0_2$
  12. $[d_{2n+1}]^0_2 \rightarrow [\ ]^+_2d_{2n+1},\ [d'_{2n+1}]^0_2 \rightarrow [\ ]^+_2d'_{2n+1}$

  • The rules in *Check* are:

  13. $[r_{1,n+1}]^+_2 \rightarrow [\ ]^-_2r_{1,n+1}$
  14. $[r_{i,n+1} \rightarrow r_{i-1,n+1}]^-_2$ $\quad 1 \leq i \leq m$
  15. $[c_i \rightarrow c_{i+1}]^-_2$ $\quad 0 \leq i < m$

16. $r_{1,n+1}[\ ]_2^- \to [r_{0,n+1}]_2^+$
17. $[c_m]_2^+ \to [\ ]_2^+ \text{yes}$

- The rules in *Decide* are:

18. $[c_i \to c_{i+1}]_1^0 \qquad 0 \le i < 3n + 2m + 4$
19. $[\text{yes}]_1^0 \to [\ ]_1^+ \text{yes}$
20. $[c_{3n+2m+4}]_1^0 \to [\ ]_1^0 \text{no}$

In this P system rules number 1–2 implement the *exponential space* pattern for membrane separation, whereas rules number 3–4 include the standard object duplication technique to preserve the objects when separating the membranes. For the rest, the behaviour of the system is analogous to the one from the solution with polarizations and membrane division in Subsect. 3.1. Just only rule number 9 is added to get rid of the prime objects, so that we do not have to duplicate the rules for the subsequent operations.

3.4   Solution to **SAT** Using Minimal Cooperation (with Minimal Production) and Membrane Division

Given φ a Boolean formula in CNF with m clauses and n variables, the recognizer P system $\Pi(m, n)$ of the solution that decides if φ is satisfiable or not is constructed in polynomial time from:

- A working alphabet:

$$\Sigma^*(m, n) \cup \{a_{i,k} \mid 1 \le i \le n, 1 \le k \le i\}$$
$$\cup \{t_{i,k}, f_{i,k} \mid 1 \le i \le n, i \le k \le n + p + 1\}$$
$$\cup \{\beta_k \mid 0 \le k \le n + 2p + 2\}$$
$$\cup \{c_j \mid 1 \le j \le m\}$$
$$\cup \{d_j \mid 0 \le j \le m\}$$
$$\cup \{T_i, F_i \mid 1 \le i \le n\}$$
$$\cup \{x_{i,j,k}, \bar{x}_{i,j,k}, x_{i,j,k}^* \mid 0 \le i \le n, 1 \le j \le m, 1 \le k \le n + p\}$$
$$\cup \{\alpha, \text{no}, \text{yes}\}$$

- A set $\{1, 2\}$ of labels for the membranes.
- An initial membrane structure and contents of the membranes $[\alpha \, \beta_0 [d_0 \, a_{i,1} \, T_i^p \, F_i^p]_2]_1$ (the input membrane is the one labelled 2).
- A set of rules *Generate* $\cup$ *Remove* $\cup$ *Compute* $\cup$ *Check* $\cup$ *Decide* where:
  - The rules in *Generate* are:

1. $[a_{i,i}]_2 \to [t_{i,i}]_2[f_{i,i}]_2 \qquad 1 \le i \le n$
2. $[a_{i,k} \to a_{i,k+1}]_2 \qquad 2 \le i \le n, 1 \le k \le i - 1$
3. $[t_{i,k} \to t_{i,k+1}]_2 \qquad 1 \le i \le n - 1, i \le k \le n - 1$
   $[f_{i,k} \to f_{i,k+1}]_2$

- The rules in *Remove* are:

    4. $[t_{i,k} \, F_i \rightarrow t_{i,k+1}]_2$
       $[f_{i,k} \, T_i \rightarrow f_{i,k+1}]_2$ $\quad 1 \leq i \leq n, n \leq k \leq n+p-1$

- The rules in *Compute* are:

    5. $[x_{i,j,k} \rightarrow x_{i,j,k+1}]_2$
       $[\bar{x}_{i,j,k} \rightarrow \bar{x}_{i,j,k+1}]_2$ $\quad 1 \leq i \leq n, 1 \leq j \leq p, 0 \leq k \leq n+p-1$
       $[x^*_{i,j,k} \rightarrow x^*_{i,j,k+1}]_2$

    6. $[T_i \, x_{i,j,n+p} \rightarrow c_j]_2$
       $[T_i \, \bar{x}_{i,j,n+p} \rightarrow \#]_2$
       $[T_i \, x^*_{i,j,n+p} \rightarrow \#]_2$
       $[T_i \, x_{i,j,n+p} \rightarrow \#]_2$ $\quad 1 \leq i \leq n, 1 \leq j \leq p$
       $[T_i \, \bar{x}_{i,j,n+p} \rightarrow c_j]_2$
       $[T_i \, x^*_{i,j,n+p} \rightarrow \#]_2$

- The rules in *Check* are:

    7. $[d_i \, c_{i+1} \rightarrow d_{i+1}]_2$ $\quad 1 \leq i \leq m-1$

- The rules in *Decide* are:

    8. $[\beta_i \rightarrow \beta_{i+1}]_2$ $\quad 0 \leq i \leq n+2p+1$
    9. $[d_m]_2 \rightarrow [\ ]_2 d_m$
    10. $[\alpha \, d_m \rightarrow \text{yes}]_2$
    11. $[\beta_{n+2p+2} \, \alpha \rightarrow \text{no}]_2$
    12. $[\text{yes}]_1 \rightarrow [\ ]_1 \text{yes}$
    13. $[\text{no}]_1 \rightarrow [\ ]_1 \text{no}$

Note that for this solution a different *input alphabet* is needed:

$$\Sigma^*(m, n) = \{x_{i,j,0}, \bar{x}_{i,j,0}, x^*_{i,j,0} \mid 1 \leq i \leq n, 1 \leq j \leq m\}$$

Then, given a Boolean formula $\varphi = C_1 \wedge \cdots \wedge C_m$, before starting a computation of $\Pi(m, n)$ an object $x_{i,j}$ (respectively, $\bar{x}_{i,j}$) has to be put inside its input membrane for any clause C_j and any variable x_i such that x_i is in C_j (respectively, $\neg x_i$ is in C_j). If neither x_i nor $\neg x_i$ appear in C_j, then an object $x^*_{i,j,0}$ has to be put inside its input membrane.

In this P system rules number 1–2 implement the *exponential space* pattern with division rules. This way, rules number 3 are able to synchronize objects $t_{i,k}$ and $f_{i,k}$ for the next stage. Rules number 4 remove the wrong "truth assignment objects" to keep only the objects that represent the real truth assignment of such a membrane. Rules number 5–6 synchronize $cod(\varphi)$ with the rest of the system and compute the clauses that are satisfied by the corresponding truth assignment.

Rules number 7 implement the *all present* pattern with minimal cooperation, and finally rules number 8–10 return the answer by means of the *no if not yes* pattern.

4   Conclusions

Many variants of P systems are powerful enough as to permit the existence of (theoretical) efficient solutions to hard problems. Indeed, a plethora of such solutions to **NP**-complete, **PP**-complete, **PSPACE**-complete problems and the like can be found in the membrane computing literature.

A careful analysis of those solutions reveals that a number of techniques and constructions are repeatedly applied. Following what is recommended practice in software engineering, it is advisable to devise abstractions of those techniques and constructions. These design patterns may speed up the elaboration of solutions to new problems and increase the confidence in their correct functioning.

This paper aims to promote the developing of design patterns for solutions to hard problems within membrane computing. As a starting point, three of them are introduced, namely: the *exponential space* pattern, to create an exponential number of membranes in linear time; the *all present* pattern, to check if all of a number of objects are present in a membrane; and the *no if not yes* pattern, to supply the no object when the yes object has not appeared in a membrane at a specific computation step.

To highlight the advantages attained from the utilization of design patterns, several solutions to the SAT problem are given. Although the variants of P systems considered work with different features, the proposed design patterns can be implemented in all of them, what we exploit to use the same structure for each of the solutions.

There are three clear lines for future work:

- Provide implementations of the design patterns in variants of P systems other than P systems with active membranes, for example, P systems with symport/antiport rules or tissue P systems.
- Abstract more design patterns from existent or new solutions. In particular, a review of the solutions to **PP**-complete and PSPACE-complete problems that can be found in the literature (for example [14–18]) shows that other types of patterns are required. Namely, for the former, the ability to "count" is needed, whereas for the latter a hierarchical separation of the space is usually performed.
- Apply the design patterns to obtain efficient solutions to new hard problems.

Acknowledgments. The authors are very grateful to Mario J. Pérez-Jiménez for his unconditional support, unlimited generosity, patience and enthusiasm, and particularly for his skillful advising and guiding as their "scientific father".

The authors also acknowledge the support from research project TIN2017-89842-P, cofinanced by Ministerio de Economía, Industria y Competitividad (MINECO) of Spain, through the Agencia Estatal de Investigación (AEI), and by Fondo Europeo de Desarrollo Regional (FEDER) of the European Union.

References

1. Fortnow, L., Homer, S.: A short history of computational complexity. Bull. Eur. Assoc. Theor. Comput. Sci. (EATCS) **80**, 95–133 (2003)

2. Păun, Gh.: Computing with membranes. J. Comput. Syst. Sci. **61**(1), 108–143 (2000)
3. Păun, Gh.: Membrane Computing. An Introduction. Natural Computing Series. Springer, Heidelberg (2002). https://doi.org/10.1007/978-3-642-56196-2
4. Păun, Gh., Rozenberg, G., Salomaa, A. (eds.): The Oxford Handbook of Membrane Computing. Oxford University Press, Oxford (2009)
5. Păun, Gh.: P systems with active membranes: attacking NP-complete problems. J. Autom. Lang. Comb. **6**(1), 75–90 (2001)
6. Pérez-Jiménez, M.J., Romero-Jiménez, Á., Sancho-Caparrini, F.: Complexity classes in models of cellular computing with membranes. Nat. Comput. **2**(3), 265–285 (2003)
7. Pérez-Jiménez, M.J., Riscos-Núñez, A., Romero-Jiménez, Á., Woods, D.: Complexity: membrane division, membrane creation. In: Păun et al. [4], chap. 12, pp. 302–336
8. Garey, M.R., Johnson, D.S.: Computers and Intractability. A Guide to the Theory of NP-Completeness. W. H. Freeman, New York (1979)
9. Gutiérrez-Naranjo, M.Á., Pérez-Jiménez, M.J., Romero-Campero, F.J.: A uniform solution to SAT using membrane creation. Theor. Comput. Sci. **371**(1–2), 54–61 (2007). https://doi.org/10.1016/j.tcs.2006.10.013
10. Pan, L., Ishdorj, T.O.: P systems with active membranes and separation rules. J. Univers. Comput. Sci. **10**(5), 630–649 (2004). https://doi.org/10.3217/jucs-010-05-0630
11. Pérez-Jiménez, M.J., Romero-Jiménez, Á., Sancho-Caparrini, F.: A polynomial complexity class in P systems using membrane division. J. Autom. Lang. Comb. **11**(4), 423–434 (2006)
12. Valencia-Cabrera, L., Orellana-Martín, D., Martínez-del Amor, M.Á., Riscos-Núñez, A., Pérez-Jiménez, M.J.: Reaching efficiency through collaboration in membrane systems: dissolution, polarization and cooperation. Theor. Comput. Sci. **701**, 226–234 (2017). https://doi.org/10.1016/j.tcs.2017.04.015
13. Valencia-Cabrera, L., Orellana-Martín, D., Martínez-del Amor, M.Á., Riscos-Núñez, A., Pérez-Jiménez, M.J.: From distribution to replication in cooperative systems with active membranes: a frontier of the efficiency. Theor. Comput. Sci. **736**, 15–24 (2018). https://doi.org/10.1016/j.tcs.2017.12.012
14. Porreca, A.E., Leporati, A., Mauri, G., Zandron, C.: Elementary active membranes have the power of counting. Int. J. Nat. Comput. Res. **2**(3), 35–48 (2011). https://doi.org/10.4018/jncr.2011070104
15. Leporati, A., Manzoni, L., Mauri, G., Porreca, A.E., Zandron, C.: The counting power of P systems with antimatter. Theor. Comput. Sci. **701**, 161–173 (2017). https://doi.org/10.1016/j.tcs.2017.03.045
16. Alhazov, A., Pérez-Jiménez, M.J.: Uniform solution of, QSAT using polarizationless active membranes. In: Durand-Lose, J., Margenstern, M. (eds.) MCU 2007. LNCS, vol. 4664, pp. 122–133. Springer, Heidelberg (2007). https://doi.org/10.1007/978-3-540-74593-8_11
17. Sosík, P.: The computational power of cell division in P systems: beating down parallel computers? Nat. Comput. **2**(3), 287–298 (2003). https://doi.org/10.1023/A:1025401325428
18. Alhazov, A., Martín-Vide, C., Pan, L.: Solving a PSPACE-complete problem by recognizing P systems with restricted active membranes. Fundam. Inform. **58**(2), 67–77 (2003)

Spiking Neural P Systems:
Theoretical Results and Applications

Haina Rong[1], Tingfang Wu[2], Linqiang Pan[2(✉)], and Gexiang Zhang[1]

[1] School of Electrical Engineering, Southwest Jiaotong University,
Chengdu 610031, China
{ronghaina,zhgxdylan}@126.com
[2] Key Laboratory of Image Information Processing and Intelligent Control of
Education Ministry of China, School of Automation, Huazhong University of Science
and Technology, Wuhan 430074, Hubei, China
{tfwu,lqpan}@hust.edu.cn

Abstract. Spiking neural P systems, namely SN P systems, are a class
of distributed and parallel neural-like computation models, inspired from
the way neurons communicate by means of spikes. It has been shown
that SN P systems have powerful computation capability and significant potential in real-life applications, and they have received more and
more attraction from the scientific community. This paper firstly introduces the formal definition of standard SN P systems and some notions
which are often used in this field. Then, the theoretical results about the
computation power and efficiency of SN P systems are surveyed. The
applications of SN P systems are recalled by summarizing the literature
about the real-life applications of SN P systems. Finally, some hot topics
and further research lines on SN P systems are provided.

1 Introduction

Natural computing is the computational version of the process of extracting
ideas from nature to develop computation systems, or using natural materials
(e.g., molecules) to perform computation. Typical examples of natural computing
include well-known neural computing inspired by the functioning of the brain,
evolution computing inspired by Darwinian evolution of species, swarm intelligence inspired by the collective behavior of groups of organisms, and so on.

Membrane computing is a new branch of natural computing, which was initiated by Gh. Păun in 1998. The area of membrane computing aims to abstract
computing ideas from the structure and the functioning of the living cell as
well as from the cooperation of cells in tissues, organs, and other populations
of cells [38], e.g., constructing computation models and designing algorithms
for optimization. The abstracted parallel and distributed computation models
in the area of membrane computing are called membrane systems, also called
P systems. Since P systems have powerful capability in parallel processing and
significant potential in various applications, this area has attracted more and

C. Graciani et al. (Eds.): Pérez-Jiménez Festschrift, LNCS 11270, pp. 256–268, 2018.
https://doi.org/10.1007/978-3-030-00265-7_20

more people's interest. The area of membrane computing was listed by Thompson Institute for Scientific Information (ISI) as an emerging research front in computer science in 2003.

According to the membrane structure, membrane systems fall into three main categories: (1) cell-like P systems which have a hierarchical arrangement of membranes as in a cell; (2) tissue-like P systems which have several one-membrane cells as in a tissue; (3) neural-like P systems which have several neurons as in a neural net.

This paper will survey a kind of neural-like P systems, called spiking neural P systems (SN P systems, for short), which emphasize on a specific type of cell, i.e. the neuron.

The human brain is a complex information processing system, where more than a trillion neurons work in a cooperation manner to perform various tasks. Therefore, the human brain structure and functioning, from neurons, astrocytes, and other components to complex networks, is a gold mine for inspiring efficient computing devices. Inspired by the neurophysiological behavior of neurons sending electrical impulses (spikes) along axons from presynaptic neurons to postsynaptic neurons in a distributed and parallel manner, Ionescu et al. proposed SN P systems in 2006 [19]. SN P systems have become an attractive and promising research direction in the community of membrane computing [61]. Since the introduction of SN P systems, much attention has been paid to various topics, such as the establishment of SN P systems variants from different biological inspirations, computation power, computation efficiency, and applications.

In the past twelve years, there are lots of theoretical results and applications published in journals or conference proceedings. However, a few papers ([35] is one of them in Chinese) focused on the survey of the main results of SN P systems in theory and applications. This paper is to briefly summarize the development and main results achieved in computation models, computing power and efficiency of SN P systems, and the applications in fault diagnosis of electric power systems, combinatorial and engineering optimization, signal classification, etc.

The organization of this paper is as follows. Section 2 reviews the standard SN P system and its various variants. Section 3 summarizes the theoretical results of SN P systems reported in literature. Main applications of SN P systems are presented in Sect. 4. Future research lines are listed in Sect. 5.

2 Spiking Neural P Systems and Variants

A standard spiking neural P system (shortly, SN P system), of degree $m \geq 1$, is a construct of the form

$$\Pi = (O, \sigma_1, \ldots, \sigma_m, syn, out),$$

where:

- $O = \{a\}$ is the singleton alphabet (a is called spike);

- $\sigma_1, \ldots, \sigma_m$ are neurons, of the form

$$\sigma_i = (n_i, R_i), 1 \le i \le m,$$

where:
(a) $n_i \ge 0$ is the initial number of spikes contained in the neuron;
(b) R_i is a finite set of rules of the following two forms:
  (i) $E/a^c \to a; d$, where E is a regular expression over $\{a\}$, $c \ge 1$, and $d \ge 0$ is the delay time, that is, the interval between applying the rule and releasing the spike;
  (ii) $a^s \to \lambda$, for some $s \ge 1$, with the restriction that $a^s \notin L(E)$ for any rule $E/a^c \to a; d$ of type i) from R_i;
- $syn \subseteq \{1, 2, \ldots, m\} \times \{1, 2, \ldots, m\}$ are synapses between neurons, with $(i, i) \notin syn$ for $1 \le i \le m$;
- $in, out \in \{1, 2, \ldots, m\}$ indicate the input and output neurons, respectively.

The rules of type are called spiking rules (also called firing rules). A spiking rule $E/a^c \to a; d$ in neuron σ_i is eanbeld if the following conditions are satisfied: (1) the content of neuron σ_i is described by the regular expression E associated with the rule, e.g., if neuron σ_i contains k spikes, then $a^k \in L(E)$; (2) the number of spikes in neuron σ_i is not less than the number of spikes consumed by the rule, i.e., $k \ge c$. The application of this rule means that neuron σ_i consumes c spikes, and produces one spike after a delay of d steps. If $d = 0$, then the produced one spike emitted by neuron σ_i is replicated and sent immediately to all neurons σ_j such that $(i, j) \in syn$. If $d \ge 1$, assume that the rule is applied at step t, then at steps $t, t+1, \ldots, t+d-1$, the neuron is closed, so that it cannot receive new spikes from neurons which have synapses to the closed neuron (if any of these neurons tries to send a spike to the closed neuron, then the particular spike is lost). At step $t + d$, the neuron fires and becomes open again, so that it can receive spikes (which can be used at step $t + d + 1$, when the neuron can apply rules again).

The rules of type (ii) are called forgetting rules. A forgetting rule $a^s \to \lambda$ in neuron σ_i is eanbeld only if the neuron contains exactly s spikes. The application of such a rule means that neuron σ_i removes all s spikes, but produces no spike.

If a rule $E/a^c \to a; d$ has $E = a^c$, then it can be written in the simplified form $a^c \to a; d$.

If a rule $E/a^c \to a; d$ has $d = 0$, then it can be written in the simplified form $E/a^c \to a$.

In standard SN P systems, only one spike can be produced by a spiking rule in one time, which is always called a standard spiking rule. With the goal of simplifying the results about universality of SN P systems, Chen et al. proposed extended SN P systems [9], where several spikes can simultaneously be produced by a spiking rule in one time, which is called an extended rule. Specifically, extended rules are of the form $E/a^c \to a^p; d$, where E is a regular expression over $\{a\}$, $c \ge 1$, and $p, d \ge 0$, with the restriction $c \ge p$. The meaning of such a rule is that if the content of the neuron is described by the regular expression E, then c spikes are consumed and p spikes are produced. Because p can be 0 or greater than 0, extended rules are a generalization of both standard spiking and forgetting rules.

It is assumed that a global clock exists in an SN P system, marking the time for the whole system (for all neurons of the system). In each time unit, if a neuron σ_i have enabled rules, then it must apply (at most) one of the enabled rules. In this way, a situation may appear: neuron σ_i contains two enabled rules $E_1/a^{c_1} \rightarrow a; d_1$ and $E_2/a^{c_2} \rightarrow a; d_2$, and these two rules have $E_1 \cap E_2 \neq \emptyset$. If so, one of them is nondeterministically chosen to be applied. Thus, the rules are used in a sequential manner at the level of each neuron, but neurons function in parallel with each other.

The state of an SN P system at a given time is described by the number of spikes present in each neuron and the number of steps to count down until it becomes open (this number is zero if the neuron is already open). That is, the configuration of system Π is of the form $\langle r_1/t_1, \ldots, r_m/t_m \rangle$ for $r_i \geq 0$ and $t_i \geq 0$, where r_i indicates that neuron σ_i contains r_i spikes, and it will become open after t_i steps, $i = 1, 2, \ldots, m$. With this notation, the initial configuration of system Π is $\langle n_1/0, \ldots, n_m/0 \rangle$. By using the rules as described above, one can get a sequence of consecutive configurations. Each passage from a configuration C_1 to a successor configuration C_2 is called a transition and denoted by $C_1 \Longrightarrow C_2$. Any sequence of transitions starting from the initial configuration constitutes a computation. A computation halts if it reaches a configuration where all neurons are open and no rule is enabled. With any computation, halting or not, one associates a spike train, that is, a binary sequence with occurrences of digit 1 (resp., 0) indicating that the output neuron sends one spike (resp., no spike) out of the system.

When an SN P system works as a number generator, the result of a computation can be defined in several ways. With any spike train containing at least two spikes, the time interval between the first two being emitted is considered as the computation result [19]. This way of defining the result of a computation has been extended in [37]: generalizing to the first the time intervals between the first k spikes of a spike train, or the time intervals between all consecutive spikes, or only alternately the time intervals between all consecutive spikes, etc.

The way of defining the result of a computation in membrane computing can also be introduced in SN P systems. That is, one can also consider the result of a computation as the total number of spikes sent into the environment by the output neuron when the computation halts [6].

An SN P system can also work as a number acceptor [19]. In general, a number is introduced in the form of the time interval between two spikes entering the system. If the computation eventually halts, then this number is said to be accepted by the system.

Moreover, the result of a computation can be also defined as the spike train itself [7]. In this way, an SN P system is used as a binary string language generator defined on the binary alphabet $\{0, 1\}$.

3   Theoretical Results of Spiking Neural P Systems

These results mainly concern two aspects: computation power and computation efficiency. We start by briefly presenting some results of the first type.

For standard SN P systems, Ionescu et al. proved that these systems are Turing universal (also say computationally complete), that is, equivalent with Turing machines, when they are used as number generators or number acceptors [19]. Moreover, if a bound is given on the number of spikes present in any neuron along a computation, then a characterization of semilinear sets of numbers is obtained; and a characterization of finite sets can be obtained by standard SN P systems with one neuron.

From both mathematical and computer science points of view, it is always desirable to make the construction of SN P systems as simple as possible without the loss of computing power, i.e. a normal form. Ibarra et al. first investigated the influence of some ingredients of SN P systems on the computation power of these systems, such as the regular expressions used in spiking rules, the delay in spiking rules, and forgetting rules [18]. It was proved that in the case of removing the delay in spiking rules or forgetting rules, standard SN P systems are Turing universal. Afterwards, Pan et al. improved these results and proved that standard SN P systems are still Turing universal with the restrictions: (1) the delay in spiking rules and forgetting rules are not used, (2) each neuron contains at most two rules, and (3) the rules in the neurons using two rules have the same regular expression which controls their firing [28].

The resource (here, in terms of the number of neurons) needed for constructing universal computing devices of various types has been heavily investigated in computer science, e.g., Siegelmann et al. constructed a universal recurrent neural network by using 886 neurons [44]. This issue was also considered in SN P systems. Gh. Păun et al. constructed a universal SN P system having 49 neurons in the case of using extended rules and having 84 neurons in the case of using standard rules for SN P systems used as a device of computing functions; as a number generator, a universal SN P system with standard rules having 76 neurons, and one with extended rules having 50 neurons were obtained [36]. The comparison result shows that SN P systems have a "desired" computation power while using less resource. Following the research line of small universal computing devices, some bio-inspired features and mathematical strategies have been introduced into universal SN P systems for computing natural numbers and functions, in order to reduce the number of neurons. Some known results are shown in Table 1.

Besides used as number generators/acceptors and function computing devices, SN P systems can also be used as language generators. In a standard SN P system, the output neuron sends at most one spike into the environment in one time, thus the time instances when one spike exits the output neuron are marked with the digit 1, and the time instances when no spike is emitted by the output neuron are marked with the digit 0. In this way, the system can generate the binary string languages defined on the binary alphabet $\{0, 1\}$. In this definition, it was proved that the generative capacity of standard SN P systems

Table 1. The known results of Turing universal SN P systems with small numbers of neurons.

	Number of neurons for computing functions	Number of neurons for computing natural numbers	Type of rules
Bio-inspired features			
Weighted synapses [34]	38	36	Standard
Rules on synapses [47]	30	-	Extended
	39	-	Standard
Rules on synapses with high capacity neurons [50]	-	6	Extended
Request rules [46]	28	4	Extended
Colored spikes [49]	-	3	Extended
Mathematical strategies			
Combined modules [65]	41	41	Extended
	67	63	Standard
Cooperating rules	59 [25]	-	Standard
	-	8 [45]	Extended
High capacity neurons	-	10 [32]	Extended
"Super" neurons with an infinite number of rules [26]	-	4	Extended

is rather restricted, even some finite languages cannot be generated by these systems. However, by using morphism and projection, standard SN P systems can generate recursively enumerable languages [7].

For extended SN P systems, because several spikes can exit at the same time, the time instances when the output neuron emits i spikes are marked with the symbol b_i. In this way, extended SN P systems can generate any language defined on an arbitrary alphabet. It was proved that extended SN P systems can directly generate recursively enumerable languages [9].

In standard SN P systems, all neurons function in parallel at the level of the system (i.e., the system works in the synchronous manner), while at most one rule can be applied at the level of each neuron (i.e., the system works sequentially) [19]. Inspired by computer science theories, SN P systems working in different modes were investigated, such as non-synchronized (i.e., asynchronous) mode [6], that is, a neuron can apply or not apply its rules in any step; sequential mode: at each step of a computation, one (resp. all) of the neurons with the maximum/minimum number of spikes among the neurons that are active will fire [17,22]; exhaustive mode: whenever a rule is enabled in a neuron, it is used as many times as possible for the number of spikes from that neuron [20,33].

With the inspirations of different biological phenomena, various new types of SN P systems were proposed. For example, inspired by the functioning of inhibitory impulses among biological neurons, Pan et al. introduced anti-spikes and inhibitory synapses into SN P systems, and proved a series of normal forms of SN P systems with anti-spikes [27,48]. Inspired by the fact that astrocytes play an important role in the functioning and interaction of neurons, and astrocytes have excitatory and inhibitory influence on synapses, Hoogeboom et al. proposed SN P systems with astrocytes [31]. It was proved that SN P systems with astrocytes using simple neurons (all neurons have the same rule, one per neuron, of a very simple form) can achieve Turing universality. With the goal of identifying an easy way to determine the applicability of rules, Wang et al. proposed SN P systems with weights, which are inspired by the fact that a biological neuron can fire only when its membrane potential reaches or exceeds its threshold potential [51]. It was proved that SN P systems with weights are universal. Motivated by the excitatory or inhibitory nature of Ranvier nodes in biological neurons, Chen et al. constructed axon P systems [10]. Afterwards, Zhang et al. proved that four nodes (respectively, nine nodes) are enough for axon P systems to achieve Turing universality as number generators (respectively, function computing devices) [64]. Based on such a neurobiological fact that in the chemical synapse transmitting, there are multiple ion channels in a synapse, Peng et al. proposed SN P systems with multiple channels, and proved that such systems are universal [41].

Moreover, with mathematical and computer science motivations, many new types of SN P systems were also proposed. Based on the self-organizing and self-adaptive feature of artificial neural networks, Cabarle et al. introduced structural plasticity into the framework of SN P systems [4]. SN P systems with structural plasticity were proved to be universal. Afterwards, Song et al. proved that SN P systems with structural plasticity without any synapse at the beginning of a computation can also achieve Turing universality [57]. Incorporating ideas from nonstatic (i.e. dynamic) graphs and networks, Cabarle et al. proposed SN P systems with scheduled synapses, where synapses in such systems are available only at a specific schedule or duration [3]. SN P systems with scheduled synapses were proved to be universal. With mathematical motivation, Wu et al. consider a combination of basic features of cell-like P systems and of SN P systems, that is, consider cell-like P systems with only one kind of objects and spiking rules as those in SN P systems, called cell-like SN P systems [59]. It was proved that cell-like SN P systems with four membranes can achieve Turing universality. In order to simplify the integration-and-fire conditions of SN P systems, Wu et al. exploited polarizations $+, 0, -$ to control the application of rules instead of regular expressions [58]. It was proved that SN P systems with three kinds of polarizations are universal. Inspired by the way that components communicate with each other by a request-response pattern in parallel-cooperating grammar systems, Pan et al. proposed SN P systems with communication on request [30]. It was proved that SN P systems with communication on request are universal when two types of spikes are used.

Another topic on SN P systems is to study their computation efficiency, that is, to study whether SN P systems can solve computationally hard problems in a feasible time. Under the assumption that $P \neq NP$, Leporati et al. proved that a deterministic SN P system of a polynomial size cannot solve an NP-complete problem in a polynomial time, i.e., Milano theorem for SN P systems [14]. Hence, some features need to be introduced into SN P systems in order to enhance the efficiency of such systems. Generally, there are three kinds of features introduced into SN P systems to solve computationally hard problems as follows.

(1) Pre-computed resources (here, in terms of exponential number of neurons): Chen et al. first exploited SN P systems with pre-computed resources to solve in a constant time the NP-complete problem SAT in a semi-uniform way [8]. Leporati et al. provided semi-uniform and uniform solutions to the numerical NP-complete problem Subset Sum by using SN P systems with exponential size pre-computed resources [23]. Afterwards, Ishdorj et al. shown that the two PSPACE-complete problems QSAT and Q3SAT can be solved in a polynomial time by SN P systems with pre-computed resources in a uniform way. All the systems constructed above work in a deterministic way [21].

(2) Nondeterminism: Leporati et al. provided the solutions to SAT problem and Subset Sum problem in a semi-uniform or uniform way by using nondeterministic SN P systems but without pre-computed resources [14]. In [13], standard SN P systems without the delay feature and having a uniform construction were obtained.

(3) Neuron division and neuron budding: inspired by neural stem cell division, Pan et al. introduced the features of neuron division and neuron budding into the framework of SN P systems, which can generate exponential workspace in linear time. It was shown that SN P systems with neuron division and neuron budding solve computationally hard problems by means of a space-time tradeoff in a polynomial time, which is illustrated with an efficient solution to SAT problem [29]. Afterwards, Wang et al. exploited SN P systems only with neuron division to provide a uniform solution to SAT problem in a polynomial time [52].

4   Applications of Spiking Neural P Systems

This section presents an overview of SN P systems from the perspective of real-life applications with respect to engineering optimization, fault diagnosis of electric power systems, image processing, and signal identification.

The design of optimization algorithms can build a bridge between SN P systems and real-life applications. In [62], an extended SN P system (ESNPS) was proposed by introducing the probabilistic selection of evolution rules and multi-neurons output and a family of ESNPS, called optimization SN P system (OSNPS), were further designed through using a guider to adaptively adjust rule probabilities to approximately solve combinatorial optimization problems. In [54], OSNPS was used to solve the fault section estimation problem in an electric power system by formulating it into an optimization problem. Thus, OSNPS can search output fault sections in an automatic way when the status information of protective relays and circuit breakers coming from a supervisory control and data acquisition system is considered as the input. Several types of fault cases consisting of a single fault, multiple faults and multiple faults with incomplete and uncertain information in an electric power system can be accurately diagnosed in the simulation experiments.

The application for diagnosing the faults in an electric power system is an attractive research direction and is well investigated in the past years through introducing an algebraic fuzzy reasoning approach into SN P systems called fuzzy reasoning SN P systems (FRSNPS) [39,55]. The most attractive aspect of FRSNPS is that they can offer an intuitive illustration based on a strictly mathematical expression, a good fault-tolerant capacity due to its handling of incomplete and uncertain messages in a parallel manner, a good description for the relationships between protective devices and faults, and an understandable diagnosis model-building process [56]. Until now, FRSNPS have been successfully used to diagnose the faults existing in transformers [39], power transmission networks [40,56], traction power supply systems of high-speed railways [53], metro traction power systems [16], fault classification of power transmission lines [43] and fault lines detection in a small current grounding system [42].

As many problems in the processing of digital images have features which make it suitable for techniques inspired by nature, in [12], a novel link between SN P systems and Digital Imagery was presented, by providing an implementation of the parallel Guo and Hall algorithm in SN P systems to solve the skeletonization problem.

The learning ability for SN P systems is the fundamentals to be used for classification. In [15], the first attempt was made by using the framework of SN P systems to implement Hebbian learning. In [11], SN P systems were used to identify nuclear export signals and the promising experimental result with accurate rate 74.18 % was obtained.

Software for experimental simulations have been developed for SN P systems and their variants, as in [1,2,5,24,60].

5   Concluding Remarks and Future Research Lines

By introducing some further biologically-inspired features into SN P systems, it is worth developing new computation models which are "more realistic"to get closer to the brain. Moreover, to bring enough further biologically-inspired features to SN P systems may possibly model and simulate processes taking place in the "real" brain.

Most of the aforementioned SN P systems were proved to be Turing universal. In the area of SN P systems, a challenging and interesting problem is to look for classes of SN P systems which are not equivalent with Turing machines, but also not computing only semilinear sets of numbers. From the point of view of theory, such classes of systems are rather significant, because of the possibility of finding classes of systems with decidable properties. Moreover, from the point of view of applications, these classes of systems are also attractive, because of the possibility of finding properties of the modeled processes by analytical, algorithmic means.

The computation efficiency of SN P systems deserves further efforts. It is interesting to introduce new ingredients in the area of SN P systems to generate an exponential workspace in polynomial time, by trading space for time in solving **NP**-complete problem and **PSPACE**-complete problem.

There are many ingredients of usual P systems which were not considered for SN P systems, e.g., promoters, inhibitors, membrane creation. Thus, with mathematical motivation, considering these ingredients in the framework of SN P systems might also make sense.

Future application work on SNP systems could be focused on the *killer real applications* [63]. There are many possibilities like fault diagnosis with FRSNPS, OSNPS for engineering optimization and classification with the SNP systems with learning ability. Several important topics on FRSNPS were listed in [56]. The extension of OSNPS to numerical optimization problems is an ongoing task. How to develop a learning network with SNP systems is also a challenging topic.

Acknowledgments. This work was supported by National Key R&D Program of China for International S&T Cooperation Projects (No. 2017YFE0103900), National Natural Science Foundation of China (61320106005, 61672437, 61702428, and 61772214) and Sichuan Science and Technology Program (2018GZ0085, 2018GZ0185, 2017GZ0159).

References

1. Barbuti, R., Maggiolo-Schettini, A., Milazzo, P., Tini, S.: Compositional semantics of spiking neural P systems. J. Log. Algebr. Program. **79**(6), 304–316 (2010)
2. Cabarle, F.G.C., Adorna, H.N.: On structures and behaviors of spiking neural P systems and petri nets. In: Csuhaj-Varjú, E., Gheorghe, M., Rozenberg, G., Salomaa, A., Vaszil, G. (eds.) CMC 2012. LNCS, vol. 7762, pp. 145–160. Springer, Heidelberg (2013). https://doi.org/10.1007/978-3-642-36751-9_11
3. Cabarle, F.G.C., Adorna, H.N., Jiang, M., Zeng, X.: Spiking neural P systems with scheduled synapses. IEEE Trans. Nanobioscience (2017). https://doi.org/10.1109/TNB.2017.2762580
4. Cabarle, F.G.C., Adorna, H.N., Pérez-Jiménez, M.J., Song, T.: Spiking neural P systems with structural plasticity. Neural Comput. Appl. **26**(8), 1905–1917 (2015)
5. Carandang, J.P., Villaflores, J.M.B., Cabarle, F.G.C., Adorna, H.N., Martinez-del-Amor, M.A.: CuSNP: spiking neural P systems simulators in CUDA. Rom. J. Inf. Sci. Technol. **20**(1), 57–70 (2017)
6. Cavaliere, M., Ibarra, O.H., Păun, G., Egecioglu, O., Ionescu, M., Woodworth, S.: Asynchronous spiking neural P systems. Theor. Comput. Sci. **410**(24–25), 2352–2364 (2009)
7. Chen, H., Freund, R., Ionescu, M., Păun, G., Pérez-Jiménez, M.J.: On string languages generated by spiking neural P systems. Fundam. Inform. **75**(1–4), 141–162 (2007)
8. Chen, H., Ionescu, M., Ishdorj, T.O.: On the efficiency of spiking nNeural P systems. In: Proceedings of the 8th International Conference on Electronics, Information, and Communication, Ulan Bator, Mongolia, pp. 49–52 (2006)

9. Chen, H., Ionescu, M., Ishdorj, T.O., Păun, A., Păun, G., Pérez-Jiménez, M.J.: Spiking neural P systems with extended rules: universality and languages. Nat. Comput. **7**(2), 147–166 (2008)

10. Chen, H., Ishdorj, T.O., Păun, G.: Computing along the axon. Prog. Nat. Sci. **17**(4), 417–423 (2007)

11. Chen, Z., Zhang, P., Wang, X., Shi, X., Wu, T., Zheng, P.: A computational approach for nuclear export signals identification using spiking neural P systems. Neural Comput. Appl. **29**(3), 695–705 (2018)

12. Díaz-Pernil, D., Peña-Cantillana, F., Gutiérrez-Naranjo, M.A.: A parallel algorithm for skeletonizing images by using spiking neural P systems. Neurocomputing **115**, 81–91 (2013)

13. Leporati, A., Mauri, G., Zandron, C., Păun, G., Pérez-Jiménez, M.J.: Uniform solutions to SAT and subset sum by spiking neural P systems. Nat. Comput. **8**(4), 681–702 (2009)

14. Leporati, A., Zandron, C., Ferretti, C., Mauri, G.: On the computational power of spiking neural P systems. Int. J. Unconv. Comput. **5**, 459–473 (2009)

15. Gutiérrez-Naranjo, M.A., Pérez-Jiménez, M.J.: A spiking neural P system based model for Hebbian learning. In: Frisco, P., Corne, D.W., Păun, Gh. (eds.) Proceedings of WMC9, Edinburgh, UK, pp. 189–207 (2008)

16. He, Y., Wang, T., Huang, K., Zhang, G., Pérez-Jiménez, P.J.: Fault diagnosis of metro traction power systems using modified fuzzy reasoning spiking neural P systems. Rom. J. Inf. Sci. Technol. **18**(3), 256–272 (2015)

17. Ibarra, O.H., Păun, A., Rodríguez-Patón, A.: Sequential SNP systems based on min/max spike number. Theor. Comput. Sci. **410**(30–32), 2982–2991 (2009)

18. Ibarra, O.H., Păun, G., Păun, G., Rodríguez-Patón, A., Sosík, P., Woodworth, S.: Normal forms for spiking neural P systems. Theor. Comput. Sci. **372**(2–3), 196–217 (2007)

19. Ionescu, M., Păun, G., Yokomori, T.: Spiking neural P systems. Fundam. Inform. **71**(2), 279–308 (2006)

20. Ionescu, M., Păun, G., Yokomori, T.: Spiking neural P seystems with an exhaustive use of rules. Int. J. Unconv. Comput. **3**(2), 135–153 (2007)

21. Ishdorj, T.O., Leporati, A., Pan, L., Zeng, X., Zhang, X.: Deterministic solutions to QSAT and Q3SAT by spiking neural P systems with pre-computed resources. Theor. Comput. Sci. **411**(25), 2345–2358 (2010)

22. Jiang, K., Song, T., Pan, L.: Universality of sequential spiking neural P systems based on minimum spike number. Theor. Comput. Sci. **499**, 88–97 (2013)

23. Leporati, A., Gutiérrez-Naranjo, M.A.: Solving subset sum by spiking neural P systems with pre-computed resources. Fundam. Inform. **87**(1), 61–77 (2008)

24. Macías–Ramos, L.F., Pérez–Hurtado, I., García–Quismondo, M., Valencia–Cabrera, L., Pérez–Jiménez, M.J., Riscos–Núñez, A.: A P–Lingua Based Simulator for Spiking Neural P Systems. In: Gheorghe, M., Păun, G., Rozenberg, G., Salomaa, A., Verlan, S. (eds.) CMC 2011. LNCS, vol. 7184, pp. 257–281. Springer, Heidelberg (2012). https://doi.org/10.1007/978-3-642-28024-5_18

25. Metta, V.P., Raghuraman, S., Krithivasan, K.: Small universal spiking neural P systems with cooperating rules as function computing devices. In: Gheorghe, M., Rozenberg, G., Salomaa, A., Sosík, P., Zandron, C. (eds.) CMC 2014. LNCS, vol. 8961, pp. 300–313. Springer, Cham (2014). https://doi.org/10.1007/978-3-319-14370-5_19

26. Neary, T.: A boundary between universality and non-universality in extended spiking neural P systems. In: Dediu, A.-H., Fernau, H., Martín-Vide, C. (eds.) LATA

2010. LNCS, vol. 6031, pp. 475–487. Springer, Heidelberg (2010). https://doi.org/10.1007/978-3-642-13089-2_40

27. Pan, L., Păun, G.: Spiking neural P systems with anti-spikes. Int. J. Comput. Commun. Control **4**(3), 273–282 (2009)

28. Pan, L., Păun, G.: Spiking neural P systems: an improved normal form. Theor. Comput. Sci. **411**(6), 906–918 (2010)

29. Pan, L., Păun, G., Pérez-Jiménez, M.J.: Spiking neural P systems with neuron division and budding. Sci. China Inf. Sci. **54**(8), 1596–1607 (2011)

30. Pan, L., Păun, G., Zhang, G., Neri, F.: Spiking neural P systems with communication on request. Int. J. Neural Syst. **27**(08), 1750042 (2017)

31. Pan, L., Wang, J., Hoogeboom, H.J.: Spiking neural P systems with astrocytes. Neural Comput. **24**(3), 805–825 (2012)

32. Pan, L., Zeng, X.: A note on small universal spiking neural P systems. In: Păun, G., Pérez-Jiménez, M.J., Riscos-Núñez, A., Rozenberg, G., Salomaa, A. (eds.) WMC 2009. LNCS, vol. 5957, pp. 436–447. Springer, Heidelberg (2010). https://doi.org/10.1007/978-3-642-11467-0_29

33. Pan, L., Zeng, X.: Small universal spiking neural P systems working in exhaustive mode. IEEE Trans. Nanobioscience **10**(2), 99–105 (2011)

34. Pan, L., Zeng, X., Zhang, X., Jiang, Y.: Spiking neural P systems with weighted synapses. Neural Process. Lett. **35**(1), 13–27 (2012)

35. Pan, L., Zhang, X., Zeng, X., Wang, J.: Research advances and prospect of spiking neural P systems. Chin. J. Comput. **31**(12), 2090–2096 (2008). (in Chinese)

36. Păun, A., Păun, G.: Small universal spiking neural P systems. BioSystems **90**(1), 48–60 (2007)

37. Păun, G., Pérez-Jiménez, P.J., Rozenberg, G.: Spike trains in spiking neural P systems. Int. J. Found. Comput. Sci. **17**(04), 975–1002 (2006)

38. Păun, G., Rozenberg, G., Salomaa, A. (eds.): The Oxford Handbook of Membrane Computing. Oxford University Press, Inc., New York (2010)

39. Peng, H., Wang, J., Pérez-Jiménez, M.J., Wang, H., Shao, J., Wang, T.: Fuzzy reasoning spiking neural P system for fault diagnosis. Inf. Sci. **235**, 106–116 (2013)

40. Peng, H., et al.: Fault diagnosis of power systems using intuitionistic fuzzy spiking neural P systems. IEEE Trans. Smart Grid (2017). https://doi.org/10.1109/TSG.2017.2670602

41. Peng, H., et al.: Spiking neural P systems with multiple channels. Neural Netw. **95**, 66–71 (2017)

42. Rong, H., Ge, M., Zhang, G., Zhu, M.: A novel approach for detecting fault lines in a small current grounding system using fuzzy reasoning spiking neural P systems. Int. J. Comput. Commun. Control **13**(2), 458–473 (2018)

43. Rong, H., Zhu, M., Feng, Z., Zhang, G., Huang, K.: A novel approach for fault classification of power transmission lines using singular value decomposition and fuzzy reasoning spiking neural P systems. Rom. J. Inf. Sci. Technol. **20**(1), 18–31 (2017)

44. Siegelmann, H.T., Sontag, E.D.: On the computational power of neural nets. J. Comput. Syst. Sci. **50**(1), 132–150 (1995)

45. Song, T., Pan, L.: A small universal spiking neural P system with cooperating rules. Rom. J. Inf. Sci. Technol. **17**(2), 177–189 (2014)

46. Song, T., Pan, L.: Spiking neural P systems with request rules. Neurocomputing **193**, 193–200 (2016)

47. Song, T., Pan, L., Păun, G.: Spiking neural Psystems with rules on synapses. Theor. Comput. Sci. **529**, 82–95 (2014)

48. Song, T., Pan, L., Wang, J., Venkat, I., Subramanian, K.G., Abdullah, R.: Normal forms of spiking neural P systems with anti-spikes. IEEE Trans. Nanobioscience **11**(4), 352–359 (2012)
49. Song, T., Rodríguez-Patón, A., Zheng, P., Zeng, X.: Spiking neural P systems with colored spikes. IEEE Trans. Cogn. Dev. Syst. (2017). https://doi.org/10.1109/TCDS.2017.2785332
50. Song, T., Xu, J., Pan, L.: On the universality and non-universality of spiking neural P systems with rules on synapses. IEEE Trans. NanoBioscience **14**(8), 960–966 (2015)
51. Wang, J., Hoogeboom, H.J., Pan, L., Păun, G., Pérez-Jiménez, M.J.: Spiking neural P systems with weights. Neural Comput. **22**(10), 2615–2646 (2010)
52. Wang, J., Hoogeboom, H.J., Pan, L.: Spiking neural P systems with neuron division. In: Gheorghe, M., Hinze, T., Păun, G., Rozenberg, G., Salomaa, A. (eds.) CMC 2010. LNCS, vol. 6501, pp. 361–376. Springer, Heidelberg (2010). https://doi.org/10.1007/978-3-642-18123-8_28
53. Wang, T., Zhang, G., Pérez-Jiménez, M.J., Cheng, J.: Weighted fuzzy reasoning spiking neural P systems: application to fault diagnosis in traction power supply systems of high-speed railways. J. Comput. Theor. Nanosci. **12**(7), 1103–1114 (2015)
54. Wang, T., Zeng, S., Zhang, G., Pérez-Jiménez, M.J., Wang, J.: Fault section estimation of power systems with optimization spiking neural P systems. Rom. J. Inf. Sci. Technol. **18**(3), 240–255 (2015)
55. Wang, T., Zhang, G., Pérez-Jiménez, M.J.: Fuzzy membrane computing: theory and applications. Int. J. Comput. Commun. Control **10**(6), 904–935 (2015)
56. Wang, T., Zhang, G., Zhao, J., He, Z., Wang, J., Pérez-Jiménez, P.J.: Fault diagnosis of electric power systems based on fuzzy reasoning spiking neural P systems. IEEE Trans. Power Syst. **30**(3), 1182–1194 (2015)
57. Wang, X., Song, T., Gong, F., Zheng, P.: On the computational power of spiking neural P systems with self-organization. Sci. Rep. **6**, 27624 (2016)
58. Wu, T., Păun, A., Zhang, Z., Pan, L.: Spiking neural P systems with polarizations. IEEE Trans. Neural Netw. Learn. Syst. (2017). https://doi.org/10.1109/TNNLS.2017.2726119
59. Wu, T., Zhang, Z., Păun, G., Pan, L.: Cell-like spiking neural P systems. Theor. Comput. Sci. **623**, 180–189 (2016)
60. Zeng, X., Adorna, H., Martínez-del-Amor, M.Á., Pan, L., Pérez-Jiménez, M.J.: Matrix representation of spiking neural P systems. In: Gheorghe, M., Hinze, T., Păun, G., Rozenberg, G., Salomaa, A. (eds.) CMC 2010. LNCS, vol. 6501, pp. 377–391. Springer, Heidelberg (2010). https://doi.org/10.1007/978-3-642-18123-8_29
61. Zhang, G., Pérez-Jiménez, M.J., Gheorghe, M.: Real-life Applications with Membrane Computing. Springer, Berlin (2017)
62. Zhang, G., Rong, H., Neri, F., Pérez-Jiménez, M.J.: An optimization spiking neural P system for approximately solving combinatorial optimization problems. Int. J. Neural Syst. **24**(5), Article no. 1440006 (2014)
63. Zhang, G., et al.: Real applications of membrane computing models. In: Gheorghe, M., et al. (eds.) Multidisciplinary Creativity: Homage to Gheorghe Paun on his 65th Birthday, pp. 173–185 (2015)
64. Zhang, X., Pan, L., Păun, A.: On the universality of axon P systems. IEEE Trans. Neural Netw. Learn. Syst. **26**(11), 2816–2829 (2015)
65. Zhang, X., Zeng, X., Pan, L.: Smaller universal spiking neural P systems. Fundam. Inform. **87**(1), 117–136 (2008)

Aggregating Parallel Multiset Rewriting Systems

Dragoş Sburlan[(✉)]

Faculty of Mathematics and Informatics, Ovidius University of Constanţa,
Mamaia 124, Constanţa, Romania
dsburlan@univ-ovidius.ro

Abstract. In this paper we introduce a new computational model inspired by the processes involved in cell fusion – a biological mechanism that allows cells to combine into one cell. We are interested in the early stages of the cell fusion when a fusion pore is opened between two adjacent cells, which allows the passing of biochemicals between the cells involved. The process is reversible as the pore may close in certain circumstances, performing in this way an "incomplete" fusion. However, during the short existence of the pore we may assume the existence of three regions: one that contains the "shared" biochemicals that pass through the pore (they comply to the rules and conditions from both interacting cells) and other two corresponding to the remaining of biochemicals in the interacting cells (they comply to the corresponding original rules and conditions of the interacting cells). We investigate the computational power of the model when non-cooperative multiset rewriting rules are used.

1 Introduction

Biological membranes delimit the cells, allowing the separation between the inside and the outside of an organism, cell or organelle. In this way, by using a selective permeability, they are able to control which substances enter and/or leave. In general, membranes consist of a bilayer of lipid molecules and other elements as proteins and sugars. Membrane proteins play an important role by maintaining the structural integrity of the membrane and by mediating the flow of substances through membranes.

An important cellular process that aggregates uninuclear cells to form a multinuclear cell is the cell fusion. Of a significant importance in this process is the existence of specific proteins on the surface of cells which mediate the merging of the cell membranes. According with the lineage of the cells involved in a fusion there are known homotypic and heterotypic cell fusions. Cell fusion can be achieved by using a pulsed voltage which causes the cells' membranes which are in contact to permeate, or by using polyethylene glycol as dehydrating agent which determines the destabilization of the membranes, or even by using a virus. Destabilized cell membranes allow the merging of the lipid bilayers of membranes being in close contact and consequently of their cytoplasms.

© Springer Nature Switzerland AG 2018
C. Graciani et al. (Eds.): Pérez-Jiménez Festschrift, LNCS 11270, pp. 269–278, 2018.
https://doi.org/10.1007/978-3-030-00265-7_21

A fusion pore is the first aqueous connection between two membranes. Fusion pore usually opens suddenly and gradually expands; however, in certain cases, the initial opening is reversible. In general, the size and expansion rate of the pore are regulated by some membrane proteins concentrated at the sites of intercellular interaction. The fusion pore allows the passing of biochemicals in both directions, hence they will be the subject of the conditions corresponding to both cells interacting.

Inspired by the structure, the functioning and interactions (like cell fusion) of biological cells, in this paper we introduce a novel computational model. In this respect, we define a complex of multiset rewriting systems whose functioning captures some of the features described above. More precisely, a complex of multiset rewriting systems (a CMRS, for short) is composed by several parallel multiset rewriting systems which can perform computations as follows: at each step, in a non-deterministic manner, a multiset rewriting system may evolve independently (as common in the membrane system field) or it may aggregate with another one and evolve. The aggregation of two multiset rewriting systems Π_1 and Π_2 means that they will share some objects and rules; this can be modeled as a tuple of three multiset rewriting systems where the "middle" one has as support for computation some shared objects from Π_1 and Π_2 and employs the rules from both systems, while the other two act on the non-shared objects of Π_1 and Π_2 with their corresponding rules. Once such step is performed the tuple is disaggregated into two multiset rewriting systems by non-deterministically splitting the resulting shared objects. The computation of the complex of multiset rewriting systems continues step by step as described above and it will be considered successful if it reaches a configuration C in which no rule can be applied in any component multiset rewriting system, no matter if it attempts to evolve independently or in aggregation with other one. The result of the computation is the number (vector of numbers) of objects present in C.

It is worth mentioning that a CMRS exhibits a highly non-deterministic behavior as non-determinism is involved both at the level of rule application and at the level of multiset rewriting interaction. Moreover, upon the disaggregation the shared objects are split non-deterministically between the participating multiset rewriting systems.

Attempts to model similar phenomena have been done in [1,2,4,7]. However, in this paper the semantics of performing the computation is slightly different. Moreover, because the computation of a CMRS implies an infinite run (because at each step the multiset rewriting systems may aggregate in any possible pair), then in order to define a successful computation and collect the results, we have used a condition which resemble adult halting.

In this exploratory paper we only present some relations (in terms of computational power) of the introduced model with the "classical" Lindenmayer systems.

1.1   Preliminaries

We assume the reader is familiar with the theory of formal languages and membrane systems. However, we recall some definitions and known results. An *alphabet* O is a finite set of *symbols*. A *string* over O is a finite sequence of symbols from O. The *empty string* is denoted by λ. The set of all strings over O is denoted by O^*. The length of $w \in O^*$ is denoted by $|w|$. In particular, $|\lambda| = 0$. The number of occurrences of the symbol $a \in O$ in the string w is denoted by $|w|_a$. A language $L \subseteq O^*$ is a set of strings.

Let $O = \{a_1, a_2, \ldots, a_n\}$ and $w \in O^*$. Then, the Parikh vector associated with w is $\Psi_O(w) = (|w|_{a_1}, \ldots, |w|_{a_n})$. For a language $L \subseteq O^*$, the Parikh image of L is denoted by $\Psi_O(L) = \{\Psi_O(w) \mid w \in L\}$. Given a family of languages FL, we denote by NFL ($PsFL$) the family of length sets (Parikh images) of the languages from FL.

Lindenmayer Systems

An ET0L system is a tuple $H = (V, T, \omega, \Sigma)$, where V is an alphabet, $T = \{T_1, \ldots, T_m\}$, $m \geq 1$, such that T_i, $1 \leq i \leq m$, are finite complete tables of non-cooperative rules over V, $\omega \in V^*$ is the axiom, and $\Sigma \subseteq V$ is the terminal alphabet. In a derivation step, all the symbols present in the current sentential form are rewritten using one (non-deterministically chosen) table. The language generated by H consists of all the strings over Σ which can be generated in this way, starting from ω. If H uses only non-erasing rules then H is said to be propagating.

By $ET0L$ we denote the family of all ET0L languages. It is known that each language from $ET0L$ can be generated by an ET0L system with only two tables.

The families of finite, regular, context-free, ET0L, and recursive enumerable languages are denoted by FIN, REG, CF, $ET0L$ and RE, respectively. It is known that $NFIN \subset NREG = NCF \subset NET0L \subset NRE$ and $PsFIN \subset PsREG = PsCF \subset PsET0L \subset PsRE$ (see [6]). It is known that $\{2^n \mid n \geq 0\} \in NET0L \setminus NCF$.

Multisets and Parallel Multiset Rewriting Systems

A *multiset* M over an alphabet O is a mapping $M : O \to \mathbb{N}$. Given $a \in O$, by $M(a)$ we denote the multiplicity of a in M. A multiset can be represented as the string $a_1^{M(a_1)} a_2^{M(a_2)} \ldots a_n^{M(a_n)}$ and moreover, all permutations of this string precisely identify the same multiset.

Let $M_1 = a_1^{M_1(a_1)} \ldots a_n^{M_1(a_n)}$ and $M_2 = a_1^{M_2(a_1)} \ldots a_n^{M_2(a_n)}$ be two multisets over O; then M_2 is a sub-multiset of M_1, denoted as $M_2 \subseteq M_1$, if $M_2(a_i) \leq M_1(a_i)$, for $1 \leq i \leq n$. We say that $M_1 = M_2$ if $M_1 \subseteq M_2$ and $M_2 \subseteq M_1$.

One can also define the following operations on multisets:

- $M_1 + M_2 = a_1^{M_1(a_1)+M_2(a_1)} \ldots a_n^{M_1(a_n)+M_2(a_n)}$;
- $M_1 - M_2 = a_1^{max\{M_1(a_1)-M_2(a_1),0\}} \ldots a_n^{max\{M_1(a_n)-M_2(a_n),0\}}$;
- $M_1 \cap M_2 = a_1^{min\{M_1(a_1),M_2(a_1)\}} \ldots a_n^{min\{M_1(a_n),M_2(a_n)\}}$.

A multiset rewriting rule is a pair (u, v) where u and v are multisets over O, $|u| \geq 1$. The rules may also be labeled in order to uniquely identify them in a set of rules; a common notation for the labeled rule $l : (u, v)$, where $l \in \mathbb{N}$ is the label, is $l : u \to v$ and denotes that multiset u is rewritten by the multiset v. For a multiset rewriting rule $l : u \to v$, let $left(l : u \to v) = u$ and $right(l : u \to v) = v$. A rule of the form $r : a \to \alpha$, where $a \in O$, $\alpha \in O^*$, is called non-cooperative.

A *labeled parallel multiset rewriting system* (in short, an MRS) is a tuple $\Pi_l = (O, \mathcal{R}, w_0)$, where $l \in \mathbb{N}^k$ is a *label*, O is an *alphabet of symbol-objects*, $\mathcal{R}$ is a set of *multiset rewriting rules*, and $w_0 \in O^*$ is the *initial multiset* of objects.

A rule $r \in \mathcal{R}$ is *applicable* to a multiset $w \in O^*$ if $left(r) \subseteq w$. A multiset of rules $\rho \in \mathcal{R}^*$ is *applicable* to a multiset of objects $w \in O^*$ if there are enough objects in w to perform all the rules from ρ with their corresponding multiplicity. More formally, if $\rho = r_1^{n_1} r_2^{n_2} \ldots r_k^{n_k}$, then ρ is applicable to w if $\Psi_O(w) - \sum_{i=1}^{n} n_i \Psi_O(left(r_i)) \in \mathbb{N}^{card(O)}$. The applicable multiset of rules ρ is *maximal* if there is no applicable multiset of rules $\rho' \in \mathcal{R}^*$ to w and such that $\rho \subset \rho'$ (in the (multi)set sense).

The system Π_l performs a computation as follows. Starting from the initial multiset of objects w_0 (the *initial configuration*) and applying iteratively on the current multiset (*configuration*) a maximal applicable multiset of rules (the rules and their multiplicities are chosen in a non-deterministic manner) one gets a sequence of consecutive configurations. The passage in the sequence from one configuration C_i to the successor configuration C_{i+1} is called a *transition* and is denoted by $C_i \Longrightarrow C_{i+1}$. A *computation* of Π_l is a finite or infinite sequence of transitions between configurations.

A configuration is a *halting configuration* if there is no applicable rule to it. A computation is *successful* if it halts, that is, the last configuration in the sequence is a halting configuration. If the multiset C_h represents the halting configuration, then $\Psi_O(C_h)$ is said to be computed by the system by means of that computation. The set of all vectors of numbers computed by Π_l is denoted by $Ps(\Pi_l)$. It is also common to count the number of objects in the halting configuration of a successful computation; in this case, Π_l computes $N(\Pi_l)$.

It is known (see [3,5]) that the family of all sets of vectors of numbers (or sets of numbers) computed by parallel multiset rewriting systems using non-cooperative rules is equal with $PsREG$ (or $NREG$, respectively).

2   Aggregating Multiset Rewriting Systems

In this section we introduce a new computational model inspired by the processes involved in cell fusion. In particular we are interested in the phenomena that occur when "incomplete" fusions are taking place between the participating cells.

Given two MRSs $\Pi_1 = (O_1, \mathcal{R}_1, w_1)$ and $\Pi_2 = (O_2, \mathcal{R}_2, w_2)$, the *aggregation* of Π_1 with Π_2 represents a tuple of labeled multiset rewriting systems (referred as an AMRS)

$$\Pi_{\Pi_1 \cap \Pi_2} = (\overline{\Pi}_1, \Pi_{(1,2)}, \overline{\Pi}_2)$$

where $\overline{\Pi}_1 = (O_1, \mathcal{R}_1, w_1 - w_1')$, $\overline{\Pi}_2 = (O_2, \mathcal{R}_2, w_2 - w_2')$, $\Pi_{(1,2)} = (O_1 \cup O_2, \mathcal{R}_1 \cup \mathcal{R}_2, w_1' + w_2')$ for some $w_1' \subseteq w_1$ and $w_2' \subseteq w_2$. The AMRS $\Pi_{\Pi_1 \cdot \Pi_2} = (\overline{\Pi}_1, \Pi_{(1,2)}, \overline{\Pi}_2)$ can also disaggregate into two parts $\Pi_1 = (O_1, \mathcal{R}_1, w_1 + \alpha)$ and $\Pi_2 = (O_2, \mathcal{R}_2, w_2 + \beta)$ such that $\alpha + \beta = w$.

A *complex of parallel multiset rewriting systems* (in short, a CMRS) is a tuple $\Delta = (\Pi_1, \dots, \Pi_k)$ where $\Pi_i = (O_i, \mathcal{R}_i, w_{(i,0)})$, $1 \leq i \leq k$, are labeled multiset rewriting systems (the labels uniquely identify the MRSs in the complex).

A *configuration* of the CMRS Δ is a tuple of multisets $C = (w_1, \dots, w_k)$ which are present in the corresponding multiset rewriting systems at a certain moment. The *initial configuration* is the tuple $C_0 = (w_{(1,0)}, \dots, w_{(k,0)})$.

Given a configuration $C = (w_1, \dots, w_k)$, the CMRS Δ performs a transition to the next configuration as follows. In a non-deterministic manner, the component MRSs perform either independent transitions (as defined above for MRSs) and/or aggregate as AMRSs. In case of AMRSs, Δ performs a transition for each MRS in the corresponding tuples and finally, disaggregates all AMRSs. The next configuration is $C' = (w_1', \dots, w_k')$ where w_i', $1 \leq i \leq k$, is the content of the corresponding MRS Π_i. An additional requirement states that once an MRS Π is involved into an AMRS in a given transition, then in the next transition Π has to perform independently. A *computation* of Δ is an infinite sequence of transitions between configurations, starting from the initial one.

A computation is considered to be successful if in the sequence of configurations there exists one, say $C = (w_1, \dots, w_k)$, such that no rule can be applied by any component MRS or by any AMRS that can be constructed by aggregating two MRSs; the result (output) of a successful computation of Δ is $\sum_{i=1}^{k} \Psi(w_i)$ (or, if we count only the number of objects, $\sum_{i=1}^{k} |w_i|$). The set of such vectors (or numbers) computed in this way by Δ for any successful computation is denoted by $Ps(\Delta)$ (or by $N(\Delta)$).

Example 1. Let us consider the following complex of multiset rewriting systems $\Delta = (\Pi_1, \Pi_2, \Pi_3)$ where:

$$\Pi_1 = (O_1, \mathcal{R}_1, w_{(1,0)}) \qquad \Pi_2 = (O_2, \mathcal{R}_2, w_{(2,0)}) \qquad \Pi_3 = (O_3, \mathcal{R}_3, w_{(3,0)})$$

$$O_1 = \{a, b, c, \#\}; \qquad O_2 = \{a, b, c, \#\}; \qquad O_3 = \{a, b, c, c', \#\};$$

$$\begin{array}{lll}
\mathcal{R}_1 = \{a \to bb, & \mathcal{R}_2 = \{b \to a, & \mathcal{R}_3 = \{\# \to \#, \\
\quad b \to \#, & \quad b \to c, & \quad a \to c, \\
\quad \# \to \#, & \quad a \to \#, & \quad b \to \#, \\
\quad c \to \#\}; & \quad c \to \#, & \quad c \to c'\}; \\
& \quad \# \to \#\} &
\end{array}$$

$$w_{(1,0)} = a. \qquad\qquad w_{(2,0)} = \lambda. \qquad\qquad w_{(3,0)} = \lambda.$$

The system Δ performs its computation as follows. The initial configuration of Δ is $C_0 = (a, \lambda, \lambda)$ hence Δ has several possible transitions to perform as described below:

1. Π_1 performs a transition independently, hence by applying the rule $a \to bb$ it produces the multiset bb. Because the systems Π_2 and Π_3 do not contain any object, in this computational step, they will not execute any rule hence they will not perform a transition independently. Moreover, if Π_1 and Π_2 aggregate and form the AMRS $\Pi_{\Pi_2 \cdot \Pi_3}$, then also in this case no rule from Π_2 or Π_3 will be executed. Consequently, the next configuration will be $C_{(1,0)} = (bb, \lambda, \lambda)$. In what follows, Π_1 can evolve independently or aggregate with Π_2 or Π_3. If Π_1 evolves independently or if it aggregates with Π_3 then the rule $b \to \#$ is executed. Consequently, the object $\#$ will be generated and because the rule $\# \to \#$ is present in each MRS (hence it will always be applied in the subsequent transitions), the computation will not be successful. However, Π_1 may also aggregate with Π_2 and the computation may follow again different branches (the computation is similar as below).

2. Π_1 aggregates with Π_2 (it may also aggregate with Π_3 but the computation will be similar as below) and form the tuple $\Pi_{\Pi_1 \cdot \Pi_2} = (\overline{\Pi}_1, \Pi_{(1,2)}, \overline{\Pi}_2)$, where $\overline{\Pi}_1 = (O_1, \mathcal{R}_1, w_1 - w_1')$, $\overline{\Pi}_2 = (O_2, \mathcal{R}_2, w_2 - w_2')$, $\Pi_{(1,2)} = (O_1 \cup O_2, \mathcal{R}_1 \cup \mathcal{R}_2, w_1' + w_2')$. The following sub-cases are possible:

   (a) $w_1 - w_1' = a$, $w_2 - w_2' = \lambda$, and $w_1' + w_2' = \lambda$. In this case $\overline{\Pi}_1$ will execute the rule $a \to bb$ while $\overline{\Pi}_2$ and $\Pi_{(1,2)}$ will not execute any rule (because there are no objects). It follows that upon disaggregation, Π_1 will contain the multiset bb while Π_2 the multiset λ. Consequently, the next configuration will be $C_{(1,1)} = (bb, \lambda, \lambda)$. In the next step, Π_1 has to perform independently, hence the rule $b \to \#$ will be executed and the computation will not be successful.

   (b) $w_1 - w_1' = \lambda$, $w_2 - w_2' = \lambda$, and $w_1' + w_2' = a$. In this case $\Pi_{(1,2)}$ will non-deterministically select for application one of the rules $a \to bb$ or $a \to \#$. If the rule $a \to \#$ is applied then the object $\#$ will be generated; because the rule $\# \to \#$ is present in each MRS (hence it will always be applied in the subsequent transitions), the computation will not be successful. However, if the rule $a \to bb$ is applied instead, then it follows that upon disaggregation of $\Pi_{(1,2)}$ there will be again several possible outcomes:
   - the next configuration will be $C_{(1,2)} = (bb, \lambda, \lambda)$. In this case, because Π_1 was involved into an AMRS, in the next transition it has to make a transition independently. Consequently, the rule $b \to \#$ will be applied and the computation will not be successful.
   - the next configuration will be $C_{(1,4)} = (b, b, \lambda)$. This case produces also an unsuccessful computation since the rule $b \to \#$ will be applied by Π_1 in the next transition.
   - the next configuration will be $C_{(1,3)} = (\lambda, bb, \lambda)$. In this case, in the next transition Π_2 will perform independently and will execute the rule $b \to a$; it follows that the next configuration will be $C_{(2,3)} = (\lambda, aa, \lambda)$.
     However, in the next transition Π_2 may aggregate with Π_3. In this case, if there exists an object a that is not rewritten by the rule $a \to c$, then the object $\#$ will appear. However, in case that all the objects a are rewritten into objects c, then it means that we have a successful

computation and Δ computes the number 2. Coming back to configuration $C_{(2,3)}$, it may also happen that Π_2 aggregates with Π_1. Then it follows that one possible outcome is the configuration (λ, b^4, λ); from this configuration Π_2 will perform independently and consequently, the next configuration of Δ will be (λ, a^4, λ). Repeating the same cycle for k times the resulting configuration will be $(\lambda, a^{2^k}, \lambda)$. Finally, by aggregating Π_2 with Π_3 as above, it follows that Δ computes the number 2^k.

Consequently, the set of numbers computed by Δ is $N(\Delta) = \{2^n \mid n \geq 0\}$.

The following result shows that the computation of an arbitrary ET0L system can be simulated by a complex of multiset rewriting systems whose component MRSs uses only non-cooperative multiset rewriting rules.

Proposition 1. *The length set of any language from ET0L can be generated by a CMRS system $\Delta = (\Pi_1, \Pi_2, \Pi_3, \Pi_4)$ where Π_i, $1 \leq i \leq 4$, are multiset rewriting systems using only non-cooperative multiset rewriting rules.*

Proof. It is known that any ET0L language can be generated by an ET0L system with only two tables (see [6]). Without any loss of generality let $L \in$ ET0L and $H = (V, T, \omega, \Sigma)$ be an ET0L system such that $T = \{T_1, T_2\}$ and $L(H) = L$.

Let $\overline{V} = \{\overline{a} \mid a \in V\}$ and $\overline{\overline{V}} = \{\overline{\overline{a}} \mid a \in V\}$ and the morphisms

- $\overline{h} : V \to \overline{V}$, such that $\overline{h}(a) = \overline{a}$,
- $\overline{\overline{h}} : V \to \overline{\overline{V}}$, such that $\overline{\overline{h}}(a) = \overline{\overline{a}}$.

Starting from the definition of H we construct a complex of multiset rewriting systems $\Delta = (\Pi_1, \Pi_2, \Pi_3, \Pi_4)$ such that $\Psi(\Delta) = \Psi(H)$ as follows:
$\Pi_1 = (O_1, \mathcal{R}_1, w_{(1,0)})$ where

$\quad O_1 = V \cup \overline{V} \cup \overline{\overline{V}} \cup \{\#, d_1, d_2\},$
$\quad \mathcal{R}_1 = \{a \to \overline{h}(\alpha) \mid a \to \alpha \in T_1, \alpha \neq \lambda\} \cup \{a \to \overline{\overline{h}}(\alpha) \mid a \to \alpha \in T_2, \alpha \neq \lambda\}$
$\qquad \cup \{a \to d_1 \mid a \to \lambda \in T_1\} \cup \{a \to d_2 \mid a \to \lambda \in T_2\}$
$\qquad \cup \{\overline{h}(a) \to \# \mid a \in V\} \cup \{\overline{\overline{h}}(a) \to \# \mid a \in V\} \cup \{d_1 \to \#, d_2 \to \#\}$
$\qquad \cup \{\# \to \#\},$
$\quad w_{(1,0)} = \omega;$

$\Pi_2 = (O_2, \mathcal{R}_2, w_{(2,0)})$ where
$\quad O_2 = O_1,$
$\quad \mathcal{R}_2 = \{\overline{h}(a) \to a \mid a \in V\} \cup \{a \to \# \mid a \in V\} \cup \{\overline{\overline{h}}(a) \to \# \mid a \in V\}$
$\qquad \cup \{d_1 \to \lambda, d_2 \to \#\},$
$\quad w_{(2,0)} = \lambda;$

$\Pi_3 = (O_3, \mathcal{R}_3, w_{(3,0)})$ where
$\quad O_3 = O_1,$
$\quad \mathcal{R}_3 = \{\overline{\overline{h}}(a) \to a \mid a \in V\} \cup \{a \to \# \mid a \in V\} \cup \{\overline{h}(a) \to \# \mid a \in V\}$

$\cup \{d_1 \to \#, d_2 \to \lambda\},$
$w_{(3,0)} = \lambda;$

$\Pi_4 = (O_4, \mathcal{R}_4, w_{(4,0)})$ where
$\quad O_4 = O_1 \cup \{a' \mid a \in \Sigma\},$
$\quad \mathcal{R}_4 = \{a \to a' \mid a \in \Sigma\} \cup \{a \to \# \mid V \setminus \Sigma\}$
$\quad\quad \cup \{\overline{\overline{h}}(a) \to \# \mid a \in V\} \cup \{\overline{\overline{h}}(a) \to a \mid a \in V\}$
$\quad\quad \cup \{\# \to \#\} \cup \{d_1 \to \lambda, d_2 \to \lambda\}$
$\quad w_{(4,0)} = \lambda.$

The system Δ simulates the computation of H as described below. The system Π_1 contains three types of rules: rules which correspond to table T_1 of H (which "paint" the objects via the morphism $\overline{h}$); rules which correspond to table T_2 of H (which "paint" the objects via morphism $\overline{\overline{h}}$); rules that are responsible of generating the $\#$ object (which determine an unsuccessful computation) if independent computation of Π_1 is performed several steps in a row. The system Π_2 (and similarly, Π_3) contains rules that paint back the objects from $\overline{V}$ into their corresponding counterparts from V and rules that produce the object $\#$ if a "wrong" aggregation is performed. The system Π_4 contains the rules needed to finish the simulation of H.

At the beginning of computation, assuming that $w_{(1,0)} = \omega \neq \lambda$, Π_1 can proceed non-deterministically either individually or in aggregation with Π_2, Π_3, or Π_4.

In case Π_1 evolves in the first step individually then there are several possibilities:

- all objects from $w_{(1,0)}$ are rewritten by rules of type $a \to \overline{h}(\alpha)$ or $a \to \overline{\overline{h}}(\alpha)$. It follows that the resulting multiset of Π_1, say $w_{(1,1)}$, will contain objects from $\overline{V} \cup \overline{\overline{V}}$. Next, if Π_1 evolves again independently then the object $\#$ is produced (a rule of type $\overline{h}(a) \to \#$ or $\overline{\overline{h}}(a) \to \#$ is applied) and the computation becomes unsuccessful. Consequently, in order to get a successful computation Π_1 has to aggregate with another MRS. There are several possibilities:
  1. Π_1 aggregates with Π_2.
     In this case $w_{(1,1)}$ is divided into two multisets $w_{(1,1)} = u + v$ such that u is the subject of the rules $\mathcal{R}_1$ and v is the subject of the rules $\mathcal{R}_1 \cup \mathcal{R}_2$. If $u \neq \lambda$ then again the object $\#$ is generated (a rule of type $\overline{h}(a) \to \#$ or $\overline{\overline{h}}(a) \to \#$ is applied) and the computation becomes unsuccessful. The same outcome is also achieved if v contains objects from $\overline{\overline{V}}$. However, if $u = \lambda$ and $v \in \overline{V}^*$, it may happen that all the objects from v are rewritten by the rules of type $\overline{h}(a) \to a$. Upon the disaggregation of this AMRS, the resulting multiset (which contains only objects from V) is again split between Π_1 and Π_2; however, if an object from V remains in Π_2 then, because in the next step Π_2 has to perform individually, it follows that $\#$ is generated (hence the computation becomes unsuccessful). In case all the objects arrive in Π_1 then they will be the subject of the rules of type

$a \to \overline{h}(\alpha)$ or $a \to \overline{\overline{h}}(\alpha)$. Moreover, in the next step Π_1 has to evolve individually, hence the computation may follow a path as the one described above. In this way Δ simulates an application (or several applications) of table T_1 by the ET0L system H.

2. Π_1 aggregates with Π_3.

   This case is similar to the one described above but it corresponds to the simulation of H when table T_2 is applied. It is worth to mention that because Π_1 may aggregate non-deterministically with Π_2 or with Π_3 then all possible computations of the ET0L system H (i.e., any possible applications of tables T_1 and T_2) can be simulated.

3. Π_1 aggregates with Π_4.

   If Π_1 initially contains a multiset $w \in \Sigma^*$, then upon the aggregation with Π_4, the multiset w is split into u and v (that is $w = u + v$) and such that on u there are acting the rules from $\mathcal{R}_1$ and on v the rules from $\mathcal{R}_1 \cup \mathcal{R}_4$. There are several possible computational paths:

   - if $u = \lambda$ then the objects from v trigger the rules of type $a \to \overline{h}(\alpha)$, $a \to \overline{\overline{h}}(\alpha)$, and $a \to a'$. In case there are applied only the rules of type $a \to a'$, then the computation of Δ becomes successful. Consequently, Δ computes $\Psi(w)$. In case there are applied some rules of type $a \to \overline{h}(\alpha)$ or $a \to \overline{\overline{h}}(\alpha)$, then this will lead to an unsuccessful computation because in the next step, after the disaggregation of the AMRS, either Π_1 or Π_4 will generate object $\#$ (recall that in the next step they will have to perform individually, hence a rule of type $\overline{h}(a) \to \#$ or $\overline{\overline{h}}(a) \to \#$ will be applied, generating the trap object $\#$).

It is also worth to mention that in case of simulating the applications of the erasing rules from T_1 (or from T_2) by Π_1, then the objects d_1 are created (or d_2, respectively). The computation follows a similar pattern as described above also in the case of these objects. More precisely, if Π_1 evolves independently two times in a row, then the $\#$ object is generated and the computation becomes unsuccessful. However, if in a step Π_1 generates both symbols d_1 and d_2, and then aggregates with Π_2 then again the object $\#$ is generated (the same outcome is obtained if Π_1 aggregates with Π_3).

The only case when the object $\#$ is not generated is when Π_1 performs a cycle by applying either the rules corresponding to T_1 (or the ones corresponding to T_2), then aggregating with Π_2 (or with Π_3, respectively). Finally, if Π_1 contains a multiset over Σ and aggregates with Π_4 then the computation becomes successful.

We also conjecture that the following result is true.

Proposition 2. *Let Δ be an arbitrary complex of multiset rewriting systems using non-cooperative multiset rewriting rules. Then there exists an ET0L system $H = (V, T, \omega, \Sigma)$ such that $N(H) = N(\Delta)$.*

Such a result may be proved by simulating an arbitrary CMRS $\Delta = (\Pi_1, \ldots, \Pi_k)$ where $\Pi_i = (O_i, \mathcal{R}_i, w_{(i,0)})$, $1 \le i \le k$, with an ET0L system with several tables defined such that each of them contains all the rules that can be applied during a possible transition of Δ (recall that, in a step, each MRS can evolve independently or aggregate with other one and evolve). Accordingly, each table corresponds to a possible setup of independent MRSs and aggregated ones. Moreover, taking into account that the family of ET0L languages is a full-AFL then, intuitively, one has more arguments (and formal "tools" to use) in the favor of the above assertion.

3   Conclusion

A complex of multiset rewriting systems represents a biological inspired computational system consisting of several parallel multiset rewriting systems which can evolve in a non-deterministic manner independently or aggregating with others. In this respect, if two multiset rewriting systems $\Pi_1 = (O_1, \mathcal{R}_1, w_{(1,0)})$ and $\Pi_2 = (O_2, \mathcal{R}_2, w_{(2,0)})$ aggregate, then some of the existing objects from both systems (the "shared" objects) are the subject of the rules from $\mathcal{R}_1 \cup \mathcal{R}_2$ and the remaining objects are the subject of the corresponding sets of rules (i.e., $\mathcal{R}_1$ and $\mathcal{R}_2$); after applying the rules, the participating systems disaggregate by non-deterministically splitting the resulting shared objects. The computation continues as mentioned before and it will be considered successful if it reaches a configuration in which no rule can be applied in any component MRS.

We studied the computational power of complexes of multiset rewriting rules which use only non-cooperative rules. We proved that one can construct a CMRS being able to simulate the computation of any given ET0L system. Consequently, we proved that the family of sets of numbers generated by CMRSs includes $NET0L$. We also conjectured that the converse inclusion is true.

Acknowledgments. This work was supported by a grant of the Romanian Ministry of Research and Innovation, CCCDI - UEFISCDI, project number PN-III-P1-1.2-PCCDI-2017-0917/contract no. 21PCCDI/2018, within PNCDI III.

References

1. Cardelli, L.: Brane calculi. In: Danos, V., Schachter, V. (eds.) CMSB 2004. LNCS, vol. 3082, pp. 257–278. Springer, Heidelberg (2005). https://doi.org/10.1007/978-3-540-25974-9_24
2. Chen, X., Pérez-Jiménez, M.J., Valencia-Cabrera, L., Wang, B., Zeng, X.: Computing with viruses. Theor. Comput. Sci. **623**, 146–159 (2016)
3. Păun, G., Rozenberg, G., Salomaa, A. (eds.): The Oxford Handbook of Membrane Computing. Oxford University Press, Oxford (2010)
4. Păun, G.: Membrane computing and brane calculi (some personal notes). Electron. Notes Theor. Comput. Sci. **171**(2), 3–10 (2007)
5. Păun, G.: Membrane Computing. An Introduction. NCS. Springer, Heidelberg (2002). https://doi.org/10.1007/978-3-642-56196-2
6. Rozenberg, G., Salomaa, A. (eds.): Handbook of Formal Languages. Springer, Heidelberg (1997). https://doi.org/10.1007/978-3-642-59126-6
7. Song, B., Pan, L., Pérez-Jiménez, M.J.: Tissue P systems with protein on cells. Fundam. Inform. **144**(1), 77–107 (2016)

On Languages Generated by Context-Free Matrix Insertion-Deletion Systems with Exo-Operations

Bosheng Song, Fei Xu, and Linqiang Pan[(✉)]

Key Laboratory of Image Information Processing and Intelligent Control of
Education Ministry of China, School of Automation, Huazhong University of
Science and Technology, Wuhan 430074, China
{boshengsong,fei_xu,lqpan}@hust.edu.cn

Abstract. Matrix insertion-deletion systems are a class of insertion-deletion systems, where insertion and deletion rules are grouped in sequences, and it is known that such systems with two symbols context-free insertion and deletion rules are not computationally complete. In this work, matrix insertion-deletion systems with exo-operations (MIDEs, in short) are proposed, where insertion and deletion operations are applied only at the ends of a string (called exo-operations). The computation power of context-free MIDEs as language generators is investigated. We prove that context-free MIDEs of matrices size two with one symbol insertion and two symbols deletion are computationally complete, and so are systems with two symbols insertion and one symbol deletion. Moreover, if the size of matrices is three, the computational completeness can also be reached by context-free MIDEs with one symbol insertion and one symbol deletion. These results show that the computational power of MIDEs is strictly increased by introducing the exo-operations of insertion and deletion.

1 Introduction

Insertion and deletion systems are an active research branch in both DNA computing and membrane computing, which are based on two elementary operations: insertion and deletion of substrings in a string. There are two inspirations for insertion and deletion operations: one comes from the linguistics motivation and the related formal language investigations can be found in [8,9,13,15]; the other motivation comes from the field of molecular biology: a mismatched annealing of DNA sequences [16]; moreover, insertion and deletion operations are also present in the evolution processes as point mutations as well as in RNA editing (see [3–6]). In general, an insertion operation means adding a substring to a given string in a specified (left and right) context, while a deletion operation means removing a substring of a given string from a specified (left and right) context.

The computation power of insertion-deletion systems had already been investigated widely, several results about computational completeness were obtained

C. Graciani et al. (Eds.): Pérez-Jiménez Festschrift, LNCS 11270, pp. 279–290, 2018.
https://doi.org/10.1007/978-3-030-00265-7_22

by simulating various normal forms of type-0 grammars; we refer to [10, 16] for details and see [24] for the developments on insertion-deletion systems. There are several variants of insertion-deletion systems. In [14], context-free insertion-deletion systems were proposed, where insertion and deletion operations do not depend on any context (when using an insertion rule or a deletion rule, the left and right context are empty). It was shown that if the length of the inserted strings is three and that of the deleted strings is two, context-free insertion-deletion systems characterize the recursively enumerable languages, as well as the systems where the length of the inserted strings two and that of the deleted strings three [14]. If the length of the inserted or deleted strings is less than or equal to two, then such systems generate a subset of the family of context-free languages [23]. Insertion-deletion systems with one-sided contexts were also considered in [11], where the context of such systems is asymmetric and is present only from the left or only from the right side of all insertion and deletion rules. It was shown that non-completeness results were obtained for such systems of size $(1, 1, 0; 1, 1, 0)$, $(1, 1, 0; 1, 0, 1)$, $(1, 1, 0; 2, 0, 0)$ and $(2, 0, 0; 1, 1, 0)$ [11], where the first three numbers represent the maximal size of the inserted string, the maximal size of the left and right contexts, respectively; while the last three numbers represent the same information, but for deletion rules.

P systems are a class of parallel and distributed computation models inspired by the structure and the functioning of a living cell [17], and their study has been developed fast in both theoretical [21, 22] and practical aspects [18, 25]. In [11], the framework of P systems was introduced into insertion-deletion systems. With the framework of P systems, the computation power was strictly increased and the computational completeness was reached for insertion-deletion systems of size $(1, 1, 0; 1, 1, 0)$, $(1, 1, 0; 1, 0, 1)$, $(1, 1, 0; 2, 0, 0)$ and $(2, 0, 0; 1, 1, 0)$. Similar results can also be obtained for the case of graph-controlled insertion-deletion systems [7]. Matrix insertion-deletion systems were considered in [19], where insertion and deletion rules are grouped in sequences (called matrices), and either the whole sequence is used consecutively, or no rule is used. It was shown that matrix insertion-deletion systems with insertion and deletion rules of size $(1, 1, 0; 1, 1, 0)$, $(1, 1, 0; 1, 0, 1)$ and matrices of size three are computationally complete, and so are the systems with insertion and deletion rules of size $(1, 1, 0; 2, 0, 0)$, $(2, 0, 0; 1, 1, 0)$ and matrices of size two. However, insertion-deletion systems having rules of size $(2, 0, 0; 2, 0, 0)$ are not computationally complete even in the framework of P systems, graph-controlled or matrix-controlled manners.

P systems with exo-insertion and exo-deletion without contexts were considered in [1], where insertion and deletion operations are used only at the ends of a string (also called exo-operations of insertion and deletion). It was shown that P systems with exo-insertion and exo-deletion using insertion of one symbol and deletion of two symbols and systems with insertion of two symbols and deletion of one symbol are computationally complete [1]. If insertion and deletion rules using one symbol are considered, the computational completeness also holds for such P systems, but with priority of deletion rules over insertion rules [2]. These results showed that the computation power of insertion-deletion P systems is increased by applying the insertion and deletion operations at the ends of a string.

In this work, we use matrix-controlled instead of P systems as a framework, and a variant of matrix insertion-deletion systems, called matrix insertion-deletion systems with exo-operations (MIDEs, in short), is proposed. The computation power of context-free MIDEs as language generators is investigated. We prove that context-free MIDEs of matrices size two with one symbol insertion and two symbols deletion are computationally complete, and so are systems with two symbols insertion and one symbol deletion. Moreover, computational completeness can also be reached for context-free MIDEs with one symbol insertion and one symbol deletion, but using matrices of size three. These results show that the computation power of MIDEs is also increased by introducing the exo-operations of insertion and deletion.

2 Preliminaries

In this section, we recall the notions of Circular Post Machines, insertion-deletion systems and matrix insertion-deletion systems; for general information of formal languages we refer to [20].

2.1 Circular Post Machines

Circular Post Machines (CPMs, for short) were introduced in [12], here we only give the definition of Circular Post Machines of type 5, for the notions of CPMs (CPM0-CPM4), one can refer to [2].

Definition 1. *A Circular Post Machine of type 5 (CPM5, for short) is a quintuple* (Σ, Q, q_1, q_f, R), *where*

- Σ *is a finite alphabet,* $0 \in \Sigma$ *is the blank;*
- Q *is a finite set of states;*
- q_1 *and* q_f *are initial state and final state, respectively;*
- R *is a finite set of instructions with all instructions having one of the forms:*
  - $px \to q$, *where* $x \in \Sigma$ *and* $p, q \in Q$, $p \neq q_f$. *The corresponding computational step is* $pxW \xrightarrow{px \to q} qW$, $W \in \Sigma^*$.
  - $p \to yq$, *where* $y \in \Sigma$ *and* $p, q \in Q$, $p \neq q_f$. *The corresponding computational step is* $pW \xrightarrow{p \to yq} qWy$, $W \in \Sigma^*$.

From Table 1, we can see that the difference between CPMk ($0 \le k \le 4$) is only in the way the lengthening instruction works; that is, whether it introduces one of the two new symbols after the state, whether it applies to any symbol or only to the blank and whether one of the new symbols equals the one read. It is shown that all variants of CPMs (CPM0-CPM5) are computationally complete [2].

Table 1. Variants of circular post machines

CPM0	CPM1	CPM2	CPM3	CPM4	CPM5
$px \rightarrow q$	$px \rightarrow q$	$px \rightarrow q$	$px \rightarrow q$	$px \rightarrow q$	$px \rightarrow q$
$px \rightarrow yq$	$px \rightarrow yq$	$px \rightarrow yq$	$px \rightarrow yq$	$px \rightarrow yq$	
$p0 \rightarrow yq0$	$px \rightarrow xq0$	$px \rightarrow yq0$	$px \rightarrow yzq$	$px \rightarrow yxq$	$p \rightarrow yq$

2.2 Insertion-Deletion Systems

An insertion-deletion system is a construct $ID = (V, T, A, I, D)$, where:

- V is an alphabet;
- $T \subseteq V$ is the *terminal* alphabet (the symbols from $V \setminus T$ are called *non-terminals*);
- $A \subseteq V^*$ is the set of *axioms*;
- I, D are finite sets of triples of the form (u, α, v), where $u, \alpha(\alpha \neq \lambda)$ and v are strings over V.

The triples in I are insertion rules, and those in D are deletion rules. An insertion rule $(u, \alpha, v) \in I$ indicates that the string α can be inserted between u and v (corresponding to rewriting rule $uv \rightarrow u\alpha v$), while a deletion rule $(u, \alpha, v) \in D$ indicates that α can be removed from between the context u and v (corresponding to rewriting rule $u\alpha v \rightarrow uv$). We denote by $\Rightarrow_{ins}$ the relation defined by an insertion rule and by $\Rightarrow_{del}$ the relation defined by a deletion rule. By $\Rightarrow_r$ ($r \in I \cup D$) we denote the union of the relations $\Rightarrow_{ins}$, $\Rightarrow_{del}$, and by $\Rightarrow_r^*$ ($r \in I \cup D$) the reflexive and transitive closure of $\Rightarrow_r$.

The language generated by $ID = (V, T, A, I, D)$ is defined by

$L(ID) = \{w \in T^* \mid x \Rightarrow^* w \text{ for some } x \in A\}$.

The complexity of an insertion-deletion system $ID = (V, T, A, I, D)$ is described by the vector $(n, m, m'; p, q, q')$ called *size*, where

$n = max\{|\alpha| \mid (u, \alpha, v) \in I\}$, $p = max\{|\alpha| \mid (u, \alpha, v) \in D\}$,
$m = max\{|u| \mid (u, \alpha, v) \in I\}$, $q = max\{|u| \mid (u, \alpha, v) \in D\}$,
$m' = max\{|v| \mid (u, \alpha, v) \in I\}$, $q' = max\{|v| \mid (u, \alpha, v) \in D\}$.

The families of languages generated by insertion-deletion systems having the size at most $(n, m, m'; p, q, q')$ are denoted by $INS_n^{m,m'} DEL_p^{q,q'}$.

If one of the parameters $n, m, m'; p, q, q'$ is not specified, then instead we write the symbol $*$. In particular, $INS_*^{0,0} DEL_*^{0,0}$ denotes the family of languages generated by *context-free insertion-deletion systems*.

In this work, we use insertion and deletion exo-operations in context-free manner, so we can write these operations as follows: $ins_\alpha(x)$ and $del_\alpha(x)$, where $ins_\alpha(x)$ is an insertion rule applying at the left (right) end of a string, and $del_\alpha(x)$ is a deletion rule applying at the left (right) end of a string (if $\alpha = l$ or $\alpha = r$ accordingly).

2.3 Matrix Insertion-Deletion Systems

In this subsection, we give the definition of matrix insertion-deletion systems, which was proposed in [19].

A *matrix insertion-deletion system* is a construct
$\Pi = (V, T, A, P)$, where:

- V is a finite alphabet;
- $T \subseteq V$ is the *terminal* alphabet;
- $A \subseteq V^*$ is a finite set of axioms;
- $P = \{r_1, \ldots, r_t\}$, $t \geq 1$ is a finite set of sequences of rules, called *matrices*, of the form $r_i = [r_{i1}, \ldots, r_{ik_i}]$, where $k_i \geq 1$, r_{ij} is an insertion or a deletion rule over V, $1 \leq i \leq t$ and $1 \leq j \leq k_i$.

Sentential forms (also called configurations) of Π are represented as strings $w \in V^*$. For $r_i = [r_{i1}, \ldots, r_{ik_i}]$, $1 \leq i \leq t$, a transition $w \Rightarrow_{r_i} w'$ is performed if there exist words $w_1, \ldots, w_{k_i+1} \in V^*$ such that $w_j \Rightarrow_{r_{ij}} w_{j+1}$, $1 \leq j \leq k_i$, with $w = w_1$ and $w' = w_{k_i+1}$. We denote by $w \Rightarrow w'$ if there exists $r_i \in P$ such that $w \Rightarrow_{r_i} w'$. A sequence of transitions between configurations of a given matrix insertion-deletion system Π, starting from the initial configuration, is called a computation with respect to Π. The language generated by Π is defined by
$L(\Pi) = \{w \in T^* \mid x \Rightarrow^* w \text{ for some } x \in A\}$.

We say that system Π has matrices of size k, where $k = max_{1 \leq i \leq t} k_i$. We denote by $Mat_k INS_n^{m,m'} DEL_p^{q,q'}$ $(k > 1)$ the families of languages generated by matrix insertion-deletion systems having the size at most $(n, m, m'; p, q, q')$ and matrices of size at most k. By $Mat_k(e - ins_n^{m,m'}, e - del_p^{q,q'})$ we denote the class of matrix insertion-deletion systems with insertion and deletion exo-operations having the size $(n, m, m'; p, q, q')$ and matrices of size k $(k > 1)$. In this work, we consider only context-free insertion and deletion rules, that is, $m = m' = q = q' = 0$.

3 Computational Completeness

It is known that matrix insertion-deletion systems of size $(2, 0, 0; 2, 0, 0)$ for matrices of any size cannot achieve computational completeness (see [19]). In this section, we show that matrix insertion-deletion systems with exo-operations of both size $(2, 0, 0; 1, 0, 0)$ and $(1, 0, 0; 2, 0, 0)$ for matrices of size 2 are computationally complete, and so are systems of size $(1, 0, 0; 1, 0, 0)$, but for matrices of size 3.

Theorem 1. *The class of $Mat_2(e - ins_2^{0,0}, e - del_1^{0,0})$ is computationally complete.*

Proof. In order to prove the results of computational completeness, it suffices to show that any CPM5 can be simulated by a matrix insertion-deletion system with exo-operations. We consider a CPM5 $M = (\Sigma, Q, q_1, q_f, R)$, where $\Sigma = \{a_j \mid 0 \leq j \leq n\}$ is a set of symbols ($a_0 = 0$ is the blank symbol); $Q = \{q_i \mid$

$1 \leq i \leq f$} is a set of states; q_1 is the initial state and q_f is the only terminal state; let $Q' = Q \backslash \{q_f\}$. Suppose that rules in R are labelled, and denoted by $Lab(R) \subseteq (\{r_{ij} \mid 1 \leq i \leq f - 1, 0 \leq j \leq n\} \cup \{r_i \mid 1 \leq i \leq f - 1\})$, the set of labels corresponding to the rules R of the forms $q_i a_j \rightarrow q_l$, $q_i \rightarrow a_k q_l$.

We construct the matrix insertion-deletion system with exo-operations $\Pi = (V, T, \{\$q_1 a_j W\}, P)$, where $V = \Sigma \cup Q \cup V'$, $V' = \{X_{ij}^k \mid q_i a_j \rightarrow q_l \in R, 1 \leq k \leq 5\} \cup \{X_i^k \mid q_i \rightarrow a_k q_l \in R, 1 \leq k \leq 3\}$.

Initially, a CPM5 M starts a computation from a configuration $q_1 a_j W$, and the corresponding matrix insertion-deletion system Π starts computation from a string $\$q_1 a_j W$. We remark that a configuration $q_i a_j W$ of CPM5 M describes that M is in state $q_i \in Q$ having symbol $a_j \in \Sigma$ at the left end of $W \in \Sigma^*$. In what follows, we describe how Π simulates the two types of instruction forms of CPM5 M.

(A) For rule $r_{ij} : q_i a_j \rightarrow q_l$, with $q_i \in Q', q_l \in Q, a_j \in \Sigma$, we add the following matrix to P:

$r_{ij}^1 : [del_l(\$), ins_r(X_{ij}^1 X_{ij}^2)];$
$r_{ij}^2 : [del_l(q_i), del_r(X_{ij}^2)];$
$r_{ij}^3 : [del_r(X_{ij}^1), ins_r(X_{ij}^3 X_{ij}^4)];$
$r_{ij}^4 : [del_r(X_{ij}^4), del_l(a_j)];$
$r_{ij}^5 : [del_r(X_{ij}^3), ins_l(X_{ij}^5 q_l)];$
$r_{ij}^6 : [del_l(X_{ij}^5), ins_l(\$)].$

Let $q_i a_j W \xrightarrow{q_i a_j \rightarrow q_l} q_l W$ be a computation step in M, that is, by applying rule $q_i a_j \rightarrow q_l$, configuration $q_i a_j W$ is changed to $q_l W$ ($W \in \Sigma^*$). The simulation is clear. We start with the string $\$q_i a_j W$, matrices $r_{ij}^1 - r_{ij}^6$ are applied in order. Note that matrix r_{ij}^1 must be applied first, otherwise no matrix can be used, that is, we must delete the symbol $\$$ at the beginning of simulation. For the other two cases of rules, we use the same method to start the simulation. The evolution process is described as follows:

$\$q_i a_j W \Rightarrow_{r_{ij}^1} q_i a_j W X_{ij}^1 X_{ij}^2 \Rightarrow_{r_{ij}^2} a_j W X_{ij}^1 \Rightarrow_{r_{ij}^3} a_j W X_{ij}^3 X_{ij}^4 \Rightarrow_{r_{ij}^4} W X_{ij}^3$
$\Rightarrow_{r_{ij}^5} X_{ij}^5 q_l W \Rightarrow_{r_{ij}^6} \$q_l W.$

Thus, matrix insertion-deletion system with exo-operations Π correctly simulates rule $q_i a_j \rightarrow q_l$ of CPM5 M.

(B) For rule $r_i : q_i \rightarrow a_k q_l$, with $q_i \in Q', q_l \in Q, a_k \in \Sigma$. We add the following matrix to P:

$r_i^1 : [del_l(\$), ins_r(X_i^1 X_i^2)];$
$r_i^2 : [del_r(X_i^2), del_l(q_i)];$
$r_i^3 : [del_r(X_i^1), ins_r(a_k X_i^3)];$
$r_i^4 : [del_r(X_i^3), ins_l(\$q_l)].$

Let $q_i W \xrightarrow{q_i \rightarrow a_k q_l} q_l W a_k$ be a computation step in M, that is, by applying rule $q_i \rightarrow a_k q_l$, configuration $q_i W$ is changed to $q_l W a_k$ ($W \in \Sigma^*$). Suppose that we start with the string $\$q_i W$, and by applying the matrices from r_i^1 to r_i^4 in order, matrix insertion-deletion system with exo-operations Π correctly simulates rule $q_i \rightarrow a_k q_l$ of CPM5 M.

$\$q_i W \Rightarrow_{r_i^1} q_i W X_i^1 X_i^2 \Rightarrow_{r_i^2} W X_i^1 \Rightarrow_{r_i^3} W a_k X_i^3 \Rightarrow_{r_i^4} \$q_l W a_k.$

So the constructed matrix insertion-deletion system with exo-operations Π correctly simulates any derivation of CPM5 M. If $q_f W$ is the final configuration of M, correspondingly, string $\$q_f W$ will be generated by Π. At the end of the computation, we add the matrix $[del_l(\$), del_l(q_f)]$ to P and string W is obtained by matrix insertion-deletion system with exo-operations Π and this concludes the proof. $\square$

Theorem 2. *The class of $Mat_2(e - ins_1^{0,0}, e - del_2^{0,0})$ is computationally complete.*

Proof. In order to prove the results of computational completeness, it suffices to show that any CPM5 can be simulated by a matrix insertion-deletion system with exo-operations. We consider a CPM5 $M = (\Sigma, Q, q_1, q_f, R)$, where $\Sigma = \{a_j \mid 0 \leq j \leq n\}$ is a set of symbols ($a_0 = 0$ is the blank symbol); $Q = \{q_i \mid 1 \leq i \leq f\}$ is a set of states; q_1 is the initial state and q_f is the only terminal state; let $Q' = Q\backslash\{q_f\}$. Suppose that rules in R are labelled, and denoted by $Lab(R) \subseteq (\{r_{ij} \mid 1 \leq i \leq f - 1, 0 \leq j \leq n\} \cup \{r_i \mid 1 \leq i \leq f - 1\})$, the set of labels corresponding to the rules R of the forms $q_i a_j \rightarrow q_l$, $q_i \rightarrow a_k q_l$.

We construct the matrix insertion-deletion system with exo-operations $\Pi = (V, T, \{\$q_1 a_j W\}, P)$, where $V = \Sigma \cup Q \cup V'$, $V' = \{X_{ij}^k \mid q_i a_j \rightarrow q_l \in R, 1 \leq k \leq 3\} \cup \{X_i^k \mid q_i \rightarrow a_k q_l \in R, 1 \leq k \leq 5\}$.

Initially, a CPM5 M starts a computation from a configuration $q_1 a_j W$, and the corresponding matrix insertion-deletion system Π starts computation from a string $\$q_1 a_j W$. We remark that a configuration $q_i a_j W$ of CPM5 M describes that M is in state $q_i \in Q$ having symbol $a_j \in \Sigma$ at the left end of $W \in \Sigma^*$. In what follows, we describe how Π simulates the two types of instruction forms of CPM5 M.

(A) For rule $r_{ij} : q_i a_j \rightarrow q_l$, with $q_i \in Q', q_l \in Q, a_j \in \Sigma$, we add the following matrix to P:

$r_{ij}^1 : [del_l(\$q_i), ins_l(X_{ij}^1)]$;
$r_{ij}^2 : [del_l(X_{ij}^1 a_j), ins_r(X_{ij}^2)]$;
$r_{ij}^3 : [ins_l(q_l), ins_r(X_{ij}^3)]$;
$r_{ij}^4 : [del_r(X_{ij}^2 X_{ij}^3), ins_l(\$)]$.

Let $q_i a_j W \xrightarrow{q_i a_j \rightarrow q_l} q_l W$ be a computation step in M. We start with the string $\$q_i a_j W$, by using matrices $r_{ij}^1 - r_{ij}^4$ in order, rule $q_i a_j \rightarrow q_l$ is simulated correctly by matrix insertion-deletion system with exo-operations Π.

$\$q_i a_j W \Rightarrow_{r_{ij}^1} X_{ij}^1 a_j W \Rightarrow_{r_{ij}^2} W X_{ij}^2 \Rightarrow_{r_{ij}^3} q_l W X_{ij}^2 X_{ij}^3 \Rightarrow_{r_{ij}^4} \$q_l W$.

Note that rule $q_i a_j \rightarrow q_l$ can be simulated correctly only by applying the matrices from r_{ij}^1 to r_{ij}^4 one by one. If matrix r_{ij}^3 is applied first, additional symbol X_{ij}^3 is added at the right end of the string and it cannot be eliminated. Thus, matrix r_{ij}^1 must be applied first, if matrix r_{ij}^3 is applied after matrix r_{ij}^1, additional symbols X_{ij}^1, X_{ij}^3 are added in the string and they cannot be eliminated. Matrix r_{ij}^2 can be applied once after r_{ij}^1. After the application of matrix r_{ij}^2, only matrix r_{ij}^3 can be applied, while the application of matrix r_{ij}^4 requires a previous application of matrices r_{ij}^2, r_{ij}^3. On the other hand, in order to simulate rule $q_i a_j \to q_l$ correctly, each matrix must be applied exactly once. Since there is only one copy of symbol \$, matrix r_{ij}^1 will be applied only once, and one copy of symbol X_{ij}^1 is produced, hence matrix r_{ij}^2 should be applied only once. If matrix r_{ij}^3 is used for more than once, there are at least two copies of symbol X_{ij}^3 at the right end of the string, in this case, symbols X_{ij}^2, X_{ij}^3 cannot be eliminated. So matrix r_{ij}^3 is applied only once, this implies only one copy of symbols X_{ij}^2, X_{ij}^3, respectively. Thus, matrix r_{ij}^4 is executed only once.

(B) For rule $r_i : q_i \to a_k q_l$, with $q_i \in Q', q_l \in Q, a_k \in \Sigma$, we add the following matrix to P:

$r_i^1 : [del_l(\$q_i), ins_l(X_i^1)];$
$r_i^2 : [del_l(X_i^1), ins_r(X_i^2)];$
$r_i^3 : [ins_l(q_l), ins_r(X_i^3)];$
$r_i^4 : [del_r(X_i^2 X_i^3), ins_l(X_i^4)];$
$r_i^5 : [ins_l(X_i^5), ins_r(a_k)];$
$r_i^6 : [del_l(X_i^5 X_i^4), ins_l(\$)].$

Let $q_i W \xrightarrow{q_i \to a_k q_l} q_l W a_k$ be a computation step in M. Suppose that at the beginning of evolution, we have string $\$q_i W$. It is easy to check that the rule $r_i : q_i \to a_k q_l$ can be simulated correctly by applying the matrices $r_i^1 - r_i^6$ in order.

$\$q_i W \Rightarrow_{r_i^1} X_i^1 W \Rightarrow_{r_i^2} W X_i^2 \Rightarrow_{r_i^3} q_l W X_i^2 X_i^3 \Rightarrow_{r_i^4} X_i^4 q_l W \Rightarrow_{r_i^5} X_i^5 X_i^4 q_l W a_k \Rightarrow_{r_i^6} \$q_l W a_k.$

We remark that only by using the matrices from r_i^1 to r_i^6 in order, rule $q_i \to a_k q_l$ can be simulated correctly. If matrix r_i^3 is applied first, additional symbol X_i^3 is added in the string and it cannot be eliminated, so are the case for matrix r_i^5 applying first. If matrix r_i^3 is applied after r_i^1, additional symbol X_i^3 is added in the string and it cannot be eliminated. In the same way, if matrix r_i^5 is applied before r_i^3 or r_i^4, additional symbols X_i^2, X_i^5 cannot be eliminated in the string. Matrix r_i^4 involves symbols introduced by matrices r_i^2, r_i^3, so it it cannot be applied before these matrices. Similarly, matrix r_i^6 cannot be used before matrices r_i^4, r_i^5.

We also remark that each matrix must be applied exactly once. Since there is only one copy of \$, so matrix r_i^1 can be applied only once. This indicates that only one copy of symbol X_i^1 is introduced in the string, thus, matrix r_i^2 can be applied only once. If matrix r_i^3 is used for more than once, at least two copies of symbol X_i^3 are added at the right end of the string, and symbols X_i^2, X_i^3 cannot be deleted by matrix r_i^4, which demands that only one copy of X_i^3 appears at the right end of the string. This implies that there is only one copy of symbols X_i^2 and X_i^3 in the string, respectively. Hence matrix r_i^4 will be applied only once. If matrix r_i^5 is used for more than once, there will be at least two copies of X_i^5 added at the left end of the string, this will lead to additional symbols X_i^4, X_i^5, which cannot be deleted. Thus, matrix r_i^6 is executed only once.

So the constructed matrix insertion-deletion system with exo-operations Π correctly simulates any derivation of CPM5 M. If $q_f W$ is the final configuration of M, correspondingly, string $\$q_f W$ will be generated by Π. At the end of the computation, we add the matrix $[del_l(\$), del_l(q_f)]$ to P and string W is obtained by matrix insertion-deletion system with exo-operations Π (note that Π correctly simulates M if no additional symbols are introduced in the string) and this concludes the proof. $\square$

Theorem 3. *The class of $Mat_3(e - ins_1^{0,0}, e - del_1^{0,0})$ is computationally complete.*

Proof. In order to prove the results of computational completeness, it suffices to show that any CPM5 can be simulated by a matrix insertion-deletion system with exo-operations. We consider a CPM5 $M = (\Sigma, Q, q_1, q_f, R)$, where $\Sigma = \{a_j \mid 0 \le j \le n\}$ is a set of symbols ($a_0 = 0$ is the blank symbol); $Q = \{q_i \mid 1 \le i \le f\}$ is a set of states; q_1 is the initial state and q_f is the only terminal state; let $Q' = Q \backslash \{q_f\}$. Suppose that rules in R are labelled, and denoted by $Lab(R) \subseteq (\{r_{ij} \mid 1 \le i \le f - 1, 0 \le j \le n\} \cup \{r_i \mid 1 \le i \le f - 1\})$, the set of labels corresponding to the rules R of the forms $q_i a_j \to q_l$, $q_i \to a_k q_l$.

We construct the matrix insertion-deletion system with exo-operations $\Pi = (V, T, \{\$q_1 a_j W\}, P)$, where $V = \Sigma \cup Q \cup V'$, $V' = \{X_{ij}^k \mid q_i a_j \to q_l \in R, 1 \le k \le 2\} \cup \{X_i^k \mid q_i \to a_k q_l \in R, 1 \le k \le 2\}$.

We construct the matrix insertion-deletion system with exo-operations $\Pi = (V, T, \{\$q_1 a_j W\}, P)$, where $V = \Sigma \cup Q \cup V'$, $V' = \{X_{ij}^1, X_{ij}^2 \mid q_i a_j \to q_l \in R\} \cup \{X_i^1, X_i^2 \mid q_i \to a_k q_l \in R\}$.

Initially, a CPM5 M starts a computation from a configuration $q_1 a_j W$, and the corresponding matrix insertion-deletion system Π starts computation from a string $\$q_1 a_j W$. We remark that a configuration $q_i a_j W$ of CPM5 M describes that M is in state $q_i \in Q$ having symbol $a_j \in \Sigma$ at the left end of $W \in \Sigma^*$. In what follows, we describe how Π simulates the two types of instruction forms of CPM5 M.

(A) For rule $r_{ij} : q_i a_j \to q_l$, with $q_i \in Q', q_l \in Q, a_j \in \Sigma$, we add the following matrix to P:

$r_{ij}^1 : [del_l(\$), ins_r(X_{ij}^1), ins_r(X_{ij}^2)]$;
$r_{ij}^2 : [del_r(X_{ij}^2), del_l(q_i), del_l(a_j)]$;
$r_{ij}^3 : [del_r(X_{ij}^1), ins_l(q_l), ins_l(\$)]$.

Let $q_i a_j W \xrightarrow{q_i a_j \to q_l} q_l W$ be a computation step in M. We start with the string $\$q_i a_j W$, rules of type $q_i a_j \to q_l$ are simulated by consecutively using matrices $r_{ij}^1, r_{ij}^2, r_{ij}^3$. Since there is only one copy of $\$$ in the string, matrix r_{ij}^1 can be applied only once. This indicates that only one copy of X_{ij}^1 and one copy of X_{ij}^2 are introduced in the string. Hence matrix r_{ij}^2 and matrix r_{ij}^3 will be applied only once and matrix r_{ij}^3 cannot be applied before matrix r_{ij}^2.

$$\$q_i a_j W \Rightarrow_{r_{ij}^1} q_i a_j W X_{ij}^1 X_{ij}^2 \Rightarrow_{r_{ij}^2} W X_{ij}^1 \Rightarrow_{r_{ij}^3} \$q_l W.$$

(B) For rule $r_i : q_i \rightarrow a_k q_l$, with $q_i \in Q', q_l \in Q, a_k \in \Sigma$. Rule r_i is simulated as follows. We add the following matrix to P:

$r_i^1 : [del_l(\$), ins_r(X_i^1), ins_r(X_i^2)]$;
$r_i^2 : [del_r(X_i^2), del_l(q_i), ins_l(q_l)]$;
$r_i^3 : [del_r(X_i^1), ins_r(a_k), ins_l(\$)]$.

Let $q_i W \xrightarrow{q_i \rightarrow a_k q_l} q_l W a_k$ be a computation step in M. Suppose that we start with the string $\$q_i W$. It is easy to check that rule $q_i \rightarrow a_k q_l$ can be simulated correctly by using matrices r_i^1, r_i^2, r_i^3 consecutively, and each matrix must be applied exactly once.

$$\$q_i W \Rightarrow_{r_i^1} q_i W X_i^1 X_i^2 \Rightarrow_{r_i^2} q_l W X_i^1 \Rightarrow_{r_i^3} \$q_l W a_k.$$

Consequently, the constructed matrix insertion-deletion system with exo-operations Π correctly simulates any derivation of CPM5 M. If $q_f W$ is the final configuration of M, correspondingly, string $\$q_f W$ will be generated by Π. At the end of the computation, we add the matrix $[del_l(\$), del_l(q_f)]$ to P and string W is obtained by matrix insertion-deletion system with exo-operations Π and this concludes the proof.   □

4   Conclusions and Discussions

In this work, we have investigated the languages generated by matrix insertion-deletion systems with exo-operations. It has been shown that the computation power of MIDEs strictly increases in the exo-operations of insertion and deletion framework. Specifically, we have proved that MIDEs of matrices size two with one symbol insertion and two symbols deletion are computationally complete, and so are systems with two symbols insertion and one symbol deletion. Moreover, computational completeness also holds with one symbol insertion and one symbol deletion by such systems, but using matrices of size three.

In Theorem 3, MIDEs having the size $(1, 0, 0; 1, 0, 0)$ and matrices of size three are computationally complete. It remains open whether computational completeness can be obtained in the case that the size of the matrix decreases to two. If the answer is negative, it is interesting to investigate the computation power of MIDEs with priority of exo-deletion (with priority of deletion rules over insertion rules) as in [2].

The matrix insertion-deletion systems with exo-operations constructed in this work allow insertion and deletion operations to happen on left and right sides. It is of interest to investigate whether matrix insertion-deletion systems with exo-operations can reach computational completeness if insertion and deletion operations allow only on left side or only on right side.

Acknowledgements. The work was supported by National Key R&D Program of China for International S&T Cooperation Projects (No. 2017YFE0103900), National Natural Science Foundation of China (61320106005, 61425002, 61502186, 61602192, and 61772214), and China Postdoctoral Science Foundation (2016M600592, 2016M592335, and 2017T100554).

References

1. Alhazov, A., Krassovitskiy, A., Rogozhin, Y., Verlan, S.: P systems with insertion and deletion exo-operations. Fund. Inform. **110**(1–4), 13–28 (2011)
2. Alhazov, A., Krassovitskiy, A., Rogozhin, Y.: Circular post machines and P systems with exo-insertion and deletion. In: Gheorghe, M., Păun, G., Rozenberg, G., Salomaa, A., Verlan, S. (eds.) LNCS, vol. 7184, pp. 73–86. Springer, Heidelberg (2012). https://doi.org/10.1007/978-3-642-28024-5_7
3. Benne, R.: RNA Editing: The Alteration of Protein Coding Sequences of RNA. Ellis Horwood, Chichester (1993)
4. Biegler, F., Burrell, M.J., Daley, M.: Regulated RNA rewriting: modelling RNA editing with guided insertion. Theor. Comput. Sci. **387**(2), 103–112 (2007)
5. Castellanos, J., Martín-Vide, C., Mitrana, V., Sempere, J.M.: Networks of evolutionary processors. Acta Inform. **39**(6–7), 517–529 (2003)
6. Daley, M., Kari, L., Gloor, G., Siromoney, R.: Circular contextual insertions/deletions with applications to biomolecular computation. In: Proceeding of the String Processing and Information Retrieval Symposium & International Workshop on Groupware, pp. 47–54 (1999)
7. Freund, R., Kogler, M., Rogozhin, Y., Verlan, S.: Graph-controlled insertiondeletion systems. In: McQuillan, I., Pighizzini, G. (eds.) Proceeding of 12th Workshop on Descriptional Complexity of Formal Systems, vol. 31, pp. 88–98 (2010)
8. Haussler, D.: Insertion and iterated insertion as operations on formal languages. Ph.D. thesis, University of Colorado at Boulder (1982)
9. Kari, L.: On insertion and deletion in formal languages. Ph.D. thesis, University of Turku (1991)
10. Kari, L., Păun, Gh., Thierrin, G., Yu, S.: At the crossroads of DNA computing and formal languages: characterizing RE using insertion-deletion systems. In: Proceeding of 3rd DIMACS Workshop on DNA Based Computing, Philadelphia, pp. 318–333 (1997)
11. Krassovitskiy, A., Rogozhin, Y., Verlan, S.: Computational power of insertiondeletion (P) systems with rules of size two. Nat. Comput. **10**(2), 835–852 (2011)
12. Kudlek, M., Rogozhin, Y.: Small universal circular post machines. Comput. Sci. J. Moldova **9**(1), 34–52 (2001)
13. Marcus, S.: Contextual grammars. Rev. Roum. Math. Pures Appliquées **14**, 1525–1534 (1969)
14. Margenstern, M., Păun, G., Rogozhin, Y., Verlan, S.: Context-free insertiondeletion systems. Theor. Comput. Sci. **330**(2), 339–348 (2005)
15. Păun, G.: Marcus Contextual Grammars. Kluwer Academic Publishers, Norwell (1997)
16. Rozenberg, G., Salomaa, A.: DNA computing: new ideas and paradigms. In: Wiedermann, J., van Emde Boas, P., Nielsen, M. (eds.) ICALP 1999. LNCS, vol. 1644, pp. 106–118. Springer, Heidelberg (1999). https://doi.org/10.1007/3-540-48523-6_9
17. Păun, G.: Membrane Computing: An Introduction. Springer, Heidelberg (2002). https://doi.org/10.1007/978-3-642-56196-2
18. Peng, H., Wang, J., Pérez-Jiménez, M.J., Riscos-Núñez, A.: An unsupervised learning algorithm for membrane computing. Inf. Sci. **304**, 80–91 (2015)
19. Petre, I., Verlan, S.: Matrix insertion-deletion systems. Theor. Comput. Sci. **456**, 80–88 (2012)

20. Rozenberg, G., Salomaa, A. (eds.): Handbook of Formal Languages: Volume 3 Beyond Words. Springer, Berlin (1997). https://doi.org/10.1007/978-3-642-59126-6
21. Song, B., Song, T., Pan, L.: A time-free uniform solution to subset sum problem by tissue P systems with cell division. Math. Struct. Comp. Sci. **27**(1), 17–32 (2017)
22. Song, B., Zhang, C., Pan, L.: Tissue-like P systems with evolutional symport/antiport rules. Inf. Sci. **378**, 177–193 (2017)
23. Verlan, S.: On minimal context-free insertion-deletion systems. J. Autom. Lang. Comb. **12**(1–2), 317–328 (2007)
24. Verlan, S.: Recent developments on insertion-deletion systems. Comput. Sci. J. Moldova **18**(2), 210–245 (2010)
25. Zhang, G., Gheorghe, M., Pan, L., Pérez-Jiménez, M.J.: Evolutionary membrane computing: a comprehensive survey and new results. Inf. Sci. **279**, 528–551 (2014)

A Simulation Workflow for Membrane Computing: From MeCoSim to PMCGPU Through P-Lingua

Luis Valencia-Cabrera, Miguel Á. Martínez-del-Amor[✉],
and Ignacio Pérez-Hurtado

Research Group on Natural Computing, Department of Computer Science
and Artificial Intelligence,
Universidad de Sevilla, Avda. Reina Mercedes s/n, 41012 Seville, Spain
{lvalencia,mdelamor,perezh}@us.es

Abstract. P system simulators are of high importance in Membrane Computing, since they provide tools to assist on model validation and verification. Keeping a balance between generality and flexibility, on the one side, and efficiency, on the other hand, is always challenging, but it is worth the effort. Besides, in order to prove the feasibility of P system models as practical tools for solving problems and aid in decision making, it is essential to provide functional mechanisms to have all the elements required at disposal of the potential users smoothly integrated in a robust workflow. The aim of this paper is to describe the main components and connections within the approach followed in this pipeline.

1 Introduction

Since the early days of Membrane Computing two decades ago [17], the *in-depth* study of different types and variants of its computational devices, the *so-called* P systems, in terms of their computational power and complexity, has come along with the interest in the development of simulation tools to explore their properties and explode some of their most promising features, as extensively described in [21].

While the full potential and practical ability of P systems could only be exploited so far through the real implementation of some variants of these machine-oriented computing devices, the development of software simulators has always being considered worth exploring [4]. The main uses of these tools have ranged from pedagogical to research assistants to help studying properties of the computing devices and the solutions they aim to solve at both theoretical and practical levels, playing a crucial role in the design and verification of such solutions. Additionally, they have been successfully applied to aid in the decision-making process to manage real-world situations in ecological and industrial systems, providing useful predictive insights when virtually experimenting with potential scenarios making use of simulators for the corresponding models based on P systems.

© Springer Nature Switzerland AG 2018
C. Graciani et al. (Eds.): Pérez-Jiménez Festschrift, LNCS 11270, pp. 291–303, 2018.
https://doi.org/10.1007/978-3-030-00265-7_23

Within this overall scenario, the approach followed from our research group has been the coverage of a wide range of membrane computing devices. Not only the range of applications where we have applied simulators has been as broad as we could, but also the tools developed tried from the beginning to be as general, flexible, reusable and extensible as we could achieve. It was not the short-term publication that leaded our research and development efforts, but it was the intention of providing something the community could take advantage of, both for theoretical studies and practical applications. In this sense, the main lines explored have been directed towards three main ideas:

(1) **generality**, with the design of a standard language to specify P systems (P-Lingua), along with parsing, debugging and simulation tools within P-Lingua framework [5,19];
(2) **practical use**, through the development of more user-oriented tools to manage the models for both designers with a higher-level interface and additional exploration tools, and end users using custom applications based on MeCoSim [18,20] as black boxes; and
(3) **efficiency**, looking for appropriate architectures and designs in the development of software tools, that could (at least partially) benefit from the inherent parallelism in the essence of P systems through high performance platforms, as pursued by PMCGPU project [10,24].

The work presented here intends to put together all the achievements accomplished by these three main lines introduced above, and clarify the potential users about the main features and guidelines to use effectively the tools developed, hence providing new results presenting a good balance in terms of compromise between generality and efficiency, always bearing in mind practicality. In order to achieve these goals, a simulation workflow is proposed, starting from the design of a model and a customized application and finishing with the simulation in high performance platforms, as we will explain later.

The rest of the paper is distributed as follows. After this section where the general intention has been declared, Sect. 2 introduces the main features of the essential elements involved in the process just outlined. Then, in Sect. 3 the simulation workflow will be described in detail, clarifying the crucial points of the proposal and the connection among all the different ingredients taking part on this recipe. Finally, Sect. 4 summarises the most relevant achievements of this work, with some conclusions shedding some light upon the benefits, use and possible applications where this approach may help in future works.

2 Simulation Software for P Systems

This section introduces the roles played by the main elements of the workflow proposed in this work, highlighting the most important features of the tools provided by each project and some practical aspects of their use.

2.1   The Visual Environment MeCoSim

As mentioned in the introduction of this paper, one of the main aspects of the simulation in membrane computing has always been the practical application of the designs for relevant theoretical and real-life problems. This involves, in addition to solid foundations (given by the study of the computing devices in terms of computational power and complexity), the development of simulation tools aiming not only to allow technical people to develop solutions based on P systems, but also making their life easier when dealing with them, and also enabling end users to take advantage of those solutions as black boxes. This way, P-system based models for solving real-world problems could play a relevant role for this end users, assisting them in their decisions, permitting the experimentation with their scenarios of interest without further knowledge about the internal details. Regarding P systems designers, they should be able to have at their disposal some tools to handle their designs in a friendly way, with facilities to: check the correctness of their models, both from a lexical-syntactic and semantic view; populate different instances of the P systems designed; visualize properly the structure and contents of the elements created during the initialization and the step-by-step run of the simulations, and in general provide useful options helping in the tough tasks of design and verification of solutions based on P systems.

From the very beginning in 2009–2010 [18], MeCoSim was designed with the two-fold intention expressed above, to help P systems designers with the modelling and verification, and also allowing end users to have solutions in membrane computing. For the first goal, this software was always supported by the parsing, debugging and simulation engine given by P-Lingua, while the latter objective required further development to provide some mechanism where P systems designers could easily prepare end-user applications by a relatively simple configuration. Thus, MeCoSim was initially designed to enable the user defined customized interfaces, with inputs, outputs, charts, etc., adapted to each model or solution given by a family of P systems, expressed in MeCoSim language. This enables the users to enter their data for different initial conditions, instantiating the desired P systems within the family.

Apart from the initial goals, this software environment had from its conception two essential objectives: the flexibility required for the definition of any kind of custom applications and variety of P systems accepted, and the extensibility to increase its initial functionalities through the development using its plugins architecture and the integration with external packages. Thus, the seminal version of the software was enriched by the integration with different tools for the property extraction and verification of P systems [6,9] and the development of plugins for graph-based problems, definition of propositional formulas, extensions of the language accepted by the generation of parameters, connection with external simulators based on Spin [7] and several other new features for designers and end users. Extensive documentation, case studies, explicative videos, etc. about everything related with MeCoSim can be found at [22].

2.2 P-Lingua, and the pLinguaCore Library

In the heart of our proposal is P-Lingua framework [5, 23], the undeniable cornerstone of the approach. It was conceived from the beginning as an ambitious open source project within the area of Membrane computing, aiming to provide general-purpose tools for its research community, rather than focusing on specific short-term results.

Among its main goals, this project included a standard language, P-Lingua, for the specification/definition of P systems, for a variety if types and variants of such systems, through a unifying set of operators. As extensively described in [19], this language is modular, favouring structured programming, and provides a syntax very close to the format employed in the description of P systems we can find in research. In addition to the language and the tools developed to process its plain text files (with .pli extension), a whole framework was surrounding this core with debugging tools, some sp-called input and output parsers, and a complete set of simulators for the variants supported by the different versions of pLinguaCore library, the main software product including the crucial part of the framework. Some independent programs allow the compilation and run of models and solutions based on the library, starting with some useful command-line tools and finishing with MeCoSim.

Furthermore, inside the framework there is a parser that performs lexical and syntactical analysis to text files describing models in P-Lingua [5]. This is used to initialize internal structures that can serve later for the simulator in pLinguaCore or to generate an output file, in a different format, describing the same model. So far, XML exportation is supported for the majority of models. For the ones supported by PMCGPU, an specific ad-hoc binary format is generated, which aims at being a communication language between P-Lingua and the parallel standalone simulators. Moreover, a straightforward semantics processing is carried out after the syntactical analysis, in the sense that the P system features correspond to the model specified.

pLinguaCore is a framework that makes use of software design patterns to make the development of new simulators easier [5, 19]. Modularity and flexibility are the key aspects of it. Written in Java, and together with the parser, this framework provides a complete generic environment for P system simulations, from their specification, parsing, simulation and output. For each P system model, it is possible to implement different engines. We should note that the objective of pLinguaCore is not efficiency, so it might happen that the simulation of some models should take a considerable time.

2.3 PMCGPU for Accelerated Simulations

Parallel simulation of P systems is becoming a hot topic within Membrane Computing. The need of efficient simulators, along with the interest of implementing bio-inspired parallelism using High Performance Computing, has increased the interest on it. Latest attempts to parallelize simulations have been based on GPU computing [10, 11]. The multiprocessors of graphics cards provide a parallel architecture that is being harnessed as enabling technologies for many applications.

Since the introduction of CUDA in 2007 [8], parallel simulators on GPUs have been developed. The main project that covers these developments is PMCGPU (Parallel simulators for Membrane Computing on the GPU) [10,24]. Within this open-source project, one can find simulators for P systems with active membranes (codenamed PCUDA) [2,11] and for Population Dynamics P systems (ABCDGPU) [11–13,16]. There are also two specific simulators for two solutions to SAT problem, one based on P systems with active membranes (PCUDASAT) [3,11] and other on tissue–like P systems with cell division (TSPCUDASAT) [11,14]. Finally, simulators for spiking neural P systems have been recently attached to the project (cuSNP) as external developments.

Concerning PCUDA and ABCDGPU, both simulators receive as input a P system description, and return as output either a description in plain text of each transition step, or a CSV (comma–separated–values) with the information of the whole simulation (this last mode is available only in ABCDGPU [12]). The description of the P system to be simulated in both cases is based on an specific binary file. Further information about the structure of the input binary files is available in [10]. In order to ease the workflow, the binary files can be generated using pLinguaCore from a P-Lingua file, as described in the simulation workflow in Sect. 3.

In the following sub-sections, an overview of PCUDA and ABCDGPU is provided, together with general instructions for their installation, and also a short introduction to core concepts of GPU computing.

GPU Computing. Graphics Processing Units (GPUs) have evolve in the past 15 years in such a way that, today, they serve as a massively parallel co-processor for heterogeneous computing [8]. In 2007, NVIDIA introduced a new programming model that abstracts the underlying architecture of GPUs, so programmers only need to think in threads and in a memory hierarchy. Parallel programming on a GPU is like a game in which the amount of threads has to be balanced (the more the better, but doing effective work) and the access to memory has to be done by maximizing the usage of registers and cache, plus implementing coalesced access to data (contiguous threads loading consecutive positions in memory).

Threads are executed hierarchically, being arranged into synchronizing and cooperating blocks. Thread blocks also include a small but fast memory, called shared memory, that is used to efficiently store frequently used data. Current GPUs provide thousands of cores grouped in multiprocessors, and a dozen of Gigabytes of memory. The CUDA scheduler automatically assign blocks to multiprocessors, and groups of 32 threads, called warp, are launched simultaneously to the cores. All threads execute the same code, which is a function called kernel. The CPU is the one in charge of launching kernels, and of sending and retrieving data from the GPU [8].

Best design practices are to launch as much threads as possible, from 128 to 512 threads per block, making use of a reasonable amount of shared memory, let contiguous threads access contiguous portions of data, and avoid thread divergence (i.e. threads within a warp executing different instructions).

PCUDA: Parallel Simulation of P Systems with Active Membranes. The first simulator for P systems on CUDA was PCUDA [2]. In this work, the two-level parallel nature of P systems is mapped to the two-level parallelism on GPUs: membranes are assigned to thread blocks, and rules are processed by threads. Since the simulated model has no cooperation (only one object in the LHS), threads are effectively processing objects. In order to ease this work assignation, several assumptions from the input P system are taken:

(1) models are confluent, so that all computation halt and lead to the same result;
(2) only two levels in the membrane hierarchy is supported; that is, only a skin membrane and elementary membranes; and
(3) the amount of objects defined in the alphabet must be multiple of a number below 512.

The two last conditions are more technical issues, but that we plan to solve in future releases. The first condition is an important restriction for the design of the simulator: if the P system is confluent, then the computation path does not matter, and the simulator can choose to take the "cheapest" one (in terms of amount of membranes generated and evolution rules applied).

When simulating this P system, the major performance attribute is related to the object density [11]: the GPU simulator runs faster as long as more different objects appear in the regions of the P systems. If the amount of different objects is small, then the majority of threads will be idle. This can be seen from the two benchmarks executed with the simulator in [10]: a toy example designed to stress the simulator (up to 7x of speedup with a Tesla C1060), and a linear solution to SAT (up to 1.67x of acceleration).

The simulator iteratively carries out the transitions of the model until a stop configuration is reached. Moreover, it is optional to retrieve just the last configuration or the whole computation reproduced by the simulator. The input of the simulator is given by a specific binary format which is coupled to the way the internal data structures of the simulator are created. In this way, reading the file and creating the membrane and rule representations are efficiently carried out. The latest version (to date) of the binary format is available in [10].

There are two ways of generating a binary file for this simulator: manually creating a binary file (not recommended), or using pLinguaCore to create a binary file from a P-Lingua file (recommended). A version of pLinguaCore is redistributed along with PCUDA, including some examples and guiding files. The specific command to create a binary file can be seen in Sect. 3.2. Finally, 3 versions of this simulator is included in PCUDA: a slow but general sequential, slow but restricted fast and a parallel GPU but restricted simulator. The term restricted means that the last two assumptions of the three aforementioned are taken.

The source code is available in [24], and it can be installed by following the next instructions:

1. Install a CUDA Toolkit version 3.X - 4.X in the computer, and install locally the CUDA SDK. Set the `PATH` and `LD_LIBRARY_PATH` environment variables accordingly.
2. Install the counterslib package: extract the file counterslib.tar.gz inside the *common* folder of the CUDA SDK, go inside the folder and type `./compile.sh.`.
3. Unzip the file pcuda-1.0.tar.gz into the CUDA SDK folder *C/src*. Go inside the folder and type `make`. You should see the executable file inside the folder, or in *../../bin/linux/release*.

ABCDGPU: Parallel Simulation of Population Dynamics P Systems. Simulating PDP systems [1] in parallel is becoming critical, given that some models require to handle such amount of elements that sequential simulators do not give a result in an acceptable time. Although workarounds have been done to tune models and escape from performance pitfalls, parallel simulators might enable the simulation of large models with accurate algorithms such as DCBA [15]. In [13], a parallel implementation of DCBA was carried out for multicore processors, and in [16], for GPUs. Best performance was achieved with the latter, and yet using old GPU architectures. The simulator was experimentally validated with a model of the Bearded Vulture at the Catalan Pyrinean in [12].

The GPU design for ABCDGPU is parallelized by simulations (assuming that the user wants to make an statistical study from the probabilistic model) and environments. Given that rules have cooperation (more than one object appearing in the left-hand side), even between two membranes (the active membrane and its parent), the parallelization of membrane processing is voided. In turn, threads iterate over the rule blocks in tiles (groups of $N = 256$), and in each total iteration the threads execute a step of the DCBA over them. In DCBA, a distribution table is employed, but given that this table can be sparse, the simulator uses a virtual table which is based only on the rule information and two extra arrays (for row additions and column minimum calculation) [13]. Phase 1 to 3 of DCBA follows this distribution, while phase 4 parallelize rules instead of rule blocks along threads [10].

The performance of this simulator also depends on the object density, given that the membrane representation assumes that all different objects might appear at certain point [11]. For random number generation, a new library called CURNG_BINOMIAL was implemented [16]. Although this library creates unfortunately a high thread divergence, the performance is enough for most models. When the ratio of rule blocks competition is high (blocks having different but overlapping left hand sides), phase 2 becomes a bottleneck. In any case, a sequential, a multicore and a GPU simulator are available within ABCDGPU, so researchers can choose a version depending on the resources available. Reported speedups are up to 7x with stressing experiments [16], and up to 5x with a real but small ecosystem [12].

Latest version of ABCDGPU supports the generation of a CSV formatted file with the whole information of the simulator [12], so it might be possible to load it in other tools for its analysis (e.g. Excel/Calc, R, SQL, MeCoSim, etc.). As in PCUDA, in order to speedup the initialization of the simulator, a binary format is employed for the input [10]. It is coupled to the way the internal data structures are created, so there is no need of buffering information or doing extra loops, because the required information for the next item to be allocated is always available in the traversing of the file. In order to avoid the generation of binary files manually, pLinguaCore was extended with a binary generator for PDP systems. Hence, a P-Lingua file can be used as an input. A redistributable version of pLinguaCore with this binary module comes along with ABCDGPU, and the corresponding command line is described in Sect. 3.2.

The source code can be downloaded from [24], and the installation can be made by following the next instructions:

1. Install a CUDA Toolkit version 5.X or later, and install locally the CUDA SDK (to date, up to version 9.1 has been tested). Set the PATH and LD_LIBRARY_PATH environment variables accordingly.
2. Install the GNU Scientific Library (GSL) and Electric Fence.
3. Inside the folder of CUDA SDK samples, create a new folder named *8_pmcgpu*.
4. Extract the contents of abcd-gpu-1.0b.tar.gz and counterslib.tar.gz files into a new folder *8_pmcgpu/ abdcd-gpu*.
5. Go to folder *abcd-gpu*, and type make. You should see the executable file inside the folder.

3 A Complete Workflow

This section describes in detail the main components of the pipeline proposed in this work, along with the connections between them.

3.1 Model Personalization with MeCoSim

As part of the **workflow** described in this paper, given a certain problem we aim to solve, the role played by MeCoSim is the end-point where the end user will interact with the P systems designed and the simulation tools behind the scene. On the one hand, it will provide the mechanism to *configure a custom application* to handle the solution to the problem under study, where the designer will be able to debug its model and, once it is validated, the end users will run their simulations.

Thus, for a given design of a family of P system solving a certain problem, P systems designer provide a configuration file defining the custom app (in .xls or .json format), along with a P-Lingua file with the design based on the type and variant of membrane computing device chosen. This elements will be loaded in

MeCoSim, so that the end user can open the app and start running experiments. In the regular use of the application by these end users, whenever they introduce a new scenario through visual input tables in their custom interface, the data introduced is processed to generate parameters involved in the instantiation of the specific P system within the family of P systems specified in MeCoSim.

Given the specific P system instantiated, depending on the simulator selected, the system will run inside MeCoSim framework or will call some external simulator configured to run with MeCoSim. All simulators implemented within MeCoSim framework provide a step method that is called by MeCoSim consecutively until a halting condition is reached or until the given number of simulations, cycles and steps have finished. However, we cannot guarantee that every external simulator will provide the same mechanism or if this repetitive call will compromise the efficiency of the simulation. Therefore, the connection with the external simulators is based on the independent run of those simulation engines and the setting of protocols to generate the results of the simulation in some agreed format that can be later loaded in MeCoSim, thus populating the output tables and charts configured in the custom applications based on MeCoSim, remaining independent on the simulation engines ultimately used to run the simulations and their internal details, and focused instead on the user view of the information returned by the solution designed.

When the external simulators are not completely integrated (in terms of automation) with the framework provided by P-Lingua and MeCoSim, which is currently the case in many projects, we can still take advantage of the different capabilities of MecoSim to define the custom end-user application and run the models. Thus, once the P-Lingua specification for our problem is loaded in MeCoSim and the data about the scenario under interest is introduced by the end user in the visual input tables, the syntactic and semantic correctness of the file and input data is checked the specific instance of the problem (with the corresponding P system of the family behind) is created. Then, inside MeCoSim folder (mecosim-rgnc, in our home directory), a new file (modelname-parameters.pli) is automatically generated (in userfiles subfolder). Then, the specific P system can be defined as the pair consisting of the original modelname.pli representing the whole family providing the solution, plus the modelname-parameters.pli providing the accompanying parameters for the specific scenario introduced by the user. Th junction of both files will be ready to be used in th following steps of our workflow.

3.2   Simulation with PMCGPU Through P-Lingua

As discussed in Sect. 2.3, PMCGPU incorporates simulators for two P system models: active membranes and Population Dynamics. The other simulators are ad-hoc for specific solutions to SAT. Therefore, the workflow has two paths, depending on the P system model to be simulated.

P Systems with Active Membranes. In order to simulate a P system with active membranes with PCUDA, first, a P-Lingua file describing the model is required. In the previous step of this workflow, it is explained how a P-Lingua file can be generated with MeCoSim, which includes all required parameters. This generated file has to be copied to the computer where PCUDA has been installed, inside the folder *pcuda/plingua*. The binary file can be created out of the P-Lingua one by executing the following instruction (please replace "inputFile" by the name of the corresponding P-Lingua file):

```
java -jar pparser.jar inputFile.pli inputFile.bin
```

Once a binary file has been generated without errors (in *pcuda/plingua/? inputFile.bin*, if the last instruction was executed literally), it is time to take the next step and use the simulator. In the current version of PCUDA, we have to provide some help to the simulator and define:

- #membranes: Number of membranes that the model will generate (an upper bound)
- #objects: Number of objects defined in the alphabet
- #threadPerBlock: Number of threads per block, defined as T such that $T*n = \#objects$ and $0 < T \leq 512$.

Having at hand all of this information, we can then launch the simulator by one of the following instructions (depending on the version to run):

- The sequential simulation: `./pcuda -s -i inputFile.bin`
- The fast sequential simulation: `./pcuda -f -i inputFile.bin -m #membranes -o #objects -b #threadPerBlock -t 1`
- The parallel simulation on the GPU: `./pcuda -p -i file.bin -m #membranes -o #objects -b #threadPerBlock -t 1`

If the computer has more than one GPU, it is possible to choose which one will run the simulator, by setting up the environment variable by typing `export DEFAULT_DEVICE=x`, where x is the id of the GPU to use for the simulation. This id can be consulted by using the tool *nvidia-smi* or the SDK example *deviceQuery*). A limit to the number of transition steps can be imposed using the parameter "-l". In order to store the whole output of the simulator, just use the standard output forwarding as > *outputFile.txt*. Finally, one can choose to show all transition steps or just the final one with the verbosity parameter "-v 2" or "-v 1", respectively. The format uses a similar syntax than the output given by pLinguaCore. For more information, show the help dialogue by typing `./pcuda -h`.

Population Dynamics P Systems. Once a complete P-Lingua file (including all parameter definitions) has been generated with MeCoSim, we have all at hand to carry out the simulation with ABCDGPU. Next step is to copy the desired P-Lingua file into the computer where the GPU simulator has been installed, and place it in the folder *abcd-gpu/plingua*. In order to generate the binary file with pLinguaCore, the next command has to be executed (replace "inputFile" with the corresponding file name):

```
java -jar pLinguaCore.jar plingua inputFile.pli -bin
inputFile.bin
```

If the binary has been generated without errors, the following parameters have to be chosen:

- #simulations: Number of simulations to run (around 25–100).
- #steps: Number of transitions steps to run.
- #cycles: Number of transitions that conform a cycle. The simulator will output information only after every cycle.
- #cores: Only if the multicore simulator is used, select the amount of cores to use in the system.

Once the parameters have been set, it is time to execute the simulator. Use one of the following instructions to run one version:

- The sequential simulator: ./abcdgpu -f plingua/inputFile.bin -s #simulations -t #steps -v 1 -c #cycles -O 0
- The multicore simulator: export OMP_NUM_THREADS=#cores; ./abcdgpu -f plingua/inputFile.bin -s #simulations -t #steps -v 1 -c #cycles -O 0
- The GPU simulator: ./abcdgpu -f plingua/inputFile.bin -I 1 -s #simulations -t #steps -v 1 -c #cycles -O 0

In all cases, a CSV file is generated with the information at every end of a cycle (set #cycle = 1 to output at every transition step). The name of the output file is equal to the input file but with .csv extension. This CSV file can be processed by any platform supporting this format: R, Python, C, Excel/Calc, etc. In the near future, this output file can be reincorporated into MeCoSim, so similar analysis can be performed than when using only pLinguaCore within the simulation framework. Finally, the CSV file contains the following columns: *SIMULATION, STEP, ENVIRONMENT, MEMBRANE, OBJECT, MULTIPLICITY*. When deleting the parameter "-O 0", the output will be a plain text file describing every transition, as made in PCUDA. The format uses a similar syntax than the output given by pLinguaCore.

4 Conclusions and Perspectives

Simulation tools are indispensable in Membrane Computing. In this concern, software developments within the Research Group on Natural Computing at the University of Seville have led to three main projects with different aims: MeCoSim (for applications of Membrane Computing), P-Lingua (for flexible description and simulation of P systems), and PMCGPU (for accelerating P system simulations with GPUs and parallel platforms).

In this paper, we have shown a workflow to interconnect all of them in order to perform fast simulations of P systems (for either with active membranes and PDP systems). It goes from the top level, at the applications and end users without P system expertise, to the bottom level, executing simulations on parallel hardware. P-Lingua acts as a wrapper to communicate both sides. Future work involves further developments and implementations of models, more applications and an automatic integration of all the tools, so that the whole pipeline can run efficiently and transparently to end users.

Acknowledgments. The authors are very grateful to Mario J. Pérez-Jiménez for his unconditional support, unlimited generosity, patience and enthusiasm, and particularly for his skilful advising and guiding as their "scientific father".

The authors also acknowledge the support from the research project TIN2017-89842-P, cofinanced by "Ministerio de Economía, Industria y Competitividad" (MINECO) of Spain, through the "Agencia Estatal de Investigación" (AEI), and by "Fondo Europeo de Desarrollo Regional" (FEDER) of the European Union.

References

1. Cardona, M., et al.: A computational modeling for real ecosystems based on P systems. Nat. Comput. **10**(1), 39–53 (2011)
2. Cecilia, J.M., García, J.M., Guerrero, G.D., Martínez-del-Amor, M.A., Pérez-Hurtado, I., Pérez-Jiménez, M.J.: Simulation of P systems with active membranes on CUDA. Brief. Bioinform. **11**(3), 313–322 (2010)
3. Cecilia, J.M., García, J.M., Guerrero, G.D., Martínez-del-Amor, M.A., Pérez-Hurtado, I., Pérez-Jiménez, M.J.: Simulating a P system based efficient solution to SAT by using GPUs. J. Log. Algebr. Program. **79**(6), 317–325 (2010)
4. Díaz-Pernil, D., Graciani, C., Gutiérrez-Naranjo, M.A., Pérez-Hurtado, I., Pérez-Jiménez, M.J.: Software for P systems. In: Păun, Gh., Rozenberg, G., Salomaa, A. (eds.) The Oxford Handbook of Membrane Computing. Oxford University Press, pp. 437–454 (2009)
5. García-Quismondo, M., Gutiérrez-Escudero, R., Pérez-Hurtado, I., Pérez-Jiménez, M.J., Riscos-Núñez, A.: An overview of P-Lingua 2.0. In: Păun, G., Pérez-Jiménez, M.J., Riscos-Núñez, A., Rozenberg, G., Salomaa, A. (eds.) WMC 2009. LNCS, vol. 5957, pp. 264–288. Springer, Heidelberg (2010). https://doi.org/10.1007/978-3-642-11467-0_20
6. Gheorghe, M.: 3-COL problem modelling using simple Kernel P systems. Int. J. Comput. Math. **90**(4), 816–830 (2013)
7. Ipate, F., et al.: Kernel P systems: applications and implementations. Adv. Intell. Syst. Comput. **212**, 1081–1089 (2013)
8. Kirk, D.B., Wen-Mei, W.H.: Programming Massively Parallel Processors: A Hands on Approach. Morgan Kauffman (2010)
9. Lefticaru, R., et al.: Towards an integrated approach for model simulation, property extraction and verification P systems. In Martínez, M.A., Paun, Gh. Pérez, I., Romero, F.J. (eds.) Proceedings of the Tenth Brainstorming Week on Membrane Computing, vol. 1, pp. 291–318 (2012)
10. Martínez-del-Amor, M.A.: Accelerating membrane systems simulators using high performance computing with GPU, Ph.D. thesis, University of Seville (2013)
11. Martínez-del-Amor, M.A., García-Quismondo, M., Macías-Ramos, L.F., Valencia-Cabrera, L., Riscos-Núñez, A., Pérez-Jiménez, M.J.: Simulating P systems on GPU devices: a survey. Fundam. Inform. **136**(3), 269–284 (2015)
12. Martínez-del-Amor, M.A., Macías-Ramos, L.F., Valencia-Cabrera, L., Pérez-Jiménez, M.J.: Parallel simulation of Population Dynamics P systems: updates and roadmap. Nat. Comput. **15**(4), 565–573 (2016)

13. Martínez-del-Amor, M.A., Karlin, I., Jensen, R.E., Pérez-Jiménez, M.J., Elster, A.C.: Parallel simulation of probabilistic P systems on multicore platforms. In: García, M., Macías, L.F., Păun, Gh., Valencia, L. (eds.) Proceedings of the Tenth Brainstorming Week on Membrane Computing (BWMC 2012), vol. 2, pp. 17–26 (2012)

14. Martínez-del-Amor, M.A., Pérez-Carrasco, J., Pérez-Jiménez, M.J.: Characterizing the parallel simulation of P systems on the GPU. Int. J. Unconv. Comput. 9(5–6), 405–424 (2013)

15. Martínez-del-Amor, M.A., et al.: DCBA: simulating population dynamics P systems with proportional object distribution. In: Csuhaj-Varjú, E., Gheorghe, M., Rozenberg, G., Salomaa, A., Vaszil, G. (eds.) CMC 2012. LNCS, vol. 7762, pp. 257–276. Springer, Heidelberg (2013). https://doi.org/10.1007/978-3-642-36751-9_18

16. Martínez-del-Amor, M.A., Pérez-Hurtado, I., Gastalver-Rubio, A., Elster, A.C., Pérez-Jiménez, M.J.: Population dynamics P systems on CUDA. In: Gilbert, D., Heiner, M. (eds.) CMSB 2012. LNCS, pp. 247–266. Springer, Heidelberg (2012). https://doi.org/10.1007/978-3-642-33636-2_15

17. Păun, G.: Computing with membranes. J. Comput. Syst. Sci. 61(1), 108–143 (2000). And Turku Center for Computer Science-TUCS Report No 208

18. Pérez-Hurtado, I., Valencia-Cabrera, L., Pérez-Jiménez, M.J., Colomer, M.A., Riscos-Núñez, A.: MeCoSim: a general purpose software tool for simulating biological phenomena by means of P systems. In: Li, K., Tang, Z., Li, R., Nagar, A.K., Thamburaj, R. (eds.) IEEE Fifth International Conference on Bio-inspired Computing: Theories and Applications (BIC-TA 2010), vol. 1, pp. 637–643 (2010)

19. Pérez-Hurtado, I.: Desarrollo y aplicaciones de un entorno de programación para Computación Celular: P-Lingua. Ph.D. thesis. University of Seville (2010)

20. Valencia-Cabrera, L.: An environment for virtual experimentation with computational models based on P systems. Ph.D. thesis. University of Seville (2015)

21. Valencia-Cabrera, L., Orellana-Martín, D., Martínez-del-Amor, M.A., Pérez-Jiménez, M.J.: From super-cells to robotic swarms: two decades of evolution in the simulation of P systems. Bull. Int. Membr. Comput. Soc. Number 4, 65–87 (2017)

22. MeCoSim website. http://www.p-lingua.org/mecosim

23. The P-Lingua website. http://www.p-lingua.org

24. The PMCGPU project website. http://sourceforge.net/p/pmcgpu

An Implementation of Elementary Arithmetic with Virus Machine

Xiaoshan Yan[1], Xiangrong Liu[1]([✉]), Xiangxiang Zeng[1,2],
and Alfonso Rodríguez-Patón[2]

[1] Department of Computer Science, Xiamen University,
Xiamen 361005, Fujian, China
yanxiaoshan@stu.xmu.edu.cn, {xrliu,xzeng}@xmu.edu.cn
[2] Departamento de Inteligencia Artificial, ETSIINF,
Universidad Politécnica de Madrid, 28040 Madrid, Spain
arpaton@fi.upm.es

Abstract. In recent years, the popularity of natural computing has been on the increase. Recently, it has inspired a novel biological computational model, called virus machine, which incorporates concepts from virology and theoretical computer science. The virus machine computational paradigm is based on the manner in which viruses replicate and transmit from one host cell to another. It is represented as a heterogeneous network consisting of three subnetworks: a virus transmission network, an instruction transfer network, and an instruction-channel control network. In this paper, elementary arithmetic operation systems are built based on virus machine. Specifically, adder, subtractor, multiplier, and divider are constructed using virus machines. This work can be viewed as a first step towards a "CPU" in wet.

1 Introduction

Combining computation theory with biological systems has resulted in fresh ideas and novel computing systems. This is evidenced by the numerous natural computing methods, such as DNA computing [2,24], membrane computing [17, 20,21], permutation machines [3], and multicell bacterial computing [14,15].

Over the years, these computing systems have been widely used to solve mathematical problems, particularly NP-hard problems, by taking full advantage of parallel computing. For example, Adleman developed a system that solved the seven-point Hamiltonian path problem using DNA computation in 1994 [1]. Subsequently, Braich et al. solved a 20-variable instance of the NP-complete three-satisfiability (3-SAT) problem on a simple DNA computer in 2002 [6]. Prior to that, the maximal clique problem was also solved by means of DNA molecules followed by a series of selection processes [19]. More recently, Xu et al. developed a new unenumerative DNA computing model for a graph vertex coloring problem with 12 vertices without triangles [23], and Chang described a DNA-based algorithm for solving quadratic congruence and factoring integers [8]. In addition, it has been shown that DNA computers can be used to construct

© Springer Nature Switzerland AG 2018
C. Graciani et al. (Eds.): Pérez-Jiménez Festschrift, LNCS 11270, pp. 304–317, 2018.
https://doi.org/10.1007/978-3-030-00265-7_24

various Turing machines [5,16]. In the field of Membrane Computing, a time-free tissue P system solved the Maximum Clique Problem and the Hamilton Path Problem in polynomial time [18]. Further, the spiking neural P system, one of the P systems well known in membrane systems, was proven to be universal [7,22].

Logical operations and arithmetic operations, especially addition and subtraction, are the most fundamental operations in computing systems. Recently, DNA algorithms that perform eight relational algebra (calculus) operations-specifically, Cartesian product, union, set difference, selection, projection, intersection, join, and division-on biomolecular relational databases have been proposed [9]. Further, the arithmetical operations of complex vectors have been implemented by means of DNA-based algorithms [10]. Full addition and subtraction using strands of DNA have also been demonstrated [8]. Spiking neural P systems have also been used to perform four basic arithmetic operations [25], and individual studies on multipliers based on spiking neural P systems are also being conducted [12,13]. Regarding the arithmetic operations performed in simple P systems, it is worth mentioning the membrane systems implementing the arithmetic operations by using various encodings leading to a low complexity for each of these operations [4].

Virus machine [11] has been proved to be Turing complete in its computing mode without restrictions. This paper presents several basic arithmetic operations conducted using virus machine. Because virus machine is a new computational model, its body of research is limited. However, elementary arithmetic is not only the most important part in computing systems, but can also be a breakthrough point for virus machine research.

The remainder of this paper is organized as follows. Section 2 presents preliminaries that will be used in the remainder of this paper, including the formal definition of virus machine. Section 3 outlines the construction of the arithmetic operating models of virus machine and graphically illustrates the structure of each model: a model for addition [11] is presented in Sect. 3.1, a subtractor in Sect. 3.2, a multiplier in Sect. 3.3, and a divider in Sect. 3.4. Finally, Sect. 4 presents conclusions and outlines future research.

2   Virus Machine

Virus machine operates based on the transmissions and replications of viruses. It is a heterogeneous network consisting of three subnetworks: a virus transmission network, an instruction transfer network, and an instruction-channel control network, as illustrated in Fig. 1. The processing units in virus machine, called hosts, are placed in the nodes of the virus transmission network, which is a weighted directed graph (D_H in Fig. 1). The arcs of the graph represent the transmission channels of the viruses. The weight of the arc indicates the number of viruses that will be added to the tail host of the channel after one round of transmission and replication. The instruction transfer network is also a weighted directed graph (D_I in Fig. 1), wherein nodes represent control instruction units.

Each arc of the graph represents an optional instruction transfer path, and the weight of the arc relates to the option. The instruction-channel control network is an undirected graph (G_C in Fig. 1), wherein each edge represents the control relationship from an instruction to a channel situated between two hosts (or between a host and the environment).

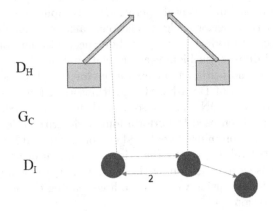

Fig. 1. Structure of a virus machine.

The basic rules of a virus machine are as follows. For the virus transmission network, each channel is closed by default. The channel is opened only when the instruction associated with it through the instruction-channel control network is activated. In this case, the head host of the channel will send one virus (only one), and the tail host will receive n viruses (where n is the weight of the opened channel). However, if the number of viruses in the head host of the channel is zero, there is no transmission of viruses. For the instruction transfer network, instructions are activated in sequence. When two instruction transfer paths exist for one instruction, if the instruction is not attached to a channel, the instruction path is selected in a nondeterministic manner. On the other hand, when the instruction is attached to a channel, if the number of viruses in the head host of the channel is more than one, the instruction transfer path with the highest weight is selected; if the number is zero, the path with the lowest weight is selected; if both weights are equal, the path is selected in a nondeterministic manner. Note that each instruction is attached to at most one channel in the virus transmission network. The virus machine starts from an initial configuration and generates a result only in the halting configuration, called the computing mode.

Chen et al. proved the universality of the virus machine in the computing mode by simulating register machines [11]. However, it has a limit because the number of viruses present in any host has an upper bound during computations.

The formal definition of a virus machine of degree (p, q), $p \geq 1$, $q \geq 1$ is a tuple [11]:

$$\Pi = (\Gamma, H, I, D_H, D_I, G_C, n_1, \ldots, n_p, i_1, h_{out})$$

where,

- $\Gamma = \{v\}$ is the singleton alphabet;
- $H = \{h_1, \ldots, h_p\}$ and $I = \{i_1, \ldots, i_q\}$ are ordered sets such that $v \notin H \cup I$ and $H \cap I = \emptyset$;
- $D_H = (H \cup \{h_{out}\}, E_H, w_H)$ is a weighted directed graph, where $E_H \subseteq H \times (H \cup \{h_{out}\}), (h, h) \notin E_H$ for each $h \in H$, out-degree $(h_{out}) = 0$, and w_H is a mapping from E_H onto $\mathbb{N} \setminus \{0\}$ (the set of positive integer numbers);
- $D_I = (I, E_I, w_I)$ is a weighted directed graph, where $E_I \subseteq I \times I, w_I$ is a mapping from E_I onto $\mathbb{N} \setminus \{0\}$ and, for each vertex $i_j \in I$, the out-degree of i_j is less than or equal to two;
- $G_C = (V_C, E_C)$ is an undirected bipartite graph, where $V_C = I \cup E_H$, and $\{I, E_H\}$ is the partition associated with it (i.e., all edges go between the two sets I and E_H). In addition, for each vertex $i_j \in I$, the degree of i_j is less than or equal to one;
- $n_j \in \mathbb{N} (1 \leq j \leq p)$ is the initial number of viruses in the input host h_j;
- i_1 is the start of instructions; and
- $h_{out} \notin I \cup \{v\}$ and h_{out} is denoted by h_0 in the case where $h_{out} \notin H$.

A virus machine of degree (p, q) as defined above is constructed using an ordered set of p hosts labelled with $h_1, \ldots, h_p$ and an ordered set of q control instruction units labelled with $i_1, \ldots, i_q$. The symbol $h_{out}(h_{out} \in H)$ represents the output region of the system, but $h_{out} = h_0$ if the region refers to the environment. Further, the output region can receive viruses from the system but cannot send viruses to the system.

A virus machine of degree $(2, 3)$ is illustrated Fig. 1. It has two hosts and three control instructions; each host is depicted as a rectangle and each instruction is depicted as a circle. In the virus transmission network and the instruction transfer network, each arrow with a positive integral weight (weight = 1 is not marked) represents a transfer path. The instruction-channel control network's edge is depicted as dotted lines.

A computation of a virus machine Π is a sequence of configurations: (a) the first term is the initial configuration of the system; (b) for each $n \geq 2$, the n-th term of the sequence is obtained from the previous term in one transition step; (c) if the sequence is finite, called halting computation, then the last term is a halting configuration (no instruction will be activated).

3   Solving Four Basic Arithmetic Operations with a Virus Machine

3.1   A Virus Machine for Addition

A virus machine that adds two natural numbers is presented in this section. In [11] there are virus machines with input, while here they are not.

The virus machine is constructed with the form:

$$\Pi = (\Gamma, H, I, D_H, D_I, G_C, n_1, n_2, i_1, h_{out})$$

where,

- $\Gamma = \{v\}$;
- $H = \{h_1, h_2\}, h_{out} = h_0$;
- $I = \{i_1, i_2, i_3\}$;
- $D_H = (\{h_0, h_1, h_2\}, E_H, w_H)$,
  where $E_H = \{(h_1, h_0), (h_2, h_0)\}$
  and $w_H(h_1, h_0) = w_H(h_2, h_0) = 1$;
- $D_I = (I, E_I, w_I)$,
  where $E_I = \{(i_1, i_1), (i_1, i_2), (i_2, i_2), (i_2, i_3)\}$
  and $w_I(i_1, i_1) = w_I(i_2, i_2) = 2, w_I(i_1, i_2) = w_I(i_2, i_3) = 1$;
- $G_C = (I \cup E_H, E_C)$,
  where $E_C = \{\{i_1, (h_1, h_0)\}, \{i_2, (h_2, h_0)\}\}$;
- n_1, n_2 are the initial numbers of viruses in the input hosts h_1, h_2;
- i_1 is the start of instructions; and
- h_{out} has zero viruses initially.

The virus machine defined above is illustrated in Fig. 2. It can compute the addition of two natural numbers n_1 and n_2.

The system carries out computation as follows, with inputs n_1, n_2 in hosts h_1, h_2:

In the first step, instruction i_1 is activated, causing the channel $h_1 \to h_0$ to open. Then, h_1 sends one virus to the environment. After the transmission, the environment has one virus because the weight of the channel is one. Then, the instruction transfer path with the highest weight will be selected, that is $i_1 \to i_1$, if the number of viruses in h_1 is $n_1 - 1$, which is greater than zero. At step 2, instruction i_1 is then activated $n_1 - 1$ times, resulting in the transmission of all n_1 viruses from h_1 to the environment. At step 3, instruction i_1 is activated, but the number of viruses in h_1 is zero. Thus, the instruction transfer path with the lowest weight is selected, that is $i_1 \to i_2$. At step 4, instruction i_2 is activated and causes the channel $h_2 \to h_0$ to open. Thus, h_2 sends one virus to the environment. After the transmission, the environment has $n_1 + 1$ viruses. Similarly, instruction i_2 is activated $n_2 - 1$ times, making all n_2 viruses transmit from h_2 to the environment. At step 5, instruction i_2 is activated, but the number of viruses in h_2 is now zero. Thus, the instruction transfer path with the lowest weight is selected, that is $i_2 \to i_3$. At step 6, instruction i_3 is activated. Because this instruction is not attached to a channel, there is no virus transmission. There is also no subsequent instruction, so this is also a halting configuration.

At this point, the number of viruses in the environment is $n_1 + n_2$; that is, the output of the system is $n_1 + n_2$, which is the sum of n_1 and n_2.

3.2   A Virus Machine for Subtraction

A virus machine that subtracts two natural numbers is described in this section. The virus machine is constructed with the following form:

$$\Pi = (\Gamma, H, I, D_H, D_I, G_C, n_1, n_2, i_1, h_{out}), n_1 \geq n_2$$

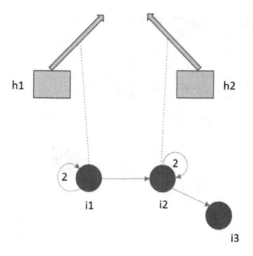

Fig. 2. A virus machine for addition.

where,

- $\Gamma = \{v\}$;
- $H = \{h_1, h_2, h_3\}, h_{out} = h_0$;
- $I = \{i_1, i_2, i_3, i_4\}$;
- $D_H = (\{h_0, h_1, h_2\}, E_H, w_H)$,
  where $E_H = \{(h_1, h_0), (h_1, h_3), (h_2, h_3)\}$
  and $w_H(h_1, h_0) = w_H(h_1, h_3) = w_H(h_2, h_3) = 1$;
- $D_I = (I, E_I, w_I)$,
  where $E_I = \{(i_1, i_2), (i_2, i_1), (i_2, i_3), (i_3, i_3), (i_3, i_4)\}$
  and $w_I(i_2, i_1) = w_I(i_3, i_3) = 2, w_I(i_1, i_2) = w_I(i_2, i_3) = w_I(i_3, i_4) = 1$;
- $G_C = (I \cup E_H, E_C)$,
  where $E_C = \{\{i_1, (h_1, h_3)\}, \{i_2, (h_2, h_3)\}, \{i_3, (h_1, h_0)\}\}$;
- n_1, n_2 are the initial numbers of viruses in the input hosts h_1, h_2;
- i_1 is the start of instructions; and
- h_{out} has zero viruses initially.

The virus machine defined above is illustrated in Fig. 3. It can compute the subtraction of two natural numbers n_1 and n_2.

The system computes as follows with inputs n_1, n_2 in hosts h_1, h_2:

In the first step, instruction i_1 is activated, causing channel $h_1 \rightarrow h_3$ to open. Thus, h_1 sends one virus to h_3. Then, the instruction transfer path is $i_1 \rightarrow i_2$. At step 2, instruction i_2 is activated, causing channel $h_2 \rightarrow h_3$ to open. Thus, h_2 sends one virus to h_3. Then, the instruction transfer path with the highest weight will be selected, that is $i_2 \rightarrow i_1$, if the number of viruses in h_2 is $n_2 - 1$, which is greater than zero. At step 3, instructions i_1 and i_2 are activated in turn $n_2 - 1$ times, causing altogether n_2 viruses to transmit from h_1 to h_3, as well as causing all n_2 viruses to transmit from h_2 to h_3. This results in h_1

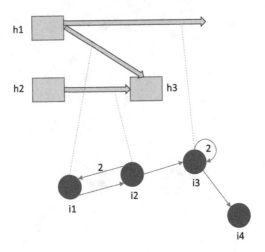

Fig. 3. A virus machine for subtraction.

having $n_1 - n_2$ viruses and h_2 having zero. At step 4, instruction i_2 is activated. However, because the number of viruses in h_2 is zero, the instruction transfer path with the lowest weight is selected, that is, $i_2 \rightarrow i_3$. At step 5, instruction i_3 is activated, causing channel $h_1 \rightarrow h_0$ to open. In addition, h_1 sends one virus to the environment. After the transmission, the environment has one virus. Then, the instruction transfer path with the highest weight will be selected, that is $i_3 \rightarrow i_3$, if the number of viruses in h_1 is greater than zero. At step 6, instruction i_3 is activated $n_1 - n_2 - 1$ times, causing all $n_1 - n_2$ viruses to transmit from h_1 to the environment. Then, instruction i_3 is activated. However, because the number of viruses in h_1 is zero, the instruction transfer path with the lowest weight is selected, that is, $i_3 \rightarrow i_4$. Finally, instruction i_4 is activated. However, because the instruction is not attached to a channel, there is no virus transmission. Further, as there is no next instruction, this is also a halting configuration.

At this point, the number of viruses in the environment is $n_1 - n_2$; that is, the output of the system is $n_1 - n_2$. Table 1 presents the computation outlined above.

Host h_s of the system contains exactly $a_{s,t}$ viruses at instant t. The control instruction unit u_t is activated at step $t+1$ (otherwise, if $u_t = \#$, then no instruction is activated). e_t denotes the number of viruses sent to the environment up to instant t. These declarations also apply to Tables 2 and 3.

3.3   A Virus Machine for Multiplication

A virus machine that multiplies two natural numbers is described in this section. The virus machine constructed as the following form:

$$\Pi = (\Gamma, H, I, D_H, D_I, G_C, n_1, n_2, i_1, h_{out})$$

Table 1. The computation process in the virus machine subtractor.

Instruction	$a_{1,t}$	$a_{2,t}$	$a_{3,t}$	u_t	e_t
	n_1	n_2	0	i_1	0
i_1	$n_1 - 1$	n_2	1	i_2	0
i_2	$n_1 - 1$	$n_2 - 1$	2	i_1	0
...	...	...	...	...	...
i_1	$n_1 - n_2$	1	$2 \times n_2 - 1$	i_2	0
i_2	$n_1 - n_2$	0	$2 \times n_2$	i_3	0
i_3	$n_1 - n_2 - 1$	0	$2 \times n_2$	i_3	1
...	...	...	...	...	...
i_3	0	0	$2 \times n_2$	i_4	$n_1 - n_2$
i_4	0	0	$2 \times n_2$	#	$n_1 - n_2$

where,

- $\Gamma = \{v\}$;
- $H = \{h_1, h_2, h_3, h_4\}, h_{out} = h_0$;
- $I = \{i_1, i_2, i_3, i_4, i_5\}$;
- $D_H = (\{h_0, h_1, h_2, h_3, h_4\}, E_H, w_H)$,
  where $E_H = \{(h_1, h_3), (h_2, h_4), (h_4, h_2), (h_4, h_0)\}$
  and $w_H(h_1, h_3) = w_H(h_4, h_2) = w_H(h_4, h_0) = 1, w_H(h_2, h_4) = 2$;
- $D_I = (I, E_I, w_I)$,
  where $E_I = \{(i_1, i_1), (i_1, i_3), (i_3, i_4), (i_4, i_3), (i_4, i_2), (i_2, i_1), (i_2, i_5)\}$
  and $w_I(i_1, i_1) = w_I(i_2, i_1) = w_I(i_4, i_3) = 2, w_I(i_1, i_3) = w_I(i_3, i_4) = w_I(i_4, i_2) = w_I(i_2, i_5) = 1$;
- $G_C = (I \cup E_H, E_C)$,
  where $E_C = \{\{i_1, (h_2, h_4)\}, \{i_2, (h_1, h_3)\}, \{i_3, (h_4, h_2)\}, \{i_4, (h_4, h_0)\}\}$;
- n_1, n_2 are the initial numbers of viruses in the input hosts h_1, h_2;
- i_1 is the start of instructions; and
- h_{out} has zero viruses initially.

The virus machine defined above is illustrated in Fig. 4. It can compute the multiplication of two natural numbers n_1 and n_2.

The system computes as follows with inputs n_1, n_2 in hosts h_1, h_2:

In the first step, instruction i_1 is activated, causing channel $h_2 \to h_4$ to open. Thus, h_2 sends one virus to h_4. After the transmission, h_4 has two viruses because the weight of the channel is two. Then, the instruction transfer path with the highest weight will be selected, that is, $i_1 \to i_1$, if the number of viruses in h_2 is $n_2 - 1$, which is greater than zero. At step 2, instruction i_1 is activated $n_2 - 1$ times, causing all n_2 viruses to transmit from h_2 to h_4. This results in h_4 having $2 \times n_2$ viruses and h_2 having zero. At step 3, instruction i_3 is activated, causing channel $h_4 \to h_2$ to open. This results in h_4 sending one virus to h_2. After the transmission, h_2 has one virus. At step 4, instruction i_4 is activated, causing channel $h_4 \to h_0$ to open. Thus, h_4 sends one virus to the environment. After

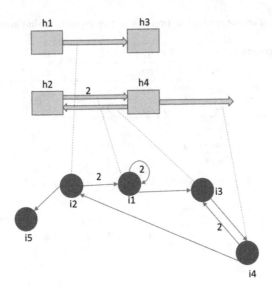

Fig. 4. A virus machine for multiplication.

the transmission, h_4 has $2 \times n_2 - 2$ viruses, and the environment has one virus. Then, the instruction transfer path with the highest weight will be selected, that is $i_4 \rightarrow i_3$, if the number of viruses in h_4 is greater than zero. At step 5, instructions i_3 and i_4 are activated in turn $2 \times n_2 - 2$ times, causing $n_2 - 1$ viruses to transmit from h_4 to h_2, and another $n_2 - 1$ viruses to transmit from h_4 to h_0. This results in h_2 having n_2 viruses and the environment having n_2 viruses. At step 6, instruction i_2 is activated. However, because the number of viruses in h_4 is zero, the instruction transfer path with the lowest weight is selected, that is, $i_4 \rightarrow i_2$. Channel $h_1 \rightarrow h_3$ is then opened, and h_1 sends one virus to h_3. After the transmission, h_3 has one virus. Then, the instruction transfer path with the highest weight will be selected, that is $i_2 \rightarrow i_1$, if the number of viruses in h_1 is greater than zero. The system will perform the above procedure until h_1 has no virus. Finally, instruction i_5 is activated. However, because the instruction is not attached to a channel, there is no virus transmission. Further, as there is no next instruction, this is also a halting configuration.

At this point, the number of viruses in the environment is $n_1 \times n_2$; that is, the output of the system is $n_1 \times n_2$. Table 2 presents the computation procedure outlined above.

3.4   A Virus Machine for Division

A virus machine that divides two natural numbers is described in this section. The virus machine constructed as the following form:

$$\Pi = (\Gamma, H, I, D_H, D_I, G_C, n_1, n_2, i_1, h_{out})$$

Table 2. The computation process in the virus machine multiplier.

Instruction	$a_{1,t}$	$a_{2,t}$	$a_{3,t}$	$a_{4,t}$	u_t	e_t
	n_1	n_2	0	0	i_1	0
i_1	n_1	$n_2 - 1$	0	2	i_1	0
i_1	n_1	$n_2 - 2$	0	4	i_1	0
...	...	...	...	...	...	...
i_1	n_1	0	0	$2 \times n_2$	i_3	0
i_3	n_1	1	0	$2 \times n_2 - 1$	i_4	0
i_4	n_1	1	0	$2 \times n_2 - 2$	i_3	1
...	...	...	...	...	...	...
i_3	n_1	n_2	0	1	i_4	$n_2 - 1$
i_4	n_1	n_2	0	0	i_2	n_2
i_2	$n_1 - 1$	n_2	1	0	i_1	n_2
...	...	...	...	...	...	...
i_4	1	n_2	$n_1 - 1$	0	i_2	$n_1 \times n_2$
i_2	0	n_2	n_1	0	i_5	$n_1 \times n_2$
i_5	0	n_2	n_1	0	#	$n_1 \times n_2$

where,

- $\Gamma = \{v\}$;
- $H = \{h_1, h_2, h_3, h_4, h_5\}, h_{out} = h_0$;
- $I = \{i_1, i_2, i_3, i_4, i_5, i_6\}$;
- $D_H = (\{h_0, h_1, h_2, h_3, h_4, h_5\}, E_H, w_H)$,
  where $E_H = \{(h_1, h_0), (h_1, h_3), (h_3, h_5), (h_2, h_4), (h_4, h_2)\}$ and $w_H(h_1, h_0) = w_H(h_1, h_3) = w_H(h_3, h_5) = w_H(h_2, h_4) = w_H(h_4, h_2) = 1$;
- $D_I = (I, E_I, w_I)$,
  where $E_I = \{(i_1, i_2), (i_1, i_3), (i_2, i_1), (i_2, i_6), (i_3, i_3), (i_3, i_4), (i_4, i_4), (i_4, i_5),$
  $(i_5, i_1)\}$ and $w_I(i_1, i_2) = w_I(i_2, i_1) = w_I(i_3, i_3) = w_I(i_4, i_4) = 2, w_I(i_1, i_3) = w_I(i_2, i_6) = w_I(i_3, i_4) = w_I(i_4, i_5) = w_I(i_5, i_1) = 1$;
- $G_C = (I \cup E_H, E_C)$,
  where $E_C = \{\{i_1, (h_2, h_4)\}, \{i_2, (h_1, h_3)\}, \{i_3, (h_4, h_2)\}, \{i_4, (h_3, h_5)\},$
  $\{i_5, (h_1, h_0)\}\}$;
- n_1, n_2 are the initial numbers of viruses in the input hosts h_1, h_2;
- i_1 is the start of instructions; and
- h_{out} has zero viruses initially.

The virus machine defined above is illustrated in Fig. 5. It can compute the division of two natural numbers n_1 and n_2.

The system computes as follows with inputs n_1, n_2 in hosts h_1, h_2:

In the first step, instruction i_1 is activated, causing channel $h_2 \rightarrow h_4$ to open. This results in h_2 sending one virus to h_4. After the transmission, h_4 has one virus because the weight of the channel is one. Then, the instruction transfer

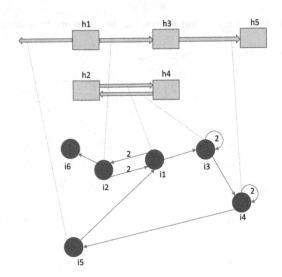

Fig. 5. A virus machine for division.

Table 3. The computation process in the virus machine divider.

Instruction	$a_{1,t}$	$a_{2,t}$	$a_{3,t}$	$a_{4,t}$	$a_{5,t}$	u_t	e_t
	n_1	n_2	0	0	0	i_1	0
i_1	n_1	$n_2 - 1$	0	1	0	i_2	0
i_2	$n_1 - 1$	$n_2 - 1$	1	1	0	i_1	0
...	...	...	...	...	...	...	...
i_1	$n_1 - n_2 + 1$	0	$n_2 - 1$	n_2	0	i_3	0
i_3	$n_1 - n_2 + 1$	1	$n_2 - 1$	$n_2 - 1$	0	i_3	0
...	...	...	...	...	...	...	...
i_3	$n_1 - n_2 + 1$	n_2	$n_2 - 1$	0	0	i_4	0
i_4	$n_1 - n_2 + 1$	n_2	$n_2 - 1$	0	1	i_4	0
...	...	...	...	...	...	...	...
i_4	$n_1 - n_2 + 1$	n_2	0	0	$n_2 - 1$	i_5	0
i_5	$n_1 - n_2$	n_2	0	0	$n_2 - 1$	i_1	1
i_1	$n_1 - n_2$	$n_2 - 1$	0	1	$n_2 - 1$	i_2	1
...	...	...	...	...	...	...	...
i_2	0	$n_1 - n_1\%n_2$	$n_1\%n_2$	$n_1\%n_2$	$n_1 - n_1/n_2 - n_1\%n_2$	i_6	n_1/n_2
i_2	0	$n_1 - n_1\%n_2$	$n_1\%n_2$	$n_1\%n_2$	$n_1 - n_1/n_2 - n_1\%n_2$	#	n_1/n_2

path with the highest weight is selected, that is $i_1 \rightarrow i_2$, if the number of viruses in h_2 is $n_2 - 1$, which is greater than zero. At step 2, instruction i_2 is activated, causing channel $h_1 \rightarrow h_3$ to open. This results in h_1 sending one virus to h_3. After the transmission, h_3 has one virus. Then, the instruction transfer path with the highest weight is selected, that is $i_2 \rightarrow i_1$, if the number of viruses in

h_1 is $n_1 - 1$, which is greater than zero. At step 3, instructions i_1 and i_2 are activated in turn $n_2 - 1$ times, causing all n_2 viruses to transmit from h_2 to h_4. This results in h_1 having $n_1 - n_2 + 1$ viruses, h_2 having zero, h_3 having $n_2 - 1$, and h_4 having n_2 viruses. At step 4, instruction i_1 is activated. However, because the number of viruses in h_2 is zero, the instruction transfer path with the lowest weight is selected, that is, $i_1 \rightarrow i_3$. At step 5, instruction i_3 is activated, causing channel $h_4 \rightarrow h_2$ to open. This results in, h_4 sending one virus to h_2. After the transmission, h_2 has one virus. Then, the instruction transfer path with the highest weight will be selected, that is $i_3 \rightarrow i_3$, if the number of viruses in h_4 is greater than zero. At step 6, instruction i_3 is activated $n_2 - 1$ times, causing all n_2 viruses to return to h_2. At step 7, instruction i_3 is activated. However, because the number of viruses in h_4 is zero, the instruction transfer path with the lowest weight is selected, that is, $i_3 \rightarrow i_4$. At step 8, instruction i_4 is activated $n_2 - 1$ times, causing all viruses to transmit from h_3 to h_5. At step 9, instruction i_4 is activated. However, because the number of viruses in h_3 is zero, the instruction transfer path with the lowest weight is selected, that is, $i_4 \rightarrow i_5$. At step 10, instruction i_5 is activated, causing channel $h_1 \rightarrow h_0$ to open. This results in h_1 sending one virus to the environment. After the transmission, h_1 has $n_1 - n_2$ viruses, and the environment has one virus. The instruction transfer path is then $i_5 \rightarrow i_1$. At this point, the first round is complete. h_1 now has $n_1 - n_2$ viruses, h_2 has n_2, and h_3 and h_4 both have zero. The procedure outlined above is repeated until h_1 has no virus. Then, instruction i_2 is activated. However, because the number of viruses in h_1 is zero, the instruction transfer path with the lowest weight is selected, that is, $i_2 \rightarrow i_6$. Finally, instruction i_6 is activated. However, as the instruction is not attached to a channel, there is no virus transmission. Further, because there is no ensuing instruction, this is also a halting configuration.

Division in fact relies on subtraction. At this point, the number of viruses in the environment is n_1/n_2; that is, the output of the system is n_1/n_2. In addition, the number of viruses in h_3 is $n_1 \% n_2$; that is, the remainder. Table 3 presents the computation outlined above.

4   Conclusions and Future Work

Virus Machine is a new biological computing model inspired by the manner in which viruses are transmitted and replicated. The model comprises three subnetworks: a virus transmission network, an instruction transfer network, and an instruction-channel control network.

This paper designed four virus machine systems that respectively implement elementary arithmetic operations: an adder comprising two hosts and three instructions, a subtractor comprising three hosts and four instructions, a multiplier comprising four hosts and five instructions, and a divider comprising five hosts and six instructions. The details of the computation procedures were also presented in tables.

The elementary arithmetic virus machine solutions presented here can be implemented in various other forms-designing even simpler systems for these elementary arithmetic operations would be an interesting challenge. It is important to determine if the upper bound of the virus machine has any impact on the elementary arithmetic system. Further, designing virus machine systems for more difficult problems, such as factoring of integers and NP-hard problems, is being considered for future work.

Acknowledgements. The work was supported by the National Natural Science Foundation of China (Grant Nos. 61472333, 61772441, 61472335), Project of marine economic innovation and development in Xiamen (No. 16PFW034SF02), Natural Science Foundation of the Higher Education Institutions of Fujian Province (No. JZ160400), Natural Science Foundation of Fujian Province (No. 2017J01099), President Fund of Xiamen University (No. 20720170054), Project TIN2016-81079-R, (MINECO AEI/FEDER, Spain-EU) and InGEMICS-CM project (B2017/BMD-3691, FSE/FEDER, Comunidad de Madrid-EU). X. Zeng is supported by Juan de la Cierva position (code: IJCI-2015-26991).

References

1. Adleman, L.M.: Molecular computation of solutions to combinatorial problems. Science **266**(5187), 1021–1024 (1994)
2. Benenson, Y., Paz-Elizur, T., Adar, R., Keinan, E., Livneh, Z., Shapiro, E.: Programmable and autonomous computing machine made of biomolecules. Nature **414**(6862), 430–434 (2001)
3. Bhatia, S., Laboda, C., Yanez, V.F., Haddock, T.L., Densmore, D.: Permutation machines. ACS Synth. Biol. **5**(8), 827–834 (2016)
4. Bonchis, C., Ciobanu, G., Izbasa, C.: Encodings and arithmetic operations in membrane computing. Theory Appl. Models Comput. **3959**, 621–630 (2006)
5. Boneh, D., Dunworth, C., Lipton, R.J., Sgall, J.: On the computational power of DNA. Discret. Appl. Math. **71**(1–3), 79–94 (1996)
6. Braich, R.S., Chelyapov, N., Johnson, C., Rothemund, P.W., Adleman, L.: Solution of a 20-variable 3-SAT problem on a DNA computer. Science **296**(5567), 499–502 (2002)
7. Cavaliere, M., Egecioglu, O., Ibarra, O.H., Ionescu, M., Păun, G., Woodworth, S.: Asynchronous spiking neural P systems: decidability and undecidability. Theor. Comput. Sci. **219**(24), 197–207 (2013)
8. Chang, W.L.: Fast parallel DNA-based algorithms for molecular computation: quadratic congruence and factoring integers. IEEE Trans. Nanobiosci. **11**(1), 62–69 (2012)
9. Chang, W.L., Vasilakos, A.: Molecular algorithms of implementing bio-molecular databases on a biological computer. IEEE Trans. Nanobiosci. **14**(1), 104–111 (2014)
10. Chang, W.L., Vasilakos, A.V., Ho, M.: The DNA-based algorithms of implementing arithmetical operations of complex vectors on a biological computer. IEEE Trans. Nanobiosci. **14**(8), 907–914 (2015)
11. Chen, X., Pérez-Jiménez, M.J., Valencia-Cabrera, L., Wang, B., Zeng, X.: Computing with viruses. Theor. Comput. Sci. **623**, 146–159 (2016)
12. Diaz, C., Frias, T., Sanchez, G., Perez, H., Toscano, K., Duchen, G.: A novel parallel multiplier using spiking neural P systems with dendritic delays. Neurocomputing **239**, 113–121 (2017)

13. Diaz, C., Sanchez, G., Duchen, G., Nakano, M., Perez, H.: An efficient hardware implementation of a novel unary spiking neural network multiplier with variable dendritic delays. Neurocomputing **189**, 130–134 (2016)
14. Gupta, V., Irimia, J., Pau, I., Rodriguez-Paton, A.: Bioblocks: programming protocols in biology made easier. ACS Synth. Biol. **6**(7), 1230–1232 (2017)
15. Gutiérrez, M.E., Gregorio Godoy, P., Pérez, D.P.G., Muñoz, L.E., Sáez, S., Rodriguez Paton, A.: A new improved and extended version of the multicell bacterial simulator gro. ACS Synth. Biol. **6**(8), 1496–1508 (2017)
16. Kari, L., Gloor, G., Yu, S.: Using DNA to solve the bounded post correspondence problem. Theor. Comput. Sci. **231**(2), 193–203 (2000)
17. Liu, X., Li, Z., Liu, J., Liu, L., Zeng, X.: Implementation of arithmetic operations with time-free spiking neural P systems. IEEE Trans. Nanobiosci. **14**(6), 617–624 (2015)
18. Liu, X., Suo, J., Leung, S.C.H., Liu, J., Zeng, X.: The power of time-free tissue P systems: Attacking NP-complete problems. Neurocomputing **159**(1), 151–156 (2015)
19. Ouyang, Q., Kaplan, P.D., Liu, S., Libchaber, A.: DNA solution of the maximal clique problem. Science **278**(5337), 446–449 (1997)
20. Pan, L., Zeng, X., Zhang, X.: Time-free spiking neural P systems. Neural Comput. **23**(5), 1320–1342 (2011)
21. Păun, G.: Computing with membranes. J. Comput. Syst. Sci. **61**(1), 108–143 (2000)
22. Song, T., Pan, L., Wang, J., Venkat, I., Subramanian, K.G., Abdullah, R.: Normal forms of spiking neural P systems with anti-spikes. IEEE Trans. Nanobiosci. **11**(4), 352–359 (2012)
23. Xu, J., et al.: An unenumerative DNA computing model for vertex coloring problem. IEEE Trans. Nanobiosci. **10**(2), 94–98 (2011)
24. Yang, J., Jiang, S., Liu, X., Pan, L., Zhang, C.: Aptamer-binding directed DNA origami pattern for logic gates. ACS Appl. Mater. Interfaces **8**(49), 34054–34060 (2016)
25. Zeng, X., Song, T., Zhang, X., Pan, L.: Performing four basic arithmetic operations with spiking neural P systems. IEEE Trans. Nanobiosci. **11**(4), 366–374 (2012)

A Kernel-Based Membrane Clustering Algorithm

Jinyu Yang[1], Ru Chen[1], Guozhou Zhang[1], Hong Peng[1(✉)], Jun Wang[2], and Agustín Riscos-Núñez[3]

[1] School of Computer and Software Engineering, Xihua University, Chengdu 610039, Sichuan, China
ph.xhu@hotmail.com
[2] School of Electrical and Information Engineering, Xihua University, Chengdu 610039, Sichuan, China
[3] Research Group of Natural Computing, Department of Computer Science and Artificial Intelligence, University of Seville, 41012 Sevilla, Spain

Abstract. The existing membrane clustering algorithms may fail to handle the data sets with non-spherical cluster boundaries. To overcome the shortcoming, this paper introduces kernel methods into membrane clustering algorithms and proposes a kernel-based membrane clustering algorithm, KMCA. By using non-linear kernel function, samples in original data space are mapped to data points in a high-dimension feature space, and the data points are clustered by membrane clustering algorithms. Therefore, a data clustering problem is formalized as a kernel clustering problem. In KMCA algorithm, a tissue-like P system is designed to determine the optimal cluster centers for the kernel clustering problem. Due to the use of non-linear kernel function, the proposed KMCA algorithm can well deal with the data sets with non-spherical cluster boundaries. The proposed KMCA algorithm is evaluated on nine benchmark data sets and is compared with four existing clustering algorithms.

1 Introduction

Membrane computing, introduced by Păun [1], was inspired by the structure and functioning of living cells and their cooperation in tissues, organs, and biological neural networks [2]. Membrane computing is a class of distributed parallel computing models, known as P systems or membrane systems. In the past, a variety of variants of P systems have been proposed [3–11], and they have been applied to real-world problems, for example, robots [12,13], image processing [14–17], signal processing [18–20], fault diagnosis [21–25], ecology and system biology [26–28].

Clustering is a class of machine learning techniques, which is the task of finding natural partitioning within a data set such that patterns within the same cluster are more similar than those within different clusters. Membrane clustering algorithms (MCA) are a kind of partitioning clustering algorithms realized in

© Springer Nature Switzerland AG 2018
C. Graciani et al. (Eds.): Pérez-Jiménez Festschrift, LNCS 11270, pp. 318–329, 2018.
https://doi.org/10.1007/978-3-030-00265-7_25

the framework of membrane computing. In recent years, a number of membrane clustering algorithms have been developed. Zhao et al. [29] discussed an improved clustering algorithm that used a cell-like membrane system to realize classical k-medoids algorithm. In Peng et al. [30], an evolution-communication membrane system has been used to propose a fuzzy cluster approach, called Fuzzy-MC. Two automatic membrane clustering algorithms were discussed [31,32], where an object representation with control bits and a membrane system with active membranes, respectively, were used to realize the corresponding automatic clustering mechanisms. Peng et al. [33] presented a multiobjective fuzzy clustering approach based on tissue-like membrane systems. The experimental results on a lot of benchmark datasets have shown that compared to the existing clustering algorithms, membrane clustering algorithms offer a more competitive approach due to three advantages: good clustering performance, better convergence and stronger robustness. However, the existing membrane clustering algorithms have a shortcoming: their cluster boundaries are spherical. Therefore, these membrane clustering algorithms may suffer a low clustering quality for the data sets with non-spherical cluster boundaries.

To overcome the critical shortcoming, this paper introduces kernel methods [34] into membrane clustering algorithms and proposes a kernel-based membrane clustering algorithm, called KMCA. Based on the principle of kernel methods, data samples are mapped to a high-dimensional feature space by a non-linear kernel function, and then KMCA algorithm is realized in the high-dimensional feature space. Due to the use of nonlinear kernel function, KMCA algorithms have a non-spherical cluster boundary. Meanwhile, KMCA algorithms can hold the advantages of membrane clustering algorithms, for example, good clustering performance, better convergence and stronger robustness, even if for the data sets with non-spherical cluster boundaries.

The remainder of this paper is organized as follows. Section 2 discusses in detail the proposed kernel-based membrane clustering algorithm. Experimental results are provided in Sect. 3. Conclusions are given in Sect. 4.

2 KMCA Algorithms

2.1 Kernel Clustering Problems

Let $X = \{x_1, x_2, \ldots, x_n\}$ be a data set of n data points in R^d, where $x_i = (x_{i1}, x_{i2}, \ldots, x_{id})$, $i = 1, 2, \ldots, n$. The data set X is partitioned into k clusters, $C_1, C_2, \ldots, C_k$. Denote by $z_1, z_2, \ldots, z_k$ the centers of the k clusters, respectively. In classical k-means algorithm, the objective function to be optimized is as follows:

$$J_m(z_1, z_2, \ldots, z_k) = \sum_{i=1}^{k} \sum_{x_j \in C_i} ||x_j - z_i||^2 \tag{1}$$

Based on the principle of kernel methods, data set X is mapped into a high-dimension feature space by a nonlinear function $\phi(x)$.

Let $Y = \{\phi(x_1), \phi(x_2), \ldots, \phi(x_n)\}$ be the mapped data set. In the feature space, the distance between $\phi(x_i)$ and $\phi(x_j)$ can be computed as follows:

$$d(\phi(x_i), \phi(x_j)) = ||\phi(x_i) - \phi(x_j)|| = \sqrt{K(x_i, x_i) - 2K(x_i, x_j) + K(x_j, x_j)} \quad (2)$$

where $K(x_i, x_j)$ is called kernel function. The widely used kernel functions are: linear kernel function, polynomial kernel function, Gaussian kernel function and sigmoid kernel function. Gaussian kernel function is defined by

$$K(x_i, x_j) = \exp\left(-\frac{||x_i - x_j||^2}{2\sigma^2}\right) \quad (3)$$

where $\sigma > 0$ is the width of Gaussian kernel. Therefore, kernel clustering problem can be viewed as the following optimization problem:

$$\min_{z_1, z_2, \ldots, z_k} J(z_1, z_2, \ldots, z_k) = \sum_{i=1}^{k} \sum_{x_j \in C_i} \left(K(x_j, x_j) - 2K(x_j, z_i) + K(z_i, z_i)\right) \quad (4)$$

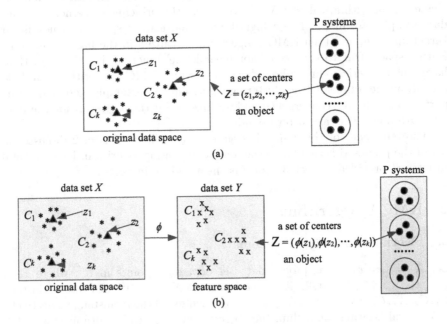

Fig. 1. (a) MCA algorithm; (b) Proposed KMCA algorithm

2.2 Basic Idea

Figure 1(a) shows the principle of the existing membrane clustering algorithms (MCA), where an object in P systems is used to denote a set of candidate cluster centers. Based on the objective function (1), a P system is considered to determine the optimal cluster centers. However, a shortcoming that MCA algorithm suffers from is that it may fail to deal with the data sets with non-spherical cluster boundaries.

To overcome the shortcoming, this paper presents a kernel-based membrane clustering algorithm, KMCA. In KMCA, data set X in original data space is mapped to a high-dimension feature space by a non-linear map ϕ, shown in Fig. 1(b). Assume that Y is the mapped data set in the feature space, i.e., $Y = \{\phi(x_1), \phi(x_2), \ldots, \phi(x_n)\}$. KMCA algorithm will design a tissue-like P system to solve the kernel clustering problem (3), i.e., determining an optimal set of cluster centers. Although cluster boundaries obtained by tissue-like P system are still spherical in the feature space, KMCA algorithm can well handle the data sets with non-spherical cluster boundaries due to using nonlinear mapping ϕ that is expressed implicitly by kernel function.

2.3   Algorithm Implementation

The proposed KMCA algorithm is based on a tissue-like P system, which is designed to solve the kernel clustering problem (3). The tissue-like P system consists of q cells, and is defined as follows

$$\Pi = (O, w_1, \ldots, w_q, R_1, \ldots, R_q, R', i_0) \tag{5}$$

where

(1) O is a finite non-empty alphabet (of objects);
(2) $w_i(1 \leq i \leq q)$ is finite set of objects initially present in cell i;
(3) $R_i(1 \leq i \leq q)$ is finite set of evolution rules in cell i;
(4) R' is finite set of communication rules of the form $(i, u/v, 0)$, which denotes communication rule between cell i and the environment, $i = 1, 2, \ldots, q$;
(5) i_0 indicates the output region of the system.

In what follows, we describe in detail several components of the tissue-like P system.

(1) *Object presentation*

The role of the designed tissue-like P system is to search the optimal cluster centers, so its each object is used to express a group of candidate cluster centers. Let $Z = \{z_1, z_2, \ldots, z_k\}$ is a set of candidate cluster centers, and each center z_i is a d-dimension vector, $z_i = (z_{i1}, z_{i2}, \ldots, z_{id}) \in R^d$, $i = 1, 2, \ldots, k$. Thus, each object in cells can be formally expressed by

$$Z = (z_{11}, z_{12}, \ldots, z_{1d}, z_{21}, z_{22}, \ldots, z_{2d}, \ldots, z_{k1}, z_{k2}, \ldots, z_{kd}) \tag{6}$$

In the designed tissue-like P system, each cell has a best object, and denote by Z_{best}^i the best object in ith cell, $i = 1, 2, \ldots, k$. There is an object in the environment, Z_{best}, which is the best object in entire system.

(2) *Evaluation mechanism*

In the designed tissue-like P system, an improved velocity-position model is used to evolve the objects in cells. The improved velocity-position model can be described as follows.

$$\begin{cases} V_i = w \cdot Z_i + c_1 r_1 (P_i - Z_i) + c_2 r_2 (Z_{best}^i - Z_i) + c_3 r_3 (Z_{best} - Z_i) \\ Z_i = Z_i + V_i \end{cases} \quad (7)$$

where P_i is the best position of object Z_i found so far, w is inertia weight, c_1, c_2, c_3 are learning factors, and r_1, r_2, r_3 are three random real numbers in [0,1]. In the implementation, the following decreasing strategy of inertia weight is used:

$$w = w_{max} - (w_{max} - w_{min}) t / t_{max} \quad (8)$$

where $w_{max} = 0.9$, $w_{min} = 0.4$, and t_{max} is maximum computing step number (or maximum iteration number).

(3) *Communication mechanism*

The tissue-like P system uses communication mechanism to achieve the exchange and sharing of objects between each cell and the environment. The communication mechanism usually is provided by communication rules. In the tissue-like P system, the used communication rule is described as follows:

$$< i, Z_{best}^i / Z_{best}, 0 >, i = 1, 2, \ldots, q \quad (9)$$

The communication rule indicates that Z_{best}^i in cell i is transported into the environment to update its best object, and Z_{best} in the environment is transported into cell i for object evolution at next step.

(4) *Halting and output*

The designed tissue-like P system adopts a simple halting condition, namely, maximum computing step number. The tissue-like P system will continue to execute until the halting condition is reached, thus, the system halts. When the system halts, the best object stored in the environment ($i_0 = 0$) is regarded as final computing result, namely, the determined optimal cluster centers.

3   Experimental Results

3.1   Data Sets

In order to evaluate the proposed KMCA algorithm, nine widely used benchmark data sets from UCI [35] machine learning repository were used in experiments, shown in Table 1. Simulation experiment is implemented in python [36] on a Microsoft Window computer.

Table 1. The data sets used in experiments

Data set	Number of data points (n)	Data dimension (d)	Number of clusters (k)
Wine	178	13	3
Lung cancer	32	56	3
Seeds	210	7	3
Lenses	24	4	3
Hayes-roth	132	5	3
Dermatology	366	33	6
Iris	150	4	3
Leuk	72	40	3
Zoo	101	16	7

3.2 The Compared Methods

In experiments, the proposed KMCA algorithm was compared with four existing clustering algorithms, which are illustrated as follows.

(1) K-means (KM): a classical k-means algorithm.
(2) K-means+PSO (KM+PSO) [37]: a k-means algorithm optimized by particle swarm optimization (PSO).
(3) Kernel k-means (KKM) [38]: a kernel-based k-means algorithm.
(4) Kernel k-means+PSO (KKM+PSO) [39]: a kernel-based k-means algorithm optimized by particle swarm optimization (PSO).

3.3 Parameter Setting

For the proposed KMCA algorithm, parameters of tissue P system are assigned: the number of cells $q = 3$, the number of objects in each cell $m = 100$, and maximum number of iterations is 100. In KM+PSO and KKM+PSO, population size is $m = 100$, maximum number of iterations is 100, and $c_1 = c_2 = 2.0, w = 1$. In KMCA, KKM and KKM+PSO, Gaussian function is used as kernel function, and the same parameter δ is used for each data set, but the different parameters δ are used in the different data sets: $\delta = 0.5$ for Wine, $\delta = 2.5$ for Lung cancer and Leuk, $\delta = 0.07$ for Iris, $\delta = 9$ for Zoo, $\delta = 0.13$ for Seeds, $\delta = 1$ for Lenses and Dermatology, and $\delta = 0.1$ for Hayes-roth.

3.4 Performance Measures

To measure the clustering quality of these clustering algorithms, two internal indexes and three external indexes were used in experiments. Internal index is used to indicate the clustering effect of data, while external index illustrates the accuracy of data clustering. In external index, n_{ij} denotes the number of samples that are actually in jth class but are classified into i class. $n_{i+} = \sum_j n_{ij}$ denotes the number of samples that are classified into i class in experiment. $n_{+j} = \sum_i n_{ij}$ denotes the number of samples that are classified into j class in the actual situation. The five indexes are as follows.

(1) Silhouette index (SI) [40]

Suppose that a denotes the average kernelized distance between a point and other points from the same cluster, and b is minimum average kernelized distance between a point and the points from other clusters. $SI \in [-1,1]$ is the average of Silhouette widths of all samples. Generally, the higher SI means the better clustering quality. The Silhouette widths is defined by $SI = \frac{b-a}{\max\{a,b\}}$.

(2) CS measure [41]

CS measure can effectively measure the clusters with different densities and sizes. Generally, the smaller CS has the better clustering partition, i.e., better clustering effect. using a Gaussian Kernelized distance measure and transforming to the high dimensional feature space, CS measure is defined as follows.

$$CS = \frac{\sum_{i=1}^{k} [\frac{1}{n_i} \sum_{x_i \in C_i} \max_{x_q \in C_i} \{2(1 - K(x_i - x_q))\}]}{\sum_{i=1}^{k} \min_{j \in \{1,\dots,k\}, j \neq i} \{2(1 - K(m_i - m_j))\}} \tag{10}$$

where $m_i = \sum_{x_j \in C_j} \frac{x_j}{n_j}$.

(3) Accuracy [42]

The clustering accuracy is defined by $p = \frac{\sum_i n_{ii}}{n}$.

(4) Adjusted rand index (ARI) [43]

$ARI \in [-1,1]$. Generally, larger ARI value means that the clustering result is the more consistent with the actual situation. ARI index is defined by

$$ARI = \frac{\sum_{i,j} \binom{n_{ij}}{2} - [\sum_i \binom{n_{i+}}{2} \cdot \sum_j \binom{n_{+j}}{2}] / \binom{n}{2}}{\frac{1}{2} [\sum_i \binom{n_{i+}}{2} + \sum_j \binom{n_{+j}}{2}] - [\sum_i \binom{n_{i+}}{2} \cdot \sum_j \binom{n_{+j}}{2}] / \binom{n}{2}} \tag{11}$$

(5) Adjusted mutual index (AMI) [44]

Adjusted mutual index is defined by

$$AMI = \frac{MI - E(MI)}{\max(H(U), H(V)) - E(MI)} \tag{12}$$

where $MI(U,V) = \sum_{i=1}^{|U|} \sum_{j=1}^{|V|} p(i,j) \log(\frac{p(i,j)}{p(i)p'(j)})$, $p(i,j) = \frac{|U_i \cap V_j|}{N}$, $H(U) = \sum_{i=1}^{|U|} p(i) \log p(i)$, $p(i) = \frac{|U_i|}{N}$ and $H(V) = \sum_{j=1}^{|V|} p'(j) \log p'(j)$, $p'(j) = \frac{|V_j|}{N}$.

3.5   Experimental Results

In the experiments, the proposed KMCA algorithm and four compared algorithms were executed on nine data sets. Since these clustering algorithms contain some stochastic/random factors, they have been independently executed 20 times on each data set. For each performance measure and each data set, averages and standard deviations of the results obtained by these algorithms were computed, respectively. The average value indicates the average performance of each algorithm, while standard deviation reflects the robustness of the algorithm.

Tables 2, 3, 4 and 5 give the averages and standard deviations of 20 times for the five algorithms in terms of five performance measures, respectively.

Table 2. Comparison results of the proposed and compared algorithms in terms of SI and CS indexes

Data sets	Internal index	KKM	KKM+PSO	KMCA
Wine	SI	0.2808(0.0008)	0.2826(0.0005)	**0.2827(0.0003)**
	CS	1.3376(0.0047)	1.288(0.0044)	**1.2842(0.0018)**
Lung cancer	SI	0.0662(0.0478)	0.1059(0.0132)	**0.1156(0.0005)**
	CS	3.0802(0.9787)	2.743(0.1793)	**2.5796(0.0901)**
Seeds	SI	0.0685(0.0047)	0.069(0.0001)	**0.06928(0.0001)**
	CS	**0.9834**(0.0726)	1.0(2.4e-05)	1.0(**1.1e-05**)
Lense	SI	0.3536(0.0338)	0.3924(0.0)	**0.3924(0.0)**
	CS	1.151(0.102)	1.1337(0.0)	**1.1337(0.0)**
Hayes-roth	SI	**0.0112**(0.0009)	0.0103(0.002)	0.0107(**0.0008**)
	CS	1.0(**0.0**)	**0.9373**(0.1364)	1.0(3e-06)
Dermatology	SI	0.1927(0.031)	0.2233(**0.0073**)	**0.2245**(0.0087)
	CS	1.5852(0.4746)	**1.2882(0.0769)**	1.3109(0.0942)
Iris	SI	0.0610(0.0064)	0.0655(0.0016)	**0.0656(0.0004)**
	CS	**0.8833**(0.1590)	1.0001(4e-05)	1.0(**0.0**)
Leuk	SI	0.0715(0.0118)	0.0791(0.0002)	**0.0792(0.0001)**
	CS	**1.0286**(0.1728)	1.0375(0.0026)	1.0373(**0.0025**)
Zoo	SI	0.4498(0.0662)	0.4787(0.0277)	**0.5029(0.0256)**
	CS	1.5972(0.3879)	1.4062(0.1259)	**1.3673(0.1183)**

Table 2 shows comparison results of the five clustering algorithms in terms of SI and CS indexes on nine data sets. For SI index, apart from Hayes-roth, KMCA can achieve the best performance on each of eight data sets. Meanwhile, compared with KKM and KKM+PSO, KMCA has the smallest standard deviations on eight data sets except Dermatology. For CS index, KMCA has the best performance on Wine, Lung cancer, Lense and Zoo, and achieves the smallest standard deviations on seven sets except Hayes-roth and Dermatology. The comparison results indicate that KMCA has the better performance compared with KKM and KKM+PSO, however, the advantage is not obvious based on results on CS index.

Tables 3, 4 and 5 provide the comparison results of five clustering algorithms on nine data sets in terms of three external indexes, including clustering accuracy, adjusted rand index and adjusted mutual index. It can be obviously observed from Tables 3, 4 and 5 that compared with other four clustering algorithms,

Table 3. Comparison results of the proposed and compared algorithms in terms of clustering accuracy

Data sets	KM	KM+PSO	KKM	KKM+PSO	KMCA
Wine	0.8533(0.1706)	0.9648(0.0039)	0.9477(0.0073)	0.9654(0.0036)	**0.9657(0.0016)**
Lung cancer	0.4781(0.0648)	0.5625(0.0453)	0.4984(0.0659)	0.5641(0.0413)	**0.5828(0.0247)**
Seeds	0.8021(0.1461)	0.886(0.004)	0.8762(0.0503)	0.895(0.0046)	**0.8967(0.0034)**
Lense	0.5833(0.152)	0.5375(0.107)	0.5896(0.1105)	0.8063(0.0622)	**0.8312(0.0596)**
Hayes-roth	0.4492(0.0585)	0.4095(0.0692)	0.4564(0.0807)	0.4966(0.0618)	**0.5087(0.0525)**
Dermatology	0.6396(0.1521)	0.7963(**0.071**)	0.6334(0.1573)	0.8004(0.0748)	**0.8344**(0.082)
Iris	0.7977(0.1153)	0.88(**0.0**)	0.7993(0.1100)	0.8907(0.0129)	**0.894**(0.0029)
Leuk	0.9153(0.1094)	0.9583(**0.0**)	0.8708(0.1394)	0.9708(0.0041)	**0.9715**(0.0030)
Zoo	0.7475(0.076)	0.7401(0.0769)	0.7223(0.0988)	0.7554(0.0717)	**0.7728(0.065)**

Table 4. Comparison results of the proposed and compared algorithms in terms of adjusted rand index (ARI)

Data sets	KM	KM+PSO	KKM	KKM+PSO	KMCA
Wine	0.7102(0.2504)	0.8946(0.0122)	0.8462(0.0206)	0.8962(0.0112)	**0.8972(0.0051)**
Lungcancer	0.0682(0.0870)	0.1193(0.0458)	0.0822(0.0765)	0.1187(0.0454)	**0.1282(0.0176)**
Seeds	0.6092(0.1673)	0.694(0.0125)	0.6873(0.0478)	0.7142(0.0105)	**0.7181(0.0079)**
Lenses	0.1953(0.2004)	0.1059(0.15)	0.1513(0.13)	0.5415(0.0674)	**0.5686(0.0646)**
Hayes-roth	0.0539(**0.0422**)	0.0073(0.0642)	0.078(0.0803)	0.103(0.0711)	**0.1258**(0.056)
Dermatology	0.5742(0.2084)	0.7617(**0.0713**)	0.5759(0.1821)	0.7695(0.0737)	**0.7975**(0.0846)
Iris	0.6331(0.0968)	0.7021(**0.0**)	0.6302(0.0956)	0.7205(0.0279)	**0.7291**(0.0064)
Leuk	0.8232(0.1505)	0.8803(**0.0**)	0.7661(0.1823)	0.9148(0.0115)	**0.9167**(0.0083)
Zoo	0.7211(0.1017)	0.5864(0.1186)	0.6972(0.1284)	0.6994(0.0744)	**0.73(0.0696)**

Table 5. Comparison results of the proposed and compared algorithms in terms of adjusted mutual index (AMI)

Data sets	KM	KM+PSO	KKM	KKM+PSO	KMCA
Wine	0.6990(0.2361)	0.8696(0.0104)	0.8242(0.0205)	0.8709(0.0101)	**0.8716(0.0050)**
Lungcancer	0.1006(0.1141)	0.1814(0.0458)	0.0904(0.0917)	0.1752(0.054)	**0.1907(0.017)**
Seeds	0.5762(0.1628)	0.6619(0.009)	0.654(0.0493)	0.6777(0.0086)	**0.6812(0.0066)**
Lenses	0.2761(0.164)	0.2104(0.1661)	0.2291(**0.1171**)	0.4424(0.1246)	**0.4925**(0.1194)
Hayes-roth	0.0563(**0.0496**)	0.004(0.0638)	0.0945(0.088)	0.125(0.0816)	**0.1494**(0.0591)
Dermatology	0.6952(0.185)	0.8811(0.021)	0.7114(0.1363)	0.8835(**0.0192**)	**0.8892**(0.0224)
Iris	0.6395(0.0788)	0.7050(**0.0**)	0.6113(0.1214)	0.7137(0.0202)	**0.7233**(0.0044)
Leuk	0.7955(0.1502)	0.8542(**0.0**)	0.7450(0.1723)	0.8878(0.0112)	**0.8896**(0.0081)
Zoo	0.7409(0.0549)	0.7194(0.0667)	0.7426(0.0649)	0.7679(0.0417)	**0.7939(0.0289)**

KMCA achieves the best performances on nine data sets. Moreover, KMCA also has the smallest standard deviations on seven data sets except Iris and Leuk.

In summary, KMCA can achieve a good clustering performance and also is a robust clustering algorithm.

4   Conclusions

This paper discussed a kernel-based membrane clustering algorithm, KMCA, based on the principle of kernel methods. The proposed KMCA algorithm is suitable to handle a challenge of the existing membrane clustering algorithms: it fails to deal with the clustering on the data sets with non-spherical cluster boundaries. In principle, samples in original data space are mapped to a high-dimension space via a non-linear kernel function, and then membrane clustering algorithm is used to cluster the mapped data sets. As usual, a tissue-like P system is designed to determine the optimal cluster centers in the high-dimension space. Based on the principle of kernel methods, all computations are completed in original data space according to the used kernel function. Therefore, although membrane clustering algorithms have spherical cluster boundary, the proposed KMCA can deal with the data sets with non-spherical cluster boundaries. Experimental results on nine benchmark data sets demonstrate the advantage over other clustering methods

Acknowledgment. This work was partially supported by the National Natural Science Foundation of China (No. 61472328), Chunhui Project Foundation of the Education Department of China (Nos. Z2016143 and Z2016148), the Innovation Fund of Postgraduate, Xihua University (No. ycjj2018184), and Research Foundation of the Education Department of Sichuan province (No. 17TD0034), China.

References

1. Păun, Gh.: Computing with membranes. J. Comput. Syst. Sci. **61**(1), 108–143 (2000)
2. Păun, Gh.: Membrane Computing: An Introduction. Springer, Berlin (2002). https://doi.org/10.1007/978-3-642-56196-2
3. Cavaliere, M.: Evolution–communication P systems. In: Păun, Gh., Rozenberg, G., Salomaa, A., Zandron, C. (eds.) WMC 2002. LNCS, vol. 2597, pp. 134–145. Springer, Heidelberg (2003). https://doi.org/10.1007/3-540-36490-0_10
4. Freund, R., Păun, Gh., Pérez-Jiménez, M.J.: Tissue-like P systems with channel-states. Theor. Comput. Sci. **330**(1), 101–116 (2005)
5. Bernardini, F., Gheorghe, M.: Population P systems. J. Univ. Comput. Sci. **10**(5), 509–539 (2004)
6. Păun, Gh., Păun, R.: Membrane computing and economics: numerical P systems. Fundam. Inform. **73**(1–2), 213–227 (2006)
7. Ciencialová, L., Csuhaj-Varjú, E., Kelemenová, A., Vaszil, G.: Variants of P colonies with very simple cell structure. Int. J. Comput. Commun. Control **IV**(3), 224–233 (2009)
8. Ionescu, M., Păun, Gh., Yokomori, T.: Spiking neural P systems. Fundam. Inform. **71**, 279–308 (2006)
9. Song, T., Pan, L., Păun, Gh.: Spiking neural P systems with rules on synapses. Theor. Comput. Sci. **529**, 82–95 (2014)
10. Peng, H., et al.: Competitive spiking neural P systems with rules on synapses. IEEE Trans. NanoBiosci. **16**(8), 888–895 (2018)

11. Peng, H., et al.: Spiking neural P systems with multiple channels. Neural Netw. **95**, 66–71 (2017)
12. Buiu, C., Vasile, C., Arsene, O.: Development of membrane controllers for mobile robots. Inf. Sci. **187**, 33–51 (2012)
13. Wang, X., et al.: Design and implementation of membrane controllers for trajectory tracking of nonholonomic wheeled mobile robots. Integr. Comput.-Aided Eng. **23**(1), 15–30 (2016)
14. Zhang, G., Gheorghe, M., Li, Y.: A membrane algorithm with quantum-inspired subalgorithms and its application to image processing. Natural Comput. **11**(4), 701–717 (2012)
15. Díaz-Pernil, D., Berciano, A., Peña-Cantillana, F., Gutiérrez-Naranjo, M.A.: Segmenting images with gradient-based edge detection using membrane computing. Pattern Recogn. Lett. **34**(8), 846–855 (2013)
16. Peng, H., Wang, J., Pérez-Jiménez, M.J.: Optimal multi-level thresholding with membrane computing. Digit. Sig. Process. **37**, 53–64 (2015)
17. Alsalibi, B., Venkat, I., Al-Betar, M.A.: A membrane-inspired bat algorithm to recognize faces in unconstrained scenarios. Eng. Appl. Artif. Intell. **64**, 242–260 (2017)
18. Zhang, G., Liu, C., Rong, H.: Analyzing radar emitter signals with membrane algorithms. Math. Comput. Model. **52**(11–12), 1997–2010 (2010)
19. Peng, H., Wang, J., Pérez-Jiménez, M.J., Riscos-Núñez, A.: The framework of P systems applied to solve optimal watermarking problem. Sig. Process. **101**, 256–265 (2014)
20. Wang, J., Shi, P., Peng, H.: Membrane computing model for IIR filter design. Inf. Sci. **329**, 164–176 (2016)
21. Xiong, G., Shi, D., Zhu, L., Duan, X.: A new approach to fault diagnosis of power systems using fuzzy reasoning spiking neural P systems. Math. Problems Eng. **2013**(1), 211–244 (2013)
22. Wang, J., Shi, P., Peng, H., Pérez-Jiménez, M.J., Wang, T.: Weighted fuzzy spiking neural P system. IEEE Trans. Fuzzy Syst. **21**(2), 209–220 (2013)
23. Wang, T., et al.: Fault diagnosis of electric power systems based on fuzzy reasoning spiking neural P systems. IEEE Trans. Power Syst. **30**(3), 1182–1194 (2015)
24. Peng, H., Wang, J., Shi, P., Pérez-Jiménez, M.J., Riscos-Núñez, A.: Fault diagnosis of power systems using fuzzy tissue-like P systems. Integr. Comput.-Aided Eng. **24**, 401–411 (2017)
25. Peng, H.: Fault diagnosis of power systems using intuitionistic fuzzy spiking neural P systems. IEEE Trans. Smart Grid **9**(5), 4777–4784 (2018)
26. Gheorghe, M., Manca, V., Romero-Campero, F.J.: Deterministic and stochastic P systems for modelling cellular processes. Natural Comput. **9**(2), 457–473 (2010)
27. García-Quismondo, M., Levin, M., Lobo-Fernández, D.: Modeling regenerative processes with membrane computing. Inf. Sci. **381**, 229–249 (2017)
28. García-Quismondo, M., Nisbet, I.C.T., Mostello, C.S., Reed, M.J.: Modeling population dynamics of roseate terns (sterna dougallii) in the Northwest Atlantic Ocean. Ecol. Model. **68**, 298–311 (2018)
29. Zhao, Y., Liu, X., Qu, J.: The K-medoids clustering algorithm by a class of P system. J. Inf. Comput. Sci. **9**(18), 5777–5790 (2012)
30. Peng, H., Wang, J., Pérez-Jiménez, M.J., Riscos-Núñez, A.: An unsupervised learning algorithm for membrane computing. Inf. Sci. **304**, 80–91 (2015)
31. Peng, H., Wang, J., Shi, P., Riscos-Núñez, A., Pérez-Jiménez, M.J.: An automatic clustering algorithm inspired by membrane computing. Pattern Recogn. Lett. **68**, 34–40 (2015)

32. Peng, H., Wang, J., Shi, P., Pérez-Jiménez, M.J., Riscos-Núñez, A.: An extended membrane system with active membrane to solve automatic fuzzy clustering problems. Int. J. Neural Syst. **26**(2), 1–17 (2016)
33. Peng, H., Shi, P., Wang, J., Riscos-Núñez, A., Pérez-Jiménez, M.J.: Multiobjective fuzzy clustering approach based on tissue-like membrane systems. Knowl.-Based Syst. **125**, 74–82 (2017)
34. Shawe-Taylor, J., Cristianini, N.: Kernel Methods for Pattern Analysis. Cambridge University Press, Cambridge (2004)
35. UCI. http://archive.ics.uci.edu/ml/datasets.html
36. Python. https://www.python.org/
37. Merwe, D.W., Engelbrecht, A.P.: Data clustering using particle swarm optimization. In: 2003 Congress on Evolutionary Computation (CEC 2003), pp. 215–220 (2003)
38. Zhang, R., Rudnicky, A.I.: A large scale clustering scheme for kernel k-means. In: Proceedings of 16th International Conference on Pattern Recognition, vol. 4, pp. 289–292 (2002)
39. Wei, X.H., Zhang, K.: An improved PSO-means clustering algorithm based on kernel methods. J. Henan Univ. Sci. Technol.: Nat. Sci. **32**(2), 41–43 (2011)
40. Rousseeuw, P.J.: Silhouettes: a graphical aid to the interpretation and validation of cluster analysis. J. Comput. Appl. Math. **20**(20), 53–65 (1987)
41. Chou, C.H., Su, M.C., Lai, E.: A new cluster validity measure and its application to image compression. Pattern Anal. Appl. **7**(2), 205–220 (2004)
42. Congalton, R.G., Green, K.: Assessing the Accuracy of Remotely Sensed Data: Principles and Practices. CRC Press, Boca Raton (2009)
43. Hubert, L., Arabie, P.: Comparing partitions. J. Classif. **2**(1), 193–218 (1985)
44. Zhang, J., Niu, Y., He, W.: Using genetic algorithm to improve fuzzy k-NN. In: International Conference on Computational Intelligence and Security, pp. 475–479 (2008)

Author Index

Printed in the United States
By Bookmasters